A Military History of Germany

'Wollen wir die Nation selbst zum Heer, oder wollen wir die Soldaten zu Bürgern machen?'
Karl von Rotteck, 1816

'Der Soldat darf nicht denken, sonst denkt er Unsinn.'
Wilhelm II to Bismarck

'Wo es keinen Staatsbürger in Zivil gibt, darf man auch keinen in Uniform erwarten.'
Bundeswehrgeneral Koestlin

A Military History of Germany

from the eighteenth century
to the present day

MARTIN KITCHEN

The Citadel Press : *Secaucus, N. J.*

To Corinna and Susie

Contents

Maps

Acknowledgement

The first three maps are reproduced by courtesy of Martin Gilbert, from his *Recent History Atlas* published by Weidenfeld and Nicolson.

Introduction

Ideally the military establishment in any country should be controlled and directed by the sovereign power, which in turn must be devoted to truly rational, humane and democratic goals. The German experience has witnessed both the flaunting of sovereign power by the military and the perversion of sovereign power for inhuman, irrational and criminal ends, and thus offers the unique possibility of insight into the causes and nature of militarism.

Militarism is the excessive influence of the military over the economic, social, political and cultural values of society. It is the predominance of the military over the political. It is an aggressive and reactionary means of domination, an attempt to counteract the forces of social change and to secure the particular interests of specific social groups. It is not a phenomenon peculiar to any particular form of social organization, but can occur in any society in which there is a separate warrior class. But like any other such concept it is historical, and as such is subject to change. With the growth of the military apparatus and the complexity of advanced societies it becomes increasingly hard to separate the military from the civilian, and military thinking infects every aspect of life. Militarism ceases to be the simple preponderance of the military over the civilian, and becomes an insidious cancer which threatens the vitality of a social organization. As President Eisenhower pointed out: 'The military establishment, not productive of itself necessarily must feed on the energy, productivity, and brainpower of the country, and if it takes too much, our total strength declines.' At no time has the problem of militarism been more dangerous nor the need to solve it more pressing than today. The colossal expense of modern armies and their possession of weapons that have the capacity to destroy life on our planet make it imperative that they be rigorously controlled, diminished and, hopefully, abolished. The economy of death must be replaced by the economy of life.

In no other country has militarism played a more important or longer role than in Prussia and Germany. The military history of Germany can thus illuminate the changing nature of militarism under different forms of social organization: under declining feudalism, under industrialization, under parliamentary democracy, under fascism and under advanced capitalism. A historical and functional study of German militarism is necessary for an understanding of the genesis and praxis of contemporary militarism, and hopefully it may make a contribution to the struggle against it.

Characteristic of the early history of German militarism, particularly in its Prussian form which is the main object of this study, is the close connection between the feudal aristocracy and the army. Indeed militarism was the means by which that class maintained its unique position against the forces of change. At the end of the fifteenth century struggles between the peasantry and the nobility became increasingly virulent and there were a number of instances of open revolt. In the Peasants War of 1525 this anti-feudal rebellion was crushed and the powers of the landowning aristocracy strengthened. The peasants had not been supported by the burghers in the towns, and Martin Luther, for all his sympathy for the common man, provided the aristocracy with a powerful ideology to use against the peasants. Thus the Peasants War and the Reformation strengthened the position of the aristocracy. It was saved from the threat from the peasantry and the burghers, and through the secularization of the church lands was able to strengthen its economic position. In Prussia the junkers seized the common lands and forced the peasantry to work on their estates as landless serfs. Demesne farming replaced peasant farming, enabling the aristocracy to profit from the increasing demand for agricultural produce in western Europe. The peasants were

2

reduced to the serfdom of *Leibeigenschaft*. With the decline of the towns the aristocracy was able to win further privileges, among them the abolition of the tariffs on grain.

The misery and suffering of the Thirty Years War were borne in large measure by the peasants and the townspeople; the aristocracy and the princes emerged relatively stronger than ever. The power of Kaiser and Reich had been irreparably broken and Germany dissolved into three hundred little sovereign states. Some of the princes, among whom Frederick William, the 'Great Elector' of Brandenburg, was one of the most outstanding, were able to use the resulting chaos and confusion to strengthen and consolidate their state power. The Great Elector was determined to secure his sovereignty, to weld his dispersed territories together into a unified state, to break the independent power of the aristocracy and to crush discontent in the towns and on the land. He could not hope to crush the aristocracy, so he co-opted it. In return for its financial support and its reluctant approval of his policies, Frederick William I granted the aristocracy further rights and privileges. Its control over its estates and the peasantry, with unrestricted police, legal and economic powers, was formally recognized by the monarchy, and remained in force until the reforms of Stein. The aristocracy thus was able to crush the peasantry which had become increasingly restless as a result of the Thirty Years War and the loss of their rights to the landowners. In this way the latter's substantial privileges were guaranteed in return for their co-operation.

In 1640 at the beginning of the Great Elector's rule, the Brandenburg army consisted of a mere 3,000 men. By 1678 he had increased it to 45,000 men and had created a force which had defeated the Swedes at Fehrbellin, establishing Brandenburg as a military power which could not be ignored. Initially the army had been recruited from foreign mercenaries and adventurers. Frederick William tried to recruit an increasingly large number of natives, but he met with the fierce resistance of the estate owners. They complained about the drunken and brutal behaviour of the recruiting officers who threatened to destroy the economy by forcing skilled men into the army. The Great Elector was therefore obliged to grant special exemptions to landowners, craftsmen, tenant farmers and

3

agricultural labourers, and had to recruit his army largely from rural vagabonds and domestic servants. An increasing number of junkers became officers in the army, attracted by the profits that could be made by the manipulation of company funds and by the fact that the army was becoming once again socially respectable and was no longer regarded as a band of marauding savages as it had been during the Thirty Years War. But it was not until the days of his son that the army was to have an officer corps in which the Prussian aristocracy predominated. In order to provide the revenue for this expanding army in a country which had been severely damaged by the Thirty Years War, the Great Elector encouraged state-financed manufactories which were often run by foreigners, the work force often being made up of beggars and criminals who were forced to work in these enterprises. After the repeal of the Edict of Nantes thousands of highly skilled Huguenots came to Brandenburg and made a major contribution to the development of industry.

The Great Elector's son used the army that he inherited largely for self aggrandizement, his reward coming in 1701 when he became 'King in Prussia' as Frederick I. To meet his massive expenditures both on the army and on pomp and ceremony, the king increased taxation. He was most ingenious in finding new things to tax. One of the more bizarre taxes was a 'virginity tax' on unmarried women. But even these measures did not save the state from near-bankruptcy at the time of his death in 1713.

Frederick William I was devoted to the army, and earned the nickname given to him by George I: *'le roi sergent'*. He was determined to end the extravagance and waste of his father, but at the same time increased the size of the army to 64,000 men in 1725 and to 89,000 at the time of his death in 1740. His one great extravagance was his regiment of enormously tall grenadiers, his *'lange Kerle'*, 2,400 men from all over Europe with a pipe and drum band press-ganged in the Gold Coast. The 'lange Kerle' were so unruly that on several occasions they were fired upon with live ammunition to keep them in order whilst drilling. The discipline in the rest of Frederick William's army was equally ferocious, causing frequent desertions. Recruiting methods were primitive, and the expansion of the army caused a number of serious economic problems which were not brought under control until the reign of Frederick the Great. Most important of all, Frederick William I completed the process of co-opting the aristocracy into the officer corps. The army became increasingly attractive to the junkers as the revenues from their estates declined in the early eighteenth century, and the king encouraged them to join the army by giving them the monopoly of high ranks and granting them further favours and privileges. By 1739 all the thirty-four generals were aristocrats, and of 211 staff officers only eleven were not noblemen. Frederick William, whose own coarse behaviour was legendary, summed up his attitude towards the officer corps as follows: *'On purgea dans chaque régiment le corps des officiers de ces gens dont la conduite ou la naissance ne répondait point au métier de gens d'honneur qu'il devait faire, et depuis la délicatesse des officiers ne souffrit parmi leurs compagnons que ces gens sans reproche.'*

The Prussian kings thus achieved a far-reaching militarization of society. As army officers the aristocrats were controlled by the king, but in return for the loss of their full autonomy they were given considerable privileges both in the army and on their estates. The brutal discipline of the army affected social relationships throughout the kingdom so that the whole state was, in Graf Manteuffel's words, like a gallery. The economy of the country was geared to the needs of maintaining a large army. Symbolic of the importance of the army was the fact that King Frederick William I was the first European monarch always to wear military uniform. In its early form, therefore, Prussian militarism was a vital ingredient in the absolutist state. It was the means by which the king asserted and strengthened his sovereignty *'wie ein rocher de bronze'* against a potentially fractious nobility. But it was also the means by which that nobility preserved its own privileged position against the demands of the new age of industrialism, capitalism, and the rights of man. Thus it held together an authoritarian and increasingly antiquated social order. It helped to create a powerful state, but one which was increasingly incapable of overcoming its internal problems and contradictions. It is to these questions that we now turn.

1

The German Army in the Eighteenth Century

The Prussian state of the eighteenth century was based on the army. The needs of the army determined to a considerable extent the social, political and economic life of the country. The nature, the development and the stabilization of Prussia's socio-economic structure was thus closely linked to the military system. It was not simply that Prussia, with its long frontiers which were so difficult to defend, could survive only with a powerful army, or that this curious collection of states could be welded into a modern state only by force of arms, or even that the king could not assert his authority without an obedient army. It was that the army determined the social and economic development of the country. Indeed it can be argued that the Prussia of Frederick the Great was held together only by the army. For all his appearance as an enlightened and modern monarch, Frederick II ruled over a hopelessly antiquated state, based on the mediaeval estates of aristocrats who monopolized the power, burghers who were without any political rights and a peasantry most of whom were serfs. This feudal ruin was propped up and preserved by the army, and thus the state could hardly be reformed and modernized without the defeat and destruction of the army.

The size of the army placed an intolerable burden on the Prussian people. About one sixth of the men fit to serve were actually under arms, or in other terms about four per cent of the total population. Although Prussia was the thirteenth largest state in Europe in terms of population, it had the third largest

6

army. Two thirds of the budget was spent on the army. The Prussian bureaucracy devoted most of its time and energy to maintaining it. The economic effects of this large military force were considerable, for the army provided the largest single market and the Prussian economy was geared to its needs. Economic life was therefore militarized and bureaucratized, and as the historian Otto Hintze has pointed out, Prussian mercantilism was the natural economic consequence of a society placed on a permanent war footing.

Eighteenth-century Prussia was an agricultural country, and it was therefore the countryside that had to bear the main burden of the army. It was the agricultural areas that had to provide the bulk of the taxes to finance the army, and it was the peasant who had to pay them. The army was recruited from the country-side, the aristocracy serving as officers, the peasantry as private soldiers. The social relationships of the countryside were thus transferred to the army: aristocrats were born officers, and serfs made subservient and obedient soldiers. Frederick II was insistent that this close link between the social structure of the country and the organization of the army was the only guaran-tee of the army's military efficiency. Conversely the survival of a fiercely authoritarian feudal order on the land was to a consider-able degree dependent on the strengthening of the distinctions between lord and peasant by the Prussian military system. The social structure of the country and the rank system in the army therefore served to strengthen one another, and a challenge to one was felt of necessity to be a danger to the other.

The major problem, however, was that the strain placed on the rural economy due to the exigencies of military policy was so great that it threatened to collapse. The problem of supporting a large army with a backward rural economy became increasingly difficult to solve. One of the most disruptive aspects of military policy in the early decades of the century was the fact that the peasants had no idea when they would be called upon to do their military service, and once they were in the army they were placed under military discipline for the rest of their lives. As life in the Prussian army was rigorous and brutal the peasants would do almost anything to avoid having to serve. Self-inflicted mutilation, bribery or flight were the usual methods of attempt-ing to escape from the king's drill sergeants. So determined was

7

the resistance to military service that the recruiting officers resorted to increasingly brutal methods, to a point where the slaughter of peasants was not uncommon. Even men who were unfit for duty, either by natural or induced causes, had to bribe the recruiting officers with considerable sums of money, often so great that they were left utterly destitute. The alternatives of facing a lifetime of hardship and suffering in the army, or of being left financially ruined by the recruiting officers left the peasant with no real choice but to flee in order to avoid the latter. News that the recruiting officers were in the vicinity spread rapidly, and it was not unusual for whole villages to take to the road in the hope of finding some more peaceful and secure existence elsewhere.

The situation became so bad that the rural economy was severely disrupted, and the army was not getting the recruits it needed. The efficiency of the feudal estates was seriously impaired, for an appreciable portion of the work force could be press-ganged into the army at a moment's notice, and often at critical times such as the harvest. As the land became increasingly depopulated, and as those who remained on the land were so often ruined by having to bribe the recruiting officers, the revenues from taxation were drastically reduced, as was the income of the feudal estates. The king, the aristocracy, the army and the peasantry all had their reasons to be dissatisfied with this inefficient and callous system. It became increasingly obvious that some reform was essential.

If the rural economy was to be given some relief the amount of time that the soldiers actually spent in the army would have to be significantly reduced. After a period of initial training soldiers were sent home on leave for the better part of the year, and were thus able to contribute fully to the economic life of the country. Since most officers were either landowners or sons of landowners they were more than willing to allow their soldiers to return to the land, for their own prosperity depended on a flourishing agriculture. As a result of this new system officers were able to make significant economies and so could afford to recruit foreign mercenaries. These initial changes, brought about largely by the officers themselves, resulted in a considerable increase in the number of foreigners serving in the

Prussian army, and did ease the burden of military service which had weighed so heavily on the peasantry.

Frederick William I is represented in popular history as being a mixture between an absurd buffoon and a sadistic tyrant, yet in spite of his coarseness, his miserliness and his almost pathological love for the army he was a man of very considerable administrative talents. The *ad hoc* reform of military organization which had been instigated by the officer corps in order to protect their economic interests as landowners was altogether too unsystematic for his tastes. In a series of decrees in May and September 1733 he established the canton system which was to form the basis of the Prussian military system until the reforms of the Napoleonic era. The canton system became the subject of a carefully fabricated legend, when men like Scharnhorst argued that it established the principle of universal military service in Prussia, and that it was proof that the Hohenzollern dynasty was committed to this idea. This was a useful propaganda weapon for Scharnhorst in 1810, but it does not correspond to historical reality. The canton system was the result of a deal between the crown and the aristocracy which gave considerable advantages to the latter and lessened some of the problems of the former. It was the formalization of an already existing situation, and far from being universal in scope it applied almost solely to the countryside.

The canton system was in effect the transference of the social relationships of a feudal society into military terms. In the western provinces, where the social structure was quite different, the system could not be applied, and hence the outbursts in Frederick William's *Political Testament* against the 'stupid cattle who are as malicious as the devil' and the 'false intriguers who drink like beasts and who have nothing else in their empty heads', in other words men whose crime in the king's eyes was to be born under a less rigid social order, and who therefore did not easily fit into the Prussian military system. Within the cantons regimental lists were made on which all young men who were fit for military service were enrolled. Under the new system soldiers served for eighteen months to two years in the army, then when this period of basic training was completed the cantonist returned home, normally spending only two months in each year back in the regular army. The Prussian

9

peasantry was thus either enrolled for military service serving full-time, or was in what amounted to a reserve army. The canton system was certainly not without its hardships and injustices, but it was now at least predictable and it was generally felt to be a considerable improvement on the old system which most people found intolerable.

The reforms of 1733 certainly improved the lot of the peasantry as far as their direct military obligations were concerned, but it did very little to relieve the appalling financial burden of taxation for military purposes which fell so heavily on the rural poor. The peasants were obliged to pay two separate taxes to meet the expenses of the army: the 'contribution', which was a combined poll and land tax, and 'cavalry money', a tax which replaced the old requirements to provide forage but which was even more onerous. In addition the peasants were obliged to sell forage to the army at an uneconomic price and to allow the cavalry to graze their horses during the summer months. Taxation, which was very heavy in the eastern provinces, was even more severe in the west. As it was extremely difficult to apply the canton system to the western provinces, since the social structure was quite different with a large class of small independent farmers, westerners were exempted from military service but were obliged to pay additional taxes as a compensation. Throughout the country the peasants could still be called away from the land, even at critical points in the farming year, in order to help with transport for the army or to build fortifications. This too could be a major source of hardship to a peasantry which was living very close to the subsistence level. The extent to which the peasantry was afflicted by the military system can be clearly seen in one example which is frequently quoted in the literature. In 1756 a peasant in Nether-Pomerania paid a yearly tax for contribution and cavalry money of 18 talers. His total yearly income was 22 talers.

Thus although the reforms of 1733 were an improvement, the military system still imposed an almost intolerable strain upon the already impoverished peasantry. Hence it is hardly surprising that desertion was a major problem. In some areas villages were obliged to maintain a twenty-four hour watch for deserters, and heavy fines and penalties were imposed if they were discovered to be derelict in their duties. All soldiers were obliged to wear uniform, even during the ten months in the year which they spent at home, and those who were due to be called to the colours were forced to wear special insignia. Thus as virtually all grown men were subject in one way or another to military law a deserter was in effect anyone who travelled without permission from the authorities, a point which was underlined in the fact that the law refered specifically to 'the desertion of soldiers and peasants'. In this way the military system helped to keep the peasants subservient and unfree and reinforced the rigidity of social divisions on the land.

This aspect of the military system was emphasized by the fact that until 1763 the cantons were subdivided into company cantons under a company captain. These captains, the vast majority of whom came from the junker class, were absolute masters over the fate of militarily eligible peasantry. In 1763 the company cantons were abolished, and the duties of the company captain were performed by the civilian *Landrat* assisted by a staff officer. But the principle remained the same: the militarization of the peasantry was used to strengthen the feudal order.

As the officer corps was almost exclusively aristocratic the canton system did not unduly interfere with the rights of the junkers. The junker was absolute master of his estates, the peasants were subservient to him, their relationship with the king was mediated by him. The junker had the same rights over the peasant as the officer over his men, and these rights were firmly anchored in the law. The authority of the crown reinforced the power of the officers over the men; it stopped at the gates of the junker estates. The brutality of military discipline was matched by the severity of the punishments meted on the peasantry by the junkers. Both were sanctioned by the crown as necessary for social stability and military efficiency. Frederick the Great's remark that men should be more frightened of their officers than of the enemy admirably sums up this attitude and eloquently betrays the extent to which eighteenth-century Prussia was a society on the defensive, its antiquated social order propped up by a harsh military system.

The social order and the military system in Prussia were thus closely bound together so that a change in the one was bound to have a profound effect on the other. In the western provinces, where the social order was quite different, the military system could not be applied. Similarly the profound changes in the economic structure of Prussia, which resulted in a brisk trade in junker estates, threatened to undermine the position of the aristocracy, for the movements of the capital market were becoming as important as impeccable lineage. The great increase in the cost of land led to an intensification of labour and thus to even more harsh discipline. The old landed order was giving way to agricultural capitalism and social relationships were undergoing a profound change which was to be formalized in the reform period. By the late eighteenth century therefore the military system was becoming increasingly out of step with economic and social developments, and reform could not be long postponed.

The Prussian kings were well aware that this particular form of military organization depended on the stability of the social order on the land. Although the junkers were the foundation on which the army was based, they could not be allowed to become too powerful, for they would then destroy the last vestiges of independence of the peasantry. As agriculture became more scientific and more heavily capitalized the economic position of the peasantry became increasingly precarious, and without active intervention by the state the Prussian peasantry were threatened with extinction, just as the English smallholders were destroyed by the enclosure movement in the course of the century. Thus in a series of edicts in 1709, 1714 and 1739 Frederick I and Frederick William I laid the foundations of the *Bauernschutz*, the attempt to preserve an economically secure and effective peasantry. It was the peasantry which paid the bulk of the taxation which supported the army, and they were also called upon to provide supplies and to work for the military. Equally important was the fact that it was the peasantry which provided the majority of the soldiers. The protection of the peasantry was therefore also the protection of soldiers. Without a viable peasant class there could be no support for the army and no reliable soldiers. The peasant, secure in his holdings, protected against unfair competition and with a preordained position in society, was as much the basis of the Prussian army as was the aristocrat, and for this reason he had to be protected in a world which was becoming increasingly hostile to him. Frederick II was fully aware of this fact and issued further edicts for the preservation of the peasantry. In one of these edicts the principle was clearly enunciated that whoever chased a peasant away from his land was as guilty as a man who forced a soldier to desert, and this was indeed a logical corollary of the law which treated peasants who left the land without permission as deserters.

During the course of the eighteenth century the old order on the land came increasingly under attack. The rigid feudal structure was severely hampering the development of an efficient modern economy. Critics were demanding the removal of all restrictions on the free play of market forces, and argued that Prussia's social order, far from being the source of her strength, was causing her to lag behind other European states and Prussia was becoming alarmingly antiquated and inefficient. The aristocracy was predictably opposed to any such changes, and argued that the abolition of feudal service and dues without massive compensation from the state would be grossly unjust. They were able to win the support of Frederick the Great for this dubious argument, for the king was as determined to maintain the position of the aristocracy as he was that of the peasantry. The junkers provided the king with his officers and his civil servants, and since in the lower ranks of the officer corps and the bureaucracy expenditure invariably exceeded income, an economically secure aristocracy was essential if the system was to be perpetuated. Thus once more the exigencies of military policy had a profound effect on the social and economic structure of Prussia.

In spite of the provisions of the *Bauernschutz* and the determination of the Prussian kings to maintain a strong class of peasants, the military system, by reinforcing the power and authority of the junkers, was bound to weaken the relative position of the peasants. The more unscrupulous landowners were able to use the military system to their personal advantage. It was not unusual for junkers to seize the holdings of their peasants when they were away doing their military service. The junkers' private servants could be replaced by peasants while the former were in the army, and the holdings of those who had been forced into service were then added to the land-lord's estates. Thus before the emancipation of the serfs there was already a sizeable rural proletariat and the beginnings of a profound social revolution that no royal edict could halt. The junkers themselves were also beginning to realize that their own prospects for economic gain were severely hampered by the provisions of the *Bauernschutz*, and that perhaps the abolition of feudal ties on the land might bring them considerable advantages. The peasants could not be fully exploited until they became free wage labourers, and their privileges could be destroyed only by liberating them from serfdom. But for the time being the old system was preserved, for the Prussian kings had no intention of reforming the army, and it was not until 1806 when reform could no longer be postponed that the system of land tenure was radically changed.

Although the peasants were protected as a class, though not as individuals, they were totally subservient to the aristocracy. The junker had almost absolute power over the peasants. Politically, economically and legally the peasant was delivered up to the aristocracy, and he had no right of appeal to the crown. The power of the aristocracy was further reinforced by the fact that the local representative of central authority, the *Landrat*, was also a representative of the aristocracy, and the officer corps of the army was almost exclusively aristocratic. The relationship between the aristocracy and the army was the outward and visible signification of the class structure of Prussia and of the attitude of the aristocracy to the state.

Until the time of Frederick William I the aristocracy was mistrustful and often hostile towards the monarchy and the army was not yet fully integrated into society. Sons of the aristocracy were more likely to serve in foreign armies than to serve the king of Prussia, and the links between the aristocracy and the Hohenzollern dynasty were still weak. It was Frederick William I who more than any other Prussian ruler forced the aristocracy into the army and drastically reduced their freedom. He forbade the junkers to travel abroad or to enter the service of a foreign prince. If they disobeyed these edicts they were to be treated as deserters, just like the humblest of their peasants. Their sons were forbidden to attend foreign universities and forced into the cadet schools and thence into the regular army. This series of edicts was reinforced by further similar enactments by Frederick the Great who was determined that the aristocracy should, in return for the very real privileges which they enjoyed, be utterly subservient to the requirements of the monarchy. He was particularly concerned that the aristocracy should not enter trade and commerce but should remain a class apart. If they were to follow such bourgeois pursuits they would, he argued, lose their sense of honour and as a class might turn away from the profession of arms which was their natural and appropriate calling.

This policy of Frederick William I was one of almost deliberate confrontation with the aristocracy, a determined attempt to establish royal absolutism. At first there was widespread discontent among the junkers, but this never reached the point at which a revolt against the crown might have seemed likely. The aristocracy came to realize that their own position could best be maintained by close co-operation with the monarchy. Furthermore serving in the army quickly became a way of life for them, and they were soon filled with pride in their regimental traditions and their own contributions to the army. The number of aristocrats serving in the army greatly increased in the course of the century, from 3,116 at the time of the accession of Frederick II to nearly 8,000 on the eve of the battle of Jena. Most of the officers served from twenty to thirty years in the army, so that the majority of them were truly professional soldiers rather than country gentlemen with military interests.

The Prussian kings thus succeeded in forcing the aristocracy into the army, breaking their independent power and establishing their unchallenged authority. But this created a profound contradiction in the economic and social structure of the country. Neither Frederick William I nor Frederick the Great wished to create a separate officer class. The object of their policy was to recruit the officer corps from a strong and firmly established landed aristocracy so that there would be an identity between the military system and rural society. Yet the very fact that an increasingly large proportion of the junkers spent most of their lives as professional soldiers meant that they were unable to devote their time to their estates, and thus their economic position became threatened. The military policy of Prussia seemed threatened by its own success.

Forced to leave his estates to serve in the army, often heavily taxed, and his work force often critically depleted to meet the needs of the military, the junker had real cause for grievance

15

against the army. The official lists of complaints of the aristocracy in 1740, the *Gravamina*, cite the depopulation and exploitation of the land by the military and the high-handed behaviour of the officers as principal grievances. Frederick the Great, with his particular love for the aristocracy and his brilliance as a military commander, did much to encourage the complete identification between the aristocracy and the officer corps. The officer corps became the first estate of the country, officers taking precedence over their civilian equivalents. The aristocratic nature of the officer corps was further signified by the fact that no badges of rank were worn so that their social equality was emphasized, whatever their differences of rank. Throughout the eighteenth century ninety per cent of the officer corps were aristocrats, and sons of bourgeois landowners who became officers could be ennobled after ten years of service. In exceptional cases, usually for outstanding bravery on the battlefield, non-commissioned officers could become officers, and after years of service they also were ennobled. In this way non-noble officers, although a minute percentage of the officer corps, were absorbed into the aristocracy, and the social homogeneity of the officer corps was hardly disturbed.

The East Elbian aristocracy became reconciled with the army, and a large percentage of them spent most of their lives, from cadet to major or colonel, in the army. The army thus shaped their life style, and the junker became a curious mixture of officer and country gentleman, quite unlike the aristocrat of the western provinces who was not closely associated with the army. The junkers were doubly privileged. They monopolized the officer corps which became the first estate in the land, and in order that there might be an adequate supply of officers their economic position was bolstered and reinforced by the monarchy. On his estates and in the army he was born to command; the peasant was born to obey. This unique double role enabled the junkers to survive many of the vicissitudes of the modern age, and to shape German history to a degree which would not otherwise have been possible.

It was characteristic of the absolutist monarchs to increase the royal demesne at the expense of the aristocracy, and Frederick William I who had no special love for the nobility was no exception. But he realized, however grudgingly, that such a policy would serve only to undermine the economic position of the officer corps and weaken the ability of the country to pay for his excessively large army, and therefore he called a halt to this scheme. Frederick II pursued a policy of direct support for the nobility, feeling that only if a strong and independent class of aristocratic landowners were maintained could the old Prussia be preserved. There was a clear contradiction between royal absolutism and the imperatives of military policy, but for the Prussian kings the needs of the army took precedence.

In the course of the eighteenth century it became increasingly tempting for the junkers to sell land. They were short of capital which was badly needed for the modernization of their estates, and at the same time there was a growing class of prosperous merchants and entrepreneurs who wished to buy land so that they might lead the lives of respectable country gentlemen. Frederick William I had been concerned that the aristocracy might be tempted to sell off their estates, and thus endanger his military policy. He therefore forbade the aristocracy to sell land without royal assent. This edict was strengthened by Frederick the Great, and in the code of law of 1796 it was laid down that only nobles had the right to own noble estates. Frederick II insisted that an aristocracy without land was no longer an aristocracy, and if they were allowed to sell their estates to the bourgeoisie they might just as well cease to exist as a class.

These measures were purely defensive; they did nothing to save the landed aristocracy from economic decline. The intolerable strain placed on the rural economy by Frederick the Great's incessant wars made more drastic measures imperative. In the 1770s and 1780s a series of credit institutions were established in an attempt to overcome the chronic shortage of capital in agriculture. These institutions enabled the junkers to mortgage up to half their estates at four per cent and to circulate the mortgage bonds as cash. Yet in spite of this cheap credit, the active support of the monarchy and the sinecure positions in the army and the bureaucracy, the junkers found it increasingly difficult to keep their heads above water. From the 1760s onwards the sale and speculation in estates flourished, and the aristocracy found itself ever more indebted to the bourgeoisie. In this situation it proved impossible to keep the junker estates exclusively in junker hands, regardless of the provisions of the law. By 1800 about ten per cent of noble estates were in the hands of bourgeois landowners.

The army was able to help the rural economy by the extent of its purchases. Junker officers bought supplies from junker estates, very often at advantageous prices, and the army offered to the landowners a secure, regular and controlled market. But the greatest opportunity for enrichment was offered in the army itself by the manipulation of company funds, by the acceptance of bribes and by the fact that the army was run as a business enterprise for the profit of the officers. Company commanders were given a certain sum of money from the war chest in order to maintain their companies. Every year they were obliged to present their companies for review to ensure that the money had been correctly spent. This system gave the company commanders plenty of opportunity to cut corners and to appropriate a sizeable part of the funds for their private use. The usual way of saving money was to recruit peasants from the company commander's own estates. The men could then be sent on leave to work on his own estates. While on leave they were not paid by the army, so he could take all the funds that would otherwise have gone in pay and extra bonuses. Frederick the Great corrected some of the abuses in this system, but even he was unable to change the fact that the company was regarded as the private business concern of the commander, and virtually his own private property. It was estimated that a company of infantry was worth 2000 talers, and there are instances of companies being bought and sold and of compensation paid to the widows and orphans of company commanders who had been killed.

Company commanders not only could make substantial savings through careful book-keeping and parsimony, there were also other lucrative possibilities open to them. Officers frequently accepted bribes to allow men to go home on leave. Company captains had to give men permission before they were allowed to marry, and it was a standard joke in the Prussian army that one got a wife for 1 taler and 14 groschen. Some stern moralists complained that this led to sexual licence and immorality, but the approved remedy was to flog unmarried mothers so that the principle cause of the problem was concealed. Another favourite trick was to save money on supplies, by cutting down rations and even by reducing the amount of material in uniforms.

Company captains could thus make a comfortable living out of these dubious practices, and the authorities were willing to turn a blind eye. More senior officers in the Prussian army were able to amass considerable fortunes in the course of their military careers. Senior positions in the civil service, and the office of *Landrat*, were often reserved for ex-officers. Officers were granted many kinds of tax exemptions, and unlike the men they were still paid when on leave. Other officers were given grants of land or large cash payments by the king in return for special services or outstanding achievement. One such general, Bogislav Friedrich von Tauentzien who came from an impoverished junker family, was able to retire with a fortune of at least 150,000 talers.

The rewards of military service were in a sense compensation for the sacrifices which the junkers were called upon to make for the army. Conversely they were given special rights and privileges as landowners in order that they might be encouraged to play their part in the military system. But this system came more and more under attack. Years before the battle of Jena men like Stein felt that the exclusively aristocratic officers' corps was an absurdity, and it was apparent that the old economic system on the land was unlikely to survive the competition of manufacturing capitalism. Shortly before his death Frederick II expressed his fears that the Prussian system was about to collapse. In rather self-conscious imitation of Louis XIV he said: 'I am afraid that after me there will be a *pêle-mêle*. The ferment has begun everywhere, and the gentlemen in command help it along. . . . The masses are beginning to push from below, and when they get going all hell will break loose.' The situation was to a considerable extent due to the strain placed on the economy by Frederick's wars. The Seven Years War left Prussia on the verge of ruin, and the lot of the common people was so wretched that spontaneous and ill-organized riots were not infrequent.

The Prussian economic system was geared to the needs of the army and economic growth was stunted by the fact that the

19

military system was rooted in a feudal social order. Fierce protectionism, monopolies, rigorous controls on exports and imports and substantial subsidies did much to help those sectors of the economy which were important to the military effort, but in the long run they were harmful to the full and healthy development of industry and commerce. Before the Seven Years War the state played a predominant role in industry and the development of a vigorous bourgeoisie was severely hampered. The state had a grain monopoly and controlled the export of wool, and the overwhelming importance of the army to the economy made it particularly difficult for capital to accumulate in the manufacturing sector. The catastrophic effects of the Seven Years War and a steady growth in population in the latter part of the century made it clear that reform was needed. Efforts were made to stimulate the economy by encouraging investments in the private sector. An increasing number of machines were imported from England and in 1785 the first German-built steam engine was put into operation in Hettstedt in the Mansfeld coal district. In 1789 the first coke-fired smelter was built in Silesia. In the 1790s there was the beginning of the machine building industry in Germany. Agronomists such as Johann Christian Schubart and Christian Reichart made a significant contribution to improvements in agricultural output, and the credit banks enabled the junkers to apply some modern techniques to agriculture. By 1800 there was vigorous activity in the Prussian and German economy, but it was certainly not of the order that would mark the beginning of an industrial revolution.

Frederick II had thus removed some of the restrictions on the development of the forces of production and his successors continued in this tradition, but there was a strict limit to this development. The feudal relationships underlying the production system could not be changed without altering the social structure of Prussia and thus threatening the basis of the military system. If the middle class was not restrained and controlled it would threaten the hegemony of the aristocracy. The junkers attempted to modernize the economy and to use elements of modern capitalism to their own advantage and to strengthen their own position. This curious amalgam of feudalism and capitalism was to affect the whole course of

German economic and social development in the nineteenth century and beyond.

The limitations of the Prussian economy, the social structure of the country and the relations between junker and peasant all had a profound effect on the strategy and tactics of the Prussian army. Frederick II was in no sense a revolutionary innovator in the art of war, and for there to be such a revolution there had first to be an economic and social revolution to produce a new general of genius, as the French Revolution produced Napoleon. Frederick's genius, like Napoleon's, was his ability to exploit to the utmost the possibilities of the means available to him.

The financial resources available to the Prussian kings were extremely limited, and therefore the size of their armies and the length of time they could remain in the field were restricted. The bulk of the Prussian army consisted of demoralized men, often the dregs of society, press-ganged foreigners and prisoners of war, unwilling peasants and unreliable mercenaries, the whole motley crew held together by violent brutal discipline and ferocious punishments. Although in some regiments a certain local pride was developed, and in certain instances respect for the company commander or the king, it would be a mistake to exaggerate the strength of such local patriotism or to see in it the first dawn of nationalism. In any case no such feelings motivated the foreigners who comprised about half the Prussian army at the time of Frederick II. After the Seven Years War the king no longer paid money to the company captains in order to recruit foreigners: this was now done directly by the recruiting officers. The result was a marked decline in the recruits from abroad. Previously, although the company captains had appropriated a large percentage of the funds for their own private use, they had at least insisted on fairly high standards so that their companies would not look too disgraceful at the annual review. Under the new system standards were lowered, with disastrous consequences for the army, because the king's recruiting officers had even less scruples about putting funds into their own purses.

Not surprisingly in view of its composition, the major problem facing the army was that of desertion. This had a profound effect on tactics. The army could scarcely afford to march by night or to move through woods or forests, for fear that a large number of men would take the opportunity to desert. The army therefore had to move in one large mass, in open country, and could manoeuvre effectively only on flat ground. It could only march extremely slowly – seventy-five paces per minute was considered an absolute maximum – and changes in formation were virtually impossible. The cavalry was used largely to police the army when it was on the move and to hunt down deserters. Reconnaissance patrols often failed to return and headed for home, with the result that intelligence in the army was extremely limited. Frederick II thus often had only the vaguest notion where the enemy was, and frequently lost contact with other sections of his army. Although he tried to develop the hussars as a light cavalry specializing in reconnaissance work he was able to achieve very little, and the hussars did not come into their own until the Napoleonic period. This extraordinarily cumbersome army could be seriously endangered by a mere handful of soldiers firing on a flank from adequate cover – the speciality of the pandours of the Austrian army – for it was incapable of hand-to-hand combat in difficult terrain.

A further major problem facing Frederick II's armies was that of provisions. The Prussian army was usually quite well fed, and it therefore marched with large quantities of food and fodder which was stored in magazines left at intervals of about five marching days. Such stores were extremely vulnerable to attack, and loss of a magazine could have very serious consequences on the outcome of a campaign. Eighteenth-century armies were too small to set up an elaborate administration for the exploitation of occupied territory, as occurred under Napoleon, and there was thus a limit to the degree to which they could live off the land. Most of the supplies had to be carried with the armies, and the inadequacy of the means of transport in central Europe further hindered their progress. To this vast quantity of material was added the baggage of the officers, which enabled them to campaign in considerable comfort and even luxury. Although Prussian officers did not live in the field in quite the same style as French officers, nevertheless the amount of paraphernalia they took around with them was a further factor slowing down the progress of the army. Unlike the Napoleonic armies, the Prussians took heavy tents with them for the men. An infantry regiment of about eight hundred men needed sixty pack horses for the tents alone.

Such difficult logistic problems coupled with the frequency of desertions had considerable implications for the development of Frederick II's strategy. It was dangerous to move too far away from Prussia, or from the magazines established *en route*. In the *General Principles of War*, which Frederick the Great wrote in 1748, he argued that Charles XII, the Emperor Charles VI and the French in Bohemia in 1742 all came to grief because they wandered too far away from their home base. The aim of his strategy could not be the total destruction of the enemy forces as it was for Napoleon, but swift blows which disrupted lines of communication, partial victories and the establishment of firm bases on enemy territory. It was very rare for even the greatest victories to be followed up so that the enemy army was destroyed, because the risk of desertion was particularly high. Thus most operations were very limited in scope. A campaign was won by a series of tactical victories coupled with diplomatic moves, the eighteenth-century variation of the 'strategy of attrition' as opposed to Napoleon's 'strategy of annihilation'.

Such were the limitations of eighteenth-century warfare, but Frederick II's military genius helped him to overcome them to a considerable degree. Unlike most of the military theoreticians of the time who sought to reduce the art of war to a set of axiomatic principles so that a true science of war might be developed, Frederick II preferred to run risks, to attack when many of his generals urged caution and to fight a battle rather than indulge in endless and sophisticated text book manoeuvres. There were severe limits on strategic offensives, as we have seen, but it was the tactical offensive which was Frederick II's speciality. The Austrian army believed in fighting defensive battles, and under skilful generals like Daun they were a most imposing force. Frederick developed the art of fighting an offensive battle to its highest point until the art of war itself was revolutionized.

The Prussian army on the battlefield was never very large, seldom more than 40,000 men. The battles were usually fought in open ground, on a narrow front of about two miles. From a suitable vantage point the whole battle could be observed.

The army fought in close order, shoulder to shoulder in three lines, with the officers in the rear, their swords drawn to deal summarily with any stragglers. In such a battle order the ferocious drill of the Prussian army came into its own. The footsoldiers were reduced to mindless robots, executing to perfection their battlefield movements and using to deadly effect the musket drill which had become second nature to them. The Old Dessauer (Leopold of Anhalt-Dessau) developed a complicated system of parade ground drill, whereby each regiment was divided into eight platoons, each platoon firing in sequence, all three ranks firing simultaneously. On the battlefield the precision of this drill began to fail, and Frederick preferred to march the infantry up to the enemy, let loose a salvo at close range and finish the job with the bayonet.

Eighteenth-century linear tactics were developed to the highest point by Frederick II with his 'oblique order of battle'. The ideal tactic was to attack the enemy on the flank, because extended lines rendered the flanks particularly vulnerable. Since the Prussian army was usually smaller than that of the enemy it was deployed across a narrower front. As a result the risk of being outflanked was far greater, and it was extremely difficult for the Prussians to outflank their opponents. The oblique order of battle was an attempt to overcome this deficiency. As the front attacked, one flank was held back so that the front executed a wheeling motion. The attacking flank was strengthened so that it would descend on the enemy lines like a hammer blow, punch a hole in the lines and then begin to roll up the enemy front. The success of this tactic was sometimes remarkable, a relatively weak Prussian force causing havoc to a strong enemy – the Battle of Leuthen is a classic example.

On paper the oblique order of battle is exceedingly simple. In practice it depended on iron discipline, strong will and endless drill. If the enemy had sufficient warning it was relatively simple for them to strengthen the point where the attack was likely to fall, and then the other weak Prussian flank was likely to be seriously endangered. If the weak flank of the oblique attacking line was allowed to move forward too much it became too heavily involved in fighting and the whole point of the manoeuvre was lost. But if the weak flank did not engage the enemy sufficiently, then the point at which the attack was aimed could be further strengthened. The ideal degree of the angle of attack was often exceedingly hard to calculate, and even more difficult to achieve under battle conditions. If the first attack failed it was almost impossible to re-form and attack again, and the extent to which infantry reserves and cavalry could be used to support the initial attack was strictly limited. In the hands of less gifted men the oblique order of battle could all too easily degenerate into an empty formula. It was Frederick II's particular genius that he never allowed this method to dictate the course of his battles. He was quick to improvise and adapt any tactic to the exigencies of the moment. Thus for him the oblique order of battle was a powerful and valuable tool; it was not simply a recipe for inevitable success. The failure of his successors was due in part to their overlooking the flexibility of Frederick II's system and their attempt to find in his battles some universal secret for military success.

Even during his lifetime there were ample signs that these tactics, however sophisticated they might have become, were no longer adequate. Significant improvements in artillery and hand weapons resulted in terrible casualties being inflicted on the closed lines of the Prussian army. By the end of the Seven Years War artillery had become an important factor in warfare, and the outcome of an engagement could depend on the field artillery. Frederick II was well aware of the significance of artillery and worked hard to improve the Prussian artillery, and to ensure that better gun carriages and roads were made so that the artillery could be moved more swiftly. He was able to increase the number of guns so that there were seven per thousand infantrymen – a considerable amount if it is remembered that Napoleon had only two guns per thousand at the Battle of Wagram. Although the artillery was still extremely cumbersome, inaccurate and slow firing, it was nevertheless able to inflict crippling damage on the Prussian lines. At battles such as Liegnitz, Torgau and Burkersdorf the Prussian army showed that it could fight effectively in more open formations, yet such developments which pointed clearly to the future were never exploited. The Prussian army stuck to tactics which were already outmoded because fighting in open order, with considerable reliance on skirmishers, would lead to a critical increase in desertions. Eighteenth-century tactics reached their peak under Frederick II, but they were already inadequate for the requirements of the time. Further technological improvements in guns and artillery were soon to render them useless. Linear tactics were the military expression of a socio-economic order which had become outmoded. If Prussia was to survive, reforms both of the military system and of society itself could no longer be postponed.

2

The Birth of Reform

During the Seven Years War there were many indications that traditional linear tactics had become inadequate for the needs of modern warfare, but it was not until the American War of Independence and the first campaigns of the French revolutionary wars that it became apparent that for there to be radical changes in warfare there had also to be fundamental changes in society. The new warfare was thus the result of a new social order, and not until the feudal-absolutist state was destroyed could the full resources of the nation be mobilized for a total war effort.

The sharpshooters of the American War of Independence showed the importance of marksmanship and mobility in the 'little war', but their contribution should not be exaggerated. The larger engagements in the war were fought along conventional lines, both sides using traditional tactics. Nevertheless the implications of the extensive use of *tirailleurs* and light infantry were tremendous and were discussed in the military literature in Europe. In most European armies efforts were made to strengthen the light infantry and to render the traditional tactics more flexible, but it was only in the Russian army, particularly under imaginative generals such as Suvorov, that the strategic-operative and tactical principles of the new warfare were seriously developed. In all cases, however, there were severe limitations, for nations of serfs and unfree peasants did not provide the material for effective skirmishers and highly trained and intensely motivated light infantrymen. The French

27

Revolution, which destroyed the privileges of the aristocracy and proclaimed the rights and equality of man, removed the social barriers to the development of a truly modern army. French nationalism, which resulted in the identification of the people with the state, was the result both of revolutionary enthusiasm and of a determination to defend the revolution against the counter-revolutionary intervention of the European states. These strong feelings paved the way for the *Conscription générale* of 23 August 1793. Universal service for the duration of the war was thus proclaimed and was enthusiastically supported by the masses. With universal service the French army was organized along different lines. Distinctions between troops of the line and the national guard were abolished, and a professional army thus became essentially an army of volunteers. Such an army had tremendous enthusiasm but totally lacked the clockwork precision of the old armies. The revolutionary army achieved an astonishing degree of mobility by dispensing with tents and heavy baggage and by living off the land. The tactics were improvised, but they learnt to use their *tirailleurs* and their attacking infantry columns with deadly effect, and by fighting from cover on difficult terrain they were able to disrupt the linear tactics of their opponents.

The superiority of the French army was due to greater mobility, more flexible tactics and the unparalleled enthusiasm and heroism of the troops. In armaments the two sides were virtually equal. The French musket was slightly lighter and marginally more accurate than the Prussian model, but it was just as slow and cumbersome to load and had the same range and the same effect. Similarly the French artillery was lighter and more mobile, but otherwise very much the same as the Prussian. It was morale rather than technology that was the true dividing line between the two sides. The French were fighting for the achievements of the revolution, for the protection of their country with which they had come to identify themselves. The Prussians and their allies were forced into fighting a war in which they had no vital interest. The officer corps of the French army had been transformed. One third of the old officer corps had emigrated. The remainder had been ruthlessly weeded out, so that the officers were young, effective and enthusiastic, and promotion depended on service and bravery, not privilege and birth. By contrast, of about 8,000 officers in the Prussian army in 1806 only 695 were non-noble. Of 142 generals 4 were over the age of eighty, 13 were over seventy and 62 were over sixty. Of the 945 captains and majors in the infantry 2 were over seventy, 18 over sixty and 119 over fifty. Twenty-five per cent of the regimental commanders were over the age of sixty. In short the Prussian army was grossly over-aged and the officers were selected for their social origins rather than their abilities.

With a more capable officer corps and high morale among the troops the French were able to allow army commanders, divisional commanders and even regimental commanders to use a considerable degree of initiative on the battlefield. They were thus able quickly to adapt their tactics to new and un-expected situations, and did not have slavishly to follow a pre-ordained battle plan. As a consequence staff work became increasingly important, and the French developed a corps of highly trained and experienced officers to assist the com-manders.

The Prussians were slow to realize the full implications of the revolution. In 1791, with Austria and Saxony, they agreed to intervene against it. The campaign began the following year with the coalition armies full of confidence. They were fighting for monarchy against revolution, and felt that they would have little trouble in restoring law and order in a country which had shown gross insubordination towards its rightful superiors, and which had little to protect it but a rag-tag and undisciplined army, 'miscellaneous gutter-snipes' in the words of the allied commander, the Duke of Brunswick. On 20 September 1792 these illusions were brutally shattered at the Battle of Valmy. The French army withstood a ferocious artillery barrage which lasted for an hour, and then unleashed a counter-attack in column formation which resulted in the routing of the counter-revolutionary army, which was then forced back over the Rhine. By October Speyer, Worms, Mainz and Frankfurt am Main were in French hands. Goethe, who witnessed the artillery duel at Valmy, wrote in his description of the campaign in France: 'this is the beginning of a new epoch in world history.'

The rulers of Prussia were unwilling to think of Valmy in

quite such cosmic terms, partly because they preferred to put the blame on the shortcomings of individuals and squabbles among the allies rather than on more fundamental weaknesses in the military system, and partly because Prussia was heavily engaged in Poland. Faced with the threat of the French Revolution, Prussia, Austria and Russia had settled their differences over Poland, and were now determined to squash the reform movement which threatened to emulate the French example. The further partition of Poland was resisted by a growing patriotic movement on whose behalf Tadeusz Kosciuszko negotiated with the Jacobins in Paris for support for a Polish insurrection. The Prussian ruling class was divided between those who saw the main threat from France and the majority, which included Frederick William II, who felt that a swift peace should be concluded with France so that Poland could be destroyed. In spite of fierce resistance the Poles were unable to resist the combined forces of the Prussians and the Russians, and in 1795 Poland was once more partitioned so that it was now completely divided up between Prussia, Austria and Russia.

Thus by 1795 Prussia had won substantial areas of Poland but at a terrible price. Its army had been badly mauled by the French and had suffered a number of humiliating set-backs at the hands of the Polish patriots. It had won peace and neutrality by the Peace of Basel, but the position of the French had been greatly strengthened so that Prussia was virtually defenceless against a French attack, and the French were able to play Prussia off against Austria in the following years. Prussia seemed satisfied. The peace left it as the major power in northern Europe, and in the *Reichsdeputations-hauptschluss* of 1803 it was rewarded for its benevolent neutrality by territories which amounted to five times the area lost to France on the left bank of the Rhine. In 1805 Prussia was given permission to march into Hanover. Its gains in Poland had been considerable and gave it the false notion of indeed being a great power. All these factors gave to the Prussian government an unwarranted sense of security and contributed to the inadequacy of the attempts that were made to carry out a long overdue reform of the army.

The Prussian army was not entirely impervious to criticism, and modest attempts were made before the catastrophe of 1806 to remedy some of the more obvious shortcomings of the system. There were also a number of highly intelligent and perceptive officers who were aware that radical changes were needed and who pushed for further reforms. But they were very much a minority. General Boyen argued that there were only three types of officer in the Prussian army in 1806: the old soldiers who had fought with Frederick the Great and who were obsessed with outmoded tactics and mindless drill, those who had been commissioned after the Seven Years War and who, now that they were in command of regiments, were obsessed with making money out of their commands and feared that war might spoil these operations; and lastly the young officers who had served in Poland and who laboured under the sad delusion that the Prussian army was invincible. The reformers thus faced a vast mass of self-satisfied, complacent, ultra-conservative and unprofessional officers who refused to see any real need for change and who were either so set in their ways that they wanted little more than a quiet life or, if they were young, were anxious to show their valour on the battlefield, but if possible against a less imposing foe than the French.

Reform attempts before 1806 had been modest. In 1788 Frederick William II established a reform commission under Field Marshal von Möllendorf, but the report, published in June of the same year, did not make any far-reaching suggestions. The commission was largely concerned with the disruptive effect on the economy of abuses of the military system though it did suggest that the term of service should be reduced. The canton law of 1792, which incorporated some of the suggestions of the Möllendorf commission, resulted in little change. The principle of universal service was boldly enunciated, only to be immediately contradicted by the assertion that 'other functions are at hand which are not less important for the support of the body politic, so exemptions from this rule exist, dependent upon the decision of the representatives of the state, who shall consider which classes will serve the defence of the land, and which are qualified for exemption'. Yet the very fact that the canton law reaffirmed the principle of universal service was to provide a strong argument to the reformers that universal service should be implemented in practice. Before 1806, however, it was little more than an empty formula.

31

Towards the end of the century critics of the military system began to publish their ideas quite extensively in a number of military journals, most of which managed to escape the censors. In 1801 Scharnhorst left the Hanoverian army and came to Berlin to become head of the Academy of Officers. Shortly after his arrival he founded the Military Society which provided a valuable forum for the reformers. Meetings were held each week, papers were read and discussed and a wide range of military and political questions were tackled. The officers who attended these meetings included many who were to play an important part in the military reforms after 1806. The society paid close attention to developments in France, and was sharply critical of the notion that Frederick II had found a set of infallible answers to all the problems of warfare.

The most distinguished critics of the army in this period were von Behrenhorst and von Bülow. In his *Observations of the Art of War*, published in 1798 and 1799 von Behrenhorst poured scorn on the Frederican manoeuvres which, he argued, were suitable only for the parade ground. By turning the soldier into a mindless robot his true soldierly nature and his dignity as a human being were denied and his effectiveness as a solider was greatly diminished. Behrenhorst argued that if the solider were given greater freedom his enthusiasm would be awakened and the army could draw on the moral and spiritual resources of the nation. He strongly criticized the ideas of those theorists who argued that warfare could be reduced to a set of mathematical principles which could be applied like the laws of physics, and insisted that the psychological and moral aspects of war were of critical importance. The implications of his arguments were quite clearly that the army could not be reformed without a fundamental reform of the state.

Behrenhorst's pupil, von Bülow, developed many of these arguments, but he denied that chance and randomness dominated the battlefield. He set out to discover the laws that determined the new warfare, the clash between mass armies fired with patriotic enthusiasm. The decisive factor for Bülow was mobilizing the masses and using them to maximum effect according to the principles he had established. The tactics of this new type of warfare would be based on the *tirailleurs*, the 'little war' would become 'total war' and the old linear tactics would have to be abandoned, for they were the 'tactics of serfs'. Bülow argued for 'human tactics' against 'clockwork tactics', and yet his ideas were often over-simplified and schematic. In spite of his dogmatism and naivety he had a profound effect on Clausewitz, and even the famous aphorism that war is merely the continuation of politics by other means is based on one of Bülow's dicta.

Both Behrenhorst and Bülow understood and accepted the principles behind Carnot's *levée en masse* of 1793, but the implications of these insights were disturbing. The notion of thinking soldiers rather than parade-ground puppets, of mass armies fired with deadly enthusiasm, of promotions as rewards for outstanding service, were all ideas which were repugnant to the aristocratic officers of the Prussian army who had been reared in the Frederican tradition. As the full implementation of these ideas was clearly unthinkable the army contented itself with a number of half-hearted and minor reforms. The importance of light infantry was given somewhat belated recognition – it was not until 1787 that separate fusilier battalions were created. Each infantry company was then required to train ten men as sharpshooters, but this was clearly inadequate so that in 1805 royal permission was given to create separate light infantry battalions from the men in the third rank in the line. By 1806 the Prussian army was still chronically short of light infantry, and these compromise solutions had resulted in confusion and uncertainty.

The reformers all insisted that education was of paramount importance for the new methods of warfare, and that if officers were to be allowed greater initiative then they would clearly have to be better trained. Artillery and engineering schools were established before 1806, and in 1803 the training of staff officers was improved. Officers were selected by examination and were given a grounding in theory, and at the same time they paid frequent visits to their regiments so that they did not become mere theoreticians. Yet in spite of these improvements most senior officers were highly suspicious of the staff, and were extremely loath to take any advice from them. More important was the fact that a number of remarkable men were appointed to the staff. In 1804 Scharnhorst was given command of the western division of the General Quartermaster Staff, and he was able to appoint a number of his friends from the Military Society as adjutants, among them men of such distinction as Boyen, Müffling and Rühle. Yet even they were unable to have much impact on an army which had become so hostile to the idea of reform.

The most far-reaching proposal for the reform of the army before 1806 came from von Knesebeck, who published a report in 1803 which argued strongly for universal service so that the whole country would become involved in the army, rather than the military representing a small fraction of the population. He argued that exemptions from military service should be allowed only in truly exceptional circumstances and that the full burden should not rest solely on the rural population. His suggestion was that every year the army should release 128,397 men and replace them with recruits who would later be released in like manner, so that a substantial reserve army would be established. For the leaders of the army, steeped in the traditions of Frederick the Great, such notions were altogether too unprofessional, smacking of jacobinism and the *levée en masse*. They were therefore abandoned, but the notion of a substantial reserve army which would play an active part in the field in any future campaigns lived on to become an important ingredient in the thinking of the reformers after 1806.

The chronically indecisive politics of Prussia coupled with this reluctance to begin the long overdue reform of the army was profoundly depressing to the reformers. Prussia was isolated, and when in the course of peace negotiations with England Napoleon offered that Hanover, which was occupied by Prussian troops, should be returned to Britain, Prussia mobilized its army. On 8 October 1806 the ultimatum from Prussia expired and the war began. The Prussian commander-in-chief, the Duke of Brunswick, failed to exploit the fact that the French army was dispersed, and chances for at least initial successes were lost. Napoleon, who rightly said that the Prussians had no idea what they wanted to do, quickly outmanoeuvred his enemy and on 14 October 1806 the Prussian army was destroyed at the twin battle of Jena and Auerstädt. Once again the French had moved with lightning speed and in one crushing battle had destroyed the enemy. The Prussian army had hardly begun to move. They marched at seventy-five paces per minute, and there had been a long and ponderously serious discussion in army circles as to whether it would be possible to increase the marching speed to seventy-six paces. The French by contrast marched at 120 paces per minute. The extraordinarily slow speed of the Prussian army was partly due to the amount of equipment it dragged around with it. Even the great advocate of light infantry, General York, went into the field with two extra uniforms, ten pairs of gloves, four pairs of trousers and waist-coats, an extra hat, cloaks, miscellaneous personal clothing, four pairs of leather breeches, fifteen pairs of stockings, eight nightgowns, five night caps, three table cloths, thirty-six napkins, a mattress, five pillows, a red silk bed cover, two bed pans, a set of china and silver, cooking utensils, a coffee grinder, eight razors, twelve glasses and twenty-five bottles of liquor – and all of this for a brief campaign.

The Prussian army began a retreat which soon degenerated into panic-stricken flight. Sections of the army surrendered without even fighting, and a number of fortresses were surrend-ered to the French without a shot being fired. The defence of Colberg by Gneisenau was almost the only example of a determined attempt to resist the French. In Berlin the governor, Count von der Schulenburg, issued his notorious order on 17 October 1806: 'The king has lost a battle, the prime responsibility of the burghers is for quiet.' Stein had the presence of mind to leave the capital with the cash box of his ministry. The remaining bureaucrats prostrated themselves before Napoleon who entered the city five days later on 25 October. After two further battles in 1807 at Preussisch-Eylau and Friedland Prussia was forced in the Peace of Tilsit to surrender all her territories west of the Elbe, renounce her Polish acquisitions and pay an indemnity of 146 million francs. Having been roundly defeated, having lost half her territory and having been saddled with a crippling indemnity, Prussia ceased to be a great power.

The Prussian defeat had been swift and shattering, but it had been foreseen by men like Scharnhorst who up until the very last moment urged the king to reform the army drastically, for otherwise defeat would be inevitable. As late as April 1806 Scharnhorst submitted a memorandum on army reform, for he was fully aware that Prussia with its senile and unimaginative commander-in-chief and its vacillating cabinet was heading for disaster. He argued that in modern warfare questions of morale were more important than sterile parade-ground manoeuvres, that self reliance was as important as rigid discipline and that warfare could not be reduced to a set of formalistic axioms which ignored the vital role of the men who did the actual fighting. Scharnhorst, like Clausewitz, was fully aware of the importance of the sociological dimension of warfare, and a profound humanism pervades the thinking of this great military genius. Scharnhorst called for the mobilization of the entire people to resist invasion. The army was to be inspired by bravery, a sense of honour and just rewards for the brave and the effective, regardless of their social background. All the barbarous and humiliating punishments which rendered life in the Prussian army so utterly miserable for the common soldier should be abolished. For the defence of the country the army would have to draw on the moral reserves of the nation: great men such as Napoleon were needed only to inspire an army to fight wars of aggression and conquest. These ideas were later to be taken up and developed by socialist writers such as Engels, Bebel, Liebknecht and Rosa Luxemburg in their theories of the people's army. Scharnhorst wrote: 'We are beginning to value the art of war more than military virtues – this was always the undoing of peoples. Bravery, self-sacrifice, and resoluteness are the foundations of the independence of a people; if our heart no longer beats for these then we are lost, even in the course of great victories.'

Scharnhorst's memorandum was first greeted with horror, then placed aside. Such 'jacobin' sentiments could not be expressed to the king and were quite unacceptable to the army. In desperation Scharnhorst joined an opposition group which included Stein, Prince Louis Ferdinand, Phull and Schrötter, who went to the king in the summer of 1806 to beg him to implement far-reaching reforms in the army and in the state. Far from regarding this as the act of devoted patriots, the king felt that it was gross insubordination and a flagrant disregard for his prerogative powers. The approach was thus rebutted.

The reformers could only watch helplessly the destruction of Prussia, and the disgraceful performance of the Prussian army filled them with anger and despair. Scharnhorst was enraged at the behaviour of the commanders with their 'fat bellies and thin skulls' and felt it a disgrace to have to fight alongside such 'miserable, stupid and cowardly men'. The Duke of Brunswick he described as 'seventy years old, deaf, forgetful and in every way a weak man'. He continued right up until the Peace of Tilsit to urge reform, but to no avail. The only compensation in those wretched months was the brilliant success of his tactics at Preussisch-Eylau, which saved the Prussian army from certain destruction and left the battle undecided. This showed that Scharnhorst was not merely a critic of the old army but also an outstanding field commander.

Scharnhorst, like Stein and Hardenberg, was not a Prussian. He was born in 1755 in Hanover, the son of a poor farmer. He made a career as an artillery officer in Lower Saxony, until he moved to Berlin in 1801. He was a determined, almost stubborn man who lacked the chameleon-like diplomatic skills of Hardenberg, but was less haughty and less short-tempered than Stein. As a foreigner and a man of simple background he had little patience with the Prussian junkers. Although he had fully absorbed all the niceties of Frederican tactics he was quick to understand the true nature and the implications of the French Revolution, particularly its effect on military strategy and tactics. Almost instinctively he identified with the jacobin notion of a nation at arms, and with extraordinary dedication and determination he set about applying these principles to the Prussian army. To an exceptional degree he combined the talents of battle commander, administrator, politician and theoretician. He was both far-sighted and intensely practical, combining a rich imagination with a complete command of the minute details of administration. He was such an exceptional, talented and attractive man that his biographer, Max Lehmann, can perhaps be excused his excessive enthusiasm and his occasional flights of fancy.

The defeat of the Prussian army had shown that the reformers' contention that the army needed drastic overhauling could no longer be denied. The economic consequences of the defeat were such that even the most pusillanimous of the opponents of reform realized that changes would have to be made if the French were ever to be removed. On 21 November 1806 Napoleon decreed the Continental System from Berlin, in an

attempt to cut England off from the continental market.
He hoped that he would thus be able to destroy the British
economy, starve the British by stopping supplies of grain from
the continent and enable the French bourgeoisie to take over
those markets which had been dominated by the British. The
Continental System initially had a disastrous impact on the
Prussian economy. The junkers were no longer able to export
grain, wood and wool to Britain. The Silesian linen industry
was forbidden to export to Italy, Spain and the non-European
countries with the result that the industry was virtually destroyed. The ship building industry was particularly hard hit. French
policies resulted in a sharp rise in the price of articles such as
cotton, sugar, tobacco and coffee, which had an immediate
effect on the cost of living. Raw material and even manufactured
goods were subject to a number of controls and quotas which
further hampered the Prussian economy. The silk industry
was unable to compete with the French and was destroyed.
Grain prices fell by sixty to eighty per cent, shipping dropped
sixty per cent and the silk, linen and cloth trades lost fifty per
cent of their markets.

The French occupation speeded up a process which had
already become apparent in the latter part of the eighteenth
century. The social structure of the country was no longer
adequate to its economic function. The feudal order on the
land could not meet the demands of modern agricultural
capitalism, and now the economic position of the junkers had
been further weakened. The burden of the occupation weighed
heavily on all classes. The peasants and the urban workers
were further exploited by their own ruling class and by the
French, and were faced with ever rising costs. The merchants
and manufacturers were hurt by the loss of markets and of
transit trade. All classes were saddled with the indemnity.
The drastic reduction in the size of the army and the bureaucracy left many aristocrats without a job. The crisis was now so
acute that it was not merely the economic sphere that was
affected; the political structure of the country was in danger,
and the possibility of revolutionary change was now a real
threat. Faced with this situation many of the ruling elite,
who had become heavily compromised by their failures,
argued that the only feasible policy was co-operation with the

French. Further conflict would lead to the total destruction of Prussia, and reform would open the flood gates of revolution. On the other hand the reformers argued that only by careful reform could a solution be found without recourse to violence, and the object would be to create a new society in which the citizens identified with the state, or in the phraseology of the legal commentators the *societas civilis* would become one with the *res publica*. The object of such reforms was to create a society which would be capable of paying the indemnity and which would have the strength and resources to liberate the country from the French.

On 9 October 1807 an edict was published which announced that on St Martin's day (11 November) 1810 all forms of serfdom would be abolished, and that there would be 'only free men'. With the abolition of hereditary bondage, the freedom to buy and sell land, the abolition of the exclusive rights of the guilds and the freedom to choose a profession, the way was opened for the development of the productive forces. Reforms of city administration, the schools, contract law and taxation and the separation of justice from the administration helped to create a society of free men who would create a new state on principles quite different from those of the old hierarchical and authoritarian society. But the reformers sadly underestimated the power and influence of the old elite. Freeing the peasants did not settle the question of land tenure. In 1811 a new edict decreed that peasants who were hereditary tenants could become freeholders if they gave up one third of their property to the landowner. Those peasants who held tenure for life were obliged to give up one half of their property to the junker. By 1865 the peasants had been forced by these means to give up more than two and a half million acres to the junkers. Many of the peasants were forced to sell off their remaining lands, for they were too small to support one family, and the junkers were able to buy up their property for modest amounts. The result of the liberation of the serfs was the 'Prussian way' to modern agricultural methods: the junkers maintained their dominance, increased the size of their estates and were able to draw on the expropriated peasants to employ them as agricultural labourers. The 'liberation' of the serfs was thus equally the liberation of the junkers from whom many of the restrictions of the feudal order had been burdensome and who were now able to exploit to the full the possibilities of large-scale agriculture. Meanwhile reform of the army had begun. Scharnhorst was appointed in 1807 to head a commission to propose a reorganization of the army. The commission was split between the reformers and those who were either sceptical or opposed to reform. Scharnhorst was supported by Gneisenau, the son of an Austrian officer who had joined the Prussian army in 1786 at the age of twenty-six, and who had become nationally famous for his defence of Colberg. The most radical and outspoken of the reformers was Major von Grolman. He was supported by Count Götzen who was a member for only a short time in 1808. Boyen, a protégé of Scharnhorst, was also a member. The reformers were supported by two civilians on the commission, Stein, the architect of the civilian reforms, and Könen, the auditor general. Clausewitz gave his expert advice and support to the reformers and drafted some of the position papers.

The two most outspoken opponents of the reformers were von Lottum and von Bronikowsky, but the latter was soon replaced by Boyen. Von Massenbach was a conservative and slow cavalry officer whose opposition to Scharnhorst was never particularly effective. Far more trouble was created by Borstell who was exceptionally sensitive to criticism and detested Scharnhorst to such an extent that he had eventually to be replaced by Götzen. Thus the reformers had a clear majority in the commission, but Lottum was the king's adjutant and therefore had direct access to him. Even more important, the commission was opposed by the majority of the officer corps, and this made it extremely difficult effectively to implement the suggestions made by the commission.

The military commission was entrusted with the task of examining all aspects of military policy, but the king instructed it to pay particular attention to the punishment of those who had been cowardly or incompetent during the war, an investigation of the feasibility of opening the officer corps to the bourgeoisie, the problem of exemptions and mercenaries and the reform of military law and punishments.

The task of investigating the general conduct of officers in the campaign of 1806-7 was relegated to a special commission, the Superior Investigating Commission, which set about its work with ponderous seriousness. The commission produced 606 volumes, each of over 700 pages, of reports which provide fascinating material on the army of the period. By 1813 when the war broke out again the commission had not even finished examining the year 1806. The task of investigating the conduct of individual officers was largely entrusted to the regiments. In each regiment a tribunal was established of officers of proven merit, and the result was an extensive purging of the officer corps, each officer being tried by his peers. By 1809 according to the statistics of the historical division of the General Staff, of 142 generals in 1806 17 had been cashiered, 86 honourably dismissed and only 22 remained on active duty. Only two of those who remained. Blücher and Tauentzien, had commands in 1813. Of the 885 staff officers 50 were cashiered, 584 honourably dismissed and 185 remained in the service. Of the 6,069 junior officers 141 were cashiered, 3,924 resigned voluntarily and 1,584 remained in the army. To protect officers against libellous accusations certificates of good conduct were issued to those who had fought with distinction during the past campaign. This was necessitated by the public outcry against the army for its failures and the incessant demands for scapegoats. But although the work of the investigating commission was carried out in a somewhat hectic and hysterical atmosphere there is ample evidence that the job was done thoroughly and fairly. It was neither a formalistic bureaucratic exercise nor an over-emotional response to defeat and humiliation, but a sober attempt to correct manifest abuses and shortcomings within the officer corps. It was carried out without creating a vast bureaucratic apparatus and without in any way undermining military discipline. The commission's work was most beneficial to the regeneration of the army.

It was not enough merely to remove the incompetent from the officer corps. Officer selection and promotion had to be based on ability rather than birth and length of service. In November 1808 the principle that promotions in the senior ranks could only be according to length of service was abolished, ending a system which even Frederick II had criticized as leading to a decrepit and unimaginative leadership. This reform was the necessary corollary of a law of 6 August 1808 which was drafted by Grolman and which stipulated that anyone with

41

the right education and qualities could become an officer. The wording of the law, which is often rhapsodic, gives an excellent indication of the reformers' thinking.

Service cannot be monopolized by birth; for if birth is given too many rights then many undeveloped and unused strengths will slumber on the lap of the nation, and the soaring wings of genius will be crippled by these oppressive conditions. . . . We shall open the triumphal gates to the bourgeois, through which prejudice only wishes the aristocrat to enter. The new age needs more than old titles and parchments, it needs fresh deeds and strength.

Such ideas were dangerous and subversive in the eyes of the aristocratic opposition, and as thousands of officers had been dismissed or obliged to resign their commissions after the Peace of Tilsit many of them were exceedingly hard-pressed and therefore more outspoken in their opposition. Their spokesman was York who poured scorn on the assumptions on which the reforms were based. 'We are now concerned with every miserable subject, for because Pope Sixtus V was a swineherd in his youth they are afraid that some holy pig-keeper might pass unnoticed.' To Prince William he uttered the solemn warning: 'If your Royal Highness takes away the rights of me and my children, what are yours based upon?' But Scharnhorst remained steadfast. He had no intention of destroying the aristocracy as such, but of ending privileges which could no longer be justified. To the king he wrote: 'If aristocratic children with their crass lack of knowledge and their feeble childishness alone should have the privilege of becoming officers and if men with knowledge and courage are placed under them without any chance of promotion, then the aristocracy is helped, but the army will become bad and will be the laughing stock of the other educated estates.'

Henceforth anyone might become an officer provided that he met certain minimum educational standards. Officer cadets had to begin their military training as privates, not as corporals as had previously been the custom. Each regiment formed a committee of officers which selected the cornets. Potential officers, privates and NCOs were allowed to put their names forward to this committee, but clearly the fact the regiments themselves were able to select their own cornets meant that they tended to become self-perpetuating cliques, and this was a powerful antidote to the reformers' determination to open up the officer corps to the middle class. A special committee in Berlin was then empowered to select a certain number of the cornets and recommend them for a commission as lieutenant. The law also required that all officers due for promotion should take special examinations which tested not only their military knowledge but also their general education. As many officers had been dismissed by the investigating committee, and as Napoleon had severely restricted the size of the army, very few new officers were commissioned between 1808 and 1813, so that these reforms had little impact. The democratic principles of 1808 were further modified in 1813 when the officer corps was expanded, and the aristocracy was thus able to maintain its predominance. The principles of 1808 were also of limited nature, because the educational requirements were such that they virtually excluded all but the middle class and the aristocracy. NCOs with sufficient educational background were few and far between.

The most radical suggestion of all came from Hardenberg. He suggested that NCOs should be elected by the privates, and subalterns by the NCOs. But these ideas were roundly denounced even by the most radical of the reformers who feared that it would seriously undermine military discipline. They wished to create a sense of comradeship by allowing regiments to select their own officer candidates. This idea was a particularly weak point in the reform of officer selection, for it diminished the importance of the educational requirements and gave the middle class little chance of access to the officer corps.

Scharnhorst, who placed particular emphasis on the education of officers, would have dearly liked to abolish the cadet schools which were havens of aristocratic privilege and had little educational value. Faced with determined opposition he was able to reform the curriculum only to a certain extent, and henceforth all cadets had to pass the cornet examinations just like any other potential officer. The reformers had to concede the demand that only the sons of officers be admitted to the cadet schools, and this had the effect of keeping them almost exclusively aristocratic. Thus the cadet schools remained, in the eyes of the reformers, 'incubators of aristocratic pride, caste consciousness and obscurantist snobbery'. However a step forward was made in the education of officers with the foundation in 1810 of the General War School, which was later to be called the War Academy. The school was to help realize some of Scharnhorst's dreams of a well educated and professional officer corps, and was to train generations of staff officers.

The reformers believed that men were rational beings, amenable of argument, and yet capable of great sacrifice to a cause which they felt to be just. The ferocious discipline of the Prussian army in which men were almost beaten to death for trivial infringements of discipline was clearly a denial of this belief, and therefore it needed drastic reform so that military justice could be based on rational principles. As Clausewitz pointed out, if men were freed from serfdom and if the old mercenary system was abolished, then the number of desertions from the army would decrease, for Prussians could fight for their beliefs and ideals just as much as Frenchmen. Thus the old barbarous punishments would have to be abolished. If discipline were bearable, then the people would no longer dread their military service. In 1808 the vicious practice of running the gauntlet was abolished, and beatings were to be performed only by special disciplinary units after proper investigation, not on the spur of the moment by sadistic officers. Gneisenau was the most eloquent spokesman for the abolition of flogging, and in a widely quoted newspaper article he insisted that 'freedom of the back . . . seems to be the essential precondition of universal military service'. These two principles were closely connected in the new articles of war published on Frederick William III's birthday. They reaffirmed the principle of universal military service and also made military punishments far more humane. Deserters were no longer shot but given ten years' imprisonment. All severe punishments had to be recommended by duly constituted military courts and confirmed by the king, and death penalties had to be approved by the king.

There is no doubt that the new articles of war represented a major advance. Discipline was to be founded on rational understanding rather than brute force. Free men could no longer be treated like animals. But however lofty these ideals in practice, the change was not so great. There is ample evidence to suggest that corporal punishment continued to be widely used by officers and NCOs, and in April 1813 there was even a popular demonstration against an officer who was guilty of beating his men. The main weakness of these reforms was that although officers were instructed to treat their men as human beings there were totally inadequate means of enforcing these requirements. Officers who were discovered beating their men, usually with the flat of their swords, were simply given a written or personal reprimand. If the officer persisted and was given frequent reprimands he could be sentenced to a period of house arrest in the mess, a punishment that was seldom particularly unpleasant.

If the army were indeed to become the 'nation in arms' and if soldiers were to be 'citizens in uniform' so that the full strength of the country could be realized in the army, then it was obvious that there had to be a reform of military law. In 1809 a law stated that only military personnel could be brought before a court martial, and that soldiers involved in civic suits were to be brought before civilian courts. All criminal charges were brought to court martial. The reform went only half way to meet the problem. The families and dependants of military personnel were no longer subject to courts martial, nor were ex-soldiers, but criminal cases, even if they had nothing whatever to do with military matters, were still heard by military courts. The army was simply not prepared to accept the logic of the notion of 'citizens in uniform' and was determined that its dirty linen should not be washed in public and that its own legal proceedings should not be open to public scrutiny. This system had the effect of protecting the officer corps, for the standard disciplinary procedure for officers was to bring the case in front of a court of honour of his peers. The assumption was that as the officer corps was likely to remain predominantly aristocratic, the concept of honour would be sufficient guarantee for the behaviour of officers. It was easy to take the step from this dubious notion to asserting that infractions of the law should be regarded as infractions of a code of honour. Thus formal justice for officers was deemed unnecessary, and provisions were made only for courts of honour. The army successfully fought off the attempt to bring its legal proceedings under civilian scrutiny, and however well intended the courts of honour might initially have been, they were soon to be abused and used to protect the officer corps and to cut it off from civil society.

None of these reforms were likely to be particularly effective without an efficient administration of the army, and the reformers, civilian as well as military, were well aware of the need for a central administrative agency. Stein's great memorandum of November 1807 for the reorganization of the government proposed a war ministry which would combine the functions of command and administration. Frederick William III was fearful that such a ministry would undermine his royal power of command and raised several objections which resulted once again in a compromise that was far from being completely satisfactory. The ministry was divided into two sections, a War Department under Scharnhorst and a Military Economy Department under Lottum. Both men were given the right of direct access to the king so that neither could be considered as the minister. As Lottum was a conservative the effectiveness of the ministry was greatly diminished by the clashes between him and Scharnhorst. It was not until 1814 that the king appointed Boyen minister of war, so that in the critical period before 1813 the army was without an effective central body, a factor which was detrimental to the reformers. Of great significance was the fact that the cabinet order of July 1808 which created the war ministry decreed that the head of the War Department should also be head of the general staff, so that Scharnhorst was *de facto* minister of war and chief of the General staff.

The general staff consisted of little more than thirty-one officers and an office. As yet it was of little significance, but a beginning had been made. In 1809 Frederick William III, pushed by the conservatives and the French, dismissed Scharnhorst from the War Department, but he remained as chief of the general staff. He resigned this position for a time in 1812, and his place was taken by von Rauch. Scharnhorst still remained in close contact with the staff officers who devoted their time and energy to making sure that the army did everything possible to prepare for a war of liberation. Although few in number the staff officers were enthusiastic, determined and well trained and made a major contribution to the effectiveness of the army in 1813.

Central to Scharnhorst's military thinking was the idea of universal service. To a degree it was necessitated by self defence. Just as France instituted universal service in 1793 in order to protect the revolution against the counter-revolutionaries, so universal service was needed in Prussia to protect the state against France. To a humanist like Scharnhorst only a real and serious threat to national survival could justify placing free men under military discipline. With his brilliant insights into the connections between social structure and military system, without which no army can be understood, he realized that universal service would have to be tied to social reform. In military terms the reform of the state and the army was intended 'to raise the spirit of the army, to give it life, to unite the army and the nation and to give it direction towards its great and important destiny'. This in turn could not be achieved without giving to the nation a sense of independence and without destroying the old prejudices and social forms which restricted its growth. In order that the principle of universal service might be implemented the canton system would have to be abolished, for it excluded virtually all but the peasantry from military duty, and if the canton system were to go then the foreign mercenaries would also no longer be required.

Scharnhorst's idea was to divide those who were liable for military service into two sections, the standing army and the militia. Those who did not have the financial means to buy arms and a uniform and to pay for their keep during their military service were to go into the standing army where everything would be provided free. Those who were able to pay for these things were drafted into the militia. This unsatisfactory compromise was the result of the chronic shortage of money. It was simply the cheapest way of increasing the size of the army, and the reformers were unhappy with the fact that it perpetuated the system of exemptions for the wealthy which had been one of the worst aspects of the old system. The militia was required to spend two months training per year in the initial period, which was to be reduced to one month. It was designed to play a supportive role to the regular army in time of war.

Even though the military reorganization committee recommended these measures unanimously, it was considered too radical a departure for the king and his ultra-conservative advisers to accept. But it was not only the ultras who were opposed to the scheme: enlightened reformers such as Altenstein and Niebuhr were convinced that universal service would mark the end of all culture, disrupt the economy and place an undue burden on the middle class. Even Stein was dubious about the principle of universal service, and although he agreed that the towns should contribute as much to the army as the country, he nevertheless argued that certain professions should be exempted. In fact it was Napoleon who settled the question by forbidding the militia, but there is little doubt that this action was greeted with sighs of relief by the king, the conservatives and influential sections of the middle class. The problem now facing the reformers was how to make a 'people's army' out of a standing army.

The failure of the militia scheme meant that the old canton laws of 1792 remained in force until 1813. Attempts by the reformers to circumvent the Treaty of Paris by expanding the Civil Guard, (*Bürgergarde*) which had been instituted in the towns by Napoleon, were frustrated by the king. The only way to increase the reserves was therefore to make sure that as many as possible of those on the canton rolls were indeed trained. This was to be done by the *Krümper* system. Every month three to five men were sent on leave from each company in the infantry and foot artillery, their places to be taken by recruits. By means of this constant turnover it was hoped that a substantial reserve of well trained men could be created. The idea came from Scharnhorst, but he was careful to present it to the king as the brain child of a crusty old Frederican general so that the monarch would not be immediately suspicious. Nationalist historians created the legend that the *Krümper* system enabled the Prussians to train a reserve army of 150,000 men, and this legend was so widely believed that provisions against the recreation of such a system were incorporated into the Treaty of Versailles. In fact it was far less successful than was imagined. The Prussian army with reserves numbered 53,523 in 1807 and 65,675 in 1813; the difference between the two figures cannot be accounted for solely by the *Krümpers*. In large measure it was due to bringing the regiments up to full strength. The *Krümper* system, however, should not be totally discounted as a reaction to the excessive claims of the nationalists. The size of the Prussian army was greatly reduced by Napoleon's drafting a large part of it to assist in the invasion of Russia, and considerable numbers of Prussian troops were also used by the French for coastal defence. The *Krümper* system helped to offset some of these losses.

With the partial success of the reforms changes had to be made in the tactical training of officers and men. Gradually constant drill was replaced by exercises in the field, target shooting and training in sharpshooter tactics. In 1812 new training regulations were published based on the experience gained. They were the work of a commission which included Scharnhorst, Clausewitz and York, the latter a conservative general who was a specialist in light-infantry tactics. The outstanding feature of the regulations was their flexibility and their common sense approach. As late as 1856 Engels was to write that the Prussian regulations were still the best in the world in spite of the fact that they were nearly fifty years old. This was a striking tribute to Scharnhorst's genius. Prussian tactics were now a mixture of the old linear formation, battalion columns and *tirailleur* tactics as used by the French. They managed to combine effective fire power with a strong attacking force. Artillery tactics were modified so as to give maximum support to the infantry, preparing the way for an attack or helping in defence. The co-ordination of the two arms had become considerably more effective. Cavalry tactics were also changed so as to make the cavalry subordinate to the infantry, and they no longer enjoyed the independent role they had played under Frederick II. Disgruntled cavalry officers were later to insist that Scharnhorst, a mere gunner, misunderstood the nature of the cavalry. Others insisted that with greatly increased fire-power the cavalry was bound to be reduced to a supporting role. The fierce debate on the usefulness of the cavalry begins in Prussia in 1812, and still continues in the historical literature.

Even more difficult than changing the tactics of the Prussian army was the problem of altering the strategic and operational thinking of the senior officers. In spite of the dismissal and pensioning of such a large proportion of the senior ranks, the generals were mostly of a conservative and unimaginative cast of mind. Scharnhorst's solution to this problem was to train a new generation of highly qualified staff officers who would instil a new spirit into the army. The new strategic principles can be briefly summarized: the maximum utilization of the resources of the country and of maximum military strength at the beginning of operations; the army should march divided and come together only on the field of battle; a determination to engage the opponents in battle as quickly as possible under optimum conditions; swift mobilization and utilization of reserves; the use of every opportunity to divide the enemy forces or to make the enemy use up its strength in long marches; pursuit of the enemy after a defeat in battle so that when possible his forces might be completely destroyed. These principles, developed by the reformers to a point of considerable sophistication, were the most that could be achieved until major advances in communications and transport made it possible for men like Moltke to develop them further.

The effective application of these principles required officers of considerable ability, discipline and independence, and a high degree of enthusiasm and determination. The reformers had to fight against enormous odds in the war of 1813, and the degree to which they were successful is testimony to their outstanding abilities. They were able to triumph over a reactionary court, incomplete military reforms, the relatively small size of the Prussian army and an unsympathetic coalition. Determined to overcome every obstacle which stood in their way, they were able to show the validity of their strategic and operational ideas by their significant contribution to the defeat of Napoleon.

The repressive policies of the French in Prussia were such that popular pressure was mounting for a war of liberation. As early as 1806 the Nürnberg bookseller, Palm, had been shot by the French for agitation against the occupying forces, and he had become something of a national martyr. The Spanish guerilla war of 1808 acted as a great impetus to the patriots, and a number of secret societies, the best known of which is the *Tugendbund*, were formed to work for the overthrow of French domination. The commandant of Berlin, Count Chasot, formed a committee which was in close contact with the reformers, and which tried to co-ordinate all anti-French activities. In 1808 Gneisenau presented the king with a memorandum on the possibility of an insurrection in northern Germany. The document was remarkably radical: it called for a free constitution, the dispossession of all those princes and aristocrats who refused to support the insurrection and complete freedom from all feudal dues for those peasants who fought in the campaign. These plans were far from being unrealistic pipe-dreams. Both Scharnhorst and Gneisenau were well aware that a popular revolt on its own would never succeed without close liaison with the regular army, and that Prussia alone was not strong enough to defeat France. An insurrection called for close co-operation between the regular and irregular forces, and between Prussia and her allies. The king and the junkers were afraid of the revolutionary dimension of these schemes and preferred to be subservient to the French to running the risk of social upheaval. The patriots still hoped for an alliance with Austria, which was preparing for war, but their hopes were dashed in September 1808 when the king's plenipotentiaries signed the humiliating treaty with the French. In November that year Stein was dismissed, largely at the instigation of the reactionary court party, and the reformers lost a powerful support. York summed up the attitude of the conservatives: 'one idiot has been crushed, the other nest of vipers will be destroyed by their own poison.'

In 1809 war resumed between Austria and France, and in May Napoleon suffered his first defeat at Aspern. News of the victory was greeted enthusiastically in Prussia, and the reformers again pressed the king to join with Austria to drive the French from Germany. A number of actions against the French were planned. Chasot was in close liaison with two officers who organized 2,500 peasants to attack the French garrison in Magdeburg. There were various spontaneous actions against the French in Berlin and the Prussian estates refused to pay taxes to the French. Further inspiration to the reformers was given by the revolt of the Tirolese peasants under Andreas Hofer who fought fiercely against the invaders. But the king refused to budge, and the crushing defeat of the Austrians at Wagram destroyed any hope of an effective uprising in Prussia. The year did see one dramatic military action in Germany. The commander of the 2 Brandenburg Hussar regiment, Ferdinand von Schill, who had played an important role with Gneisenau and the civilian Nettelbeck in the defence of Colberg in 1807, marched his regiment to Westphalia and began to harass the French, all without permission from the authorities. In a dramatic rush across Germany he was able for a time to seize Halle and later Stralsund, where he was killed during the French assault on the city. Similarly Duke Frederick William of Brunswick formed his 'Black Band', and supported by Austrian troops was able to hold Leipzig and Dresden. After Wagram the duke continued a desperate battle until he was forced to flee to England where he formed a German legion which fought on the continent in 1813. Neither Schill nor the Duke of Brunswick was able to inspire a popular revolt in Prussia, and after Wagram such an action would almost certainly have led to disaster. The experience of 1809 made the court party even more suspicious of the reformers and Prussian policy became more conservative and pusillanimous.

In February 1812 Prussia offered half her army to assist Napoleon's attack on Russia. Many of the reformers, chief among them Gneisenau, left Prussia in disgust and went to Russia to offer their services for the defeat of France. A quarter of the Prussian officer corps resigned. Scharnhorst requested early retirement, but this was refused. Because of his strong feelings for the institution of the monarchy he did not leave the country, but went to join Blücher in Breslau where he was soon surrounded by his gloomy disciples.

Gneisenau had urged the king to: 'Trust in fortune! Trust the gods! Step into the boat, in spite of the crashing and the storm, as heroically as Caesar!' He called on him to organize an uprising to attack the French in the rear as they marched into Russia. The king had commented that this was very nice as poetry but he had no desire to instigate a repeat performance of the revolt of the Maccabees. The rage and frustration of the reformers did not last long. Russia was invaded in July and in December the remnants of the French army were back in East Prussia. On 30 December 1812 General York signed the Convention of Tauroggen which declared the neutrality of the Prussian troops which had been under Russian command. On 8 January Russian troops entered Königsberg to an enthusiastic welcome from the citizens. Shortly afterwards Stein arrived in the city and, supported by the Russians, he persuaded York, who had been dismissed by the king for his insubordination in signing the Convention of Tauroggen without royal consent, to urge the extraordinary *Landtag* to agree to join in the fight against the French. The *Landtag* agreed, again without the assent of the crown, to establish a territorial army (*Landwehr*) at its own expense, and approved the principle that every fit person under the age of forty-five was liable for military duty. So great was the response to these moves in East Prussia that the king and the court party were forced to give way and break the alliance with Napoleon. The Prusso-Russian treaty was signed at Kalisch on 28 February 1813 by Scharnhorst and Kutusov, and on 16 March Prussia officially declared war on France.

With the resumption of the war in 1813 the way was open for the implementation of the ideas which the reformers had been urging since 1806. In two edicts of 3 and 9 February 1813 Scharnhorst established the principle of universal service. The first of these edicts established the voluntary *Jäger* detachments. The *Jäger* were to be recruited from those volunteers who were able to pay for their own equipment and uniforms, and thus they came largely from the middle class, although some *Jäger* were equipped by subscriptions from patriots. The reason for these particular formations was not so much to save money for there were after all only some 12,000 *Jäger*, but rather to fire the enthusiasm of the middle class for the army and to create a volunteer army where the imperative to serve should be moral rather than legal. Scharnhorst saw in this system the outline of the army of the future. Promotions and appointments as officer or NCO were to a considerable extent conditional on the approval of subordinates. The officer was *primus inter pares* rather than a figure of absolute authority. Scharnhorst hoped that the *Jäger* detachments would be the breeding ground of future officers and prove the military efficacy of a democratically organized army. He paid close attention to the development of the *Jäger*, but when he was mortally wounded at the battle of Gross-Görschen and the development of the *Jäger* detachments was no longer subject to his close scrutiny, the units began to change their attitude. Officers of the line were frequently replaced by *Jäger* who quickly gained a reputation for excellence. The *Jäger* detachments thus rapidly became watered down and served as little more than recruiting grounds for officers in the infantry regiments. In 1814 the volunteer *Jäger* detachments were disbanded. The *Jäger* regiments of the nineteenth century, elite light infantry regiments, therefore had nothing whatever to do with the original innovatory and progressive plans of Scharnhorst.

The principle of universal service had been annunciated in the edict of 9 February 1813. Once war had been declared on France it was possible to create the militia which had been forbidden in 1808. Scharnhorst knew full well that the king was opposed to the creation of a militia (*Landwehr*) and that Napoleon's actions against it were welcomed by him. He had therefore taken the precaution of writing into the Treaty of Kalisch the stipulation that Prussia was required to provide militia forces. All men between the ages of seventeen and forty who were physically fit for military service were required to enrol for duty in the *Landwehr*. Those who volunteered were given certain preferential treatment. If there were fewer than 120,000 volunteers recruits would be drafted by lots. No exemptions were allowed except for priests, teachers and some civil servants.

The *Landwehr* was far from being the democratic army of contemporary aristocratic propaganda and of historical legend. Officers were chosen by a committee in each district (*Kreis*) consisting of two junkers, a burgher and a peasant, the two latter being appointed by the government. Even such an unrepresentative body was not allowed to make final decisions, and all appointments had to be subject to royal review. Even a man like Gneisenau with his romantic democratic notions was horrified to find that his tailor had been commissioned in the *Landwehr* and made certain that this 'mistake' was corrected.

The military effectiveness of the *Landwehr* was limited. Some units fought with great distinction and courage, others collapsed at the first exchange of fire. Patriotic enthusiasm, though often high, was simply not enough to overcome insufficient training and lack of experience. Gneisenau was particularly concerned about the *Landwehr* in the Silesian army, and gave orders that strict discipline should be enforced to hold the *Landwehr* together. Colonel Steinmetz, who had been with Gneisenau at Colberg, reported after the successful battle of Katzbach: 'The Command-

54

ing Officers of the battalions have been punished with stern warnings, several officers have been arrested, the majority of the *Landwehr* has been demoted to the second class, made to march past with their badges reversed, punished with hunger and beatings; the only thing left to do now is to have them shot.' The shortcomings of the *Landwehr* were instantly seized upon by the conservatives who insisted that they proved that 'democratic institutions' were worthless and even dangerous. In fact the reverse was true. The failures of the *Landwehr* were in large measure due to the fact that it was too much a poor imitation of the standing army rather than something new and innovatory. The *Jeunesse dorée* in the *Jäger* were magnificently equipped, admittedly at their own expense, and were showered with honours, welcomed as heroes, hymned by the poets and immortalized by the historians. It is therefore hardly surprising that they were able to enjoy a 'loving and paternal' discipline. The *Landwehr* by contrast was manned largely by the poor and dispossessed. The typical *Landwehr* man was a Silesian weaver, wretchedly clothed, often barefoot, with obsolete equipment, poorly fed, and with no protection against rain and snow. It is therefore hardly surprising that morale was not particularly high, and it was certainly not improved by harsh discipline. What is truly remarkable is the great contribution which the *Landwehr* made to the liberation in spite of all these difficulties, and the degree to which it was held in popular esteem. It was the affection shown towards the *Landwehr* by the people which convinced the conservatives that it was indeed a revolutionary force.

The final act in the attempt to create a 'People's Army' was the edict of April 1813 calling for the creation of a home guard, the *Landsturm*. This edict was the logical consequence of the reformers' belief that the full resources of the nation should be mobilized for war. For revolutionary romantics like Ernst Moritz Arndt it was the revival of the Old Germanic practice of the military community (*Wehrgemeinde*) which was the natural and national response to the French Revolution. For Gneisenau the *Landsturm* was part of the close identity of the army with the nation, a relationship which was so intimate that he believed that the army could fight even against the wishes of the king. The edict, drafted by Jakob Bartholdy who had fought with the partisans in the Tirol, obliged all male citizens between the ages of fifteen and sixty who were not in either the regular army or the *Landwehr* to fight as guerillas in the manner of the irregular forces in the Vendee, Spain, Russia and the Tirol. The *Landsturm* was not uniformed, and therefore could not be treated as an army by the enemy. *Landsturm* men would thus not be taken prisoner. They were to specialize in sabotage, scorched earth and sniping.

The notion of a *Landsturm* was exceedingly alarming to the conservatives. Arming the people was tantamount to jacobinism. The weapons that were used against the invader could all too easily be turned against the enemy at home. Tempers ran high. War Councillor Scharnweber, a fervent opponent of the *Landsturm*, became so outspoken in his criticisms that great tact was needed to prevent him from fighting a duel with Gneisenau. In the end the *Landsturm* was never properly implemented, partly because of conservative opposition and partly because the French were soon driven from Prussia. In some areas in the east the peasants organized impromptu *Landsturm* units which were reasonably effective. The intellectuals were also fired with patriotic enthusiasm. Friedrich Köppen wrote:

The professors of Berlin University formed their own troop, and constantly practised their weapon drill. The small hunch-backed Schleiermacher, who could hardly carry a pike, on the extreme left, Savigny who was as tall as a tree, stood on the right wing; the energetic and puckish Niebuhr drilled so that his hands, which were only used to hold a quill, were covered in large callouses; the ideologically valiant Fichte appeared armed to the teeth, two pistols in a wide belt, a long sword trailing behind him, and in the entrance of his apartment lances and shields were placed for him and his son. Old Schadow led the hordes of artists, Iffland the heroes of the stage; the latter were usually costumed and armed in an adventurously mediaeval or fantastically theatrical manner: scaling helmets and *Pickelhaube*, broadswords and even cudgels appeared on the scene; on the parade ground one saw the warlike accoutrements of Talbot and Burgundy, or Wallenstein and Richard Coeur de Lion. Iffland actually appeared with the breastplate and shield of the Maid of Orleans, which caused considerable amusement.

As Köppen pointed out the idea of the *Landsturm* was sublime, but it is one short step from the sublime to the ridiculous.

Scharnhorst's death in June 1813, the result of a shot in the leg, was a serious loss to the reformers. But a worthy successor was found in Gneisenau who was appointed chief of general staff, and served in the campaign as chief of staff to Blücher who commanded the Silesian army. Gneisenau was a more romantic and radical person than Scharnhorst; he was more impetuous and lacked Scharnhorst's respect for the monarchy. He had served in America as a mercenary when his Ansbach-Bayreuth regiment was hired to the British Government. It was in America that he learnt at first hand the lessons of the importance of sharpshooting and of high morale, and he was determined to instil some of the same enthusiasm and fervour into the Prussians. Returning to Prussian service after his duties in America, Gneisenau spent many years of dull and monotonous duty and remained a figure of some obscurity. It was not until 1807 that the 47-year-old major became widely known for his leadership in the defence of Colberg. He then worked closely with Scharnhorst, the two men admirably complementing one another. Gneisenau provided much of the fire and energy, Scharnhorst the wisdom and pragmatism. The contribution of the general staff to the successes of Blücher's army were great. Blücher, a hard-drinking, womanizing and rough old soldier, was immensely popular with his troops, a warrior of the old style. He was quick to realize the intellectual superiority of Gneisenau, and was always prepared to accept his expert advice. Both men were somewhat impetuous, but Gneisenau was restrained by his senior staff officer von Müffling, a disciple of Scharnhorst, whose appraisals of the overall situation were often more sober and realistic than those of his superior. Staff work in the Silesian army approached the ideal. Blücher, Gneisenau and von Müffling were all men of exceptional strength of character and ability. They complemented one another, with the result that they were able to achieve so much more together than would ever have been possible had they worked separately.

The last great act of the reformers was the Army Law of 3 September 1814, the work of Boyen who had been appointed as Scharnhorst's successor to a reorganized war ministry. Boyen, unlike so many of the reformers, was a Prussian. He was educated in Königsberg where he was strongly influenced by

Kant. He remained throughout his life a fine example of an enlightened and humanitarian reformer who remained true to his Kantian idealism. He had played a vital role on the Military Reorganization Commission and, having failed to persuade the king to fight against the French in 1812, he left Prussia in disgust to join the Russian army. In 1813 he returned to Prussia to act as general staff chief to von Bülow. He was shortly afterwards appointed minister of war.

Boyen's law was in many ways the most lasting achievement of the reformers. It was modified to a degree in the military reforms of 1859, but in essentials it remained in force until the collapse of the monarchy in November 1918. The law firmly established the principle of universal service, even in peacetime, without the possibility of exemptions or purchasing substitutes. The only exception, and a very important one, was the stipulation that 'young men from the educated classes' who were able to pay for their own equipment were to serve for only one year. All those who were not eligible to serve as 'one year volunteers' were obliged to serve for three years with the regular army. After these three years the men were required to serve a further two years in the active reserve. The one-year volunteers, most of whom were bourgeois, were obliged to serve in the *Landwehr* on completion of their duties, and the majority of them became officers. Thus most of the *Landwehr* officers were from the middle class, and it is for this reason that the bourgeoisie had a particular affection for the *Landwehr*, while the conservatives tended to regard it as a dangerously democratic and progressive institution. Obviously not all young men who were eligible for military service were required to serve, the army would have been gigantic had that been the case. Recruits were selected by lots, a practice which was unpopular but was generally regarded as being more equitable than the old system of exemptions.

Equally important in the army law was the separation of the *Landwehr* from the regular army. After their two-year service in the active reserve men were required to serve in the *Landwehr*. The organization of the *Landwehr* was kept quite separate from the regular army, and with its bourgeois officer corps and part-time troops it was intended to bridge the gap between the people and the regular army. In this way the *Landwehr* embodied many of the ideas of the reformers. It was to a certain extent a 'people's army'; it helped to forge a link between the citizens and the state and to instil patriotic feelings into an idealistic and hopeful generation. But even its partial success was the object of severe criticism from the regular army who wished to control the *Landwehr*, and from the reactionaries who eyed it with the darkest suspicion. For them it was the culmination of a series of reforms which threatened to undermine the structure of a society from which they profited so much. Their attitude is best summed up by von der Recke who told his cronies in the Aristocrats' Club in Berlin: 'I would rather have three battles of Auerstädt than one October Edict.'

In military terms the work of the reformers was largely successful. The Prussian army made a significant contribution to the defeat of Napoleon, particularly at the battles of Leipzig and Waterloo. The army of 1813 was greatly superior to that of 1806. The reforms that had been made were promising for the future development of the army. But they were never able to be taken to their logical conclusion. Without a drastic change in Prussian society the notion of a people's army or a nation in arms could be little more than a pious hope. The contradiction between the modernity of the military system and the antiquated social structure became increasingly acute. A universal obligation to do military service was not matched by equality of civil rights and obligations. The aristocracy maintained its monopoly of commissions in the army, while bourgeois officers were under increasing attack and were forced to defend the *Landwehr* against mounting criticism. Without adequate reform of the state it was evident that the achievements of the military reformers could not be consolidated. As the political and social structure of Prussia remained in essentials unchanged these liberal and progressive ideas had only a short-term effect. It can be argued that for the reformers Napoleon's fall came too soon, and with the collapse of revolutionary France it was time to turn on the 'jacobins' at home. Having done so much to save Prussia from Napoleon, they in fact sawed off the branch on which they were sitting. It was the supreme irony of the reformers' position that their fate was so closely linked with that of their enemy. Napoleon's fall was soon to be followed by the defeat of the reform movement.

3

From Restoration to Revolution

In 1811 Gneisenau had written: 'Destiny will sweep us aside, the great and the small will once again behave in a miserable fashion, some will sacrifice themselves and be destroyed, the scoundrels who remain will rejoice and denigrate them.' He knew full well that once Napoleon had been defeated a reaction was almost bound to set in, directed towards purging the army and the administration of the state of the 'jacobins' and halting the impetus of the reform movement. His fears were amply justified.

In the last few months of the war relations between the reformers and the king became increasingly strained. Blücher and Gneisenau had heavy-handedly insisted on their own war plan and had ignored instructions from headquarters, thus causing considerable tension with the allies and no little concern to the king, who resented such rebellious subjects. They had been scornful of the efforts of the Prussian diplomatists at the Congress of Vienna, and Gneisenau had fought a rather fatuous duel with Wilhelm von Humboldt, the butt of much of their criticism. Gneisenau, Boyen and Grolman had even drawn up plans for an attack on Austria so that Germany could be remodelled under Prussian domination, plans that were to be realized fifty years later. The reformers were sharply critical of the peace treaty, Blücher even refusing orders to evacuate France, and they were deeply concerned about the steady strengthening of conservative, outmoded and particularist ideas in the Prussian court and government. They looked beyond Prussia to the vision of a reformed Germany, and beyond traditionalism and a hidebound conservatism to liberal reform and constitutional change. The king referred to Gneisenau as an 'evil and insolent fellow' and broadcast his intention to get rid of him and his radical associates.

The king was pressured both by his allies and by the conservatives at home to curb the reformers. The Tsar told his generals in Paris that the time might come when they would have to save the king of Prussia from his own army. Castlereagh warned that the King of Prussia was not in full control of the army and quoted Thomas Moore's lines: 'Woe to the Monarch who depends/Too much on his red-coated friends.' At home the reactionaries feared that the reform could all too easily lead to revolution, that the war against Napoleon could be turned into a war against the propertied. The police minister, Prince Wittgenstein, announced that 'to arm a nation is to organize revolt' and argued that the king should at once abolish universal military service and disband the *Landwehr*.

It was against the *Landwehr* that the first attacks of the restoration period were launched. The regular officers regarded the *Landwehr* as a collection of vulgar amateurs and resented their independence from the control of the regular army. The junkers protested that the lax discipline of the *Landwehr* was undermining their authority over the peasantry. They complained about the noise caused by Sunday exercises, and that their workers were forced to train in the army rather than working on their estates. They argued that all the *Landwehr* really did was to sit around in pubs drinking, and that as a military force it was useless. Worst of all, the *Landwehr* was regarded as a liberal institution, where dangerous ideas were discussed and liberal officers filled the heads of their men with revolutionary ideas. Generals such as York and Ludwig von der Marwitz argued that tactical reform had been necessary so that the Prussians could defeat the French, and they were even prepared to accept the idea of universal service which was at least a more efficient way of recruiting than the old corrupt system. But they were not prepared to accept the idea that military reform had to be the predicate of social and political reform. For Marwitz and York the army had to serve the king and the junker caste; the notion of a 'people's army' was both ludicrous and dangerous. For this reason Marwitz objected to the statue in memory of Scharnhorst erected in Berlin in 1822, complaining that he was the first administrator ever to be honoured as a general.

For the time being, however, the *Landwehr* was able to hold its own. The war had placed a great strain on the Prussian economy, which had been so badly disrupted by the Napoleonic occupation, and it was not possible to increase the standing army. The regular army of about 200,000 needed the support of the *Landwehr* which was about 500,000 strong. Reactionary generals such as Kleist von Nollendorff, von Hünerbein and von Borstell mounted a massive attack on Boyen and the *Landwehr* in 1817, arguing that it was badly organized, that its manoeuvres were incompetent, and that it was badly equipped and short of supplies. Boyen defended the *Landwehr* in a brilliant pamphlet on military organization, but by now he was very much on his own. Gneisenau had resigned from the army in 1816 having earned the nickname of Wallenstein, and Blücher and Stein had also retired. It was not to be long before Boyen, with his supporters such as Grolman and Beyme, was to be forced out of office.

The ability of the reactionaries to destroy the last vestiges of the reform movement can be understood only in relation to the total economic and political situation in Germany. The political solution of the Congress of Vienna had been to create the German Confederation, a loose association of states. The minute states of pre-revolutionary Germany had vanished, and the territorial reforms of Napoleon had been modified but not undone. Some states, such as Prussia, Bavaria, Württemberg, Baden, Saxony and even Hanover, were large enough to be able to survive, somewhat precariously, as independent states. But the division of Germany into this patchwork of states hindered the creation of a national market and so hampered economic and social development. Thus the small states could act as an effective brake on the growth of a national bourgeoisie, and were able to reassert the power of a quasi-feudal reaction. The national and progressive ideas of the wars of liberation were crushed by the particularist and retrogressive forces of the age of Metternich.

The reforms had broken many of the legal and social restraints on the growth of the productive forces. Feudal ties had been abolished on the land, at least partially, and the stranglehold of the guilds had been broken. The problem, however, remained that the Prussian economy was in no fit state to exploit these new possibilities. Once the continental system was smashed cheap British goods again flooded the German market, destroying all the small manufacturing companies which had sprung up in the hot-house atmosphere of absolute protection. The banking system was still primitive, and in spite of all the efforts of the bureaucracy such capital as there was available usually was invested in agriculture or in government. Most manufacturing was done by family firms which were particularly susceptible to crises and permanently short of capital. Thus the benefits of new inventions, and even of the new free trade areas first in Prussia, and then throughout Germany with the formation of the *Zollverein*, could not be fully exploited. Between 1815 and 1840 no new spinning machines were produced in Germany, and this branch of industry became increasingly backward and unproductive at a time when world prices were sinking. In the wool and iron industries the situation was hardly better. Heavy industry was hopelessly backward, the growth rate was minimal, and real chances for development were lost so that Germany did not even meet her own needs for industrial goods. Other more progressive nations, such as Belgium, were able to corner a large share of the market.

The combined effects of the reform and of liberal economic policy was disastrous for the small artisans and craftsmen. They were unable to compete against either British imports or the new manufacturing industries at home, and saw the origin of their misery in the reforming policies of the liberal bureaucracy. This large petit-bourgeois class demanded the restoration of their rights and privileges and protection against the economic forces of industrial capitalism. The aristocracy were quick to ally with them to form a common front against liberal and democratic reform. The breaking down of the old system had also caused a sharp increase in the number of paupers and unemployed both in the countryside and in the towns. They were to fuel an as yet somewhat inchoate radical and revolutionary movement, and from their class came calls for a fundamental redistribution of wealth and genuine democratic reform.

In agriculture the liberation of the serfs was made even

more profitable to the aristocracy. In 1816 it was announced that peasants had to pay twenty-five times the value of their yearly obligations, either in money or in land, to their landowner if they were to become free men. In most instances this meant that they lost all their land to the junkers. By the middle of the century 1.6 million peasants owned five per cent of the land, whereas the 18,000 largest estates covered sixty per cent of the land. Thus the junkers were able to keep their judicial rights over the land, seize the land of the peasants and reduce the former serfs to ill paid wage labourers. The general effect of the liberation was, to use Hans Rosenberg's phrase, the 'socialization of mass misery'. This enabled the junkers to maintain their pre-eminence, which in turn was one of the main reasons for the continuation and strengthening of the old military system of junker militarism. The junkers exploited the possibilities of the situation during the agrarian depression from 1807 to 1837. They learned how to run their estates strictly as business enterprises. Considerations of profit and loss had now replaced the certainties of a feudal mode of production; modern techniques and scientific farming had replaced the old and inefficient methods. But in spite of all their business acumen and skill the junkers looked down snobbishly on the industrialists and merchants of the west, and refused to run the risk of being regarded as 'tradesmen' and thus losing caste.

The restoration of the landed aristocracy and their conversion into a modern entrepreneurial class, the growing opposition of the artisans and petit-bourgeois to reform, the large numbers of impoverished and unemployed, and the relative weakness of the bourgeoisie were the most pronounced social characteristics of the Prussian pre-March. The bureaucracy, which still upheld the ideals of the reformers, tried to overcome the resulting social and economic tensions with a combination of liberal trade policy and mercantilist *dirigisme*. This policy pleased neither side. For the aristocracy and declining artisans it was too liberal, for the middle class it was not liberal enough. By the 1840s these disparities became even more apparent. Relative prosperity and the stimulating effect of railway construction strengthened the bourgeoisie, but this only served to show that in spite of all the economic and social changes that had taken place political power was still monopolized by the landed aristocracy. Indeed they had strengthened their position by reintroducing the guild system, restricting the freedom of the market place, hampering industrial growth and strengthening the legal privileges of the aristocracy. The rising bourgeoisie was unable to beat the landed aristocracy, and in increasing numbers they therefore decided to join them. Here were the origins of the profound imbalance in German society: a modern economic system dominated and restrained by an antiquated social order, a society divided between east and west, between agriculture and industry, between estate and class.

Given the relative strength of the classes it is hardly surprising that the aristocracy was able to strengthen its position in Prussia, and their restorative efforts were given the enthusiastic support of the Holy Alliance. The European order established by the Congress of Vienna was threatened by revolution, and little distinction was made between reform and revolution. The political order was to be placed in quarantine, any movement for change was to be instantly crushed. In Germany among the most outspoken opponents of the Holy Alliance were the students. They had fought in the Free Corps and the *Jäger*, had found excitement and adventure in the campaigns against Napoleon and dreamed of national unity and liberal freedoms. Bitterly frustrated in the dull and drab Germany of 1815 they theorized about the future of Germany and paraded the black, red and gold flag of the Free Corps and their slogan 'Honour, Freedom and Fatherland'. The student movement was in many ways hopelessly idealistic and utopian. German unity was to be achieved by education and in the realm of ideas. Many dreamed of a return to the Empire of the Hohenstaufen and to vague notions of 'German morals and habits'. Change in consciousness was to take precedence over changes in territorial demarcation. In 1817 a meeting of the student societies (*Burschenschaften*) was held at the Wartburg, ostensibly to celebrate the three hundredth anniversary of the Reformation and the fourth anniversary of the battle of Leipzig. The meeting was attended by a considerable number of students from throughout Germany. Much of the activity was a mixture of religious revival meeting and boy scout jamboree. Lutheran hymns were sung, and later a group of Berlin radicals burnt well known reactionary books and symbols of princely despotism in a large bonfire. The effect of this slightly bizarre occasion was electric. Metternich accused the unfortunate Grand Duke of Saxon-Weimar of making his small state into a haven for jacobins. The deputy Prussian minister of police told the Grand Duke that those present at the meeting were 'crazed professors and seduced students'. At the Aachen conference of the Holy Alliance in 1818 the danger of liberal movements in Germany was discussed in some detail, and it was agreed that the universities should come under close police scrutiny. On 23 March one of the radical students, Karl Sand, murdered the reactionary writer Kotzebue, whose works had been among those burnt at the Wartburg festival and who was known to be an informant to the Tsar. Metternich was determined to use this murder of a widely known figure as an excuse for repressive action against the national and liberal movements. Prussia agreed to support the Carlsbad decrees, which were presented to the Bundestag in September 1819 and which resulted from a series of somewhat one-sided discussions between Metternich and Hardenberg in Teplitz and Carlsbad. The decrees established rigorous political control of the universities, censorship of the press and the formation of a central committee in Mainz to investigate revolutionary activities throughout Germany.

Fear of revolution and these repressive actions against the liberals had a profound effect on the army. Just as Metternich was determined to rid Germany of democrats, reformers and radicals, the Prussian government was determined to purge its ranks of men of a liberal persuasion, and the army was to be made safe from any suggestion of political reform. The reformers were now fighting a losing battle, and with the Carlsbad decrees that battle was finally lost. For the reformers the Carlsbad decrees were a craven capitulation to Austria and a denial of the principles for which they stood. Humboldt led the attack from the civilian side, but Hardenberg had little difficulty in securing his resignation. For the military reformers it was Boyen who was most outspoken in his attack on the Carlsbad decrees. Thus the question of reform of the *Landwehr*, which Boyen resisted, became linked with the question of the Carlsbad decrees, and for the reactionaries the defeat of Boyen was of paramount importance.

Certain deficiencies in the *Landwehr* which were apparent in the autumn manoeuvres of 1818 were pointed out, not without relish, by its critics. Boyen's criticisms of the Carlsbad decrees, coupled with the belief that the *Landwehr* harboured many sinister revolutionaries and reformers, confirmed the conservatives' worst fears. In December 1819 the king ordered a reorganization of the *Landwehr* and its closer association with the regular army. He had long contemplated such a step, and it would seem reasonable to assume that it was Boyen's opposition to the Carlsbad decrees which finally convinced him he should act. The step was somewhat drastic. The *Landwehr* was to be inspected by officers from the regular army, all field commands were to be manned by officers of the regular army, thirty-five battalions of the *Landwehr* were abolished and the remaining brigades were to become part of regular army divisions, even in peacetime. Boyen's reaction to this step was promptly to hand in his resignation. His example was followed by Grolman. Clausewitz, who remained almost alone as a representative of the reformers, was critical of Boyen's precipitate action which he felt to be desertion of the colours and a concession of victory to the reactionaries. With both Humboldt and Boyen removed from the government the reactionaries had indeed triumphed.

The year 1819 saw the crushing defeat of the reform movement. All the hopes of 1806 that Prussia and Germany could evolve towards a modern liberal state were now dashed. For the next thirty years life in Germany was dull, repressive and bitter. For brief moments the underlying tensions and antagonisms became apparent, but for the most part the period was one of deadly monotony. Very real economic and social problems were either ignored or deliberately forced from view. The social and political structure of the country became increasingly out of phase with social and economic realities. In 1848 these tensions were to lead to an abortive revolution, an expression of the frustrations and hopes of a hide-bound society.

During this period the *Landwehr* was relentlessly obliged to conform to the regular army and was brought even more closely under the sway of the aristocratic officer corps. In the east the officer corps of the *Landwehr* was purged of its bourgeois elements. *Landwehr* officers were required to serve for several weeks with the regular army. Recruits in the *Landwehr* had to be trained by regular soldiers so that distinctions between the regular army and the *Landwehr* would become minimal. Prince William summed up this thinking admirably when he said: 'If the *Landwehr* imagines that it will be treated in any way differently from the regular army you already have the first step towards a revolutionary army.' The reformers' ideal of enlightened soldiers playing an active part in society, so that the gulf between the army and society could be bridged, was regarded as a dangerous revolutionary concept. The officer corps, both in the *Landwehr* and the regular army, were to be the main supporters of the *status quo* and be ever ready to crush the enemy at home. The army was to become an instrument of a restorative order, not a home for enlightenment and reform. The 'Boyen spirit' was soon dead, and the army quickly adjusted to its new role.

Boyen and Grolman had been perhaps over-optimistic. During the wars of liberation the officer corps had lost its exclusive aristocratic membership and had been forced to accept bourgeois officers. Thus by the end of the wars almost half the officer corps came from middle class backgrounds. Grolman was determined that the general staff officers should be trained in the spirit of Scharnhorst and the reformers. Although most of the general staff officers came from aristocratic backgrounds many of them were sympathetic to the ideas of the reformers, and their influence was significant at the higher levels of the army. They hoped that with the younger and junior officers coming from bourgeois backgrounds, and with an enlightened general staff, they would be able to further the work of reform. In fact they seriously underestimated the reaction against them. Boyen's sympathy for a liberal constitution and far-reaching political reform and Grolman's determination to make the general staff officers into idealistic crusaders excited the opposition of the court. A counter-attack, which began with the censorship of the general staff's history of the war of liberation, was to end with the resignation of both these men.

The general staff did not immediately fall into the hands of the reactionaries. Grolman's successor was Rühle von Lilienstern, a pupil of Scharnhorst, but he was replaced in 1821 by

Von Müffling, who had conveniently converted to a reactionary position. To make doubly certain that the general staff would not be a hotbed of dangerous ideas, Müffling was given increased powers so that the centralization of authority in the war ministry, which the reformers had advocated, was further weakened. In 1825 the general staff became a separate organization, although it was still to a degree subordinate to the war ministry. Within the war ministry, Department III, which dealt with personnel questions, was given a considerable degree of independence, and the head of the department, von Witzleben, who was already the king's adjutant, became the closest military adviser to the crown. This was the origin of what was to become the military cabinet. The reasons for strengthening this department are quite obvious. The crown wished to make certain that reliable men were given commissions and promotions, and this in turn meant that the artistocracy was once again to be given special privileges. Thus the proportion of bourgeois officers was gradually reduced, and officers who were suspected of liberal thinking were denied promotion.

The effect of these changes was again to cut the army off from the rest of society, and in an age which was relatively peaceful the main concern of military policy became the 'enemy within'. The army became consciously an instrument of domestic oppression. The ideas of the reformers seemed finally to have been crushed. In the general staff, however, some of the old ideas were cherished, even under a conservative like von Müffling, and a high degree of technical proficiency was maintained. But just as the regular army became increasingly removed from society around it, so the general staff became aloof from the rest of the army, and Scharnhorst's insistence that there should be constant interplay between staff work and regimental duty was forgotten. The general staff under von Müffling also tended to neglect theoretical work, but the director of the General War School, von Clausewitz, was to make an outstanding contribution to the theory of war and to train a new generation of military theorists. His masterpiece *Vom Kriege* was published posthumously in 1833. Although it laid the foundations for a modern and sociological study of war, it was to be seriously misunderstood and misinterpreted by later generations. In spite of such inspired teaching the officers graduating from the War School lacked any real understanding of the heritage of the reformers, and for all their practical and theoretical understanding they were mostly conservative and monarchical, out of touch with the progressive tendencies of the age.

The problem of the relationship between the military and society continued to be debated in the literature of the time. The reactionary position was most forcefully stated by the Prussian military engineer Blesson, who argued that the military was a separate estate and that following his oath of allegiance to the king, a soldier lost all the rights and privileges of a civilian. The soldier was in no sense a 'citizen in uniform', he was bound to unconditional obedience to the monarchy. In a pithy aphorism Blesson insisted that 'a soldier who thinks is a mutineer'. The contrary position was persuasively argued by Karl von Rotteck, a professor from Freiburg, in a book published in 1816 entitled *On Standing Armies and a National Militia*. Rotteck was committed to the idea of the 'citizen in uniform' and to an army that owed allegiance to a constitution rather than a monarch. He argued that modern military techniques had strengthened the power of both the monarchy and the army over the people, but that in spite of this power they were not able to meet the needs of a modern national state, for, as the experience of the war against Napoleon had shown, the full resources of the nation had to be tapped. A standing army was ideal for fighting aggressive wars, for repression of dissent at home, and for persuading recruits by propaganda to serve a system which was contrary to their own real interests. If the army did not reflect the society in which it was situated both socially and ideologically, then it was an alien body serving interests other than those of that society. This was the distinction which Rotteck made between liberalism and militarism, and in so doing he was in the best tradition of progressive liberal thought. Rotteck's book is a classic text which was used by German liberals in their stuggle against standing armies and for a constitutional oath.

As the main concern of the army was to combat revolutionary and reformist movements at home it is hardly surprising that the commanding generals of the nine Prussian corps were given increased powers. They were directly responsible to the

70

king and had precedence over the civilian authorities. In a series of cabinet orders the commanding generals were given far reaching police and political functions. In 1820 they were empowered to restore law and order if, in their judgement, the civilian authorities did not have sufficient means to keep the peace. They were thus able to intervene in civil strife without even being asked to do so by the police and local authorities. Harsh sentences were meted out to those who refused the orders of the military or who were insubordinate to military authority. These changes were significant in that the army was able to act, and to use the utmost violence, without having first to be requested to do so by the civil authorities. This assertion of the primacy of the military over the civilian was systematized in the Prussian law on the state of siege of 1851, which was a response to the experiences of the revolution of 1848 and was then incorporated into the imperial constitution as article 68. It was on the basis of this law that the corps commanders were given such extensive powers in the First World War. Thus the military policy of the pre-March was to shape much of the future history of civil military relations in Germany for the next hundred years.

The army intervened in a number of instances in 1830 when there was widespread unrest throughout Germany, sparked by the example of the revolution in France. The Prussian army was also employed in some of the smaller states such as Reuss-Schleitz and Reuss-Ebersbach to crush protest movements against absolutism and lack of freedom. Also in 1830 'Safety Associations' (*Sicherheitsvereinen*) of the middle class were formed throughout the country to co-operate with the military authorities to put down any unrest. Apprentices, students and workers were specifically excluded from the Safety Associations, and the split between the liberal bourgeoisie and the radicals in the working-class movement, which was to prove fatal in 1848, thus became apparent. The liberal movement was certainly not crushed in 1830. The Hambach festival of 1832 in which 30,000 people demanded the unification of Germany, popular sovereignty and the abolition of the monarchy made the Prussian authorities fear that revolution was near, and repressive policies were increased. In the following year a group of radicals, with very little popular support, attacked the police station in Frankfurt am Main as the first part of a plan to seize the Bun-

71

destag. They were dislodged by Prussian and Austrian troops. In 1840 it seemed that the liberals were about to be rewarded for their persistence and that the reactionaries would be pushed aside. The new king, Frederick William IV, was given to making brilliant and highly ambiguous speeches which gave rise to many false hopes. His vague and arcane references to constitutions and romantic murmurings about progress and the people amounted to little more than a kind of political gothic revival, but many liberals, accustomed to years of dull repression, were ready to grasp at any straw. Frederick William IV had absolutely no intention of sharing political power with the liberals, but he was prepared to make rather empty concessions. He relaxed the censorship of the press, released political prisoners, allowed exiles to return and in 1841 recalled Boyen, now seventy years old, to become minister of war once again. All these moves almost instantly backfired. The press became filled with demands for a constitution, so that censorship was soon restored. In 1841 Johann Jacoby, whose pamphlet demanding the fulfilment of the promise made by Frederick William II in 1815 was seized by the authorities, was charged with high treason and sentenced to two-and-a-half years' imprisonment, a sentence which was so obviously illegal that it was overthrown by a superior court. Similarly the *Rheinische Zeitung* edited by Karl Marx was banned in 1843. Boyen was greeted as a liberal martyr and serenaded with old *Landwehr* songs which seemed to the king to have dangerous revolutionary overtones. Boyen imagined that his appointment as war minister was a sign of royal approval for his policies, but he was soon to realize that it was an empty gesture. His orders were frequently ignored by his subordinates in the war ministry and by the commanding generals, particularly the Prince of Prussia. He attempted to revive the *Landwehr*, to strengthen the bourgeois element in its officer corps and to appoint *Landwehr* officers to staff positions. This met with such ferocious resistance that Boyen resigned, realizing that it was not possible for him to implement any meaningful reforms.

The situation was further exacerbated by the increasing social tensions occasioned by the growth of the economy. The customs union (*Zollverein*) was beginning to have an effect on the balance between the junkers and the anti-feudal forces. Liberal trade policy was restrained and hampered by the selfish interests of the junkers and a large class of artisans and hand-loom operators were caught between these two opposing forces. The most dramatic instance was the miserable plight of the Silesian weavers. In 1844 they revolted against the factory owners, and although the uprising was easily crushed their example made a deep impression and called attention to the misery and oppression of the workers in this epoch of industrialization. Of fundamental importance was the growing split between the bourgeoisie and the aristocracy in the 1840s. Encouraged by the king's pseudo liberalism the middle class of the western provinces, particularly in the industrialized Rhineland, supported the liberal reformers and placed themselves at the head of the opposition movement. They demanded a share of political power and the removal of all barriers to the development of industrial capitalism. They continued to press their demands, even when the king made it plain that he had no intention of giving way to pressure. The junkers for their part were weakened by economic developments which in turn strengthened the opposition. The liberals were able to place themselves at the head of a movement which, although divided into many conflicting interest groups, had a common aim in securing a degree of reform. As it grew in strength the numerous acts of repression and censorship served only to strengthen the arguments against the absolutist state. For the moment it seemed as if the divisions between the liberals, who wanted a constitutional monarchy, and the radical democrats, who wanted more fundamental changes, were secondary. It was not until the outbreaks of civil unrest in 1847, occasioned by the severe economic crisis of that year, that the split between the two camps became once again clearly evident.

The only solution to the economic crisis that the government could find was brute force. In numerous instances in 1847 the army was employed against hunger marchers, rioters and the unemployed. The gulf between the army and the nation had become wider than ever before, and the soldiers were regarded as enemies of the people. In the debates of the United Diet, which met to discuss economic and constitutional problems, frequent criticisms of the army were voiced. As the situation grew increasingly tense the government persisted in its belief that military force was the only way to meet the threat of reform or revolution. In doing so it undoubtedly helped to make the crisis of 1848 far more serious than it otherwise would have been.

In February 1848 Louis Philippe of France was forced into exile and a republican government seized power in Paris. A week later there were revolutionary stirrings in the Rhineland. Prince William was made military governor with plenipotentiary powers. In other parts of Germany the garrisons were strengthened in preparation for any civil unrest. In Berlin the garrison was doubled so that it consisted of some 21,000 officers and men and thirty-six guns. Throughout the country democratic demands were made, but the reactionaries who advised the king, prominent among them Prince William and Leopold von Gerlach, insisted that they were the work of outside agitators, and argued that only if the king stood firm, and used the utmost force at the slightest sign of provocation, could a serious situation be avoided. Some of his civilian advisers, however, argued that some concessions would have to be made to stem the mounting criticism of the monarchy. The king as usual dithered between these two positions, uttered more than the usual amount of ambiguous comments and unintelligible promises, and succeeded only in giving the impression that he was giving way to public pressure. This enraged the army, which was determined to resist any challenges to the system whatever the king might think, but it also aroused hopes among the people that the king might offer some real concessions to the liberals. Thus political demands grew increasingly strident, and the garrison in Berlin was further reinforced. As the tensions grew more acute a conflict became almost inevitable. An increasing number of incidents occurred between soldiers and civilians in the capital, and serious bloodshed was avoided only by the intervention of the Commandant of Berlin, General Pfuehl, who countermanded Prince William's characteristically draconian orders. News that Metternich has been toppled on 16 March convinced the king that significant concessions had to be made, and late on the night of 17 March he signed a document which promised a constitution, the lifting of the censorship and the reorganization of the German Confederation. To the reactionaries at the court it seemed that the king had pusillanimously given way to the liberals, and their depression was profound. As a concession to their objections he transferred the command of the Berlin garrison from von Pfuehl to General von Prittwitz, thus denying von Pfuehl's request that the troops be reduced in Berlin to lessen the tension in the city, and at the same time offering Prince William satisfaction for the slight he had received from the commandant. Most seriously of all this action compromised the concessions which the king had made and prepared the ground for the tragedy of 18 March.

On that day a crowd assembled at the palace, partly to show their appreciation of Frederick William's promises of reform and partly to present a set of demands. These called for the withdrawal of the troops from Berlin, the creation of an armed civil guard, the freedom of the press and the recalling of the united diet. General von Prittwitz, fearing that this was the beginning of the revolution and that the king's life might well be in danger, ordered the crowd to disperse. In the ensuing mêlée shots were fired and the soldiers cleared the *Schlossplatz* with drawn swords. The crowd withdrew, ripped up the streets and built barricades. The army tried to clear the barricades but met with little success. The soldiers had no experience of street fighting. They wasted much of their ammunition blasting away through windows and doors, and spent too much time chasing after reported snipers. The cavalry was unable to make much progress as the cobbled streets had been destroyed. The infantry was unable to storm the barricades, even though the rebels were poorly armed. Indeed they only had two antiquated pieces of artillery and they had to use stockings stuffed with marbles as shot. The barricades were so effective and numerous that many observers were convinced that they resulted from a carefully planned communist plot. The troops were quickly demoralized. Some units refused to attack the civilians, and others even joined the people. Prittwitz urged the king to withdraw the troops from Berlin and blockade the city. If the barricades could not be stormed, then the people should be starved out. The king eventually acted by publishing an address 'To my dear Berliners', in which he argued that the unrest of 18 March had been the work of outside agitators and that if the rebels were prepared to remove the barricades he would withdraw the troops from the city. This did little to clear up the confusion, for it was still not clear at what point the army would begin to withdraw. Amid the procrastination and undecisiveness of the court Prittwitz acted. He ordered the troops to leave the city so that he could prepare to blockade the rebels. The king remained in the palace debating whether or not he also should leave, but while discussions of the historical analogy of Henri IV were taking place it was announced that the *Schlossplatz* was again filled with Berliners and that the king's line of retreat was effectively cut off. Frederick William was forced to pay his respects to the 216 who had been killed in the fighting and to accept the demand for a civil guard (*Bürgerwehr*) with sole responsibility for maintaining law and order in the capital. As a final humiliation he was obliged to ride around the streets of Berlin with the red, black and gold band of the German liberals around his arm. In a final speech that day he uttered his famous words, 'Prussia merges into Germany' and announced his intention of introducing major constitutional reforms. He declared that he had placed himself at the head of the liberal movement. The crowd was enthusiastic, partly out of sympathy. The king cut such a ridiculous figure on horseback that it melted the heart of even convinced republicans such as the Socialist Wilhelm Weitling. The events of 21 March were thus something of a charade, but the Berliners were convinced that they had won a significant victory.

The army had retired to Potsdam, the officers longing to lay siege to the city and crush the rebellion. They greeted the news from Berlin with horror. The creation of a *Bürgerwehr* was regarded as a gross insult to the army, and although workers and apprentices were banned from the force it was considered a dangerously revolutionary body. On 25 March the king went to Potsdam and in front of an astonished assembly of officers he praised the Berliners and the *Bürgerwehr*. The officers rattled their sabres in disgust and some hot heads began to think in terms of a military coup. But other more perspicacious men realized that there was a considerable ambiguity, as usual, in what the king had said, and they hoped that one day Berlin would again be pacified. The king was in a curious position. As Veit Valentin points out in his history of the 1848 revolution, he had stretched out a hand in the direction of a liberal and united Germany, but this hand was 'bloodstained and shaking'.

At the same time he was running the risk of an officers' Fronde, but he was still careful to keep in close contact with the reactionaries around Gerlach. With the king playing such a doubtful role the sides began to consolidate in preparation for the decisive clash which was bound to come.

As a sop to the liberals the king appointed a new ministry which represented the right-wing liberal and conservative interests. The leading figures were two prominent big businessmen from the Rhineland, Ludolph Camphausen and David Hansemann. For the reactionaries this was further proof that the king had given way to the revolution, but in fact the Camphausen-Hansemann ministry was neither particularly liberal nor was it given any power. Indeed Frederick William IV paid more attention to his military *camarilla* in Potsdam, which included such outspoken men as von Rauch, von Neumann, von Manteuffel, Leopold von Gerlach and Count Dohna, whose influence was greatly enhanced when the king took up residence in Potsdam in April. The *camarilla* was determined to defeat the revolution militarily, and was thus particularly concerned that the army should not be infected by democratic ideas and should be separated as far as possible from the masses in Berlin. If the army was kept as a powerful instrument in the hands of the monarchy then the liberal-conservative government could be removed and the old junker order restored. The *camarilla* had adequate funds, for they had rescued the state treasury from Spandau on leaving the capital. They were also able to count on the active support of the commanding generals throughout Prussia, who became increasingly overbearing and violent, and there were numerous instances of brutal force being used against demonstrators and even against the *Bürgerwehr*. Frederick William was also determined that no inroads should be made on his power of command over the army. The Camphausen-Hansemann ministry was well aware that its own position was precarious indeed if no reforms were introduced to stop the military acting without any regard for the civil authorities. But the king interpreted these attempts to curb the excesses of the army as a vicious attack on the institution of the monarchy and the Prussian state.

The Prussian army was by no means inactive in these weeks. In March 1848 the Polish national liberation movement struck at the Prussian-occupied areas of Poland. The Camphausen-Hansemann ministry authorized the dispatch of 30,000 Prussian soldiers to crush the revolt. It was a fatal mistake of the liberals in 1848 that they did not support the Polish patriots, for the antagonism between the Germans and the Poles was seriously to undermine the work of the Frankfurt assembly and the chauvinistic anti-Polish stance of the German liberals was to make a mockery of their professed belief in national self-determination. Victory for the Poles would have seriously weakened the Prussian monarchy and its semi-feudal supporters. An alliance between German liberalism and Polish nationalism would have resulted in a powerful bulwark against the Tsar, and might even have carried the revolution to Russia. Lastly, by calling on the army to crush the Poles, Camphausen undermined his own attempts to control the army, for his insistence that political considerations should be heeded in the course of military actions in Posen was brushed aside as unwarranted and unprofessional meddling in military affairs. In spite of a heroic struggle by the ill-equipped Polish peasants, the uprising was crushed and the Prussian army went on the rampage, behaving, in the words of the Archbishop of Posen, like 'Tartar hordes'.

Prussian troops were also fighting in Schleswig-Holstein. The popular movement in the duchies opposed the efforts of the Danish king to annexe Schleswig and demanded incorporation in the German confederation. The Bundestag called upon Prussia and Hanover to support the people of Schleswig-Holstein against the Danes. Frederick William had no intention of fighting a liberal war for the unification of Germany, but just as he had been prepared to place himself at the head of the revolutionary movement in Berlin in March, so he was willing to send Prussian troops into Schleswig-Holstein in order better to direct and control the movement. The *camarilla* hoped that the Prussian expeditionary force would achieve two aims: to bring the Schleswig-Holstein free corps movement under control and to win a certain popularity in liberal circles for the Prussian army whose reputation had become badly tarnished. For all the dramatic actions such as the storming of Düppel, the Prussian commander General von Wrangel cautiously avoided any decisive battles and refused to follow up his

78

advantage over the Danes. On 26 August 1848 an armistice was concluded at Malmö in which Prussia agreed to evacuate Schleswig-Holstein, thus leaving the fate of the duchies undecided. The Prussians had gained the support of some of the liberal nationalists in Frankfurt, but those on the spot felt they had been betrayed. The *Schleswig-Holsteinische Zeitung* remarked: 'German unity is marvellous in verse, bad in prose, and in practice non-existent. . . . It was united for four weeks by mistake.'

The Prussian National Assembly met on 22 May and devoted part of its time to somewhat vague discussions of the military question. Popular feeling against the army was still running very high, and the left-wing delegates at the Assembly, pushed by the democratic clubs, demanded a people's army and the abolition of the standing army. Although a consitution had yet to be worked out, the details being bogged down in endless and somewhat futile discussion in committees of the National Assembly, the left insisted that the army should swear an oath to the constitution. The army was to be placed under the command of the German Confederation, which was in the process of being reconstructed at Frankfurt. Counter-revolutionary and reactionary officers were to be dismissed, and the cadet schools abolished. Soldiers were to have full civil liberties including the right to vote and the right to assembly.

These debates were symptomatic of a growing split in the revolutionary forces. The *Bürgerwehr*, which was designed to protect the achievements of March against the army, was rapidly becoming an instrument of repression against the people of Berlin who were disenchanted with the lack of progress in the Assembly. The workers and apprentices were demanding that the people should be armed and that the law-keeping forces should be democratized. The propertied classes were dissatisfied with the *Bürgerwehr* which they regarded as a lax and inefficient force, and were afraid that it would be unable to withstand a second revolutionary wave from below. Thus the left in the National Assembly felt that the experience of the *Bürgerwehr* showed that the army should be democratized, whereas the right argued that the incompetence of the *Bürgerwehr* showed that military efficiency and democracy were irreconcilable. On 14 June events came to a head when a crowd of workers and students stormed the armoury and then began to roam the streets armed to the teeth. The episode was badly planned, and the crowd had no leadership or goal. They found themselves in possession of the new Prussian needle gun. They did not know how to fire it and if they had known would have had little idea of what use to put it to. The bourgeois of Berlin were horrified and had visions of jacobin terror. Peace was restored by calling into the city battalions of the *Landwehr* and by the reorganization of the *Bürgerwehr* which had proved so ineffective as a special constabulary. These events helped to convince the moderate bourgeois that there was a simple choice to be made between the regular army and an armed mob. The left continued to put forward schemes for a militia, but they failed to find a sympathetic audience. The storming of the Berlin armoury was thus an understandable outburst of frustration and impatience, but was to be effectively exploited by the right to demonstrate that there was no valid alternative to the regular army.

June 1848 also saw the real beginning of a consequential counter-revolutionary campaign by the army. The mouthpiece of the reaction was the *Deutsche Wehr-Zeitung*, and the main thrusts of its attacks were directed against the national idea. The critics of the army had insisted that it should be subordinate to a central German authority, and therefore the counter-revolutionaries were outspoken in their denunciation of the idea of German unification. The most influential pamphlet written on this question was by the director of the general war department of the Prussian war ministry, von Griesheim, whose 'German Central Power and the Prussian Army' was a semi-official manifesto by the Prussian army. Griesheim argued strongly for Prussian rather than German nationalism, and launched a scathing attack on the Frankfurt parliament's demands that the Prussian army should be merged into a German army. This successor of Scharnhorst summed up his view of the relationship between the army and democracy in the much-quoted phrase: 'Only soldiers help against democrats.'

The writings of Griesheim and the *Deutsche Wehr-Zeitung* prompted discussions about the possibility of establishing a military dictatorship, and many a Prussian general dreamed of slaughtering the workers of Berlin and thus becoming the Prussian Cavaignac. This mounting aggressiveness on the part of the army did not pass unnoticed by the Prussian National Assembly, and fearing a military coup they eventually managed on 9 August to pass two resolutions demanding that the army desist from any reactionary activities and accept the notion of a constitutional system. Officers who were unable to accept these ideas would be called upon to resign their commissions. The king regarded this move by the Assembly as a sinister attack on his power of command, and called upon the Hansemann-Auerswald ministry to put an end to this attack on the army. The ministry was thus caught in a cross fire between the king and the Assembly, and rather lamely attempted to persuade the Assembly to retract the resolutions. The Assembly reacted truculently by reaffirming the resolutions, and the Hansemann-Auerswald ministry was placed in such a difficult position that it was obliged to tender its resignation. The situation was now extremely tense. The army urged the king to march into Berlin. In the capital some barricades were built. Helmuth von Moltke wrote that he would emigrate to Australia if the king did not act. Once again the king prevaricated – and Moltke remained.

The military were gaining the upper hand. The stupid and histrionic Wrangel was given command of all the troops from the Oder to the Elbe, and issued a number of menacing threats in the direction of Berlin. A provisional government was formed on 21 September 1848 under General von Pfuehl which seemed to be designed to pave the way for a military coup. But much to the disgust of the military, one of the first acts of the new government was to accept the resolutions of the Assembly which had led to the downfall of the Hansemann-Auerswald government. There was much mumbling in the army about 'sedition', 'anarchy' and 'republicanism', and General Wrangel indulged in some well publicized sabre rattling. The king's actions in these weeks are difficult to interpret. Had he lost his nerve and given in to the democrats in the Assembly, as the army feared? Or was it merely a tactical move to buy time before Berlin was occupied by the Potsdam garrison, as the republican historians argue? Whatever his initial motives were, the king began to think more and more in terms of a military coup, and in the next few days the reactionary *camarilla* undoubtedly won the king's confidence.

By the end of October the situation in Berlin seemed almost as critical as it had been on 18 March or 14 June. Windischgrätz had begun his attack on Vienna on 28 October, and the left in the Assembly knew that it was unlikely to be long before Berlin suffered a similar experience from Wrangel's troops. Amid expressions of solidarity for the Viennese revolutionaries violence again broke out in Berlin. Pfuehl was obliged to hide in the apartments of a left-wing deputy where he quietly and calmly took tea. A wit remarked, 'The swimming master [Pfuehl was an expert swimmer] was drowned in Madame Jung's teacup.' The wretched Pfuehl was dismissed. His successor was the ultra-reactionary Count of Brandenburg, a representative of the *camarilla*. The National Assembly in a somewhat impotent gesture of defiance refused to accept Brandenburg, and was promptly dismissed by the king on 9 November and ordered to re-convene on 27 November in Brandenburg. The right-wing deputies promptly left the Assembly. The left continued to meet in defiance of the order and were chased from hotel to hotel by the military until they were finally disbanded by Prussian troops on 14 November. Meanwhile on 10 November General Wrangel marched into Berlin with 40,000 troops. The radicals urged the *Bürgerwehr* to resist, but they meekly allowed themselves to be disarmed. No resistance was offered to the troops. The leaders of the *Bürgerwehr* claimed that submission was the best guarantee of freedom and argued that this lame policy could be given the impressive title of passive resistance. Wrangel's reply to this passive resistance was to declare a state of martial law. The middle class greeted the troops as saviours from the uncertainties of a National Assembly which under pressure from the left had been making some distressingly radical noises of late. Some workers urged the *Bürgerwehr* to refuse to be disarmed, and *Bürgerwehr* units from the provinces expressed their willingness to fight Wrangel's troops and restore the National Assembly. Karl Marx in the columns of the *Neue Rheinische Zeitung* called for a tax boycott. The rump of the National Assembly also demanded such an action, but those who followed their lead were promptly arrested and fined. Within a few days it became apparent that resistance was futile. General Wrangel ruled in Berlin.

Wrangel hoped that something approaching a military dictatorship would be established. But Brandenburg, who was still Minister President, persuaded the king that some concessions would have to be made, however empty and meaningless, so that Prussia would not become so seriously divided that it would not be able to meet the challenge of Austria within the German Confederation. On 5 December 1848 the National Assembly was officially disbanded and a constitution octroyed. As far as the army was concerned, the constitution left the king with an unrestricted power of command and the sole right to declare war and conclude peace. The king hinted that soldiers would be required to make an oath of allegiance to the constitution, but he was instantly flooded with protests from officers and the press was full of warnings that such a move would undermine the army and the monarchy and leave the state defenceless against the forces of revolution and democracy. This requirement was then dropped, so that the army was to a considerable extent outside the constitution, owing direct allegiance to the king whose power of command was subject to no restraints.

While these events were taking place in Prussia the Frankfurt parliament continued to debate the issue of German unity. But it had no army to back up its demands. In the German Confederation there were some thirty different armies, most of which had been forced onto the defensive in March. There was a federal army consisting of three Austrian, three Prussian, one Bavarian and three mixed army corps. The mixed army corps were manned by troops from eighteen different states. Thus without an army of its own the Frankfurt parliament relied on the toleration of Austria and Prussia. Once Berlin and Vienna had been pacified it seemed obvious that Frankfurt's days were numbered.

The military issue was debated at Frankfurt in some detail. As in Paris, Berlin and Vienna, the left demanded a people's army. The liberals agreed in principle, but the question of a definition of 'people' could not be settled. The liberals felt that a people's army would be a middle-class force, along the lines of the Prussian *Bürgerwehr*, while the democrats gave the term a wider definition. In general the liberals felt that the military question should be settled after the constitutional question, that with the creation of a unified Germany the armies could be reorganized to form a German army. The radical democrats argued that unless the people were armed the constitutional question would be settled for them. Like Bismarck they knew that the issues of the day would be decided not by majority votes but by blood and iron. Thus on 12 July 1848 the Frankfurt parliament appointed the Prussian General von Peucker as war minister of the Reich. Peucker was hardly a liberal, but he realized that some concessions would have to be made. He called upon all German troops to wear the German national colours and urged the abolition of substitution for military service, reform of military law and the introduction of the one-year volunteer system throughout Germany. These views were regarded as unacceptable by the sovereigns of Germany, not so much on the grounds of their intrinsic value as because they originated from a parliament the legitimacy of which they were not prepared to accept.

On 28 March 1849 the Frankfurt parliament finally finished its deliberations on the German constitution. The Prussian government promptly refused to accept the constitution, intending to form a German confederation under Prussian domination which would exclude Austria and crush the last remnants of the revolution. It was out of the question for the Prussians to use the new constitution for these reactionary aims, for it placed the armed forces of Germany under a central authority to which all soldiers would owe allegiance. The Frankfurt liberals had no intention of forcing the constitution on the German princes, because that would have unleashed forces which they would not have been able to control. They therefore chose to negotiate, but unwilling to call upon popular support they had to negotiate from a position of exceptional weakness. When the constitution was rejected by the governments the liberals were left helpless, and the leadership of the revolution passed into the hands of the artisans and workers of the large cities who demanded that the constitution be accepted. On 3 May 1849 fighting broke out in Dresden, the armoury was stormed, the people were armed and barricades erected in preparation for the arrival of Prussian troops, which the Saxon government had requested to help crush the revolt. The Dresden democrats, among them Richard Wagner, held out for six days until they were defeated by a vastly superior force of Saxon and Prussian troops.

Revolutionary violence spread throughout Germany. In Prussia the *Landwehr* was called upon to assist in crushing the movement for a German constitution. In a number of instances the *Landwehr* refused orders, thus confirming the very worst fears of those reactionaries who for years had demanded the abolition of that dangerously democratic force. As early as March 1848 a number of *Landwehr* men had shown their sympathy for the revolution, and had fought with the people on the barricades. Units of the *Landwehr* had refused to obey orders in the counter-revolutionary days in the autumn of 1848, and democratic '*Landwehr* Associations' grew in size and importance and opposed the policies of the Prussian government. In May 1849 during the struggle over the German constitution there were instances of bloody battles between the *Landwehr* and the regular army. The motives for the refusal of the *Landwehr* to obey orders were not so much that they were enthusiastic supporters of the democrats, but rather that the *Landwehr* had been specifically designed to meet the threat of war with a foreign power, and the idea that it should be used as a police force against democratic forces at home was contrary to its traditions. If the army were to be used for domestic repression, then the *Landwehr* was indeed an unsuitable force and the reactionaries' arguments against it were valid. Similarly the reformers of 1806 who saw in the *Landwehr* the outline of a citizens' militia which incorporated a liberal idea were remarkably prescient. In spite of the determined efforts of thirty-three years of reaction, the *Landwehr* had not lost all its liberal heritage, and if it was far from being a people's army, and even though the majority of the *Landwehr* remained loyal to the Prussian crown, it still showed a greater sympathy for the people of Prussia than for its rulers.

The centres of revolutionary violence in the west were Düsseldorf, Elberfeld, Hagen, Iserlohn and Solingen. The task of suppressing these uprisings were made all the easier by the fact that the revolutionaries were seriously divided between those who feared that perhaps some of the demands they were making of the Prussian government were going too far, and those who were calling for a republic. Friedrich Engels, who played an important role in the defence of Elberfeld, was forced to leave the city by those who feared that an attempt to establish a communist republic would turn the workers against their temporary allies among the artisans and petit bourgeoisie.

With the defeat of the revolutionary forces in the Rhineland the only remaining hope seemed to be for a national movement based on the south-west in alliance with the radical wing of the Frankfurt parliament. The parliamentarians drew back when faced with this drastic choice, and the revolutionary army of the south-west was abandoned.

In May 1849 the revolution had succeeded in Baden, the old regime was chased away and the army supported the revolutionaries. With the resources of one of the large German states the revolutionaries hoped to defend the new state against the attacks of the counter-revolutionary forces of Germany. The revolution in Baden, however, suffered from two serious weaknesses. The revolutionaries were deeply suspicious of the radical elements in Baden and were anxious that the revolution should be kept within certain limits. More serious was the fact that they were not prepared to cross the frontiers of Baden to meet the advancing Prussian army and to win support for the revolution in other parts of the country. The Baden revolution was thus too provincial and too limited in aims to have much chance of success. The campaign in Baden was heroic and hopeless. The people of Baden were supported by volunteers from Poland, France, Switzerland, Hungary and from throughout Germany. They faced the well trained regular army of Prussia and its allies, which was at least three times the size of their own forces. The Prussians were better armed, better equipped and better supplied. In early June command of the Baden forces was given to the Polish revolutionary Ludwig Mieroslawski. After a series of truly heroic engagements against vastly superior forces the fortress of Rastatt fell and the Baden army capitulated. With the defeat of the revolution in the south west the German revolution was crushed.

The failure of the revolution of 1848 greatly strengthened the old ruling class and thus preserved Prussian militarism. German unity had not been achieved by democratic reform – it was to be achieved with Prussian bayonets. The 'revolution from above' would succeed where the 'revolution from below' had failed.

The military experience of 1848-9 showed that the regular army of Prussia had been unwavering in its hostility to the revolution. The *Landwehr* had not been wholly reliable, and was to come under increasing attack from the conservatives. The liberals had failed completely to provide a viable alternative, even in theory, to the standing army. They were forced to realize that the slogan of a people's army was either a radical democratic demand with serious revolutionary consequences, or it was nothing but an empty formula which disguised the sectional interests of the urban middle class. They were thus demoralized by the knowledge that by pressing their own demands for reform they were in constant danger of being overtaken by the left. Fearing the masses, the liberals were all too willing to seek a compromise with the aristocracy and to support the junker-dominated army against the democratic forces. The issue of the relationship between the liberals and the army was to be the critical question for the next twenty years.

4

Constitutional Crisis

With the defeat of the revolution the main aims of the Prussian government were to rid the octroyed constitution of 1848 of its democratic elements and to strengthen Prussia's position in Germany. The first of these policies was largely successful, the second ended in a disastrous failure.

Universal suffrage for the lower house was abolished in May 1849 and was replaced by the three-class system which guaranteed a conservative majority. The three classes were based on the amount of taxes paid, so that the very few in the first class had as many votes as the vast majority of the population who were in the third class. As a result the elections held in the summer of 1849 returned a reactionary chamber which willingly set about the task of demolishing the constitution. The upper house was changed into a form of house of lords, and many of the members were appointed by the king. The *Bürgerwehr* was abolished and the principle of a standing army reaffirmed. The oath to the colours (*Fahneneid*) replaced the oath to the constitution. Civil liberties were severely restricted by legislation which controlled the press and limited the right of assembly. New legislation on the relationship between the junkers and their workers and servants forbade any associations of rural labour. Punishments for infractions of this law, which remained in force until 1918, were severe. The local and provincial *Landtag* which were the basis of junker authority on the land were restored, and the landed aristocracy preserved their judicial rights.

It was not possible to remove entirely the budgetary rights of the parliament, and expenditure on the army had to be approved by the lower house. The government was short of money, and it was no longer possible to return to the financial chicaneries of the pre-March. The government chose a mixture of dubious legalistic tricks and an attempt to curry popular favour for the army. It was announced that there was a 'hole in the constitution', for there was no indication of what was to happen when the lower house and the government failed to agree. This spurious argument was later to be taken up to great effect by Bismarck. The statute books were combed for taxes which were levied in perpetuity, but they were not enough to meet the growing demands of the army. Thus concessions had to be made, and the army had to argue a case in the house. As Prussian foreign policy was exceptionally feeble in the 1850s it was difficult to argue for increased military expenditure. Thus to bolster up a weak case the army made the tentative beginnings of a propaganda campaign designed to show the history of the army in the best possible light. The glorious role of the army in the wars of liberation was emphasized, but the dangerous liberal content of the reforms was studiously ignored. Historians who tried to write works which emphasized the critical aspects of the work of men like Scharnhorst were not given access to the archives, and their work was suppressed. These propaganda efforts were as yet in their infancy, but with the growth of liberal democratic forces they were to become increasingly strident. It was not until the 1890s that the army began seriously to make concessions to the spirit of the age and to leave its remoteness from everyday politics to play a direct political role in order to preserve its privileges and its unique position in the state.

Although parliament had no direct control over the army and the king's power of command remained intact, the position of the war minister gave rise to some concern in reactionary circles. The Prussian minister of war in his capacity as a member of the government, but not as an army officer, was obliged to take an oath to the constitution. As an officer, he was bound to obey the commands of the king, whose power of command was not limited by constitutional concerns. But as a minister, he was bound by article 44 of the constitution to defend actions which came under the jurisdiction of his department in the parliament. The king's military advisers were concerned that his power of command should not be in any way susceptible to parliamentary scrutiny, and therefore the war minister was required only to answer questions of a purely administrative nature in the *Landtag*. Matters of a purely military nature, which fell within the area of decisions made by the king in his capacity as supreme commander of the army, could not be discussed in parliament, and were not to be countersigned by the war minister. Thus the king's power of command, which was the cornerstone of Prussian militarism, and without which the army could not be used in an anti-democratic and absolutist way, was preserved. The war minister, however, was placed in an extremely invidious position, caught between the demands of parliamentary control and royal absolutism. If he took his obligations towards parliament seriously he was bound to lose the confidence of the crown, but if he erred in the other direction his position in parliament was likely to become untenable. The more realistic among the army leaders realized that some concessions had to be made, and they therefore agreed that the War Minister should consent to take an oath to the constitution. But they were adamant that the king's power of command should not be jeopardized. The situation of the war minister was therefore highly ambiguous, and the question of the relationship between the army and parliament was far from settled. The parliamentarians saw in this ambiguity a chance to extend constitutional controls over the army. The struggle between budgetary control and power of command was to dominate the politics of the 1850s.

If the army was prepared to make some steps in the direction of parliamentarianism, as in the case of the war minister, they were equally determined to strengthen the army as an instrument of domestic oppression ready to deal instantly with any civil unrest. The 'Law on the State of Siege' of 1851 strengthened the old law on the use of the army to combat civil unrest. It gave military commanders the right to suspend constitutional rights and to declare martial law. The war ministry's instructions on the use of weapons in the event of civil unrest, whicn was published in the same year, gave military commanders the right to use weapons against the people without having to seek the permission of the civilian authorities. It was claimed that the

Landwehr had been unreliable in 1848 and inefficient during the mobilization of 1850; it was therefore brought under closer control by the regular army. *Landwehr* regiments were in effect combined with regular regiments, given the same numbers and placed in infantry brigades. Regular officers were posted to replace *Landwehr* officers so that the two officer corps began to overlap. The two-year service in the regular army was gradually replaced by a three-year service so that, in the words of Prince William of Prussia, soldiers could fully imbibe the military spirit. In short a systematic attack was made on those institutions which still to a certain degree embodied the spirit of the reformers of 1806.

The argument for these changes was always couched in terms of military necessity. In the first place the growth of military technology necessitated a more professional army and arguments for an extended term of service had a certain cogency. Equally important was the fact that Prussia had suffered a severe humiliation in 1850, and the army was determined that such a disaster would not happen again. Frederick William, following the advice of von Radowitz, had pursued a plan for German unity in 1849-50 which threatened to lead to war with Austria. Radowitz proposed a German confederation which would exclude Austria (the *klein-Deutsch* solution) and would turn the liberal demand for national unity to the advantage of Prussia. In the course of the summer of 1849 the German states, with the exception of Bavaria and Württemberg, agreed to join in a Prussian-dominated union. Details of a constitution were worked out which left executive power in the hands of the king of Prussia, and which made only modest concessions to parliamentary democracy by proposing a lower house based on a three-class franchise on the Prussian model with strictly limited powers. This scheme was not unattractive to the right-wing liberals, the so-called 'Gotha-ers', who were prepared to abandon their liberalism for the cause of national unity.

The initial successes of Prussian policy were due in large measure to the fact that Austria was busily engaged in fighting the Hungarian nationalists. But once the Hungarians were defeated, the Austrian government under the leadership of the somewhat headstrong Schwarzenberg could devote its full attention to frustrating Prussian schemes for Germany. Austria was enthusiastically supported by Russia in its determination to destroy the German Union, for the Tsar was convinced that Radowitz was a sinister liberal and that a united Germany would be a formidable power to contend with in central Europe. Within Prussia the plans for union were also vehemently opposed by the *camarilla*, who urged Frederick William to abandon these dangerous plans. For men such as von Gerlach, Otto and Edwin von Manteuffel and the minister of war von Stockhausen, to say nothing of the majority of the senior officers, the scheme was a dangerous concession to liberalism and democracy which might well open the flood gates of revolution. If Prussia indeed merged into Germany then the junkers feared that they would lose their uniquely privileged position and be swept aside by forces which they could no longer control. They argued that the Prussian army was no match for the Austrians, the *Landwehr* was politically unreliable, the regular army too small, the financial resources of the state depleted, and the Austrians in fine fettle after crushing the Hungarians. Even if Prussia could defeat Austria there was the serious risk that Russia would intervene to stop German unity, and Prussia could not resist the combined forces of Austria and Russia. Meanwhile Austria in a trial of strength attempted to revive the old Bundestag as a rival to the Prussian-dominated union parliament in Erfurt.

After a series of long and complicated negotiations and diplomatic moves the crisis came to a head over the issue of Hesse. The people of Hesse had protested against the Elector's blatantly unconstitutional behaviour in dismissing the *Landtag*, which had refused to grant new taxes, and in declaring martial law. The Hessian officer corps had responded to this challenge by resigning their commissions *en masse*: of 257 officers 241 resigned. The Elector promptly fled to Frankfurt and called upon the Austrian-dominated Bundestag to send troops to restore order. The Prussians, fully aware of the vital strategic importance of Hesse and wishing to exclude Austria from influence in the electorate, took sides against the Elector and against Austria. This placed Frederick William in an exceedingly contradictory position, and confirmed the worst fears of the *camarilla*. The king of Prussia was supporting a rebellious people and an officer corps which put its oath to the constitution above its oath to the sovereign. In doing so he had won the support of the Prussian people against the scheming of Austria and Russia, but also for the constitutional and liberal principle involved in the Hessian affair. The Prussian army, which had only recently crushed the revolution in Germany, was not prepared to lead a popular war against Austria and Russia. The army mobilized, but there is evidence that the mobilization was deliberately retarded and sabotaged by the officers who were strongly opposed to the idea of a war which seemed to be as much for liberalism as for Prussian hegemony. Prince William argued that Prussia should go to war and that Prussia would win, but he was overruled by the *camarilla*. Frederick William shied back at the last moment and preferred to negotiate.

Historians are in general agreement that the Prussian army stood a good chance of defeating the Austrians in 1850, but it is certain that in a diplomatic duel they were bound to lose. In November at Olmütz Otto von Manteuffel gave way to Schwarzenberg and abandoned the plans for a Prussian-dominated union after negotiations in Warsaw which were singularly ineptly conducted by the Prussians. The Prussian liberals were disgusted at the 'humiation of Olmutz' and so was Prince William who regarded it as the darkest day in his life. The conservatives were delighted and the Prussian officer corps jubilant. For Helmuth von Moltke it was a great victory over democracy even though he rightly felt that the Prussian diplomats were incompetent. The army had deliberately placed domestic repression above considerations of foreign policy, their conservative ideology overriding liberal nationalism.

After Olmütz Prussia once again entered a period of bleak reaction. A leading figure of this period was the Prussian Minister of the Interior, von Westphalen, an ultra-conservative who is certainly less well known than his brother-in-law Karl Marx. The most spectacular trial of the period was the communist trial at Cologne in 1852. The dubious nature of the evidence and the activitives of the Prussian police were savagely denounced in one of Marx's most brilliant pamphlets. These two brothers-in-law are characteristic of the 1850s in that they represented the two main tendencies of the period: Westphalen the attempt to return to the pre-March and to undo even the modest achievements of 1848; Marx the movement towards progress, social change and the revolutionary consequences of modernization – on the one hand the 'christian-agrarian state', the transference of the traditions of enlightened despotism to the industrial age, on the other hand social revolution.

The social question had been raised in 1848 in dramatic form, and the economic boom of the 1850s was to set the stage for an intensification of the struggle in years to come. The economy surged ahead at a time when the social and political reaction was intensified. Economic and political forces thus moved in contrary directions. This was to make the crash of 1857 all the more serious in its consequences and was to plunge Prussia into a crisis which shook the very foundations of the state.

Industrial growth in this period was most noticeable in heavy industry, particularly in the Ruhr, and output doubled in the decade after 1848. The railway system was extended, the army playing an important part in planning new stretches of rail so that strategic considerations were taken into account. If the aristocracy feared that, in the industrialist Harkort's words, 'the locomotive is the hearse in which absolutism and feudalism are driven to the graveyard', they were able to maintain their position by the 'Prussian way' of improving and capitalizing their estates, to a large extent from the massive compensations that they were able to extract for relinquishing their feudal rights. And they built distilleries and sugar beet processing plants which were highly profitable because of government monopolies.

Industrial development had a profound effect on the army, not only through its social and economic effects, but also on armaments and transport. In the 1830s Nikolaus Dreyse had perfected a breach-loading rifle, the 'needle gun' with three times the rate of fire of the muzzle-loader and with a narrower bore. Major Priem of the war ministry had said in 1838: '60,000 men armed with this gun and led by a talented general, and his majesty the king will be able to decide where the frontiers of Prussia should be.' The problem facing Dreyse was how to mass-produce these weapons. Although they were made of cast steel and therefore suitable for industrial processing, Dreyse did not have the facilities for large-scale production. The weapons were used effectively in Saxony and Baden in 1849, but there was still some resistance from conservative generals to this new weapon. It was not until the early 1860s that the needle gun finally replaced the bronze muzzle-loader as the standard infantry weapon. With the mass production of modern rifles the fire power of the army was greatly increased. Both in attack and defence the infantry were now more effective, and any future war was bound to lead to higher casualty rates. Railways and the electric telegraph made the army more mobile and more flexible, but the full implications of these inventions were ignored. Just as in 1806 increased mobility and individual initiative were not possible without a higher degree of personal freedom. The Prussian army was loath to change infantry training to any great degree, fearing that officers might lose control over their men. Advances in technology had made a more flexible form of warfare possible, but political reaction hindered these advances in tactics and strategy.

The lesson of Olmütz was that the Prussian army was more concerned with the 'enemy at home' than with an ambitious foreign policy. The officer corps was therefore expanded, but care was taken that no dangerously liberal men were commissioned, and the aristocratic nature of the officer corps was preserved. Drill was as rigid as ever, but there was a gradual realization of the importance of individual training and education. The army was to be preserved, in the words of the director of the general war department, von Griesheim, as an island separated from society around it. Soldiers were not to be citizens in uniform, but rather citizens were to become soldiers, a separate caste without the political rights of normal citizens. In such an army education was to be an immunization against the dangerous ideas of the time. Men were to be trained to be reliable citizens of a conservative and authoritarian state. The army was to be the 'School of the Nation'. In short the ideas of the reformers had been stood on their head: the army was not to be an instrument of social change and enlightenment, but a brake on further progress, a pillar of the status quo.

Political tensions grew particularly severe in Prussia during the Crimean War, and a significant split began to develop within the ruling class. Those who favoured a policy tinged with liberalism, who wished to see a degree of compromise between the aristocracy and the bourgeoisie and who were close to the *Wochenblattpartei* favoured an alliance with England and France. The *camarilla*, which regarded Russia as a bastion of decency and strong government against the liberalism of the west, favoured an alliance with the Tsar. In this struggle the army tended to side with the *camarilla*, and the military plenipotentiary in St Petersburg was busily engaged in negotiations with the Russian court. The war minister, von Bonin, was dismissed when he made some remarks in the *Landtag* which were construed as being anti-Russian. Prince William, however, tended to favour the *Wochenblattpartei* and urged that Prussia should undertake an active foreign policy in order to regain her position in central Europe which had been so seriously weakened at Olmütz. In the end neither party won, with the result that Frederick William IV again vacillated. Prussia thus pleased none of the powers involved in the Crimean War, and in the peace negotiations in Paris it played a subordinate role. Internally Prussia had become seriously divided over Crimea. The *Wochenblattpartei* and the liberals denounced the government's policy of neutrality as being a thinly disguised pro-Russian policy which placed ideological concerns before the national interest. The *camarilla* and the majority of the officer corps bitterly resented the criticisms of the army which had been voiced in liberal circles and were determined not to allow parliamentarians to meddle in military affairs. Prussia was heading for a major political crisis.

In 1857 two events occured which precipitated the crisis. Prussia was particularly severely hit by the world economic crisis because it was coupled with an internal crisis of overproduction: rates of interest soared, the stock market collapsed. Wholesale prices in the *Zollverein* fell by thirty per cent, unemployment rose sharply. The crisis had a more critical effect on industry than on agriculture. Many smaller firms were ruined, and there was a significant number of amalgamations. Investors lost their confidence in industrial shares and tended to put their money in government bonds. Industry was thus forced to rationalize and economize. The second important event of 1857 was that the unfortunate Frederick William IV finally reached the point at which his mental state no longer enabled him to reign. Prince William of Prussia was appointed regent and entrusted with the affairs of state.

The regency seemed to mark the victory of the *Wochenblattpartei* and promised liberal reform, but this liberalism of the 'New Era' was deceptive. Prince William was to propose a far-reaching reform of the army which put the liberals in implacable opposition to the crown. The junkers hoped to preserve the power of the king against the encroachments of parliament, to strengthen the executive authority of the monarchy by increasing the army and keeping the monarch's power of command, and if possible to release the ministers from their oath to the constitution. The liberals hoped to use the crisis to secure a greater degree of control over the king and the cabinet, and to strengthen parliamentary control over the army. Thus the army was to play a central role in the constitutional conflict.

For Prince William the pseudo-liberalism of the 'New Era' was little more than a sop to the liberals to make them more receptive to the idea of army reform. But to many leading officers it was a dangerous concession likely to have disastrous consequences. Albrecht von Stosch warned that the year 1858 was likely to be a repeat performance of 1848, adding, 'the revolution in night gown and slippers is just as much at home in the fatherland, now as then'. The most outspoken proponent of this view was the chief of the military cabinet, Edwin von Manteuffel, who was prepared to offer no compromises whatsoever to the liberal bourgeoisie, and was determined to strengthen the army in a conservative sense in the course of the reforms. Manteuffel had felt that too many concessions were made in 1848, although it was largely due to his persuasive arguments that the army was not required to make an oath to the constitution. He hoped that the junkers would be able to use the crisis in order to restore royal absolutism and finally to destroy the last vestiges of parliamentary power. In order to strengthen the king's power of command Manteuffel succeeded in restructuring the military cabinet as a powerful body which was beyond any form of constitutional control.

Prince William began discussions in earnest on the question of military reform in 1858. There was general agreement, even in liberal circles, that some changes were needed. There had been no major reorganization of the army for fifty years, and although the population of the country had nearly doubled since 1820 the size of the annual intakes had remained constant. The minister of war, Albrecht von Roon, agreed that Prussia could maintain her position as a great power only if the army was reformed, and pointed an accusing finger at the *Landwehr* as the source of all the trouble. Both Roon and Manteuffel argued that the *Landwehr* was unreliable against the 'enemy at home', and that a popular war like that in 1813 for which the *Landwehr* was designed was no longer the priority for military planning. If the army was to be used against the people, then the *Landwehr* would have to be drastically modified. There were three main points in the proposed reform. First *Landwehr* should be under the command of officers from the regular army and should act as a reserve army. In other words the *Landwehr* would be made completely subordinate to the regular army. Secondly it was argued that the three-year service in the regular army would have to be enforced so that the right military and political attitudes could be drummed into the men. Lastly the size of the army would have to be greatly increased, without in any way democratizing the officer corps. This programme was in no sense original: it embodied ideas which had been discussed by those officers close to the *camarilla* for the last ten years. Indeed memoranda of Manteuffel dating back to 1849 contain all the principal ideas that he put forward in 1858, and have the same emphasis on the need to keep the army reliable to put down any unrest at home.

Thus plans for the reform of the army which had been informally discussed for years were put forward at a critical conjuncture in Prussian history. The reactionary nature of the reforms as they affected the army in its domestic role was at first somewhat obscured by the fact that it was put forward during the 'New Era'. The reaction against it was therefore all the stronger when the campaign against the proposed reforms began in earnest. The political tensions were particularly violent because the crisis occurred during an economic depression of considerable magnitude. The middle class was determined to resist the attempts of the reactionaries to turn back the clock, but fearing the possibility of serious unrest from below it was not prepared to go too far. The bourgeoisie was thus forced into a defensive position against both the aristocracy and their reactionary army reform and the workers and artisans who had suffered the most from the depression. But it was not until Bismarck came to power that the Prussian government was given the leadership that could exploit the situation to the advantage of the ruling elite by abandoning rigidly held positions and pursuing an active policy which used the opponents' weaknesses to its own advantage.

The new era had brought back von Bonin as war minister. He was an admirer of Boyen, was close to the *Wochenblattpartei* and had been forced out of office in 1854 for what were construed as liberal leanings. As minister of war he was determined to preserve the authority of his office, and was thus immediately to come into conflict with von Manteuffel, who planned to strengthen the military cabinet against the war ministry as an effective instrument of royal absolutism. Bonin opposed the reorganization of the *Landwehr* which he feared would further estrange the army from the people, and urged co-operation with the *Landtag* over army reform. Manteuffel argued that Bonin's opposition to army reform was motivated by his dislike of royal control over the army. He declared that if the military cabinet was not given complete independence from the war ministry he would resign. William, who was becoming increasingly annoyed by Bonin's intransigence and who was anxious to preserve the royal prerogative in military affairs, supported Manteuffel. Shortly afterwards relations between Bonin and Manteuffel became so intolerable that Bonin resigned.

Manteuffel and the king's adjutant general, von Alvensleben, had managed to prevent Bonin from playing an active part in the discussions on military reform, which were conducted in a small committee chaired by Albrecht von Roon. It was not until the committee had finished its work and some of the suggestions had already been put into practice, that Manteuffel was able to secure Bonin's resignation and his replacement by Roon. Roon was a staunch conservative, a confirmed monarchist who feared social revolution more than anything else. But unlike Manteuffel he was not a rigid and dogmatic reactionary. He had a more highly developed political sense and a more pragmatic caste of mind than the chief of the military cabinet. He was more interested in foreign affairs and in the position of Prussia as a great power, and was thus closer to Bismarck in his thinking than to Manteuffel. In March 1848 Roon had realized that concessions would have to be made if the aristocracy was to preserve its privileges, and that compromises with the bourgeoisie were necessary if the authority of the crown was to be preserved and a constitutional republic avoided. He agreed fully with Manteuffel that the power of the crown and the army had to be saved from liberalism, democracy and radical social change, but he saw the problem in a wider, European context. Although he was closely associated with the men of the *camarilla* he was opposed to their intransigently reactionary programme, but he felt that the *Wochenblattpartei* went too far towards seeking to accommodate the liberal bourgeoisie. Manteuffel's main political concern was the strengthening of the monarchical principle against liberalism in a battle which would take place at home, Roon thought in terms of strengthening the monarchy by making Prussia a great power in central Europe. Thus Manteuffel's obsession was the revolution of 1848, Roon's was Olmütz.

In 1860 the government placed the proposed reforms before parliament. The *Landtag* was in a highly critical mood. The promises of the 'New Era' had been shown to be chimerical, criticism of Prussian policy during the Italian War of 1859 had been strong and the Italian example had fired liberal nationalist imaginations. Fully aware of the political implications of the proposed reforms the chamber was in no mood to accept it without severe criticisms. The politicians argued that the cost of the military reforms would be so great as to place an intolerable strain on the Prussian economy, but this argument was hardly convincing as the *Landtag* happily voted an equivalent sum for the army shortly afterwards. There were the usual rousing speeches in favour of the *Landwehr* as the saviour of the nation in 1813 and as the guardian of civil liberties. The three-year service proposal was also denounced as a sinister scheme to turn the young men of Prussia into mindless robots and unthinking slaves of royal absolutism. But the *Landtag* was not entirely averse to the idea of increasing the size of the army. The liberals had urged an active policy in 1859, and realized that a national policy was impossible without adequate military support. The proposals were sent to committee, their fate still undecided.

By the time the army reforms were discussed in committee the issue had excited considerable public notice. Public opinion was strongly against the three-year service and the change in the status of the *Landwehr*. Those deputies who feared a confrontation with the government and who had rather timidly suggested that the reforms should be accepted were now beginning to have second thoughts. To the army this was a typical manifestation of democratic cowardice, and it made them all the more arrogant when they appeared as witnesses before the committee. Prince William and Roon argued that the committee had no right whatever to question the army's judgment that the reforms were essential, for it was a technical question which civilians had no competence to judge. They were therefore not prepared to make any concessions at all, and the committee's worst fears were confirmed that the reforms were designed for political just as much as military ends. Accordingly the committee prepared a report for the *Landtag* which called for a drastic reduction in funds for the proposed reforms, the retention of the two-year service in the infantry and the preservation of the *Landwehr*.

It was quite obvious that the *Landtag* would accept the recommendation of the committee and reject the military reforms. Manteuffel insisted that if the regent did not have a direct confrontation with parliament it would amount to a repeat performance of the capitulation of 18 March 1848. He was perfectly prepared to run the risk of a civil war, for the issue for him was simply whether the army was to take its orders from parliament or from the king. Prince William, however, was prepared to accept the advice of his ministers who wished to avoid a deadlock with the *Landtag* and who suggested that the proposed military reforms should be withdrawn. Manteuffel was enraged and wrote to Prince William: 'Things only work in Prussia if the king orders and the ministers obey.' The government withdrew the proposals while Manteuffel fumed in the wings, but the Finance Minister managed to secure additional funds for the army which nearly equalled the cost of the proposed reforms. Thus the army could expand, but the two-year service and the *Landwehr* would have to remain. In the struggle between Manteuffel and the government Roon had once again taken a middle position. He agreed with the ministers that an open conflict of the sort for which Manteuffel was thirsting must be avoided, but he agreed with Manteuffel that army reform should continue regardless of the attitude of the *Landtag*.

Roon believed that relative peace and quiet were needed, but he fully intended to use the money which parliament had voted to continue with the reorganization of the army. Roon's motto in these months was 'act firmly, keep firmly silent', a policy which won the approval of Manteuffel.

Manteuffel seemed to be grudgingly reconciled to a degree of compromise with the *Landtag*, which in turn agreed to the expenditure of further additional funds on the army. But in 1861 there was a marked swing to the left in Prussian politics which was to take the crisis to the next stage. A sizeable section of the liberals were no longer prepared to support the government and formed a new opposition party, the Progressive Party. William became king of Prussia in 1861 on the death of his brother, but there were a number of demonstrations against him, and even an assassination attempt by a man who argued that he had not done enough for German unity. The *Landtag* discussed proposals for constitutional reform which would clarify the issue of ministerial responsibility and thus limit the powers of the crown. The progressives made even more radical proposals for reform and demanded an energetic national policy. William seemed inclined to accept some of the proposals of the *Landtag*, but Roon in a series of angry letters to the king pointed out that the choice was now between a citizen king or a king by the grace of God. The war minister threatened the king with the displeasure of the army were he to give way to the demands of the *Landtag*, and, enthusiastically supported by Manteuffel, he called for the dismissal of those ministers who had advised the king to capitulate to the liberals.

The army now argued from a position of strength. It had been effectively reorganized and strengthened thanks to the funds granted by the *Landtag*. Now the conservatives were demanding action, for they were no longer prepared to compromise with the *Landtag* or tolerate the criticisms of the liberals. But there was division among them as to which was the best course of action. Manteuffel, Alvensleben and Prince Carl of Prussia favoured a *coup d'etat* which would restore Prussia to a pre-March absolutism. Roon felt that 'we can emerge refreshed from the mudbath of revolution', but he was realist enough to understand that Prussia could not revert to old-style reaction, but that the aim of the ultras should be to strengthen the position of the junkers within the existing system and use the constitutional mechanisms to their own advantage. Manteuffel's position was aggressive, Roon's defensive. The army should be prepared for a revolution from below, it should not initiate a coup from above. Bismarck told his friend Roon that the crisis in Prussia should be directed outside, that the position of the throne could be strengthened by an active foreign policy. But these ideas were to be developed not by Roon but by the greatest soldier of the epoch, Helmuth von Moltke, who was appointed chief of general staff in 1857.

Moltke was a man of greater intellectual ability than either Roon or Manteuffel. He rejected the narrow and rigidly reactionary views of the *camarilla* and, strongly influenced by Hegel's thought, he believed that the state should rule so that revolutions should come from 'above' and that the state should be constantly regenerated. Although he was profoundly conservative he realized that changes had to be made and he sympathized with at least some of the aims of the liberals. Thus he supported the nationalist policies of the 1848 liberals, but believed that they could be achieved only by military might and against rather than with the revolutionary forces. For the radical democrats he harboured an undying hatred, and insisted that all popular movements should be crushed by force. Moltke was fully aware of the military significance of industrial and technological advances, and was ready to exploit these achievements to the advantage of Prussia's armed strength. Such thinking was far in advance of men like Alvensleben who were obsessed with visions of charging cavalry.

It is perhaps curious that this man who shared few of the prejudices and habits of the junkers, a quiet, reserved and intellectual person, should have been the choice of the *camarilla* to succeed General Reyher as chief of the general staff. He was in fact the compromise candidate who was acceptable to both the factions in the military elite. His technical mastery of military affairs was beyond dispute, and his reticence, reliability, level-headedness and unwillingness to become involved in political brawls made him an attractive choice. In fact the army found that they had chosen a man with an iron will who was able to exploit the differences and divisions in the military and political leadership to pursue his own ends.

Moltke was deeply troubled by the crisis in Prussia because he felt that the deadlock between the government and the *Landtag* made it impossible for Prussia to pursue an active foreign policy. He followed Hegel's arguments in *The Philosophy of Right*, that the state should guarantee its independence and strengthen its position and power at the expense of other states. This was heady and idealistic stuff, and Moltke's original schemes for a national policy were singularly unrealistic. He dreamed of an understanding between Prussia and Austria which would create a powerful Germanic bloc in central Europe. With the outbreak of war in northern Italy in 1859 Moltke favoured an attack on France once the French troops reached Lombardy. This scheme brought him into direct conflict with the Prussian foreign minister, von Schleinitz, who wished to maintain Prussia's neutrality. The Austrians feared that if Prussia were to go to war with France that would greatly strengthen Prussia's position in central Europe, and this was precisely what Moltke hoped. Moltke also argued, as Bismarck was to do in 1870, that an active anti-French policy would take the wind out of the liberals' sails; but his critics in the *camarilla*, among them Manteuffel, feared that such a policy was dangerously liberal.

Although the experience of 1859 showed the deep divisions between Prussia and Austria, and although it was quite clear that were Prussia to expand her chief opponent would be Austria, Moltke still based his strategic thinking on the idea of a war against France in alliance with Austria. Political necessity forced him to consider plans for a possible war with Austria, but he was plagued with fears that in such an eventuality Russia and France would intervene with disastrous consequences for Prussia. In 1862 he began to think in terms of a short campaign against Austria which would be immediately followed by a full-scale attack on France, an outline of what in fact was to occur under Bismarck under quite different circumstances and with a considerable interval between the two campaigns. German unity was to be achieved by the defeat of France once Austria had been rendered harmless. For the ultras in Prussia such a scheme was altogether too risky. Their conservatism was such that they could seldom think in anything other than purely defensive terms. Moltke's *va banque* play, which elicited the support of nationalist liberals, could not expect to win their approval, and indeed it was ill-considered, overlooking the highly complex political ramifications of such a policy. Here Moltke was to find the perfect partner in Bismarck, who realized that the struggle for German unity was as much a political as a military problem, and who had the genius clearly to see the domestic, diplomatic and military consequences of each move. Moltke's ends could only be achieved by Bismarck's means.

Moltke's desire to project the crisis outside Prussia added a further dimension to the struggle, but in the circumstances of the time it could not provide a solution. Meanwhile the crisis over army reform grew even more intense. In a singularly provocative move William, urged on by Manteuffel, dedicated the standards of the reorganized regiments with pomp and ceremony in January 1861 at the tomb of Frederick the Great in Potsdam. Strictly speaking, once the *Landtag* had rejected the proposed reforms these regiments should have been disbanded, for they were designed to reduce the size of the *Landwehr* by incorporating parts of it into the regular army. The dedication ceremony was in many ways a triumph for the *camarilla*, because the liberals in the *Landtag* did little more than pull faces at the military. They had no intention of forcing a direct confrontation with the government, and meekly voted more funds for the army. The leftward swing of the *Landtag* later in the year further heightened the tensions.

In December 1861 the Progressives won an impressive victory in the elections, their stand against the three-year service and the *Landwehr* reforms winning them widespread popular support. Roon felt that revolution was just around the corner and called upon the king to appoint a second Brandenburg. Manteuffel heartily agreed, and saw himself in this role. The military cabinet worked out a plan for draconian action against Berlin if there was the slightest hint of civil unrest, and the plan was accepted by the king. Manteuffel was not satisfied with merely waiting upon events but argued that the people of Berlin should be provoked into action so that an excuse could be found for a military coup. Roon did not support these ideas. He feared that there was a genuine possiblity of a revolt but felt that Manteuffel's policies would simply make matters worse. He therefore argued that concessions would have to be made, and suggested that a two-year service could be accepted. Manteuffel was furious and felt that he had been betrayed. Roon had after all been completely under his sway in the early months of 1862, but now in April he was wavering and even talking of capitulating to the *Landtag*. Manteuffel talked wildly of Louis XVI and Charles I, of 1830 and 1848, but he was becoming completely isolated. The reason for this lay in the profound social changes that had taken place since the pre-March. Neither the junkers nor the bourgeoisie were willing to risk an outright confrontation, for in terms of the social reality of their position they were far closer together than was immediately apparent from their intransigent political attitudes. Both parties feared that if the crisis were to get out of control they might both be overcome by a social revolution which would destroy their privileged position. There could be no return to the junker absolutism of the pre-March, and a way would have to be found to reconcile the two factions.

Although Roon was more prepared to compromise with the *Landtag* than other leading generals, there was little he could do without their support. In looking for alternative solutions he stumbled on the idea of a war that would take people's minds off the tensions at home. As 1848 was still fresh in the memory it was perhaps natural that Roon should suggest a campaign in Schleswig-Holstein. To Theodor von Bernhardi he argued that such a policy would make the army popular again, and thus offer a way out of the crisis. Roon at this moment stood half-way between Manteuffel and Moltke; his policies were the most realistic of the three. Manteuffel's proposal for a restoration of pre-March absolutism was objectively an impossibility. Moltke's far-reaching political aims were unrealistic given the intransigence of the junkers and their hostility towards any suggestion of a compromise with the liberal bourgeoisie. Moltke's ideas would become realistic only when the domestic crisis was under control; his day would come. Manteuffel's ideas by contrast were destined for the rubbish dump of history: they could survive only in an acute crisis, and they offered no possible solution to the problems of the day. Thus Roon was the man of the moment, and his closest political contact was Bismarck. Although isolated from the king by the opposition of the *camarilla*, Roon continued to urge caution so that a conflict with the *Landtag* could be avoided. He bided his time, working for the day when Bismarck would become the king's first minister.

William was intransigent over the question of the length of service, and rejected Roon's proposal that it should be reduced to two years so that the *Landtag* would once again be prepared to vote funds for army reorganization and expansion. On 23 September 1862 by a vote of 308 to 11 the *Landtag* refused to grant any further funds for army reform. Some of the ministers felt that they could no longer remain in office. The king thought of abdication. The crown prince urged compromise. Manteuffel hoped that the time to strike was ripe. The liberals and progressives were a little shocked at their own behaviour in the chamber and had no desire to man the barricades; but the reactionaries were equally put out by the unanimity of the opposition. All was chaos and confusion. In a last desperate bid the king agreed to call on the 'mad junker' to save the situation. Roon sent his famous telegram to Paris where his friend was Prussian ambassador: '*Periculum in Mora. Dépêchez vous.*' On 24 September Otto von Bismarck-Schönhausen was appointed minister president of Prussia. He assured the king that he would secure the army reforms, regardless of the attitude of the *Landtag*.

Bismarck's future plans were outlined in his notorious 'blood and iron' speech, in which he indicated that the political and social standing of the monarchy and the aristocracy could best be preserved in Prussia by an active foreign policy, which by fulfilling part of the programme of the liberal bourgeoisie would bind them closer to a conservative state. Thus although Bismarck was known as an outspoken opponent of liberalism and democracy he was too shrewd a politician not to realize there could be no return to the policies of the period of reaction. He therefore developed his own brand of bonapartism which combined an extreme form of authoritarian government with certain concessions to liberalism and democracy. With Roon he worked out a compromise scheme for army reform which was a partial retreat from the extreme position of the *camarilla*. The army would be divided into two sections: the first third would be regular soldiers, the remaining two-thirds would be conscripts who would serve for two years. The size of the army would change with increases in the population, so that it would always be one per cent of the population. A fixed sum was to be voted per man, so that increases in the army caused by increases in population would not have to be approved by the *Landtag*. In other words, in return for the two-year service the *Landtag* was being asked to relinquish virtually all its budgetary control over the army.

These suggestions were totally unacceptable to Manteuffel, who at once began to bombard Roon with endless memoranda denouncing the War Minister for undermining royal prerogative and giving way to the chamber. Manteuffel still believed that the only solution to the crisis would be a direct fight between the aristocracy and the bourgeoisie, and that the slightest concession to the *Landtag* would amount to the creation of a parliamentary army. He was completely blind to the real intention of Bismarck's proposals and refused to budge one inch from his extreme position. Roon tried to explain to Manteuffel that there was no difference between them on ends, and that the difference was simply over means, but Manteuffel could not be convinced. Indeed he was able to persuade William that the means that Bismarck and Roon were suggesting would result in an overwhelming victory for the progressive party and the destruction of the Prussian monarchy. Roon was therefore forced to withdraw the proposed bill, and Bismarck, frustrated in his attempt to come to an arrangement with the *Landtag*, proposed a truculent policy which would be acceptable to the king's closest military advisers.

Roon and Bismarck became increasingly arrogant and scornful in their attitudes towards parliament, letting it be known that they had no intention whatever of allowing a handful of parliamentarians to interfere with the business of government. Reviving the old theory of the 'hole in the constitution', Bismarck announced that if the *Landtag* refused to grant the funds which the government needed in order to govern effectively then he would simply collect the money regardless. Civil servants who had concerns about the dubious legality of such a course of action were removed from office. By May 1863 the position had become quite intolerable. Bismarck refused to put forward a new request for funds. Roon's behaviour in the chamber was inflammatory and relations between the minister and the *Landtag* became so strained that Bismarck announced he would no longer allow ministers to appear in parliament until order could be guaranteed. Shortly after this parliament was dissolved.

Bismarck was concerned that the junkers should not become seriously politically divided. Thus once he had met with the opposition of an influential section of the aristocrats under Manteuffel he was prepared to abandon his scheme to reconcile the *Landtag* to the army reform. He had shown initially some consideration for the *Landtag*, and certainly more than the parliamentarians had expected, and this was not entirely forgotten in the following years. He knew perfectly well that the liberals were not prepared to risk extra-parliamentary action because they too were divided among themselves and they feared that they might also be destroyed in a revolution which they might not be able to control. His position was greatly strengthened once he began to hammer the *Landtag*, for this new policy reconciled him to the king and stole a large portion of Manteuffel's thunder. The more aggressive Bismarck and Roon became, the less influential were Manteuffel and Alvensleben. But the political situation was far from being satisfactory. The politicians were in a bitter mood. In the October elections the Progressives won further victories. The king was plunged into deep despondency and began to dream of guillotines. Bismarck hoped to find a way out of this situation by an active foreign policy.

He was encouraged in his foreign political adventures by the realization that the *Landtag* and their liberal supporters objected to the army mainly because they believed it to be designed solely for domestic political repression. If the army was used as an instrument of foreign policy then it was reasonable to suppose that these fears might be assuaged. However in pursuing an active foreign policy he had to be careful not to antagonize Austria, for the *camarilla* would not tolerate an anti-Austrian policy which they construed as liberal, nationalist and therefore dangerous. Similarly a strongly anti-liberal foreign policy would alienate the *Landtag* and therefore offer no solution to the constitutional crisis. The use of foreign policy to pursue domestic political goals is always extremely difficult.

In the Prussia of 1863 it seemed almost impossible. A move in any direction seemed likely to cause a violent response from some quarter, and Bismarck's first attempts were hardly encouraging.

The Polish revolt in the Russian part of Poland in January 1863 was used by Bismarck to reach an agreement with the Tsar that Prussia and Russia would co-operate to put down Polish national aspirations. The Alvensleben Convention, in which this agreement was formalized, caused a storm of protest in the *Landtag* from the Progressives, and from the radical democrats in the country there were demands for an independent Polish republic. Prussia's support for the repression of Polish national aspirations placed a considerable strain on relations with France. Von Moltke worked out details for a war plan for a Franco-Prussian conflict provoked by Napoleon III. Moltke argued that Prussia would be supported by the southern German states, and would thus gain the hegemony over central Europe. Such a policy ran quite counter to Bismarck's intentions, which were to neutralize the anti-French aspects of his Polish policy by means of an economic treaty with France and by political contacts with Napoleon III. Events in Denmark were to provide other, less risky, ways of combining an Austro-Prussian alliance with an anti-democratic bias, which would nevertheless be acceptable to many liberals.

The fate of the duchies of Schleswig and Holstein had long excited the interests of German liberals. To them the provinces were German, and they could argue with some justification that the Danish government had violated the terms of the London agreements of 1852 which guaranteed their autonomous rights. In 1863 the Danish government took advantage of the somewhat confused and uncertain state of international relations occasioned by the Polish revolt to attempt to strengthen its hold over the duchies. On 13 November 1863 the Danish parliament ratified a policy which in effect made Schleswig a Danish province and denied any autonomy to Holstein.

Protests against this move were heard throughout Germany, and volunteers proposed to fight for the independence of Schleswig and Holstein. The already exceedingly complicated issue was made all the more complex by the fact that the male line of the Danish royal house had died out. Christian von

Glücksburg had a legitimate claim to the Danish throne, but the Duke of Augustenburg claimed the duchies under the law of succession. The Duke of Augustenburg therefore placed himself at the head of a German national movement demanding the autonomy of the duchies. On 7 December 1863 the Bundestag passed a resolution demanding that the provisions of the treaties of 1851-52 be respected by the Danish government. On 23 December Saxon and Hanoverian troops entered the duchies to implement the Bundestag resolutions. The Danish army withdrew to Schleswig and Augustenburg was proclaimed Duke of Holstein.

This solution did not satisfy the German nationalists, and they continued to demand the independence of Schleswig from Denmark. Prussia and Austria were deeply suspicious of one another, each fearing that the other would use the crisis to curry favour with the nationalists. They therefore decided on a joint action, and agreed to seize Schleswig as a bargaining counter to force the Danish government to respect the terms of the London agreements. On 1 February 1864 Prussian and Austrian troops crossed into Schleswig.

The general staff under Moltke had outlined a plan for an attack on Schleswig and Holstein. Moltke argued that the campaign would have to be rapid, and the aim would be the destruction of the Danish army. He also drew up plans for action against the Saxon and Hanoverian forces should they attempt to risk resisting the invaders. The plans included an attack on the city of Hanover. Moltke was particularly concerned that if the campaign was not brought to a quick and decisive conclusion the European powers might be tempted to intervene. In fact the commander-in-chief of the joint army, the octogenarian General Wrangel, and the commander of the Prussian forces, Prince Frederick Charles, were unable to understand Moltke's plans and the campaign was painfully slow. This in turn enabled Moltke to play a more active role in the war than would otherwise have been the case, so that the importance of the general staff was greatly enhanced.

There were considerable differences of opinion among the army leaders about the campaign in Schleswig and Holstein. Moltke had some sympathy for the claims of Augustenburg, and as a solid legitimist he was shocked by Bismarck's cynicism

111

and determination to annex the duchies. But he was also alarmed that Augustenburg's support came from the liberals and democrats, and he was therefore reconciled to Bismarck's policy, the more so as it was in accordance with his desires to make Prussia a great power. Roon had serious misgivings about an alliance with the Austrians, as he felt that they could not be trusted, but like Bismarck he was utterly indifferent to the legality of Augustenburg's claim. Like Bismarck and Manteuffel, he supported the campaign because of its domestic political effect, announcing that it would 'checkmate' the revolutionary movement in Germany. Moltke placed far less emphasis on the effect on domestic politics. Thus in March 1864 when Moltke argued against an attack on the fortifications at Düppel fearing that losses would be too great, he was opposed by Bismarck, Roon and Manteuffel who insisted that a dramatic success was needed, not only to impress the foreign powers, but also for its effect on the liberals at home. The attack was a great success, and Bismarck was then able to begin armistice negotiations from a position of considerable strength. Both Moltke and Roon felt that the campaign should continue. When armistice negotiations eventually broke down, Moltke was given virtual control over military operations, and he was able to bring operations to a swift and satisfactory conclusion.

By February 1864 relations between Austria and Prussia had become somewhat strained as Wrangel had insisted on advancing beyond the borders of Schleswig into Jutland. Bismarck sent Manteuffel to Vienna to placate the Austrians. The choice of Manteuffel was dictated by the fact that he was particularly well liked and respected at the Austrian court, and Bismarck was confident that he would be able to nip in the bud any ideas the Austrians might have had of an arrangement with France. Bismarck was particularly anxious that the war with Denmark should remain the affair of Austria and Prussia alone. If the German states were to interfere then liberal nationalist demands were almost certain to be voiced. If the Western powers were to intervene then his schemes for annexation would be likely to be dashed. Manteuffel was also given instructions not to discuss northern Italy for fear that the Austrians might demand Prussian support in Italy in return for concessions in the duchies.

This idea was particularly appealing to Manteuffel because he was so taken with the success of his mission to Vienna that he began to think up scatter-brained ideas for an alliance between Prussia and Austria to crush liberalism and democracy in Germany, to combine with Russia to dismember Poland and revive the Holy Alliance, and to lend Prussian support to Austrian ambitions in the Balkans. The fact that these two latter policies were mutually exclusive escaped Manteuffel's mind, but he was rapidly off on another tack, thinking of a Prusso-Austrian attack on France, the motherland of revolution, an idea which had a certain appeal for Francis Joseph. Bismarck was not particularly interested in these musings. As long as Manteuffel made no commitments to Austria, and as long as he was successful in keeping the alliance together, there was nothing which he needed to fear. Manteuffel, while hardly noticing it, had become Bismarck's tool; his political plans were mere phantasies without the minister president's support. Bismarck was able to use Manteuffel for his own diplomatic ends, and after the failure of the armistice Moltke was fully engaged with the conduct of the war. Both men were satisfied that they were achieving their political aims of close co-operation with Austria. Bismarck was content to use them to that end, for he needed a temporary alliance with Austria. Manteuffel and Moltke were both popular with the Austrians, and their activities helped to disguise the long-term intentions of Bismarck's policy.

A preliminary peace with Denmark was signed on 1 August 1864, and final agreement was reached on 30 October. The provinces of Schleswig, Holstein and Lauenburg were placed under the direct control of Prussia and Austria, and Denmark renounced all claims to them. Thus Bismarck had triumphed. The Schleswig-Holstein question had been settled not by a popular war, but by the joint efforts of the Prussian and Austrian governments. The problem remained, however, of what was to be done with the duchies. The Austrians tended to support Augustenburg, because, in spite of the dangerously liberal aspects of his candidature, they hoped that he would be a willing client and support Austrian policies in the Bundestag. Bismarck intended to annex the provinces even if it meant a confrontation with Austria, but for the time being he was prepared to bide his time until Prussia was strong enough to challenge Austria.

The war with Denmark had passed without any serious conflict between Bismarck and the army. Moltke had opposed the attack on Düppel and had been critical of the government's policy in agreeing to an armistice. But there had been no significant breach between the minister president and the chief of general staff. Similarly differences with Wrangel had been tiresome rather than serious. Bismarck's use of Manteuffel was masterly, and he was able to count on the support of Roon. Bismarck had little reason to fear any serious difficulties with the army in the future, and he could afford to regard Roon's warning that an army could not simply be regarded as a lancet in the hands of a diplomatic surgeon as being little more than a reasonable expression of soldierly pride.

The seeming unanimity among the army leaders soon began to fray. In the summer of 1864 a conflict was to break out which was characteristic of the history of the Prussian army. It was over the question of the fields of competence of the war ministry and the military cabinet. Manteuffel was jealous of the close co-operation between Roon and Bismarck, and feared that a strengthening of the war ministry would diminish the king's control over the army and strengthen the minister president at the expense of the monarchy. Manteuffel was also sharply critical of the proposals of Bismarck and Roon for fixing the peace-time strength of the army according to a percentage of the population. He feared that any such deal with the *Landtag* would diminish the effectiveness of the army as an instrument of domestic oppression. He still dreamed of getting rid of the constitution and ruling if necessary by a military dictatorship. Thus in May 1865 he demanded the outright annexation of Schleswig and Holstein, hoping that this would provoke such a crisis that the army would have the chance to carry out a coup. Manteuffel asked the rhetorical question of the king: 'Who rules and decides in Prussia, the king or his ministers?' Bismarck had no intention of allowing his plans to be foiled by the chief of the military cabinet, and when Manteuffel began to meddle once more in foreign affairs by urging a pro-Austrian course when Bismarck was preparing the ground for the abandonment of the policy of co-operation with the government in Vienna, he decided it was time to act. Supported by Roon, who was angry at Manteuffel for his attacks, he managed to persuade the king that Manteuffel should be sent as governor of Schleswig. After many discussions and recriminations the king agreed. Just as Bismarck had sent Manteuffel off to Vienna in order to use him for his Schleswig-Holstein policy, now he was sent to Schleswig so that he could pursue his anti-Austrian policy.

In the early months of 1865, although tension between Austria and Prussia was mounting noticeably, Moltke still continued to hope for an understanding between the two powers, toying with the idea of Prussian support for Austria in Italy in return for Prussian control of Schleswig and Holstein – an idea that had already been articulated by Manteuffel. The key to an understanding of the change in Moltke's attitude towards Austria in 1865 lies in his belief that Schleswig and Holstein had to become Prussian provinces. To his military mind the strategic importance of the provinces was apparent, and if Austria were to have a base in the duchies Prussia would be greatly weakened. He was prepared to offer Austria compensation, if necessary from Prussian territory, but as tensions between the two states grew increasingly intense he began to think in terms of a possible war. At a meeting of the crown council on 29 May 1865 Moltke announced that Prussia would have to examine the possibility of a war with Austria. He still hoped for a compromise, and thus welcomed the Treaty of Gastein in August 1865 which gave control of Schleswig to Prussia and Holstein to Austria, but which also gave Prussia the right to establish a military and naval base in Kiel.

The Treaty of Gastein, by which the Austrian province of Holstein was effectively sandwiched between Schleswig and Prussia, signified the greatly strengthened position of Prussia during the past year. In spite of the Franco-Prussian trade agreement the vast majority of the German states agreed, after some often highly dubious dealings, to continue with the *Zollverein*. In April 1865 a trade agreement was reached with Austria which effectively excluded her from the German market. The intensification and concentration of production which had occurred during the economic crisis of 1857-60 now began to pay dividends. The *Zollverein* states overtook the production of France and Belgium, and the gap between Prussia and Britain began to close. The dynamism of the Prussian economy coupled with high interest rates attracted capital to Berlin, away from the Austrian banks and state loans. Although Prussia was divided between an industrial west and an agrarian east, the division between the two sectors of the economy had not yet become acute. Agricultural prices were high, land speculation brought rich rewards and the large estates were capitalized. The effect of relative prosperity in Prussia was to push the aristocracy and the bourgeoisie into an understanding, in spite of the debate over army reform which still raged and which seemed no closer to resolution than it had been before the campaign against Denmark. The aristocracy became concerned that unless some compromise was made, the increasingly critical and vocal democratic forces might succeed in winning over some of the bourgeoisie. Serious consequences would follow an open conflict between the government and the opposition. Similarly on the liberal side there was a growing awareness that there was much solid benefit to be reaped from Bismarck's great-power politics, and their opposition to the government became less pronounced. Bismarck was fully aware that an active policy for Prussian domination of Germany could be used to effect this class compromise.

During the winter of 1865-6 Moltke began work on a detailed plan for a war with Austria. The plan called for a guarantee that Russia and France would not intervene, and proposed a joint attack with Italy. The plan was cautious, calling for a limited war which was not designed to destroy Austria but to force her to accept Prussian aims. Prussia's position seemed favourable. Napoleon III was busily engaged with his adventure in Mexico, and his predilection for neutrality was brilliantly exploited by Bismarck. The smaller German states did not pose much of a threat. Their mobilization plans were such that it would take them a long time before they could be militarily effective, and as Moltke was planning a swift attack he could afford largely to discount them. He was also well aware of the fact that most of the senior officers of the smaller armies greatly admired the Prussian army, and would be singularly lacking in enthusiasm to do battle with them. Moltke envisaged an Austrian attack on Berlin and he therefore proposed a swift attack on Saxony. Saxon neutrality would be respected only if the Prussian troops were allowed to march through the country, so that they would be ready to block the Austrian advance towards Berlin.

In early 1866 Moltke became increasingly confident. At a meeting of the ministerial council at the end of March he announced that he did not think that the Austrian army was sufficiently strong to risk an offensive. He also pointed out that the Prussian army could be fully mobilized within twenty-five days, whereas the Austrians would take forty-five days. Thus the chief of the general staff began to think in terms of an all-out offensive against Austria, rather than waiting for the outcome of an initial Austrian attack. The king was highly alarmed at this idea. He insisted that the greater size of the Austrian army made caution imperative, whereas Moltke argued that the Prussians would move so rapidly that the Austrians would not get the chance to deploy their entire army. The court was also concerned about the effects of the constitutional crisis on the army, and argued that if the Prussians met with severe military setbacks there would be a social revolution at home.

Meanwhile events were moving rapidly. Prussian troops were marched in a provocative fashion into Holstein as a calculated insult to Austria. This was coupled with a proposal to reform the German Confederation in such a way as to exclude Austria. All Bismarck had to do now was to keep up the pressure on Austria, particularly in the Bundestag, so that Austria would be forced to act and would appear as the aggressor. Moltke's influence grew considerably in these weeks. On 2 June the chief of the general staff was given the right to give commands to subordinates on the movements of the field army in the name of the king. He was to all intents and purposes given full command over the army, thus solving for the duration of the war the rivalry between general staff, war ministry and military cabinet. The degree to which Moltke pressed for war in the early days of June is difficult to ascertain, for the records of the general staff have been destroyed. But there is evidence that he urged the king to act, and gave him highly coloured accounts of the dire consequences of not moving swiftly, while at the same time assuring the army commanders that there was little to fear from the Austrians.

On 11 June the Austrians called upon the Bundestag to mobilize the federal army, with the exception of the Prussian units, as Prussia had disturbed the peace of the confederation by her provocative actions in Holstein. On 14 June the Bundestag accepted a compromise proposal from Bavaria which called for the mobilization of only two army corps. Bismarck decided to act rapidly, for there was mounting opposition to Prussian policies, particularly in southern Germany which had a radical democratic emphasis. The following day he announced that Prussia could no longer accept the federal constitution. On 16 June Prussian troops marched into Saxony, Hanover and Electoral Hesse. The war had begun.

5

The Franco-Prussian War

The war with Austria was over within a few weeks. The Prussian army was deployed according to Moltke's principle of 'march separately, fight together', whereby the three armies would meet on the field of battle. This scheme had seemed to many of the more traditionally minded officers to be highly risky, and a dangerous innovation by a relatively inexperienced officer. Moltke's strategy, however, was based on a clear understanding of the new techniques and methods that were available to the army. The needle gun had greatly increased the firepower of the infantry and made Prussian units less vulnerable to attack, even from a numerically superior enemy. The railways and greatly improved roads could be used to move an army far quicker than many thought possible. The telegraph improved communications and gave individual units a far greater flexibility. The reforms of the army that had been put into effect despite the opposition of the *Landtag* had increased its efficiency. The powers given to the chief of the general staff on 2 June greatly simplified the command structure.

There were, as was to be expected, some misunderstandings and confusion in the war, particularly between the government and the army. There was no delineation of areas of competence and authority between the minister president and the chief of the general staff, which gave rise to a number of problems. Bismarck ordered General Falckenstein of the western army to advance on Frankfurt, and Moltke was forced to accept this interference with his war plan as Napoleon's intervention made it no longer necessary for Falckenstein to engage the Bavarian army. Many soldiers were also uncertain as to the exact powers of the chief of the general staff, and the recent changes in army organization had obviously not been made clear to the army as a whole. One divisional commander at the battle of Königgrätz did not even know who Moltke was. Some officers were resentful of Bismarck's interference with military affairs, but the campaign passed without any serious conflict between the civilians and the military.

In the early morning of 3 July the decisive battle of the war began at Königgrätz. Like most battles it did not go quite according to plan, and Moltke was unable to win the decisive victory for which he had hoped. The second army, which had marched from Silesia, arrived on the battlefield in the early afternoon and by crushing the right wing of the Austrian army was able to bring Prussia the victory. Faulty communications between the first and second armies and the superiority of the Austrian artillery enabled the Austrian army to withdraw towards Vienna.

The Prussian victory ended all William's reservations about the war, and he longed to enter Vienna in triumph. The officer corps were likewise determined to pursue the Austrians and smash their army in a final decisive battle. But Moltke was less sanguine. He underestimated the confusion at the top of the Austrian army, and feared that there might be a national insurrection against the Prussian army of occupation and an increasing determination to defend Vienna against the invader. Most important of all, Moltke, like Bismarck, saw the war with Austria as an episode in a chain of events which would lead to a war with France. For him the conflict was a 'cabinet war' of limited objectives, for all the brilliance and modernity of his strategy.

Two days after the battle of Königgrätz Napoleon III called for an armistice between Prussia, Italy and Austria which would lead to a peace treaty. Bismarck was willing to accept Napoleon's proposal and Moltke agreed. Moltke had no intention of destroying the Habsburg Empire, and wished to see Austria pursue an active policy in the Balkans. He did not want to run the risk of the war becoming a general European conflict. This attitude put Moltke on Bismarck's side and in opposition to the king. Thus after a series of exchanges with Napoleon III the preliminary peace was signed at Nikolsburg on 26 July and the terms were finally agreed at Prague on 23 August.

The Prussian court had an unreasonable fear of Napoleon III, and when the emperor began to make noises about compensation on the Rhine in return for support for Prussian aims in the peace with Austria, Moltke was called upon to make an exposé of the possibility of war with France. Moltke seized this opportunity to produce, at the beginning of August, a memorandum which, although it made strategic suggestions for a war with France, is of interest mainly because it contained a programme of action for the future. He called upon the government to think in terms of a war with France in the near future, a war which would lead to the unification of Germany under Prussia, and a war which the Prussian army felt confident of winning even though the French army was the strongest in Europe. Politically the memorandum urged Bismarck not to give way to any demands from France and to prepare the ground for a future war. For Moltke this was not just a question of avoiding the necessity of fighting a two-front war, but it involved preparing the country economically, politically and militarily for war with France.

Moltke was not the kind of sabre-rattling militarist who would demand war at any price, but he devoted all his energies after 1866 to planning a war with France, and he was prepared at any moment which he considered opportune to push for war. He was well aware of the many problems that he had to surmount. As in Denmark and Austria his aim was for a swift and decisive campaign, but the difficulty of achieving this goal against an enemy as powerful as France was very considerable. He was well aware of the contradictions and weaknesses of the bonapartist regime in France, but he also knew that Napoleon might be tempted to seek a way out of his dilemma at home by an aggressive policy abroad. He feared that Napoleon might play on French national sentiment to save his regime. He had little faith in the military contributions which the German states were likely to make to a Franco-Prussian war, and a Franco-Austrian alliance to undo the decisions of 1864 and 1866 was a constant nightmare to him. He was fully aware of the counter-revolutionary nature of the bonapartist regime, and was afraid that once the regime was destroyed there could well be a social revolution in France which could lead to a people's war against Prussia in the tradition of the jacobins.

The North German Confederation, formed in 1866-67, greatly strengthened Prussia's military position and thus encouraged the general staff to be more aggressive in its plans for a war against France. The king of Prussia was commander-in-chief of the armies of the new confederation. Most of the smaller contingents were absorbed by the Prussian army, but the Saxon army enjoyed a somewhat artificial independence with its own minister of war. But even in peace-time the Saxon army was under the supreme command of the king of Prussia, designated as the XII Army Corps. In 1867 approval was given to the 'law on the obligation to military service', which extended the Prussian military system to all contingents in the North German Confederation. In a series of military agreements with the South German states Prussia's influence over the military policy of Germany was greatly strengthened, but for it to be effective Prussian policy had to have an anti-French direction. If Prussia were unable to provoke the French to attack, then the military agreements, which were essentially defensive, would be of little use.

By these measures the size of the Prussian army was greatly increased. The peace-time strength of the army in 1861 was 212,650; by 1869 it was 300,000 with a wartime strength of 552,000. Success in the campaigns of 1864 and 1866 had effectively silenced liberal criticism of Bismarck and ended opposition to army reform. The *Landtag*, by declining to comment on the excuses for the unconstitutional collection of taxes in the throne speech of 5 August 1866, in effect granted Bismarck an indemnity. As a result of this the Progressive Party split, one section forming the National Liberal Party under Rudolf von Bennigsen, the other continuing in its opposition to Bismarck's policies under Schulze-Delitzsch. Within the North German Confederation there was no minister of war, and thus no constitutional link between the army and the Reichstag. Thus the king of Prussia as supreme commander was in an even stronger position than he was in Prussia itself.

Prussia came very close to going to war with France in 1867 over the Luxemburg crisis. Luxemburg had been part of the

German Confederation, but had not been absorbed by the North German Confederation. There was, however, a Prussian garrison in Luxemburg. Napoleon III had negotiated with the king of the Netherlands and had agreed to a treaty by which Luxemburg would become part of France. Bismarck worked up a storm of protest against France in which he was enthusiastically supported by the National Liberals. The Luxemburg affair was eventually referred to a conference of the great powers at London where it was agreed that the neutrality of Luxemburg should be guaranteed. Moltke pressed for war at the height of the crisis. He was certain that Austria would not intervene, and thus his old fear of a two-front war was assuaged. Anti-French feeling was running so high throughout Germany that a united war effort was possible. He declared: 'The present situation is favourable. It has a national character, so let us use it.' His plans for a campaign in France envisaged a decisive battle on the fourth or fifth day. Moltke had no desire to wait until the French army had been equipped with breach-loading rifles, and therefore argued that the opportunity should be seized for a preventive war. But in spite of all these warlike utterances, Moltke had many misgivings about the quality of the senior officers in the Prussian army whose military thinking was seriously outmoded, and he still had doubts about the military efficiency of the South German armies. Thus he was prepared to support Bismarck's efforts to seek a diplomatic solution to the crisis.

After the Luxemburg crisis Moltke paid increasing attention to the question of railway building. In order to speed up mobilization six stretches of railway were either completed or improved to hasten the movements of troops towards France. Moltke's motto, to use his own words, was: 'The character of modern military leadership in war is shown in the pursuit of a large and swift decision.' This outline of what was later to become blitzkrieg strategy was dictated by Moltke's essentially conservative world view. War had to be quick and decisive, so that it would remain fully in the control of soldiers. It was too serious a matter to be left to anyone but the professional. Peoples' wars would lead to radical social and political changes which had to be avoided at all costs. This did not imply that Moltke was an ultra. His experience as a member of the

North German Reichstag led him to respect and understand the right-wing liberals, and unlike many conservative generals he did not disapprove of the idea of a parliament. Under the leadership of Moltke the Prussian army became cognizant of the needs and aspirations of the upper bourgeoisie, and was no longer merely the servant of a reactionary monarchy. Yet for all Moltke's modernity, his understanding of modern techniques and innovations, his imaginative reorganization of staff work and his distrust of hidebound traditionalists in the officer corps, there were strict limits beyond which he would not go. The army could not be democratized, because that would put the army in the service of social forces which Moltke wished to control and contain. Similarly to use all the resources of the modern state for military ends would lead to the unleashing of passions which might get out of hand. Moltke was determined to maintain the social *status quo*, while being prepared to make concessions to a section of the middle class. He believed that a swift, decisive and limited war was therefore essential.

From 1866 to 1870 the strategic planning of the general staff was devoted to working out the details of an offensive against France. In the event of a two-front war the offensive was still to be directed against France, and after a swift victory the railways would be used to capacity to take the army across Germany to meet the Austrians. Moltke was even prepared to run the risk of an Austrian attack on Silesia, Saxony or even Berlin, for he was convinced that once France had been defeated it would be a simple matter to dislodge the invaders. This strategy made it essential for Prussia to take the initiative from the very outset, and this in turn meant that the army would put massive pressure on the government to bring any crisis with France to a head and provoke Napoleon III into an act of aggression. Moltke saw a war against France as the ideal chance to unify Germany under Prussia in a way that would necessitate few concessions to liberalism or democracy. Napoleon III for his part made it clear that he would not tolerate the unification of Germany without concessions on the Rhine. Even more important for the smooth working of Moltke's plan, Napoleon was increasingly willing to attempt to obfuscate the internal divisions of a sharply polarized French society by a chauvinistic foreign policy aimed against Prussia. The prestige of his regime could be greatly enhanced by making the Rhine the border of France. That would restore the European balance of power which had been tipped in favour of Prussia.

Thus in the crisis over the Hohenzollern candidature for the Spanish throne the forces pushing towards war, both in Paris and Berlin, were overwhelming. Moltke and Roon demanded war, and urged Bismarck to manipulate the crisis so that Napoleon would be forced to take aggressive action. Both men played an active part in the fabrication of the famous 'Ems telegram' which provoked Napoleon into war.

From the very earliest engagements of the war it was clear that the French army was inadequately prepared, unimaginatively officered and in general no match for the Prussians. Moltke's careful staff work paid high dividends, and the deployment of the three large armies in the area of the Rhine and Mosel was skilfully executed. Yet in spite of the brilliance of Moltke's leadership, which Friedrich Engels writing in the *Pall Mall Gazette* described enthusiastically as 'exemplary', he did not achieve that swift and decisive victory for which he had been planning. Part of the trouble was the operational conservatism of some army leaders, particularly of the First Army, and their reluctance to keep headquarters fully informed of their moves. But Moltke was able to maintain a high degree of overall strategic control with considerable operational flexibility, whereas the French leadership lost control of the situation, giving individual commanders excessive responsibility. In spite of the great ability of some commanders, the lack of co-ordination seriously hampered the French as they began to withdraw in the face of the Prussian advance.

Within four weeks the French army was besieged in Metz, and forced to capitulate at Sedan. Napoleon III was a somewhat pathetic prisoner of war, but still France had not been defeated and the decisive victory had eluded Moltke. The French regular army had been destroyed, the government replaced by a republic, but peace was not in sight. Moltke's theory of the decisive battle overlooked the resources available to a highly developed modern state. The new French republic had considerable economic reserves and was quickly able to equip a new army fired with an idealism for the republic and the defence of the motherland against the Prussians. This new force was to present many problems to Moltke in the months after Sedan.

As the war was prolonged its nature changed. Whereas it had been just possible to argue that the Prussians were fighting a defensive war – the chicaneries of the Ems telegram were of course not known to the public – it now became all too apparent that the war was annexationist and anti-democratic. Bismarck made the annexation of Alsace and Lorraine and the formation of a new government in Paris essential preconditions for an armistice. Although the general staff had certainly had its eye on Alsace and Lorraine when planning the war against France, Moltke had been fearful of the intervention of the great powers if such aims became known. With the guarantee of Austrian neutrality, due in part to the efforts of the Russian government, Moltke had no reason to fear a two-front war. Thus extensive annexationist demands could be made, the arguments dressed up in terms of 'military necessity' – that without Alsace and Lorraine Germany could not be defended against a France bent on revenge. The absurdity of this argument was obscured by the fact that there was such a general enthusiasm for annexations among the national liberals and the conservatives that a rational debate on the issue was almost regarded as treason. The fact that the annexation of Alsace and Lorraine would create rather than frustrate the demand for revenge was largely overlooked, as was the extremely dangerous precedent established by allowing matters of grave political consequence to be discussed in military terms.

Moltke had argued in early memoranda that annexations would steel the determination of the French to resist, but after Sedan and Metz he was confident that France had few remaining military resources on which to call. He felt that the *franc-tireur* warfare which began in August could be ended by severe measures against civilians and the death sentence for any irregular troops which were captured. As the march began towards Paris Moltke hoped that a military dictatorship would be established under General Trochu with whom diplomatic exchanges could begin on the details of a peace settlement. These hopes were soon dashed. Bismarck's demands for annexations, reparations and political changes in France were quite unacceptable to the French provisional government. This was hardly surprising as the Germans did not even regard the provisional government as legitimate. As Moltke wrote to his brother, a government which was formed by a worker jumping up on the president's chair, ringing a bell and declaring that the republic had been formed could hardly be supported by the 'propertied classes'. Both Bismarck and Moltke agreed that the only solution would be for elections to a national assembly which would restore either Napoleon III, as Bismarck wanted, or a constitutional monarchy under the orleanists, as Moltke preferred. The general staff had no intention of winning two provinces but then allowing the 'red republic' to rule France and thus present a constant danger to the Prussian autocracy. Moltke believed that the republic in no way reflected the desires and wishes of the people of France; it had come to power by some trick or deception. He imagined that the 'decent people' of Paris would welcome the Prussian army as liberators from the barbarism of the republic, and that together they would restore civilization and culture to France. Thus the war was to be continued not merely to achieve the extensive annexationist aims and exact the reparations payments, but also to secure these counter-revolutionary aims.

By December 1870 Moltke's optimism that the war would soon be over was beginning to fade. His hopes that the anti-republican forces in France would be so strong as to undermine the French war effort proved illusory. Although the newly-created French army had been defeated in a number of engagements on the Loire, it had not been crushed. Reserves continued to mount, and Moltke estimated that the French would soon be able to muster an army of over one million men. The *franc-tireurs* were beginning really to hurt the Prussian army, and they continued to inflict heavy damage in spite of savage reprisals. These reprisals in turn served to strengthen the determination of the French to resist. The war had become for them a people's war. The growing frustration of the general staff about the course of the war led to conflicts with Bismarck and the civilians.

The struggle between Moltke and Bismarck has all too often been portrayed as a classic struggle between the 'military' and the 'civilian', between politics and strategy or, in the historian Gerhard Ritter's terms, between the 'craft' of warfare and the 'art' of statesmanship. The problem with this approach is that neither politics nor warfare is 'pure': they result from the conjuncture of many social and economic forces, and they cannot be reduced to two separate and paradigmatic entities. Furthermore, concentration on the differences between Moltke and Bismarck obscures the essential similarity of their aims. The identity of these aims is of even greater significance than their differences. However acrimonious the differences between the two men might at times have been, they were the result of temporary frustrations at the course of the war after Sedan rather than a fundamental disagreement about the overall course of German policy.

The Prussian forces were harassed by irregular units, and with a large part of the army tied down defending supply lines and depots and engaged in the siege of Paris, Moltke was short of men to combat the growing French army. He therefore evolved a strategy whereby the main body of the Prussian army would remain to the north of the Loire, wait until the French army had organized itself and then smash it with a short offensive operation. The problem, in short, was to catch the French so as to be able to inflict the decisive victory on them that had been missed at Sedan. But Moltke was not optimistic, for he realized that even if the Prussians were able to win this engagement they would not be able to pursue the French. The most they were likely to be able to do was to make it difficult for the French army to re-form for some time to come.

Thus Moltke had, in effect, abandoned his hopes for a short campaign and was prepared for a war of attrition. The siege of Paris and the firmness of the Prussian army of the Loire would, he hoped, place such a strain on the provisional French government that it would collapse and be replaced by an anti-republican government which would be ready to seek peace with the Prussians. But by abandoning hopes for a swift conclusion of the campaign the chief of the general staff came into conflict with Bismarck, who was anxious to end the war as soon as possible. Bismarck was prepared to accept any measures to achieve that aim, including the bombardment of Paris regardless of the military value of such an action, the shooting of hostages and the refusal to take prisoners.

The war was not simply a war against France; it was for the unification of the Reich. Moltke and Bismarck had somewhat different views as to how the new empire should be organized. Both men were determined that their positions in the new state would be pre-eminent. Bismarck was thus prepared to make considerable concessions to the particularist sentiments of the German states, while Moltke, who wanted a unified command over all the forces in Germany, was a centralist to the point of even considering an invasion of Bavaria if the Bavarians did not co-operate fully with Prussian demands. Bismarck was anxious not to run the risk of foreign intervention, and was prepared to make concessions to the states so as better to establish his own power and authority in Prussia and in Germany. Moltke, on the other hand, argued that France had to be destroyed and Germany closely unified so that the general staff would command the strongest military power in Europe and Moltke's authority in Germany, and Germany's in Europe, would be secure.

One of the main reasons why Moltke wished to continue the war slowly and methodically was that he expected by these means to destroy the republican regime. But as the war was prolonged and the annexationist demands of the Prussians became known, opposition became more outspoken at home and abroad. The determination of the republic to defend France was far greater than he had imagined. At home criticism of the war was mounting. Bebel and Liebknecht's stand against voting for the war credits in the North German Reichstag in November 1870 was to land them in jail on a charge of high treason, but sympathy for their stand was growing. Moltke began to fear that if the war were prolonged the risk of republicanism might become greater, making a mockery of his intention to fight a war which would purge the European states of republicanism. By January 1871 he was becoming more sympathetic to Bismarck's point of view that the war should be ended as soon as possible.

If Moltke was haunted by the spectre of red republicanism so was the French bourgeoisie. The provisional government had suffered a number of military setbacks in January at Le Mans, St Quentin and on the Lisaine. The bombardment of Paris which had begun on December 27 had been violently opposed by all the military other than Roon, but Moltke had been obliged to give way to a policy which, as a student of Clausewitz with his dislike of siege warfare, he disliked. The defeats in open battle had certainly weakened the French, but they still had adequate resources with which to continue the struggle. The Prussian army was having great difficulty in controlling the area that they occupied, and Clausewitz's observation that the problems of an occupying force increase by geometrical progression, and the area occupied grows by arithmetical progression, seemed all too true. The bombardment of Paris had little military effect, as Moltke had predicted, but it steeled the resistance of the Parisians and greatly radicalized them. The provisional French government began to fear that if the war was continued there would be a further strengthening of the democratic and revolutionary forces, so that submission to the Prussians seemed better to them than the possibility of a social revolution. Thus on 28 January 1871 an armistice was signed which was to last for three weeks. A national assembly was elected, and Thiers who headed the new government began negotiations with Bismarck for a peace settlement.

Events in Paris filled Moltke with mounting concern. Intelligence reports from the capital indicated that political tensions were mounting and that an armed insurrection was a distinct possibility. Under the terms of the armistice Paris was allowed to maintain its armed National Guard, but as the situation in Paris grew ever more explosive Moltke demanded that only the reliable elements of the National Guard should be armed, so that the Thiers government could maintain order and save the city from revolutionary violence. The general staff began to think in terms of a joint operation by the French government and the Prussian army to disarm the artisans and workers of Paris.

At the beginning of March the first barricades were built in Paris and the revolutionary movement began to gather steam, Moltke approved the release of some ten thousand prisoners of war, which were to form an army with which Thiers' government at Versailles intended to crush the revolutionary movement in Paris. On 28 March the commune was officially proclaimed in Paris. Moltke, who was in Berlin at the time, ordered that the communards should be instructed that any action on their part that could be construed as a violation of the armistice would immediately lead to the resumption of military operations against Paris. Army commanders were given instructions to co-operate fully with the Versailles government in their operations against the commune. He agreed with Bismarck that the French government should be allowed to form an army of 80,000 men for the specific purpose of crushing the commune. Thiers' army was allowed to enter zones which had been designated as neutral in the armistice. A common strategy was worked out. The German army was to seal off Paris and aid the French forces with an artillery barrage. At a suggestion that the communards might reach some compromise with Thiers, Moltke ordered that in that case the Germans would have to enter Paris, disarm the National Guard and punish the communards. In spite of their heroic defence of Paris the communards had little chance of survival. Their only hope would have been to attack Versailles and attempt to win support in other parts of France, but this risk they were unwilling to take. On 28 May, two months after the commune had been proclaimed, Paris capitulated. A total of 30,000 communards were shot, and many more were sent to the jails and penal colonies of the republic. For the labour movement the commune was a heroic defeat, a powerful and inspiring myth. For Moltke and Bismarck it was a warning of what might happen if radicals and democrats were not kept under strict control. Lurid and preposterous accounts of the commune were to be powerful propaganda weapons against the left in the years to come. By insisting the whole episode was the result of the machinations of international socialism under the chairmanship of Karl Marx, Bismarck was to unleash a vigorous anti-socialist campaign throughout Europe.

The brilliant successes of the Prussian army in 1866 and 1870-71 secured for Moltke and the army leadership an unassailable position in Bismarck's empire. The army was widely respected and admired. Even the most callow young lieutenant was regarded as a superman. The general staff officers were known as 'demi-gods' and Moltke himself was pronounced immortal. This adulation of the army had disastrous consequences. The army itself believed that it was invincible and infallible, and the civilians were convinced that the general staff was in possession of secrets of such complexity and profundity that no mere civilian could ever hope to understand them. The army had solved the national question and created a great empire. As a result many liberals were prepared to silence their criticisms of the military, ignore their democratic aspirations and devote most of their time and energy to making money. This was the age of *Realpolitik* when the expression of the deepest spiritual longings of mankind for freedom and justice was spurned as woolly-minded idealism, and a sordid materialism was dressed up as a profound and realistic understanding of the world. The sabre-rattling militarist, the inflexible bureaucrat, the hard-headed industrialist and the boorish landowner ruled the day. The intellectuals seemed to lose their grip on the real world and to escape to ivory towers or they compromised with the spirit of the times by affecting an intellectual philistinism. Even the intellectuals saw themselves as soldiers. As Professor Du Bois-Reymond proclaimed in 1870: 'The University of Berlin . . . is the spiritual Household Regiment of the house of Hohenzollern . . . Historians are . . . the Mamelukes of Prussian politics.' In the intoxication of the moment of national unity and military triumph the many problems of the new empire were forgotten. The dissident national minorities of Poles, Alsatians, Danes and French could never find a home in this new and fervently nationalistic state. The social problem, the division between capital and labour, was to become increasingly severe when the boom of the *Gründerjahre* collapsed in 1873. The problems of the relations between Germany and the rest of the world were to become more complex and sensitive as Germany grew in strength and confidence. None of these problems could be solved by the bullying and authoritarian methods of a militarized state; indeed they could only be exacerbated by such displays of hubris.

For all Bismarck's concessions to particularist sentiments in the formation of the Second Reich, there could be no talk of 'Prussia merging into Germany'. The relationship of Prussia to the Reich is best summed up in the rather cumbersome German expression Prussia–Germany. Bismarck had stuck to his principle that he was a monarchist, a Prussian and a German – in that order. The German army was divided into eighteen army corps, of which thirteen were from Prussia, two from Bavaria, one from Württemberg and one from Saxony. One further army corps was a mixed contingent stationed in Alsace-Lorraine. There were thus in theory four separate armies in Germany, the king of Prussia having supreme command over all the army corps in time of war in his capacity as German emperor. But in practice the Prussian army was supreme, and the other armies followed the Prussian lead. There were a number of reasons for this. The Prussian army was the largest and most effective military force in Germany, and no one could seriously challenge its pre-eminence. The four armies considered themselves as the embodiment of the idea of the new Reich. Their loyalty to the emperor as 'Supreme Warlord' transcended local patriotism. This was to lead to frequent clashes with local patriots who accused the Bavarian, Württemberg and Saxon armies of slavishly aping the Prussians and of being unmindful of local rights and traditions. The armies countered by accusing their detractors of an outmoded particularism, of a lack of loyalty to the institutions of the Reich and sometimes even of treasonable intent.

Transfer of officers between the various armies was also used to ensure Prussian domination of the smaller armies. Some officers were posted to the Prussian army, and usually outstanding candidates were picked so that the Prussians would be impressed with the quality of the officers of the allied armies. Other officers applied for postings to the Prussian army as promotion prospects were better and the prizes for success were much greater. By contrast, there is ample evidence that the Prussian army unloaded some of its black sheep on to the other armies, usually officers who had been involved in some scandal which was not of sufficient gravity to warrant a cashiering.

The most important factor of all making for Prussian domination in the military sphere was simply that if the army was to function effectively as a unit in wartime, then there had to be a high degree of centralization so that there could be a common training programme, unified armaments and strategic planning which would apply for the whole German army rather than its component parts. The Kaiser was supreme commander of the Germany army, and he was also king of Prussia. Therefore the Prussian war ministry and general staff became, in effect, imperial institutions, even though their position was never specified as such. The Saxons, Württembergers and

Bavarians all had their own war ministries and general staffs, but the truly significant decisions were taken in Berlin. The Prussian general staff worked out the details of strategic and operational planning, and although the other armies sent officers to the general staff their role was that of observers rather than active participants in the planning. The enormous prestige of Moltke further strengthened the position of the general staff, for none would dare challenge his word, and even in his old age when he cut a somewhat ridiculous figure in an ill-fitting wig after the style of Julius Caesar, and when wicked tongues began to talk of senile decay, his reputation remained undiminished.

When the war with France was over and the peace signed and sealed, Moltke was determined to preserve much of the authority which he had gained in wartime. Bismarck was equally determined to reduce Moltke's influence and also that of the Prussian war ministry and the military cabinet, which he wanted to make Prussian rather than imperial authorities. The chancellor was only partially successful. Moltke continued to have the right to consult directly with the Kaiser, even though this right was not made official until 1883. The constitution of the Second Reich, by giving exceptional powers to the Prussian army, was bound to enhance the authority of the chief of general staff. Prussian military law henceforth applied to all contingents in Germany. The appointment of generals had to be approved by the Kaiser, and the commanding generals had the right of audience with him. Moltke was the Kaiser's principal military adviser. He thus had the right of direct access to the man who was supreme commander of all the troops in Germany. In these circumstances Bismarck was only partially successful in limiting the power of the chief of the general staff.

Since Moltke was proclaimed the 'greatest soldier of the century', it was natural that his ideas should be widely discussed and used as the basis for the training of a new generation of staff officers. Moltke himself never wrote a systematic account of his views on strategy and warfare in the light of his experience in the wars of unification. There was to be no re-working of the 'Instructions for Senior Officers', which had been written under his personal supervision in 1869. His ideas were disseminated by his followers, and all too often they were vulgarized in the process. The best known work of this sort was Wilhelm von

Blume's *Strategy*, published in 1882 and based on a course of lectures which the author had given at the Prussian War Academy. The picture which emerges from such works, and from statements made by Moltke on the nature of war, is often contradictory. War was for Moltke part of the nature of things, and however unattractive and tragic it might appear it was a fact of existence. In a much quoted phrase he wrote that everlasting peace was a dream, and not even a very nice one. There is an unattractive racialist dimension to some of his thinking. He felt that a clash between the Germanic race and the combined forces of the Romanic and Slavic races was inevitable. But his thinking about race was closer to the rationalist anthropology of the eighteenth century than to the virulent racism of the late nineteenth century. It was the different traditions, religions and economic backgrounds of the races which would lead to conflict, not any sinister inward drives of the blood. Moltke was determined that Prussia and Germany should become truly great powers. In his writings there are outlines of schemes for a *Mitteleuropa*, for German colonization and exploitation of the Balkans and the Near East. He was well aware of the considerable economic importance of Alsace and Lorraine, and he knew that Germany could never be a great power militarily if she did not have immense economic resources. Along with this expansionist emphasis was a conviction that other nations were filled with envy, fear and greed towards the German empire. This combination was to appear most markedly in the Wilhelmine era as a mixture of truculent imperialism and paranoid fears of 'encirclement'. Moltke never allowed himself such excesses, but the origins of such ideas are unmistakable in his military writings. The consequences of this view were dangerous in the extreme and perverted the military and political thinking of the general staff. Any military move by Germany's neighbours was immediately interpreted as being aimed at the security of the Reich. A similar move by Germany was always regarded as purely defensive, so that even an aggressive war could be dressed up as a preventive measure.

Behind all these ideas was the growing realization that history had not come to an end in 1871. The decision of the Franco-Prussian war was clearly not final. Another war would therefore have to be fought to settle the future of Europe. The aim of such a war would be to secure Alsace and Lorraine against any possibility of revenge by France, and to incorporate the crumbling Austro-Hungarian empire into a Prussian-dominated *Mitteleuropa*. The aggressive thrust of German politics in the 1870s was to bring France and Russia closer together, so that the inevitable war against France would probably mean a war on two fronts. This aspect of Moltke's planning became increasingly pronounced, and the German tariff war against Russia, and Bismarck's anti-Russian stand at the Congress of Berlin in 1878, further poisoned relations between the two countries.

Although Moltke was a cautious man and his view of the chances of German success in any future war was often pessimistic, and although he was realistic and rational in his understanding of the complexities of modern warfare, nevertheless his ideas became the basis of an adventurous, unrealistic and aggressive military spirit. Under Moltke's leadership the general staff developed a strategic doctrine of aggressive warfare, a powerful and rapid offensive aimed at the destruction of enemy forces, which ignored all political considerations. As Germany entered the age of imperialism those aspects of Moltke's thinking which were most in tune with the spirit of the time were emphasized and exaggerated so that it appeared that the strategic conceptions of Waldersee or Schlieffen, which were unrealistic and adventurous in the extreme, were fully in accord with the teachings of the master.

Although Bismarck, with his 'nightmare of coalitions', was determined to avoid another war, and was deeply concerned about the possibility of a Franco-Russian alliance, the general staff from 1871 thought solely in terms of a two-front war. Whereas the chancellor strove to use his exceptional diplomatic skills to avoid a war and to preserve the *status quo*, Moltke and his staff felt that it was the duty of the diplomatists to bring about a situation favourable to the successful conduct of a war which they increasingly believed to be both inevitable and desirable. A fatal split was to develop between the strategic planning of the general staff and the diplomacy of the chancellor.

The basis of all these strategic plans was a defensive action with limited troops on one front and a massive, violent and swift attack on the other. The speed of mobilization and deployment was vital, and it was felt that political, diplomatic or even legal considerations should not be allowed to slow down operations. The diplomatists were expected to create a favourable situation for a preventive war, but once the decision to mobilize had been made nothing was to be allowed to stand in the way of the army.

Even before the end of the Franco-Prussian war Moltke had begun strategic planning for a two-front war against France and Russia. An offensive would be mounted against Russia, in alliance with the Austrians, and the Germans would adopt a defensive strategy in the west until Russia had been defeated. The experience of the Franco-Prussian war was such that Moltke did not believe that a swift decision could be made in the west, and he therefore preferred to turn the initial offensive towards the east. He was soon forced to reconsider these plans when in 1873 the League of the Three Emperors brought Germany, Russia and Austria closer together in an anti-democratic alliance. War against France alone was now Moltke's concern. The republic had survived, the monarchy had not been restored and France was for Moltke 'a volcano . . . which for one hundred years has shaken Europe with its wars and its revolutions'. Although the republic had destroyed the commune and shown few signs of radicalism, it represented for Moltke all that was dangerous and insidious in the modern world. Thus war against France would serve a double purpose. It would be a war against democracy and a war to establish German hegemony over Europe.

This anti-French policy reached a peak in 1875 with the 'War-in-Sight' crisis. Increases in the French army were used as an excuse to threaten France with preventive war. The general staff worked frantically at war plans for a campaign against France, producing three different plans within the space of three months. The general staff was even prepared to fabricate information about the French army so that the crisis could be heightened. A chief of section produced a memorandum to show that the French army was to be increased by 120,000 men when in fact the size of the army was to remain the same, there were merely to be more battalions. To foreign diplomats Moltke made no secret of his desire for a preventive war with France. Such wild talk in Berlin caused a strong reaction from the powers who had no desire to see Germany crush France and further strengthen her position in central Europe. Germany now had to face the situation in which a war with France would almost certainly involve a war with Russia, and possibly even England. Bismarck was alarmed and hastily began to relax the pressure on France. This led to increasing tension between him and Moltke. The lesson which the chancellor learnt from the crisis was that the preventive-war concept was liable to isolate Germany and strengthen the alliance against her. The general staff argued that the crisis had shown that the preventive war would have to be fought against both France and Russia, and that the planning of 1875 which was directed solely against France was therefore mistaken.

The determination to fight a war on two fronts was greatly strengthened by the Dual Alliance with Austria in 1879, an alliance which was enthusiastically supported by the general staff. For Bismarck the alliance was defensive, but he was uncomfortably aware that, like any other 'defensive' alliance, it could all too easily be used for offensive purposes. It was precisely the usefulness of the alliance for a preventive war on two fronts which made it so attractive to the army, and it was this aspect of the alliance that was to be emphasized when Bismarck was no longer chancellor. Under the terms of the treaty both powers agreed to help the other if either was attacked by Russia. If one of the partners was attacked by a power other than Russia, then the other partner would remain benevolently neutral. If that other power was supported by Russia that would constitute a *casus foederis*. The alliance thus guaranteed Germany that it would have Austrian support in the event of a preventive war against France. Austria could count on German support if its policies in the Balkans were to lead it into war with Russia.

Bismarck had no intention of cutting off relations with Russia. He had felt himself obliged to enter into an alliance with Austria in 1879 because he had been forced to choose between Russia and Austria, a choice which he had assiduously tried to avoid ever since the League of the Three Emperors. Thus in 1881 he welcomed the revival of the league, because it opened up the line of communication with St Petersburg once again and he was able to regain some of the freedom of manoeuvre which he had lost in 1879. Moltke was furious at this move. The Dual Alliance offered the foundations of a strong anti-Russian policy which Moltke welcomed. He wished to work out the details of a common strategy against Russia with the Austro-Hungarian general staff, and now he saw these hopes dashed by Bismarck's intricate diplomacy and his refusal to allow discussions between the general staffs of the two allied countries.

Whereas in the early 1870s a two-front war was regarded as a theoretical possibility by the general staff, in 1879 it was regarded as an inevitability. The old plan of 1871 was revised and refined. The offensive would be mounted against Russia whose army was much weaker than that of France, and the plan assumed that the Russian army could be damaged to the extent that it would no longer be able to play a significant role in the war. Then the main offensive would be launched against France. As the French army had been reorganized and strengthened Moltke reckoned on a prolonged and hard campaign in France. As these plans were developed the size of the western army was increased, but the general staff did not wish to place too much reliance on Austria, and was therefore reluctant to leave the initial offensive in the east largely in the hands of the Austro-Hungarian army. At the same time Moltke was becoming somewhat impatient, arguing that if the war was not fought soon both Russia and France would be able to strengthen their military forces. A preventive war would have to be fought to prevent, not to cure, all of Germany's ills.

This growing aggressiveness of the general staff was emphasized by the appointment of General Waldersee in 1882 as Moltke's second-in-command and most likely successor. Waldersee is an almost classic example of the political general, of the out-and-out militarist. Up until this time his military career had been unspectacular, but he had made many valuable connections. The son of an aristocratic Prussian military family, his career was fairly conventional. He was a page at court, an officer in the guards' artillery, an adjutant to Prince Karl of Prussia and military attaché in Paris. During the Franco-Prussian war he was appointed ADC to the king of Prussia. After the war, in which he did nothing in particular but was richly decorated for it, he was given command of a regiment of Uhlans. He was then appointed chief of the general staff of the

Xth corps and from there went to the general staff in Berlin. He had made a brilliant match by marrying the widow of Prince Friedrich zu Schleswig-Holstein-Sonderburg-Augustenburg, an American lady of considerable wealth, Marie Esther Lee. His wife was a religious fanatic and a political meddler, but she was very well connected and well liked at court and had a particularly strong hold on the Kaiser's grandson, later William II.

Moltke, who was in his eighties, was no longer at the height of his powers and he relied increasingly on Waldersee's advice and support. Waldersee was in turn determined to use every opportunity which his position gave him to pursue his own political aims. He was able in 1883 to formalize the right of access to the Kaiser by the chief of the general staff, thus strengthening Moltke's position not only with respect to the chancellor and the civilians, but also in relation to the war ministry and the military cabinet. Waldersee's determination to fight a war with Russia became almost an obsession. He flooded the chancellor's office with reports of the danger of invasion from Russia, to the point that Bismarck even suggested the restoration of Poland as a buffer state against this threat. The question of war with Russia was discussed daily at the general staff, so that most general staff officers became convinced it was simply a matter of time before war broke out, and this being so it would be best to fight it soon before the Russians were given a chance to reorganize their army and mount a carefully planned assault on the Reich.

Waldersee was little concerned with Bismarck's diplomatic moves, and disregarded the revived League of the Three Emperors. Both he and Moltke believed that war with Russia was inevitable, and that no amount of diplomatic chicanery would alter this fact. He therefore at once set about improving the plans for a rapid attack on Russia, and in the next few months these ideas were improved and refined. The diplomatic support for this anti-Russian policy Waldersee found in the Dual Alliance. In the summer of 1882 talks began between the general staffs of Prussia and Austria-Hungary. Starting from the basis of a defensive alliance, the negotiations served to encourage the extremists in both Berlin and Vienna so that an agreement was reached that a preventive war was necessary and desirable. Bismarck was kept inadequately informed of these discussions, and Moltke, Waldersee and Beck, the Austro-Hungarian chief of general staff, agreed that in a war situation the speed and effectiveness of the deployment of their armies would be seriously endangered if the diplomatists were not kept at bay. Their plan was for a gigantic pincer movement against Russia, the Prussians advancing from eastern Prussia and the Austrians from Galicia. This movement would trap the Russian army in Poland. Once the area from the Austrian frontier to Brest-Litovsk had been occupied, the larger part of the German army could be released to fight against France. Beck foresaw a long-drawn-out series of operations against Russia in order to defeat her finally. This plan was highly unrealistic. It was based on a serious underestimation of the strength of the Russian army. As the Prussian and the Austro-Hungarian forces were to begin their deployment some 200 miles apart, and as the Austro-Hungarians would be far slower to mobilize, there was a real danger that the Russians might be able to inflict such a damaging blow on one or other of the allied armies that the whole plan would have to be abandoned. Equally serious was the fact that such a scheme for preventive war was at variance with Bismarck's diplomacy, so that strategic and diplomatic planning conflicted. The tendency towards an increasingly aggressive policy was given further encouragement by the Triple Alliance of 1882 which guaranteed Italian support in the event of an unprovoked war with France, and neutrality in the event of a war between Austria and Russia. At the time of the negotiations over the Roumanian treaty in 1883 Bismarck began to be seriously concerned that the Dual Alliance and its extensions might all too easily be used by the militarists in Vienna and Berlin to pursue their own ends.

But war failed to come, and Waldersee became increasingly depressed. He began to blame it all on the gerontocracy which ruled Prussia – the Kaiser was eighty-eight, the chancellor seventy and Moltke eight-five when he confided these thoughts to his diary in 1885. In 1886 the general staff began to think in terms of a war with France. Bismarck's manipulation of the 1889 Boulanger crisis offered the prospect of such a war. In February 1887 new mobilization plans were drawn up which transferred a number of troops from the eastern to the western front. Waldersee and his cronies, men like generals von Loë and von

Heuduck and the War Minister Bronsart von Schellendorf, argued that war with France was vital for the security of the Reich. They were confident that the new estimates for the German army would be matched by similar increases in the French army, and that this escalation of armaments would eventually lead to war. But before long Waldersee was back again on his anti-Russian tack. Russian concern at the worsening of relations between France and Germany, and the movement of Russian troops to the west coupled with a reorganization and increase in the Russian army, were used as excuses for the German and Austro-Hungarian general staffs to press for a preventive war to begin in the winter of 1887. The Tsar was to be faced with a simple alternative – either the Russian troops were to be withdrawn from the western frontier or Germany and Austria would go to war. Bismarck was horrified when he heard of these talks between the Prussian and Austrian military leaders. They were after all being carried out while the Tsar visited Berlin at a time when Bismarck was busily engaged in negotiations for the 'Re-insurance Treaty', by which he hoped to improve relations with Russia. In a series of sharply-worded notes to Waldersee he warned him not to meddle in politics and insisted that he could not tolerate any interference with his foreign policy. He reaffirmed that the Dual Alliance was designed by him as a purely defensive alliance to preserve the peace of Europe, and was not to be used as a vehicle for launching a two-front war. The chancellor was also deeply concerned that a future war might very well lead to revolution, and therefore had to be avoided rather than welcomed in the unthinking manner of the general staff.

The general staff was constantly held in check by Bismarck's diplomacy, and it therefore tried to find a way to avoid Bismarck's watchful eye. Waldersee encouraged the military attachés to report on political matters directly to the general staff, without informing their heads of mission as protocol demanded. In effect Waldersee tried to create his own foreign service designed to furnish the general staff with highly selective reports to support their arguments for preventive war. In the crisis year of 1887 the activities of the attachés were of considerable significance, for they provided ample material to show that relations between St Petersburg and Paris were becoming very close, and that Russia was thinking in terms of a war with Germany. This activity was clearly opposed to Bismarck's efforts to lessen the tensions in Europe and to avoid war.

The attaché in Vienna, von Deines, continued to advocate a policy of preventive war which was diametrically opposed to that of Bismarck and the German ambassador in Vienna. From Paris von Huene sent hair-raising reports during the Boulanger crisis, which insisted that war was imminent. Even when Boulanger had left the scene Huene continued in the same vein, arguing that the apparent quiet in France was a monstrous hoax designed to disguise the true intentions of the French government to seek revenge. The attaché in St Petersburg, Yorck von Wartenburg, enjoyed a peculiar position as 'military plenipotentiary', which meant that he was a member of the Tsar's retinue and was not liable to control by the ambassador. He reported directly to Waldersee and to William II, causing the German ambassador endless headaches. When he became engaged to a divorced Russian the ambassador, Schweinitz, thought that he had found a way of getting rid of him, but William II supported Yorck, and he remained at his post. Engelbrecht in Rome, Schmettau in Brussels, Goltz in Turkey and von Rechenberg in Warsaw all reported directly to the general staff, even though von Rechenberg was consul and did not hold a military appointment. They all fed Waldersee and Moltke's prejudices with their lurid reports of imminent war.

Bismarck tried to keep the attachés under control, but he was not always successful. He chose to discredit them and the general staff by showing that their assessments of foreign affairs had been consistently and seriously wrong. Thus in 1890 he could point out to the Kaiser, that, although Moltke had insisted in 1887 that the Russians were deploying their troops on their western frontier and that war was imminent, in fact relations between Germany and Russia had greatly improved and war had been avoided. Bismarck chose to check the attachés by stern reprimands and by biting irony, but it was his successor, Caprivi, who finally brought them under control.

The mounting aggressiveness of German military planning in the 1870s and 1880s was a reflection of the profound economic and social changes which took place in these years. The foundation of the Second Reich was followed by a spectacular boom.

The enormous wave of confidence and enthusiasm was reflected in a speculative boom which lasted until 1873. National unity broke down the last barriers to economic unity. The war stimulated the economy, and the trend continued in peacetime with five billion francs of reparations, of which more than half was spent on armaments, priming the pump. The annexation of Alsace and Lorraine with its rich coal and ore deposits was a further stimulus to the economy. Between 1870 and 1873 steel production rose by eighty per cent, coal production by nearly fifty per cent and industrial production by thirty-three per cent. New companies sprouted up like mushrooms and forty-nine new banks and financial institutions were formed. In 1873 this speculative bubble of the *Gründerjahre* burst and Germany entered a period of depression which was to last until 1896.

The depression was not a stagnation of the economy, nor was it a regression. There were many considerable improvements in industry which caused an increase in output, among the most significant being the Thomas-Gilchrist method of steel production, which used up far less capital than the Bessemer converter, and the use of electrical energy in industrial production. There was, however, a significant drop in the rate of growth which had been so hectic. Thus the volume of goods increased but their price sank. This was to have profound social and economic effects.

With the onset of the depression Bismarck was gradually convinced that protection was needed. The industrialists, who had been largely unable to compete with foreign, particularly British, goods, had long been clamouring for protection. The junker landowners had opposed it as they had been able to export grain, wood and wool, and were unwilling to run the risk of reprisals against German protectionism. But by the middle of the 1870s the situation had changed drastically. The import of cheap grain from the Ukraine and from North America made the eastern landowners' rye no longer competitive. Since the 1820s the big landowners in the east had greatly improved their estates, and heavy investments had been made to increase the productivity of the land. The results had been impressive, but the costs of production had risen sharply. Prussian agriculture was thus unable to match the low unit costs of Russian and North American production. The building of the railway in the American west, and the reduction of costs by the shipping lines further lowered the cost of imported grains. So now industrialists and landowners joined together and demanded protectionism, to preserve their unique social, economic and political position in Prussia and Germany.

Protectionism brought many different factions and interest groups together. The conservatives, who represented the agrarians, felt that they were faced with the alternative of protectionism or ruin. They were thus prepared to put aside their differences with those industrialists who favoured protection and who were represented in the Reichstag by the right-wing liberals. The way was open for the alliance of 'rye and iron', that uneasy union which was to characterize the politics of the Second Reich. The new alliance led to a further split in the Liberal Party. Those liberals who opposed Bismarck's systematic strengthening of the authoritarian and anti-democratic elements of the new Reich, and who remained true to the classic liberal tradition of free trade, became increasingly critical of the chancellor and refused to accept these changes in economic policy. The Catholic Centre Party was, as usual, ready to compromise its policies in return for some favours for the Church. In this instance they were prepared to accept the new tariffs provided that the anti-Catholic programme, the *Kulturkampf*, was abandoned. The *Kulturkampf*, which was associated with the left liberals, had not been a success, and Bismarck was willing to give it up in return for the Centre Party's support in the Reichstag.

Protection involved a sharp increase in indirect taxation, and therefore a rise in prices. As revenue from indirect taxation went directly to the government of the Reich and not to the states, the effect would be to make the Reich independent of the payments from the states, which were known as the matricular payments. Bismarck also wished to reduce direct taxation in the interests of what he euphemistically called the 'productive classes'. Such a reduction would further strengthen the centralizing tendencies of the change of emphasis in the tax structure, would serve to cement the conservative alliance behind the protective tariffs, and was to give to the new alignment a profoundly anti-social thrust. The effects of the depression were thus magnified by the change in the tax structure, and the conservatism of the new Reichstag alliance served to radicalize further the working class. In 1878 two attempts to assassinate the Kaiser had been manipulated by Bismarck to cement the new alliance, to split the Liberal Party and to push through the anti-socialist laws which banned the Social Democratic Party (SPD). But purging all liberals from the bureaucracy and suppressing socialist and democratic movements created more problems than they solved. The elections of 1881 showed how unpopular these measures were, and how profound was the effect of the depression. The opposition parties, the SPD and the left liberals, won many seats from the conservatives. Bismarck was now forced to rule with an uneasy coalition and began to think of alternative solutions to this unsatisfactory situation. A comprehensive social security programme was begun in order to alleviate some of the suffering caused by his economic policy. When this failed to work he began to think in terms of a *putsch* to undo the constitution which was failing to provide a working solution to the fundamental contradiction that was becoming so apparent in German society, between a modern industrial state and an antiquated social order.

If the years of the depression saw a significant change in the political climate and a polarization of society, the effects on the structure of the economy were equally profound. In the first place Germany ceased to be an agricultural country. In 1873 agriculture played the predominant role in the economy; by 1890 this primacy had vanished. In industry there was also a major structural change. Consumer goods were slowly but relentlessly losing ground to heavy industry as a result of the decrease in consumption. Heavy industry was to gain a position in the economy from which, with the stimulus of the boom years of 1897 to 1914, it was to overtake the consumer sector. During the First World War the supremacy of heavy industry was firmly and irrevocably established.

For those on fixed incomes, army officers, bureaucrats and the regularly employed, the depression years were years of affluence and comfort. Prices fell by about thirty per cent and as there was widespread unemployment caused by the cutback in industrial growth, the drastic reduction in consumption and a twenty-seven per cent increase in population, labour, particularly domestic servants, was readily and cheaply available. Those workers who were regularly employed enjoyed a substantially improved standard of living, but this was bought very dearly. Unemployment was exceedingly high, and productivity per worker increased much more sharply than increases in real wages. This had the effect of creating a labour elite, and with it the beginning of the 'democratization of consumption' characteristic of industrialized societies. This was to be an important factor during the 1890s in the move of the social democrats towards a revisionist stance, but for the time being it was of little real significance. The labour movement in the 1870s and 1880s was radicalized by the depression, and seemed to pose a very real threat to the established order. This bogey was in turn used by Bismarck to strengthen his own position, the 'red peril' being an important weapon in his political arsenal.

The tax structure was weighted in favour of the central government, and this strengthening of the Reich was further accentuated by the effects of the depression. With the onset of the depression industrial shares were less attractive to investors, who preferred the security of government bonds. As the state was able to obtain money easily the bank rate could be lowered so that government loans became cheaper. With readily available cheap money the government was able to spend considerable sums of money on armaments and on the strategic railways.

The depression greatly accelerated the process of capital concentration, and the great banks and monopolies were largely formed in these years. The four 'D-Banks', the Deutsche Bank, the Disconto-Gesellschaft, the Dresdner-Bank and the Darmstädter Bank, established their predominance in these years. As individual investors were shy of putting their money into industry the banks had to provide the badly needed capital for the improvement and modernization of industry. The Thomas-Gilchrist process in the steel industry used up considerable amounts of capital, but the big banks could meet the needs of industry, and development was thus not held up. Similarly the great advances in electrical engineering could be exploited immediately, since the banks were ready to provide the money. This close relationship between the great banks and the giant industrial concerns was the origin of German finance capital, which was to play such a vital role in the age of imperialism.

The same process of concentration and monopolization which can be observed in banking also occurred in industry. Smaller firms which were unable to compete under depression conditions, and which did not provide attractive investment prospects for bank capital, either went under or were absorbed by one of the large companies. Fierce competition, reduced profits and the necessity for extensive investment further weakened the smaller companies and hastened the process of rationalization and concentration. Close co-operation between the great concerns led to the formation of cartels. In 1886 the Rhenish-Westphalian Iron Association was formed and in 1893 the Rhenish-Westphalian Coal Syndicate, which controlled virtually all the coal production in the Rhine and the Ruhr. Expenditure on armaments greatly profited the larger concerns. The new electrical companies, Siemens and Halske and AEG, were given large contracts by the military. The most famous company of them all, Krupp, profited immensely from Prussia's wars, and was to continue to make gigantic profits from armaments both at home and abroad. Some companies converted their production from peaceful commodities to armaments, since profits in armaments were so high. The Berlin sewing machine company, Ludwig Loewe, began to produce machine-guns and was thus able to make even greater profits. Industrialists were able to convince the government that in the interests of national security and economic stability some of the most onerous costs of research and development should be borne by the taxpayers, rather than by the companies which profited from their practical application. Thus, largely due to the persuasion of Werner von Siemens, the *Physikalisch-Technische Reichsanstalt* was formed to engage in research of a theoretical and technical nature which demanded expenditure on equipment on a scale which the private companies were not prepared to support. Further institutes of this sort were established, most of which were devoted to research of an essentially military nature. In 1911 all these institutes were reorganized and reformed as the Kaiser William Society for the Advancement of Science. Here the beginnings of subsidized research, the practical application of which could bring enormous profits, can be found. The development of this particular line of activity was to be extremely rapid in the twentieth century, and was to become one of the principal characteristics of the 'military-industrial complex'.

The strains of the depression, the concentration of industry and the remarkable technical innovations were to give to German industry its particularly aggressive nature, which in turn was to be reflected in government policy. In such a climate it is hardly surprising that the government continued to press for increases in the size of the army and for larger expenditure on armaments. High profits from armaments helped to reconcile the bourgeoisie with the army, and the traditional middle-class suspicion of the military began to disappear.

Bismarck's constitution gave budgetary rights to the Reichstag to control military expenditure. This had been deemed a necessary concession so that liberals might support a Prussian-dominated and autocratic Reich. But Bismarck at once set about trying to circumvent these constitutional provisions and to remove any form of parliamentary control over the army. The solution he suggested was the 'Eternal Law' (*Aeternat*), by which the size of the army would be fixed for all time and the Reichstag would have no control over expenditure for armaments and equipment. Bismarck knew that the army was becoming increasingly unpopular, and that the 'enemies of the Reich', the social democrats, the progressives and the Centre Party, were able to gain votes by attacking the size and expense of the army. Therefore discussions of the army estimates would have to be removed from the political debate. Bismarck tried every trick to ram through the *Aeternat*. He threatened to resign, to appoint an ultra-reactionary cabinet, he warned of a war with France, and the 'red peril' was painted in lurid colours to convince the bourgeois deputies. But in the end he was forced to compromise. The national liberal Miquel, a banker and leading architect of the compromise between the junkers and the bourgeoisie, promised Bismarck the support of the national liberals for an army bill that would be in effect for a number of years, but he declared that they would not be able to support the idea of an *Aeternat*. Finally Bismarck agreed to the Seven Year bill (*Septennat*), which passed its third reading on 20 April 1874. The new law increased the size of the army by 34,000 men to 401,659 and expenditure was increased from 324·6 million marks to 378·6 million marks. Military expenditure accounted for seventy per cent of the income of the Reich. By contrast to these enormous sums a mere 16·5 million marks was spent on schools.

A second *Septennat* was passed in April 1880 amid a storm of protests which reminded Bismarck's newspaper, the *Norddeutsche Allegemeine Zeitung*, of 1848. The size of the army was increased once again, this time by 26,000 men. A further concealed increase was the requirement that men in the first class of the reserve were to engage in manoeuvres for eighteen weeks each year. In spite of decreasing costs as a result of the depression, expenditure on the army was increased by 18 million marks, thus placing an even heavier tax load on the German people.

In November 1886 Bismarck introduced the third *Septennat* to the Reichstag. It called for an increase of 41,135 men, which would necessitate an increased expenditure of 24 million marks. On the second reading in January 1887 the Reichstag would agree only to a three-year army bill. Bismarck therefore called an election, to be held within five weeks, during the carnival season. His election campaign was marked by wild anti-French pronouncements, massive manoeuvres in Alsace-Lorraine and the prohibition of the export of horses to France. As a result of this chauvinistic campaign the government won a comfortable majority in the new parliament – the 'Cartel Reichstag' – and the new estimates were swiftly passed. But this massive increase was not deemed enough. In the following year the Reichstag approved a plan for the reorganization of the army, and the chancellor was authorized to borrow 278 million marks to cover the cost. All those who were liable for military service now had to serve on the reserve until they were forty-five years old, when previously it had been until they were forty-two. The *Landwehr* was reorganized so that the reserves were better co-ordinated with the regular army. On the basis of these reforms it was estimated that Germany would be able to mobilize an army of 2·7 million men in the event of war.

The negotiations over the various army laws had brought the Prussian war minister into the very centre of politics, and it is hardly surprising that Bismarck on the basis of these experiences described the ministry as a 'difficult and unfinished constitutional construction'. In avoiding the creation of an imperial war ministry Bismarck had been paying lip service to the rights of the states, for he did not wish it to appear that Prussia was completely dominant in military affairs. But in practice the Prussian war minister acted as an imperial war minister, for it was he who had to represent the army to the Reichstag, the Bundesrat and the Prussian *Landtag*. As far as the other armies were concerned, this worked fairly satisfactorily. The Prussian war minister always consulted his colleagues in the other states, and as the army was frequently under attack in parliament they were quite willing to see a Prussian general as whipping boy. But to the Prussian army the office of war minister, and the fact that he had to appear in front of parliament, appeared a dangerous compromise with parliamentarianism and democracy and a threat to the authority of the army and to the Kaiser's power of command. Reactionaries such as General Waldersee were determined that the powers of the war minister should be drastically reduced, so that there could be no risk that parliament might gain any sort of control over the army. In 1883 the war ministry was reorganized. It lost its personnel section, and no longer had the right of military command. It was thus reduced to being little more than an administrative organization, the really important decisions being left to the general staff and the military cabinet which were in no way liable to parliamentary control. The war minister, Kameke, a soldier in whom the Boyen tradition was still alive, naturally enough resisted these moves to reduce his authority, and questioned the political sagacity of a move which was likely further to poison the relations between the army and the politicians. Kameke was gradually eased out of office and replaced by a more compliant officer, Paul Bronsart von Schellendorf, one of Moltke's demi-gods from the general staff, who agreed to the proposed reforms. But within a few years he too was beginning to find his position in the Reichstag somewhat invidious, for with so little power and authority it was extremely difficult to stand up against the attacks of the politicians. He began to tire of making endless lame excuses that he had no authority to speak on a particular issue. Bronsart's successor, however, Verdy du Vernois, was quite content to regard his role as that of sacrificial lamb.

The silencing of the war minister and the readiness of the Reichstag to accept huge increases in the size of the army were to a considerable degree the result of the compromise between the liberal bourgeoisie and the conservative junkers, which had begun in 1866 and which was finalized in 1879. Germany had been united not by the forces of liberal nationalism but by Bismarck's reactionary politics. Unification had brought great benefits to the bourgeoisie, a substantial section of whom were ready to abandon their liberal principles and embrace the reactionary Prussianism of the national liberals. In the increasing militarization of society they were to find considerable profits, even if the repression at home and the risk of war abroad were to create almost intolerable tensions. They were prepared to accept a reduction in the already minimal responsibilities of the war minster to the Reichstag, and were silent witnesses of the systematic favouring of the aristocracy in the officer corps and the weeding out of bourgeois officers. But this attempt to preserve the social exclusiveness of the army was to create insoluble problems and eventually to undermine the army's effectiveness.

The conservatives had finally been able to destroy the old *Landwehr* and to bring the remnants of this supposedly dangerous and liberal institution under the close control of the regular army. They had succeeded in this because they could draw on the 'reliable' rural population to provide malleable material for the army. But these reactionary moves were made at precisely the time when major social and economic changes were taking place which were to make them worthless. The rapid industrialization of Germany, the steady move from the country to the towns, the destruction of the old social order on the land, the growth of an organized and politically articulate urban proletariat and the radicalization of the petit-bourgeoisie made all these calculations worthless. The army was forced to recruit an increasing number of 'unreliable' elements, and this factor was to become ever more troublesome as the army was expanded and became increasingly designed as an instrument of domestic oppression. The aggressive thrust of German foreign policy, and the strategic plans of the general staff which called for a two-front war, made it impossible for the army to be reduced in size so that this problem could be overcome. Indeed the army had to be increased to meet the political and military demands of the chancellor and the chief of the general staff. It was precisely in the reserves that the increases were the greatest, and although the aristocracy was able to maintain a very high percentage of the officer corps, there were certainly not enough younger sons to officer the reserve. The answer had to be for the bourgeoisie to provide officer material which would be prepared uncritically to accept the prejudices and values of the aristocracy. Thus after 1871 a 'feudalized bourgeoisie', to use the historian Eckart Kehr's phrase, was created which filled the gaps in the officer corps which the aristocracy was unable to fill. But there were limits to this policy too, for only a section of the bourgeoisie was prepared to ape the manners of the aristocracy. In the army's estimation the limit was reached in 1913, when it was felt that the army could not be expanded beyond a certain point without running the risk of letting unreliable elements into the officer corps.

Thus the liberal *Landwehr* officer was replaced by the reactionary reserve officer. Once more the bourgeoisie had capitulated to Bismarck's Reich, and through fear of change from below it had betrayed its progressive and liberal traditions. At a time when the old elite could not hold on to its power without the active support of the bourgeoisie, the bourgeoisie had rushed to its assistance out of fear of social and political changes which might in turn have threatened their own position and their accumulation of wealth. The reserve officers were the praetorian guards of the compromise of 1879, an essential ingredient in Prussian-German militarism. This capitulation of an important section of the middle class is a vital factor in the military history of Germany, and had a fatal effect on the growth of democracy there.

6

The Wilhelmine Era

The question of whether 1888 or 1890 can be regarded as
turning points in the military history of Germany has often been
debated by historians, but as these discussions have been
carried out in very narrow terms they have almost invariably
been fruitless. In strictly military terms neither of these two
dates has much meaning, but if the history of the army is
removed from its social, economic and political *milieu* it
becomes formalistic and even unintelligible. In terms of these
broader trends 1890 was certainly a turning point, and as
German society was plagued by growing antagonisms and
contradictions it is perhaps suitable that the change should
have been signalled by two contradictory and well publicized
slogans. The first came from William II, who announced when
Bismarck was dismissed: 'The course remains the same. Full-
steam ahead!' When it became apparent that in spite of all the
steam the course was not the same, the opponents of the new
chancellor, Caprivi, coined the phrase the 'New Course' in
contrast to Bismarck's old policies which they frantically hoped
to revive.

Caprivi, like Waldersee who became chief of the general staff
in 1888, believed that a two-front war was inevitable, but unlike
Waldersee he did not believe that it should be fought as soon as
possible. In order to strengthen the Reich for this ordeal, and to
preserve the social status quo, Caprivi attempted to extend the
compromise of Bismarck's cartel to include the Centre Party
and the independents (*Freisinn*). Thus considerations of a two-

front war, and an attempt to isolate and destroy the left by means other than outright oppression – the anti-socialist laws were not renewed in 1890 – were the two basic planks in the platform of the 'New Course'.

The politics of the New Course were an imaginative attempt to deal with the problems of a social order which was no longer adequate to the needs of a modern industrial state, but the New Course was to run aground on the implacable opposition of the extreme right and the military, who feared that such compromises with the parties in the centre of the political spectrum would open the door to democracy and revolution. Their solution was repression and reaction. These were the two poles of Wilhelmine politics. Either the bourgeois parties could join together in a common struggle against the left and defend the existing order against the 'red peril' – the policy of *Sammlungspolitik* – or the government could resort to repression, the re-introduction of anti-socialist legislation and even possibly a *coup d'état* to revise or throw out the constitution. The uneasy alliance of junkers, industrialists, small entrepreneurs who feared proletarianization and the professional middle class was hardly strong enough to overcome the conflicting political interests and principles of the parties involved, and this factor Caprivi had fatally underestimated. But the policy of repression was also bound to fail, for the inexorable forces of social change could be slowed down but they could not be stopped.

It was hard economic facts more than anything else which destroyed the new course. Caprivi, the most consistently underrated of the chancellors, realized that Germany's future strength lay in the development of its industry. He hoped to develop a strong central European market by means of long-term trade agreements, and from this position of strength to encourage exports, stimulate the economy and finally get out of the doldrums of the depression. Acting in the traditions of Delbrück and the free-traders of the North German Confederation, Caprivi aimed to break down tariff barriers and stimulate international trade. He was able to make these radical proposals because of the great strides that German industry had made under the cover of the tariffs of 1879. Industry now was strong enough to be competitive on the international market, but agriculture was not. Therefore Caprivi's economic policy was to meet with the implacable opposition of the junkers. The agrarians continued to demand high protective tariffs to exclude foreign grains. As Russia was particularly affected by these tariffs an anti-Russian policy was the price the government had to pay for conservative support. The industrialists continued to press for tariff reductions, and their aggressive commercial practices alienated the British. Thus the combination of agrarian conservatism and *Weltpolitik* was to lead to the diplomatic isolation of Germany and to make the two-front war, which the generals welcomed, almost inevitable. 'Encirclement' was the result not merely of diplomatic incompetence and lack of tact; it was the necessary outcome of economic and social forces in imperial Germany.

Caprivi paid little attention to the clamourings of the conservatives. Tariffs were lowered and new markets for German industry secured. The effect on the economy was stimulating, and Germany indeed seemed to be emerging from the depression. But however successful he might have appeared, the chancellor had succeeded in alienating most of the parties, classes and groups which he had hoped to bring together. The industrialists felt that he was too conciliatory towards labour. They objected to his extension of Bismarck's social security programme and opposed the ending of the anti-socialist laws. The agrarians were angry because he had lowered the tariffs and his programme favoured the industrialists. The petit-bourgeoisie complained that he had done nothing to save them from the power of industrial capitalism, indeed that he had made their position even more precarious. Loud criticism was voiced of his dismantling of Bismarck's system of alliances, his lukewarm attitude towards imperialist adventures and his financial reform which ended a number of exemptions and privileges enjoyed by the landowners and the middle class. The liberals objected to his conservative educational policy; the left looked upon his social policy as a patronizing tokenism designed to strengthen an authoritarian regime. The army opposed Caprivi because although he had pushed through the largest increase ever in the size of the army – by 2,138 officers, 12,323 NCOs and 72,037 men – he had done so at the expense of reducing the term of service to two years in the infantry and agreeing that the army bill should be for five years rather than seven. Caprivi's attacks on the military attachés, which were far more effective than those of Bismarck, further angered the army. The fact that the chancellor was himself a general was regarded as a dangerous precedent, for it brought the army into the centre of the political struggle, and the fact that Caprivi was pursuing what was construed as a liberal policy was regarded as a betrayal of the army.

The army's struggle against the chancellor was headed by the chief of the general staff, General Waldersee. He had been appointed in 1888 when William II became Kaiser. Although for some time it had been obvious that Moltke was no longer capable of fulfilling his duties – he was stone deaf, hopelessly absent-minded and was showing distinct signs of senility – it was unthinkable that he should retire before William I died. There was general agreement in the army that he was a genius of the order of Alexander the Great, Hannibal, Frederick II or Napoleon, but some ambitious officers were all too ready to step into his shoes. William II was determined to go his own way and to free himself from the great men of his grandfather's generation. Moltke resigned in August 1888, and Waldersee was the obvious choice as successor. He had virtually run the general staff for the past six years, and was a close friend and political associate of the young Kaiser.

Waldersee's closest political associate at this time was the court preacher Stoecker. Stoecker's ideas – a mixture of radical conservatism, anti-Semitism and intolerant protestantism – were particularly appealing to William. He hoped that they might provide a solution to the social problem, for he imagined that the working class might be tempted away from socialism by bowls of soup and bibles. But Stoecker had no real support outside the court and the *déclassés* of Berlin, and for all his demagogic skills he was unable to build up a viable mass movement. Furthermore he was soon to become fatally compromised. Rumours were persistent that he kept a mistress, hardly proper conduct for the court preacher, but to make matters worse it was hinted that the lady was Jewish, so that even the authenticity of his anti-semitism was placed in doubt. For all the claims that these rumours were merely the result of a sinister Jewish plot, William saw no alternative but to ask Stoecker to resign in November 1890.

157

The other wrong horse backed by Waldersee was Hammerstein of the *Kreuzzeitung*. Hammerstein was an extreme right-wing opponent of Bismarck who insisted that the chancellor's support of the cartel was a dangerous compromise with liberalism. He wished to oust Bismarck and destroy the cartel. Bismarck went, but the Kaiser knew that there was no valid alternative to the cartel, and indeed Caprivi extended it to include the parties of the centre. Even Waldersee began to think that Hammerstein was a fanatic, but he continued to publish his ideas for a two-front war with France and Russia in the pages of the *Kreuzzeitung* through the good offices of the military correspondent, his protégé Major Scheibert. By 1889 Waldersee was trying to dissociate himself from Hammerstein, but his professions of disapproval of Hammerstein's more wild utterances were not particularly convincing.

Thus by 1890 when Caprivi was appointed chancellor Waldersee's position was weak. He was frantically trying to scramble back from a position on the extreme right which had seemed so promising in 1888, when the young Kaiser appeared determined to reverse the moderate policies of his father and when Bismarck's days were numbered. His relationship with the Kaiser became extremely strained when he dared to criticize a particularly foolish solution to a tactical exercise. William, who regarded himself as a military expert, was furious. Waldersee, who had had some hopes of being appointed chancellor after Bismarck, saw his political ambitions dashed, and now he had to endure the disapproval of the Kaiser.

Caprivi was quick to realize that Waldersee's position was weak, and he acted swiftly to end the power of the military attachés and to assert the supremacy of the foreign office. After a first warning shot at the chief of the general staff the chancellor produced the regulation of 1867 which placed military attachés under their heads of mission, and insisted that the regulation be observed. Waldersee protested that this was a monstrous attack on the army and on the Kaiser's power of command. But Caprivi had the law on his side and stuck to his position. Eventually the Kaiser stepped in with a compromise which enabled Waldersee to receive reports from the attachés in St Petersburg, Vienna, Rome and Paris because they were military plenipotentiaries, not mere military attachés, but

Waldersee had been severely reprimanded, and it was no longer possible for him to attempt to pursue a separate foreign policy. In January 1891 he was dismissed from the position of chief of the general staff, and the bitter rivalry between the general staff and the foreign office abated.

Waldersee was a classic example of the political general, and his failure is a revealing case history of Wilhelmine Germany. It was not just his personal failings which led to his undoing, his persistent meddling, his wire-pulling and his overbearing ambition, but rather his misreading of political realities. There was within Bismarck's bonapartist system a quasi-plebescitory element, a recognition of the need to maintain a degree of popular support, to balance faction off against faction, to keep a working majority in parliament and to avoid serious social conflict. Waldersee's extremism was an expression of the intolerance of the right towards this system, a frustrated impatience with a constitutional practice which seemed to be heading towards liberalism or worse. The compromise between the upper bourgeoisie and the aristocracy might have been fragile and fraught with contradictions, but it was strong enough to withstand the attempts of a political adventurer to play both sides against the centre. Waldersee failed to realise that the army had to remain behind the scenes, had to use the civilian politicians as 'lightning conductors', to adopt Ludendorff's phrase, to protect the power and privileges of the army. The army was to exercise its greatest influence during the First World War, not by establishing a military dictatorship as Waldersee had wanted, but by endless manipulations behind the scenes. The army could exercise real political power only if it maintained the pretence of being non-political.

There had been no place for a reactionary coup in 1890 when Bismarck had been dismissed, nor was there in 1894 when Caprivi resigned and Chlodwig Hohenlohe-Schillingsfürst was appointed chancellor. Hohenlohe was a man in his middle seventies who was designated as a temporary chancellor, although in fact he lasted longer than his predecessor. The New Course had failed, and Germany now entered yet another period of reaction, usually called the 'Stumm Era' after the industrialist Stumm-Halberg, who was an outspoken opponent of social security measures as suggested by Bismarck and

Berlepsch, and who demanded draconian measures against social democracy. William II, who was bitterly disappointed at the failure of his attempt to be a 'social Kaiser' and to solve the social problem by soothing words, was particularly impressed by Stumm's arguments, particularly after the Saar miners' strike of 1892.

The Stumm Era was marked by an attempt to re-introduce anti-socialist legislation. On 6 December 1894 the Reichstag met for the first time in its rather pompous new building, and the first bill to be debated was the notorious 'Revolution Bill' (*Umsturzvorlage*) which called for severe prison sentences for any critical remarks made against religion, the monarchy, private property and marriage, and which also envisaged punishment for reputed 'revolutionary actions'. The bill cast its net so wide that it was opposed by the liberals who feared that it might be used to include them, and the social democrats carried out an impressive campaign against the bill, because they knew that for them it was a matter of life or death. The bill was rejected by the Reichstag, and the Kaiser sent a telegram to the chancellor which read: 'All we have now are fire-engines for normal situations, and grapeshot as a last resort.' With the failure of the *Umsturzvorlage* the reactionaries became even more impatient. The Prussian minister of the interior, von Koeller, decided to go ahead and arrest as many leading socialists as he could find and close down party headquarters. But the storm of protest against this illegal 'Koeller-Coup' was so great that the minister was forced to resign.

The reaction continued undaunted. Berlepsch, the architect of Caprivi's social security legislation, was forced to resign in 1896. In the following year the 'Little anti-socialist law' was introduced into the Reichstag, but this bill also failed to find a majority. In 1899 a final attempt to revive the anti-socialist laws was made with the Penitentiary Bill (*Zuchthausvorlage*), which proposed an end to the right to strike and to associate, but this attempt also failed.

Unable to gain a majority in the Reichstag for such anti-socialist legislation, the government had to make do with 'reaction in small doses'. Thus in 1898 the 'Lex Aron' made all university teachers civil servants, and thus social democrats could be excluded from holding a university post in Prussia.

Workers in the post office and railways were not allowed to strike or to associate, and so it was almost impossible for socialists to become state employees.

The army spent much time muttering about a coup, and some senior officers hoped to see Waldersee return to centre stage at the head of a military dictatorship. But much of this was idle chatter, for the army knew that they had little hope of ever being allowed to instigate an overthrow of the constitution, and they had to find other ways of combating social democracy. In the course of the Wilhelmine era they developed a programme to combat socialism. On the one hand they would have to be ready at any time to crush any revolutionary attempts the socialists might be tempted to make, and on the other hand they were determined to use the period of compulsory military service to condition the men by propaganda against the evils of democracy, materialism and socialism. But the practical implementation of such a programme presented problems which seemed insurmountable. Some officers had hoped that the Kaiser might be able to wean the 'good workers' away from the socialists by a programme of limited reform, but this policy had little chance of success when Stoecker was discredited and when William II had lost any enthusiasm for the notion of becoming a 'social Kaiser'. Those who supported anti-socialist legislation had similarly seen their hopes dashed as the Reichstag refused to co-operate. The powder and lead school seemed to gain credence, and their argument that unless the army struck now it might be too late had considerable appeal. But they had little chance of ever being allowed to test their theories. The growth of social democracy seemed inexorable and there appeared to be no satisfactory way of combating it. The army came to the conclusion that the most that could be done was to preserve the army as a bastion of the conservative order so that it was ever ready to strike against the enemies of the Reich, and at the same time to make it into the 'school of the nation', where young men would be instructed in the benefits and wisdom of the established order and the dreadful dangers of socialism and democracy.

The growth of social democracy was largely due to the growth of industrialism. As the industrial sector expanded there was a large movement of population away from the rural areas to the towns. This meant that the traditional recruiting areas of the army were shrinking, and the army was obliged to take recruits from the urban areas where they were likely to have come in contact with socialist ideas. To counter this trend the army took a high percentage of its recruits from the country areas, arguing that countrymen were healthier and had better characters. Thus in 1911 when 42·5 per cent of the population of Germany lived on the land, 64·15 per cent of the recruits came from rural areas. Only 5·84 per cent of the recruits came from large towns, 7·37 per cent from middle-sized towns and 22·34 per cent from small towns. General von Liebert, the president of the league against social democracy, a powerful right-wing organization, echoed the sentiments of the army when he exclaimed: 'Thank God for the country folk.'

However biased the recruiting pattern might have been, the army was still faced with the problem that social democrats were recruited, and in their eyes they formed a sinister fifth column within the army, endlessly plotting the overthrow of the state and undermining military efficiency. Thus although anti-socialist legislation had failed to pass in the Reichstag against civilians, the army demanded legislation to combat social democracy within the ranks. The war minister was unable to get an anti-socialist law passed in the Reichstag which would apply to the army, but he was able to win the support of the Prussian ministry of state for the use of the Kaiser's power of command to combat social democracy in the army. It was argued that since the social democrats were highly critical of the army, sympathy for social democracy could be seen as an attack on military discipline, and could therefore be punished as insubordination. By further extrapolation of this dubious logic, the war minister argued that any civilian who persuaded soldiers to become social democrats was guilty of an offence, and a number of state prosecutors agreed with this interpretation of the law, even though the Prussian minister of justice felt that it was constitutionally somewhat dubious. A further problem was that soldiers could often legitimately plead, ignorance of this ban on any form of social democratic activity as orders to that effect were issued by individual commanders. To get round this problem the war minister published orders against involvement in social democratic activities annually in the official *Reichsanzeiger*, but this in turn became something of an embarrassment as it was used by the social democrats as propaganda against the army.

Not only did the army have an unsatisfactory legal basis for their crusade against social democracy, but they were also faced with the exceedingly difficult problem of enforcing the war minister's orders. The police were called upon to keep a close watch on any soldiers who might be involved with social democracy, and to attend meetings where soldiers might be present. But the police were reluctant to join in this witch-hunt, not because they in any way sympathized with the social democrats, but because they complained that they did not have enough men available to waste on this largely fruitless task. Relations between the army and the police became increasingly strained until the army eventually decided to act alone without the help of unwilling civilians. Corps commanders were invited to send annual reports on the progress of social democracy within their areas of command. These reports were usually grossly exaggerated and wildly inaccurate, designed more to show the generals' patriotism and loyalty than as an objective assessment of the aims and intentions of the social democrats. Such hair-raising diatribes served to convince the military authorities that revolution was imminent, and led them to recommend even more drastic remedies.

As the army would have to be utterly reliable in the event of the revolution which so many senior officers insisted was just around the corner, the military authorities did everything possible to prevent social democrats from becoming NCOs. As social democrats were often among the better educated, more intelligent and most efficient of the recruits, this proved to be exceedingly difficult to achieve, and the more socialists who slipped through the net the more the army was convinced that a devilish plot was afoot to undermine the army. Known social democrats were posted away from the big urban centres to small country towns where they would be less likely to come into contact with other like-minded people. Social democrats were not allowed to serve in guards regiments, for fear that these elite battalions might become infected with treasonable ideas. They were also not allowed to serve as one-year volunteers, because volunteers were more likely to be given commissions

163

in the reserve, and because it was felt that two years in the ranks would give the army a fair chance to show a young socialist the error of his ways.

The army was not content with mere defensive tactics of this sort but was determined to go on the offensive whenever possible against the forces of socialism and democracy. In March 1890 the war minister Verdy du Vernois ordered all corps commanders to keep a close watch on socialist organizations, and suggested that the Prussian law on the state of siege might be used against the socialists. This would enable the military authorities to suspend all civil liberties and arrest suspects without trial. He assured the corps commanders that they would enjoy the full support of the Kaiser if they felt compelled to use these measures, even if they were to use firearms. Suggestions were made that special units should be formed to act as strike-breakers, but there was some hesitation about this, and once the wave of strikes in 1888-89 was over there seemed to be less immediate need for such a drastic step. After the Russian revolution of 1905 these ideas gained a new urgency. The general staff undertook a study of revolutionary tactics, and the historical section was required to examine the Paris Commune and the revolutions of 1848 to see if any useful lessons could be drawn from past experience. The study, entitled *Fighting in Insurgent Towns*, was completed in 1907. The picture it painted was gloomy indeed. It insisted that the German proletariat was well organized, disciplined and adequately financed, and could count on the support of the international socialist movement. Workers had been trained by the army to use firearms and in the basic elements of tactics, and were therefore likely to be formidable opponents on the barricades. The study argued that the only effective way to meet a revolutionary outbreak would be for the army to act immediately and with the full powers to which it was entitled under the terms of the law of the state of siege. The government would have to be evacuated so that it would not be tempted to enter into negotiations with the insurgents. Reichstag deputies would no longer be able to enjoy immunity, so that there would be no repeat performance of Bebel's speech in favour of the Paris Commune. There would be no negotiations between the military and the rebels, and fighting would continue until the revolution had been completely crushed.

The report was enthusiastically received in the army, and the corps commanders at once set about issuing orders as to what to do in the event of civil unrest. The most notorious of these orders was issued by the commanding general of the VIIth corps, Freiherr von Bissing, in April 1907. Bissing ordered that weapons should be used, even against unarmed crowds or passive resisters, and that no warning shots should be fired. The order continued with the words: 'There can be only one condition – unconditional surrender. All ringleaders or whoever is caught with a weapon in his possession are to be executed. The full severity of the law is to be applied mercilessly.' Bissing's order became public knowledge, it was discussed in the opposition press, and there was an outcry against it in the Reichstag. By 1910 the war minister was forced to countermand the section in the order which called for the suspension of the Reichstag members' immunity, as this was clearly unconstitutional. But the basic ideas behind the order, which only occasionally departed from the guidelines of the general staff, were used by the war minister in 1912 when a general order was issued to all army corps on civil unrest. Although this new order was careful to point out that responsibility for law and order rested in the first instance with the police, and that the army could be called upon to act only when the civilian powers were no longer strong enough to control the situation, the definition of a real state of emergency was hopelessly vague. The army continued to be used for strike breaking, and in the course of one such action in the Ruhr in 1912 four workers were killed. The war minister's appeal for restraint was also ignored during the Zabern crisis of 1913, involving the Prussian Army and Alsatian civilians.

Within the army there was some criticism of the powder and lead school. Those who had been preaching that a red revolution was imminent ever since the anti-socialist laws failed to be renewed in 1890 did induce a certain scepticism in some quarters. There were also many political objections to an outright confrontation with the social democrats. The Kaiser was fond of making bloodcurdling remarks, like his political programme which he outlined to Bülow in 1905: 'First shoot, behead and get rid of the Social Democrats, by a bloodbath if need be, and then fight a war outside. But not beforehand, and not a tempo.' But many officers felt that this was mere bluff, and that they would never get a chance of massacring the socialist hordes. As an alternative to violence there was always the idea of the army as the 'school of the nation', in which recruits would be subjected to propaganda on the wisdom of the established order. This aspect of the army's activities became extremely important in the Wilhelmine era.

At first it was felt that the most effective weapon against social democracy in the army was the Christian religion. Socialists were generally atheists who regarded religion as the 'opiate of the people', a sinister weapon of class oppression. Thus Christianity would be a powerful antidote to socialism. Christianity, particularly in the rather stern and militarized version as propounded by army chaplains, was considered good for discipline, the basis of honour and morality and comforting on the battlefield. The motto of the army was 'With God for Kaiser and Fatherland', and it was feared that without God, Kaiser and Fatherland might get short shrift.

The chaplain general of the Prussian army was enthusiastic for the idea of an anti-socialist crusade in the army. In 1890 he wrote: 'this revolutionary power would like, above all, to overthrow the army, since the army is based on the very foundations of human order: the fear of God, loyalty to the king and obedience.' Socialism, he unconvincingly argued, was alien to the army because the army itself was a classless society. 'The social gap between rich and poor which, in its gaping width, is one of the main sources of the present socialist agitation, does not exist in our army, in which everyone who serves is judged and accepted purely according to his worth and his achievements.' The chaplain general's vision of the army as the 'nursery of the Kingdom of God', in which a united band of pious Christian soldiers lived in a state of idyllic socialism, proved somewhat difficult to realize. The publication of Moltke's *Trostgedanken* in 1892 showed that the greatest Prussian officer of them all had been a rather sensitive deist who had looked upon the protestant church with some scepticism. It was soon apparent that such ideas were prevalent in the upper echelons of the officer corps, and most senior officers had little interest in organized religion. The younger officers were largely indifferent to the church and lacked even the rationalism of their superiors. Chaplains were regarded as second-class officers and were usually ignored, and religion was a forbidden topic of conversation in the mess. Thus the only chance that the chaplains had to deliver their propaganda to the army was in their weekly sermons. But even in their sermons they were strictly limited in what they were allowed to say. They were not allowed to imply that officers and NCOs were capable of human error, for this was considered to be liable to undermine military discipline. Similarly the chaplains were not allowed to 'prick the consciences of officers and NCOs', as one chaplain put it, as this might make them hesitant to command. As the mistreatment of soldiers, particularly by NCOs, was a serious problem in the army, this was a severe limitation on the effectiveness of the chaplains. Faced with all these restrictions, the chaplains had to limit themselves to crude panegyrics in praise of the German government and to outbursts of excessive chauvinism. God was represented to the soldiery as a loyal German, whose mighty voice spoke out in favour of the navy building programme and increased armaments, and who had little sympathy for mindless dreamers who longed for everlasting peace. The Kaiser was God's representative on earth, and the Almighty gave his unconditional support to German foreign policy. It is hardly surprising that such nonsense did little to wean socialist sympathizers away from 'materialism' and back to the church, but rather it confirmed the suspicions of those who felt that the church was misusing its authority and acting as a heavy-handed advertising agency for the established order.

It soon became obvious that the chaplains had failed to impose moral and political orthodoxy on the army, and although church parades, ceremonies of the oath to the flag and political sermons continued, it was decided that special political-instruction periods should be introduced as part of the army's educational programme to convince the soldiers of the dangers of socialism and the great advantages of the existing order. 'Patriotic history' was a favoured vehicle for such propaganda, and had been introduced into the school system in 1889. History instruction was left to junior lieutenants who knew next to nothing of the subject. The text books were naturally enough highly selective – Scharnhorst and Stein were never even mentioned, and any reference to pre-March liberalism carefully avoided – and the programme soon ground to a halt.

Another absurd idea was to encourage soldiers to go and work on the land so as to counteract the trend towards industrialization and urbanization. Since, it was argued, the countryside provided the only reliable recruits for the army, it was essential to maintain and strengthen the rural economy. Thus on Saturday afternoons one-and-a-half hours were devoted to instruction in milking, mowing and ploughing. But the programme was not a success. Soldiers from the land regarded the whole thing as absurd; those from the towns found it a burden. In any case the programme had no hope of halting the inexorable march of industrial progress, and it was not likely to persuade town dwellers of the joys of rural life.

Religion, history and agriculture all failed to counteract the influence of social democracy on the army and society, and thus as a final attempt to open the soldier's eyes to the dangers of socialism special civic-instruction periods were introduced. This programme was no more successful than the other attempts, and for much the same reasons. Officers came almost exclusively from the aristocracy and the upper bourgeoisie, and were almost totally ignorant of economic conditions and the social problems of their men. Those officers, like Captain Preuss, who tried to take the programme seriously, who suggested that there should be visits to factories and working-class neighbourhoods and genuine discussion of the problems with the men, and who insisted that the real issues behind the rise of social democracy should be examined, were silenced. The men were not even allowed to ask questions during these instruction periods, because this was considered bad for military discipline and would place officers and men on the same level. Since most officers did not even know the outline of the constitution, and their supreme war-lord boasted that he had never read it, lessons in civic studies were rarely particularly sophisticated. Many social democrats in the army had been well trained by the party in political, economic and social problems and could easily counter this propaganda. By 1907 the army had to admit defeat, and the Kaiser issued a cabinet order which decreed that social and political questions should no longer be raised in the instruction periods. Officers were still permitted to indulge in diatribes against the 'social democratic movement which is against monarchy, state and religion' on the grounds that this was not political activity because it was merely upholding the institutions of the state. This attitude served to polarize further the two sides. The officer corps stood for the privileges of their caste, for their direct relationship with the Kaiser and their refusal to show any allegiance to the parliamentary institutions of the Reich. The social democrats stood for the abolition of privilege and class and for the extension and strengthening of the democratic institutions. It is quite understandable that the officers were strongly opposed to socialism, but their opposition was ill-informed and primitive, and their inability to destroy social democracy within the army made them increasingly frustrated, violent and aggressive.

The growth of social democracy which plagued the army and which seemed to threaten the basis of Wilhelmine society was to a considerable extent the result of the spectacular growth of German industry since the Caprivi tariffs. Thus the more powerful Germany became the more she seemed threatened by socialism, and it was this that gave German politics its peculiarly aggressive thrust in these years.

The basic structure of the German economy had already been established; it was now broadened and strengthened. The monopolization of the electrical and chemical industries was largely completed by the end of the 1890s. In the other branches of industry the cartels, trusts and interest groups were reorganized and strengthened. The banks in Berlin tightened their hold on the capital market and played an increasingly dominant role in the economy as controllers and pacemakers of industrial expansion. But this dramatic growth of the German economy created endless problems. Germany was no longer England's ready market, she was a formidable rival. The expansion of the German share of world trade brought her into increasing conflict with the other great trading nations, and made German industrialists determined to secure adequate sources of raw materials abroad. At home relative prosperity papered over the divisions within German society but at the same time made them more acute. Imperialism and anti-socialism were the necessary outcome of German economic expansion in the 1890s.

In 1897 the alliance between the agrarians and the industrialists was patched up once again with Miquel's *Sammlungspolitik* – the unification of the right against the threat from the left – and was cemented by Tirpitz's naval building programme. The first great naval law of 1898 and the further laws of 1900, 1906, 1908 and 1912 were enthusiastically supported by the industrialists led by Krupp and Kirdorff. They were designed to secure Germany's imperialist aims, to provide an object for chauvinist enthusiasm which would silence discontent at home and to give industry the opportunity to make even greater profits. This latter calculation was certainly true. Stumm's Dillinger Hütte, which made armour plating for battleships, declared a thirty per cent dividend in 1900. Krupp's profits from armaments were 21 million marks in 1902. Germany spent more money on armaments than any other country, and the percentage of arms that were exported was extremely high. Krupp exported forty-four per cent of the arms he produced. Between 1890 and 1912 German firms produced 655,000 rifles for the German army and exported 2,922,000. A number of important patents for the armaments industry were sold abroad, among them the sale of a time-fuse patent by Krupp to Vickers Armstrong, for which German troops were to pay dearly in 1914-18.

The alliance on the right was the result of a deal by which the agrarians were given protective tariffs and the industrialists got an extensive armaments programme and an imperialist foreign policy. But this alliance was incapable of overcoming the growing differences between the bourgeoisie and the landed aristocracy. Many industrialists and bankers came to feel that the price paid for support from the agrarian conservatives was far too high. The group around the *Hansabund* began to urge a lowering of tariffs to secure cheaper imports of raw materials, and concessions to the left to ease domestic political tensions, in other words a revival of some of the ideas of the Caprivi era. In the elections of 1912 this group triumphed, along with the social democrats, and the stability of the system seemed seriously endangered. The reactionaries fought back with the largest army estimates that had ever been proposed. This polarization and radicalization of German politics was to prove fatal in the summer of 1914 when Germany was to make her 'bid for world power'.

The growing isolation, aggressiveness and internal instability of Germany were reflected in the strategic planning of the pre-war period which was to reach its final form in the Schlieffen plan. The military leadership was determined to secure the imperialist aims and the continental domination for which the German ruling class was striving, but they seriously under-estimated the difficulty of winning a victory over the combined forces of France, Russia and Britain. Their strategic planning was highly adventurous and lacked any profound understanding of the nature of modern warfare.

The Franco-Russian alliance of the early 1890s, the result of a refusal to renew the reinsurance treaty and of the anti-Russian nature of the conservative agrarian policy, was made all the more dangerous by the Anglo-German naval rivalry which began at the end of the decade. The 'encirclement' of Germany was completed with the Anglo-French Entente of 1904 and the Triple Entente of France, Russia and Britain in 1907. Germany's ally Italy moved closer to France, so that Germany had but one ally left of any significance, Austria-Hungary, a country which was greatly weakened by increasing internal dissent.

Germany was thus faced with a likely enemy which had greatly superior armed forces and economic reserves. The aims of German imperialism were out of all proportion to the means available to achieve them, and a way out of this dilemma was suggested by the notion of a lightning war (blitzkrieg). The need for such a strategy was dictated not only by the superiority of the forces opposing Germany, but also by the realization that Germany did not have the economic resources to fight a war of attrition, whatever the military historian Hans Delbrück might argue to the contrary. The general staff was also concerned that the social democrats might take their anti-war slogans seriously and attempt to hamper mobilization by a general strike, or that in the event of a prolonged war revolution might break out at home. Thus Schlieffen insisted that a short war, and swift and drastic measures against any strikes or revolutionary outbreaks, were essential if Germany was to avoid revolution and defeat. Indeed, when given the choice between a possible revolution or defeat, the army was prepared to opt for defeat in September 1918.

As late as 1890, in one of his last speeches in the Reichstag, Moltke had warned that the next war was likely to be a long one, and that it could well be another thirty years' war. The general staff after Moltke was determined to find what Schlieffen called the 'secret of victory', a strategic master plan that would obviate the need to fight a long war which, because of her relative economic weakness, Germany was bound to lose.

The basis of Schlieffen's strategy was the theory of the battle of annihilation – the 'Cannae Doctrine' – a vast battle of encirclement which would totally destroy the enemy forces. But his belief that a campaign could be decided by one initial battle was no longer feasible. Moltke had believed that a decisive battle in the early stages could bring about the end of the war provided that it was supported by an active diplomacy, and provided that Germany would be prepared to make some concessions. Total victory as Schlieffen envisaged was no longer possible; this was the lesson which Moltke drew from the experience of 1870-71 and it should have been reinforced by an analysis of the Russo-Japanese war of 1904-5. But Schlieffen believed that the answer to these problems lay in the genius of the commanding general, not in the nature of modern warfare itself.

In order that this battle of encirclement could be successfully achieved and one opponent defeated before turning on the other, speed was essential. Thus the offensive, regardless of the cost, was regarded as the only effective way to fight a war. Such slogans as 'to fight means to attack' resulted in a disastrous underestimation of the defensive power of modern armies. Enormously increased firepower, machine-guns and barbed wire made the attack extremely costly and bloody, but the general staff continued to believe that mind, in the form of the offensive spirit, could triumph over matter.

In the interests of speed, and in order that the army might be deployed so as to encircle the enemy, considerations of international law and the neutrality of neighbouring states were ignored. The general staff was prepared to violate the neutrality of Belgium, Holland and Luxemburg. The bombardment of cities, the shooting of hostages, reprisals, the exploitation of occupied territories and the use of forced labour were all discussed as a necessary part of the blitzkrieg strategy of the time and were to be used during the war to a great extent. As a rationale for these measures, it was argued that they would all serve to shorten the war, and were therefore deeply humane.

In response to the Franco-Russian entente Schlieffen, who followed Waldersee as chief of the general staff in 1891, changed the strategic plans of the army so that the main attack was directed against France rather than Russia. He feared that if the attack was launched against Russia the enemy forces would withdraw into the endless expanses of the east, and the German army might well meet the same fate as that of Napoleon. He also knew that the French were militarily much stronger, and that therefore it was essential that France should first be brought to her knees. Schlieffen placed great importance on heavy artillery which he intended to bring up to the front to destroy the French defences, and on the development of a strategic railway in the west to speed up mobilization and to secure adequate supplies for the army as it marched into France. Realizing that valuable time would be lost breaking through the French defences, Schlieffen by 1897 began to think in terms of an advance through Belgium to turn the heavily defended front between Verdun to Belfort and to open up the whole of the north of France for the strategic deployment of the German army. Although Moltke had considered a breach of Belgian neutrality, and had argued that considerations of international law could not be allowed to stand in the way of military necessity, it was not until the time of Schlieffen that it became axiomatic that Belgium would have to be invaded if France were to be attacked. Chancellor Hohenlohe agreed with the general staff's arguments, even though the attack on Belgium was most likely to cause Britain to enter the war. The general staff had discussed the possibility of Britain fighting on the side of France ever since the Kruger Telegram of 1896, and the Anglo-German naval rivalry made such an intervention even more likely. But it was argued that if the attack on France was brought to a swift and decisive conclusion there was little to fear from a British expeditionary force, and a naval blockade of Germany would pose a serious threat only in the event of a protracted war.

173

For the next ten years the details of the attack on France were worked out, and they reached a final form in the 'Schlieffen plan' of 1905. The plan was finalized at a time when Schlieffen hoped for a preventive war. Russia was greatly weakened by her defeat by the Japanese, Britain had not properly recovered from the after-effects of the Boer War, and Holstein, the *eminence grise* of the foreign office, hoped to use the crisis over Morocco to shatter the Anglo-French Entente. If Germany was to fight a preventive war, then clearly this was an excellent opportunity. Yet even in such favourable circumstances the plan was exceptionally risky; by 1914 it was to be a gamble at extremely long odds.

The plan called for a gigantic hammer blow aimed to the west of Paris, with the bottom of the 'handle' roughly at Metz. The proportion of troops on the right wing to the left wing would be about seven to one. All the reserves would be involved in the initial attack to give the hammer greater weight. The massed forces on the right flank would march through Belgium, Luxemburg and southern Holland to the Channel coast. The army would then wheel in a huge arc and swing round to the west of Paris, hitting the French forces from the rear and crushing them against their own positions on the German border. A French retreat to the south would have to be avoided at all costs, for this would lead, Schlieffen argued, to an endless war. The French army would be trapped and destroyed in a gigantic 'super Cannae'. For such a strategy to work, the German army would have to move extremely quickly. According to the plan the right wing would have to march more than 300 miles and encircle Paris within twenty-nine days, thus placing an intolerable strain on the troops. Schlieffen and the general staff had ignored Blume's warnings in his *Strategy*, which summed up Moltke's strategic doctrines: 'Enterprises for which the means are insufficient carry the seed of failure in them', or: 'Underestimation of the opponent or the overestimation of one's own forces has often led to severe catastrophes.'

On New Year's Day 1906 William II told his commanding generals that Schlieffen had resigned and that he had no intention of going to war over Morocco. The generals were disappointed that they were not going to get the war for which they had been hoping, but they realized there was nothing they could do but follow with disgust the proceedings of the conference of Algeciras. Schlieffen was succeeded by the younger Moltke, a man who had certain perfectly justifiable reservations about his own military qualities, and who tried to compensate for his own shortcomings by a closer co-operation with Austria-Hungary whose new chief of staff, Conrad von Hötzendorf, was an outspoken advocate of preventive war. Moltke feared that the Schlieffen plan was too risky, and with the Triple Entente of 1907 he began to revise it. Troops had to be moved from the west to the east so that a German army could hold the line against a Russian advance. Moltke was also concerned that the left flank of the German army in the west – the 'handle' of Schlieffen's hammer – was too weak, and that the French might break through in Alsace-Lorraine and turn the German flank. To obviate this danger he changed the proportion of troops on the left and right flanks. He further modified the plan so that the army would not march through Holland. Dutch neutrality would thus be preserved and Germany would be able to import vital raw materials through Holland. Yet Moltke still believed that the Schlieffen plan, the essentials of which remained unchanged, was an infallible recipe for success, and that France could indeed be defeated within five or six weeks of mobilization. Moltke has often been accused of watering down the Schlieffen plan so that the plan had no chance of success, but such criticism overlooks two vital points. Moltke had to modify the plan to meet the exigencies of a new situation in which a war with France would necessarily entail a war with Russia and Britain under conditions quite different from those of 1905. But even more important is the fact that the Schlieffen plan itself was a brilliant intellectual exercise, a piece of theoretical wizardry which had a fatal fascination for generations of staff officers, but it was totally unrealistic, a desperate attempt to find a way to square the circle of German aims and German strength. For all its brilliance and daring, blitzkrieg was as doomed to failure in 1914 as it was in 1939.

If the strategic doctrine behind the plan was highly dubious, the political effects were equally disastrous. In January 1909 Moltke told the Austrian chief of staff, Conrad von Hötzendorf, that the Central Powers had no reason to worry about a two-front war, describing such a prospect as 'serious' but certainly not 'menacing'. In the course of this exchange of letters he gave Austria an unconditional guarantee that if Austria were involved in a war with Russia over the Balkans, even if the war was caused by Austria, this would be regarded by Germany as the *'casus foederis'* under the terms of the Dual Alliance of 1879. This unjustifiable reading of the intent of the treaty was approved by the German Kaiser and by the chancellor. Both Moltke and Conrad would have welcomed the chance to fight a preventive war in 1909, and they were bitterly disappointed that the diplomats thought otherwise. With the Russian mobilization in 1912 there were further talks between the two general staff chiefs. Conrad wanted to be reassured of German support for Austrian aggression in the Balkans and this was immediately forthcoming. But whereas Conrad would have preferred a localized war in the Balkans if possible, Moltke seemed positively to welcome the prospect of a Great War which would settle the question of Europe's future.

In February 1913 Moltke told the general staffs of the German armies that he had information which showed that if Russia were to mobilize in future that would amount to a declaration of war – just as under the Schlieffen plan the first day of mobilization was also the first day of hostilities, so that Germany could not mobilize without going to war. This information was passed on by the war minister to members of the Reichstag two months later. Thus a future Russian mobilization was to be regarded as a declaration of war. A further important step had been taken towards August 1914.

In his traditional New Year's address to the commanding generals in 1914 the Kaiser told them that war was likely to come that year, and some of the commanding generals eagerly passed on the message to their subordinates. The German military attaché in Vienna told Conrad that although Moltke was in favour of war, the Kaiser and the 'authorities' were really for peace whatever their bellicose remarks might suggest to the contrary. In an ensuing exchange of letters Moltke and Conrad agreed that the military position was particularly favourable to the Central Powers, with the Russian army in the middle of a somewhat frantic reform and the French army beginning to introduce the three-year service. In April the two men met in Carlsbad, and Moltke argued that the longer they waited for war the slighter would be their chances of success, and he reassured Conrad that the German army would defeat France within six weeks and would then be able to assist the Austrian army against the Russians.

Thus when the Austrian Archduke was murdered at Sarajevo, Moltke had successfully set the scene for preventive war. The Austrian government had been given a blank cheque in the Balkans. They had been assured that a Great War could be viewed with equanimity. They knew that the German general staff would welcome a war. German diplomats were also trapped by the fact that Germany had only one war plan, and the army could not mobilize without going to war. Moltke's policy had not been conducted behind the backs of the civilians, but with the approval of the government. Thus there was no difference over the aims of the army and the civilians, but only over means. However acrimonious these debates might become, particularly during the war, this central fact should not be overlooked.

Notions of a preventive war, designed to secure far-reaching imperialist aims, had been widely discussed in the literature of the time. Colonel Yorck von Wartenburg published his *Outline History of the World* in 1897, a work which was to go through ten editions in ten years and which became a standard textbook for army officers. This racist and social-Darwinist book preached the 'united states of Europe' under German domination, and argued that Germany's justifiable right to a huge empire and the oppression and exploitation of inferior peoples was frustrated by the social democrats, who would therefore have to be ruthlessly crushed. These ideas were further developed by General von der Goltz ('Goltz Pascha'), who had gained some fame in 1877 with a study of Leon Gambetta in which he called for a two-front war to establish German hegemony in Europe. He expanded his theories in *The Nation in Arms*, a book which became a best seller. In 1883 Goltz was posted to Turkey to help reform the Turkish army. He soon began to dream of a Turkish army, led by German officers, chasing the British from Egypt and marching on towards India, and he saw the German Kaiser as 'William the Conqueror' crossing the Channel to punish '*perfide Albion*'. In 1904 he wrote that Germany would have to expand from the Dutch coast to Trieste, and then fight the great battle for the domination of Europe.

The most influential of all these writers was General Friedrich von Bernhardi whose book *Germany and the Next War* ran into many editions and was published in numerous foreign languages. Like the writings of Yorck and Goltz, the book is social-Darwinist and racist. War, for Bernhardi, 'gives a biologically just decision, since its decisions rest on the very nature of things'. Thus the sole aim of the state is power and more power. Bernhardi insisted that Germany should regain her natural frontiers from the Rhine to the Ukraine. All non-Germans, particularly the Slavs, were to be expelled from Germany, otherwise Germany would be overrun by the 'Slavonic hordes'. His long-range programme called for the total defeat of France, the creation of a European confederation under German domination and the building of a vast overseas empire. At home liberalism and democracy would have to be exterminated as they were un-German, and *nouveauriche* capitalists and stockbrokers should be heavily taxed.

Many apologist historians have tried to discount the importance of these proto-fascist ideas by claiming that they were the notions of isolated cranks and that their notoriety is due only to the fact that their ideas were used in the propaganda campaigns against Germany. Nothing could be further from the truth. Goltz, Bernhardi and Yorck were important and respected men and their ideas were shared by many leading figures of the day. In an intellectual climate which produced Nietzsche, Treitschke, Houston Stewart Chamberlain and other such ultra-reactionary thinkers, it is hardly surprising that such ideas should be reflected in theoretical military works. These ideas are to be found among university professors and army officers, politicians and landowners, industrialists and shopkeepers, and far from being wild dreams they accurately reflect the aggressive and expansionist aims of Imperial Germany.

The influence of these ideas can be seen in the strategic planning of the general staff, but the army also enthusiastically supported the imperialist ambitions of such writers. The leading figure in the army's campaign for colonies was General von Liebert who was to become president of the League Against

Social Democracy, a virulent anti-socialist organization which saw the army as the last bastion against violent revolution. He was regarded as the general staff's expert on colonial affairs, and he organized meetings between the army leaders, the Kaiser, the foreign office and prominent colonialists. From 1896 to 1900 he was governor of German East Africa, and on his retirement he was appointed to the board of directors of the German Colonial Society.

German colonial expansion since the 1880s, and Liebert's propaganda, forced the general staff, though certainly with no reluctance, to pay much attention to the military problems of the colonies. The army enthusiastically supported the seizure of Kiaochow in 1897. General Waldersee was chosen to command the international force sent to put down the Boxer rebellion of 1900, and was promoted to the rank of field marshal for the occasion. Moltke saw the true nature of the expedition when he confided in his diary: 'We want to earn money, build railways, start mines, and bring European culture – that means in other words earn money. In this respect we are not an iota better than the English in the Transvaal.' Waldersee and the German expeditionary force did not in fact arrive in China until the rebellion had been suppressed, but inspired by the Kaiser's famous speech to the troops as they left from Hamburg, in which he said that the German army should behave in China 'like the Huns under King Attila', the Germans conducted a punitive expedition in which many thousands of Chinese were brutally murdered. Waldersee did little in China but quarrel with the commanders of the allied forces, have a touching reunion with a notorious Chinese courtesan who had caught his fancy many years back when she was married to a Chinese diplomat stationed in Berlin, and contract a severe bout of dysentery. He arrived back in Germany to be fêted as a conquering hero, but he was painfully aware that he had missed the boat.

The experiences of the China expedition of 1900-01 were analysed by the general staff and used as the basis for studies on the use of troops in the colonies. The results of these investigations were singularly crude. Extreme violence, gruesome reprisals and a racialist arrogance were the *leitmotivs* of the general staff's orders and regulations on the subject. From 1904 to 1907 the German army put these ideas into practice in

Southwest Africa against the Hereros and the Hottentots. The Africans rebelled against German colonial rule and at first the colonial troops were not able to cope with the situation. Reinforcements were sent from Germany, and the general staff assumed responsibility for crushing the revolt. General Trotha took over command of the troops and proposed a war of extermination against the Hereros. He suggested that men, women and small children should be driven into the waterless desert to die. Chancellor Bülow when he heard of this scheme was appalled and told the Kaiser that such a scheme was unchristian. The Kaiser replied that as the Hereros were a bunch of heathen savages such arguments were irrelevant. Trotha's plan was thus approved by the Kaiser and by Schlieffen. In August 1904 between 50,000 and 60,000 Hereros with their cattle were driven into the Kalahari Desert and were either machine-gunned by the German troops or died in the desert. Some 80,000 Hereros lost their lives in the revolt, and the general staff's official history of the campaign proudly reports that they ceased to be an independent tribe. Genocide on this scale as a deliberate act of policy was the first step towards the horrors of the Final Solution.

The army was interested not only in colonial expansion in China and Africa but also in the possibility of a German-dominated Near East. Goltz Pascha and the military attachés at the German embassy were outspoken proponents of imperialist expansion in the Middle East, and used their influence over the Turkish army to secure enormous armaments contracts for German industry. The army was also keenly interested in the construction of the Baghdad Railway. It inspired dreams of German control of the area, and even a march on India, dreams which were to become part of German policy during the First World War. Turkey was strategically vital to Germany because it controlled the Bosphorus, threatened the Suez Canal and straddled the route to India. Profits to German industry from the sale of often obsolete weapons to Turkey were gigantic – Krupp was able to sell a large number of guns which had cost 12,000 marks to make for 160,000 marks apiece. By 1914 Turkey owed Germany 500 million marks.

Defeat of the Turkish army in the First Balkan War of 1912,

a wretched advertisement for Krupp's cannons and Goltz's skill as military adviser, was used by the German government to strengthen their hold on Turkey. A military mission under General Liman von Sanders was sent to Turkey with specific instructions from the government to 'germanize' the Turkish army and to keep a tight control of its organization. Liman was instructed to secure a dominant influence over Turkish foreign policy, and was given one million marks per year for bribes. In the Kaiser's address to the mission he said: 'You are, in fact, the pioneers of the future partition of Turkey.' Liman's mission was staffed by some outstanding officers – Goltz had to make do with some very dubious characters who had in one way or another made themselves unpopular at home – and they were given key positions in the Turkish army. Liman was appointed to the Turkish war council, was given charge of all war schools and training centres, and had the right to visit any military installations. In May 1914 the Bavarian Major Kübel was sent to Turkey to inspect the railway system and to make sure that it would be suitable for warfare within six months. Kübel demanded 100 million marks for changes in the railways and began an energetic campaign which met with the stiff opposition of the railway company. Kübel was eventually removed after long negotiations when the Deutsche Bank insisted that he was ruining the prospects of the Baghdad Railway which it was financing.

For the army to indulge in this imperialist policy abroad and repressive policy at home it had to be officered by men untouched by liberal and democratic ideas. Traditionally the officer corps had come almost exclusively from the aristocracy, but with the enormous increases in the size of the army and the growth of a prosperous and established upper-bourgeoisie, the aristocracy was no longer able to supply all the needs of the army and the middle class entered the officer corps in increasing numbers. By 1913, after the last great increase in the army before the war, thirty per cent of the officer corps was aristocratic, and the limits of what was regarded as politically safe had been reached.

The army had been forced to make concessions to the middle class through sheer necessity. The great technological advances which had been made had a profound effect on warfare, and

181

the army could not do without qualified middle-class officers, for 'character' – always regarded in the army as an exclusive attribute of the aristocracy – was clearly no longer enough, particularly in the more technical arms. In 1890 when the Kaiser was still labouring under the delusion that all class divisions could be made to disappear if only a true national purpose were found, he announced that middle-class officers would be welcomed in the officer corps. In characteristic terms he declared:

I look for men who will build the future of the army not only among the offspring of the aristocratic families of the country and the sons of my gallant officers and civil servants who traditionally have formed the keystone of the officer corps, but also among the sons of honourable bourgeois families in which a love for king and country, and a heartfelt devotion to the profession of arms and to Christian culture are planted and cherished.

The Kaiser later explained to one of his generals that this move was made as part of a deliberate attempt to win over the bourgeoisie to a common front with the aristocracy against social democracy. It was the military equivalent to *Sammlungspolitik*. Both were designed to place the old order in quarantine. The influx of bourgeois officers was thus not a move in the direction of democratization, but rather an attempt to indoctrinate middle-class young men with aristocratic and conservative values. William II and his military advisers could back up their arguments with quotations from the older Moltke, who had argued that the aristocracy would not be able to survive in the modern world without making some concessions to the middle class.

It is for this reason that the question of the rising proportion of the bourgeoisie in the officer corps must be seen not merely in terms of percentages and dead statistics, but rather in terms of how far the army was able to succeed in its functional role of assimilating the bourgeoisie into the old aristocratic and reactionary elite. In this respect the army was most successful. The bourgeois officers did not introduce liberal and alien ideas into the officer corps, as the opponents of an increased bourgeois intake feared, but rather they were rapidly assimilated, and all too often copied the worst characteristics of their aristocratic comrades. The officer corps was thus an effective instrument for the feudalization of the bourgeoisie, which was one of the main features of Wilhelmine Germany. The reserve officer corps was particularly successful in this respect. The days of the liberal *Landwehr* officer were long gone; the new type of reserve officers became often rather ridiculous caricatures of the aristocratic regular officers, providing ample material for the satirists of the day.

But in spite of these successes the army was determined that this process should not be allowed to go too far. The proponents of a socially exclusive officer corps, among the most outspoken of whom was von der Goltz, published a steady stream of warnings on the dangers of watering down the officer corps with unsuitable material. Goltz argued that too much intellect was a bad thing for an officer, because it would lead to doubt and hesitation on the battlefield. Character and inborn qualities of leadership were what mattered, and here the aristocracy had a monopoly. The officer corps should thus accept only those bourgeois who were prepared uncritically to accept the ideology of the junkers and the notion that the officer corps should be a self-perpetuating clique, far removed from the sordid material realities of Wilhelmine Germany and determined to defend the old order against the demands of the new.

Such ideas found wide support in the army. As officers were selected by the regiments they naturally chose men of their own type. In the more technical arms of the service the situation was somewhat different. Engineers and medical officers had to be properly qualified, and their skills were clearly of greater importance than their pedigree. This resulted in a growing split between the technical arms and the traditional regiments, a trend which was accentuated as warfare became increasingly technical in nature, a split between 'character' and 'intellect', between aristocrat and bourgeois. Similarly the aristocrats tended to monopolize certain regiments. In 1913 no fewer than sixteen regiments were exclusively aristocratic, and sixty-one-and-a-half per cent of the Prussian regiments had more than fifty per cent aristocratic officers. Aristocrats continued to maintain their hold over senior positions in the army. In 1913 fifty-three per cent of the officers of the rank of colonel and above were aristocrats. In 1906, although educational standards had been considerably improved, sixty per cent of the officers at the general staff were aristocrats. Yet for all these divisions the most striking thing about the army was the homogeneity of its officer corps. As in all other armies, there was a tendency for the old established cavalry and infantry regiments to look down with snobbish disdain at the officers in transport or the pioneers, but on the whole the army provided an institutional means of integration for an aspiring bourgeoisie which was not provided within the political structure of the Reich.

The limitations placed on the number of bourgeois entrants to the officer corps created a severe social problem. As Bismarck had said: 'Man begins with the rank of lieutenant', and in a society in which the army played such an important role exclusion from the officer corps acted as a brake on upward social mobility and often on social betterment. A commission in the army was virtually a prerequisite for a senior position in the foreign office or the civil service, and failure to gain a commission was a severe social stigma. The reluctance of the officer corps to open its doors to a wider section of society thus had considerable economic and social consequences which transcended mere snobbery.

After the great increases in the size of the army in 1888 and 1893 a large proportion of the funds for military expenditure was devoted to the naval building programme, but in 1899 the Reichstag approved a further increase in the peacetime strength of the army from 589,000 men to 612,000 men. In the preparation of the army bill, questions of the social composition of the officer corps had played an important part. Schlieffen had pressed for a far greater increase, because the success of his strategic planning depended to a large extent on the size of the army and the weight of the blow he would be able to inflict on France. The war minister, von Gossler, had refused Schlieffen's request, arguing that the quality of the existing army should first be improved before embarking on huge increases which were likely to lower the standards of the officer corps. But it was not only the likely changes in the officer corps that concerned the war minister; an increase on the scale proposed by the general staff would automatically lead to an increase in the proportion of recruits coming from the towns. Reliable peasants would gradually give way to city dwellers who were likely to be tinged with dangerous ideas, and the army would no longer be suitable for the repression of domestic disorders. The larger the army got, the greater the danger of a liberally minded officer corps and a rank and file that was sympathetic to social democracy. The general staff, which was more concerned with fighting a war against France than it was with crushing internal dissent, continued to press for large increases in the army. In 1903 there was a further exchange of letters between Schlieffen and the war minister, von Einem. Although the arguments on both sides were by now familiar, von Einem was an even more outspoken critic of the general staff's attitude than was Gossler. Indeed he had the audacity to suggest that Schlieffen was perhaps not immortal, however much the 'demigods' at the general staff might believe the contrary, and that his strategy might even be wrong. In the following year von Einem told the budgetary committee of the Reichstag that there was no need for any further increases in the size of the army for the time being, and that its strength was sufficient to fight a successful war. The war minister studiously avoided mentioning the fact that the chief of the general staff, who was responsible for the planning and conduct of war, violently disagreed with this view.

Einem was supported by the chancellor, Bülow, in his struggle with Schlieffen, largely because Bülow had such confidence in his own abilities as a diplomatist that he did not feel that Germany would have to risk a war. The failure of German policies during the first Moroccan crisis did something to undermine even Bülow's remarkable belief in his own abilities, but he would not accept the arguments of those soldiers who were pressing for a preventive war. By 1906 he had regained much of his old confidence, and the experience of the Russian revolution of 1905 seemed to suggest that von Einem's concern about the possibility of revolution at home was something more than idle speculation. There was once again complete unanimity between the chancellor and the war minister that the army did not need to be increased.

The younger Moltke shared Schlieffen's conviction that the army would have to be substantially increased, and with the formation of the Triple Entente this became a matter of some urgency for the general staff. Von Einem remained adamant in his refusal to accept these demands. In 1909 he wrote to Moltke saying that: 'An increase in the peacetime effective strength of 6,500–7,000 men, spread over the five years from 1 April 1911, is the absolute maximum which, under present circumstances, can be demanded and which it is at all possible to achieve.' The war minister was thus using the argument that the Reichstag would not accept such an increase, which was untrue, to back up his contention that the army should not compromise its exclusiveness and its rural origins. The fact that the costs of the army had risen very steeply since the turn of the century, largely because of new weapons, gave some credence to the war minister's arguments. Moltke, however, knew that France could never be overrun in a swift blitzkrieg campaign unless there was a substantial increase in the size of the army and further modernization of arms and equipment. In 1911 Moltke therefore demanded an increase of 300,000 men, insisting with no little hyperbole that such an increase was a 'precondition for survival'. But the Kaiser and the war minister were adamant in their opposition, arguing that such an increase would be the ruin of the old army.

The general staff did not get the gigantic increase that they demanded, but they did not go away empty handed. The conservative forces in the war ministry had to make some concessions. In February 1911 the Reichstag approved an increase of 10,000 men and an additional expenditure of 104 million marks. In May 1912 it approved a further increase of 29,000 men. The greatest increase of all came the following year when the Reichstag approved an increase of 4,000 officers, 14,850 NCOs and 117,000 men. The peacetime strength of the German army was thus about 800,000 men in 1914.

The army increases between 1911 and 1913 were the result of bitter debates. The war minister, von Heeringen, repeated the familiar arguments of his predecessors. He was supported by the chancellor, Bethmann Hollweg, who feared that such an enormous increase as that suggested by the general staff would be an unnecessary provocation of Germany's neighbours. The Kaiser, as was so often the case, was unable to make up his mind and supported whoever spoke to him last. The result was a compromise which satisfied neither side. The general staff had argued that an increase of 300,000 men was essential if their strategic plan was to work. It further insisted that in an age of mass armies with modern weapons it was absurd to claim that a small, elite and well trained army was superior, because technology was reducing the importance of the individual soldier, and concern about the social composition of the army was not of such pressing importance as the war ministry seemed to think. But the general staff achieved only about one third of the increase which it deemed essential, and Ludendorff, one of the principal architects of the increases, was posted to Düsseldorf as a regimental commander to keep him away from Berlin. On the other hand the war minister had been forced to accept increases greatly in excess of what he deemed desirable. Thus right up to the outbreak of the war the argument between the war ministry and the general staff raged. The general staff felt that the increases were inadequate, the war ministry that they were excessive.

Historians have often felt obliged to take sides in this debate, arguing that at least the general staff stood for a more liberal personnel policy. But whereas it is true that the war ministry was concerned to preserve the army as a socially exclusive and reactionary body, ready at any time to crush dissent at home, it should not be forgotten that the aim of the general staff was to fight an offensive war that would establish Germany as a world power. Thus the aims of neither side were progressive or commendable.

These last estimates before the war are important in many ways. The social democrats voted for them for the first time, abandoning their traditional stance of 'for this system not one man and not one cent'. This was an important step in the party's development, which was to lead to their support for the German government during the war. The money approved by the Reichstag was used almost entirely for offensive weapons, for highly mobile heavy artillery and heavy mortars, whereas machine-guns which were regarded as largely defensive weapons were not produced in sufficient quantities. Similarly reserves of weapons, ammunition and food were quite inadequate, for the general staff insisted that the campaign would be short and decisive. Lastly the army had unleashed a large propaganda campaign for the increases and had abandoned its political aloofness to enter the political arena.

The army had failed to combat the forces of social change, its propaganda efforts within the army had been a failure and it had found that withdrawing into itself had created more problems than it solved. Now it decided to try to win public favour and support by means of propaganda. The enormously powerful and successful interest groups of Wilhelmine Germany, such as the Navy League, the Farmers' League, The Imperial League against Social Democracy and the Association of German Industrialists, gave to German society a pseudo-plebiscitory dimension, a relatively harmless alternative to universal suffrage, which acted as an anti-parliamentary alternative to bourgeois democracy. This deliberate rabble-rousing was something quite alien to the traditions of the officer corps, which had always spurned any such sordid appeals to the masses. But the phenomenal success of the Navy League, which had made millions into devotees of the naval building programme, forced them to rethink their position. By 1912 when the army was pushing for huge increases and the war ministry was not being co-operative, the more radical officers cast their restraint aside and decided to form an Army League (*Wehrverein*) based on the Navy League, to lend mass support for the proposed increases.

The Army League was a great success, in spite of the opposition of the war minister who argued that it was 'political' and therefore could not be supported by the army. Within a year it had 300,000 members. Its philosophy was simple, and was admirably summed up by its chairman General Keim: 'Active politics and offensive war have always been, since history began, the safest foundation, and guarantee of success both in politics and war.' It was a sign that the army was making certain concessions to the spirit of the age. The para-military youth and veterans' organizations, which were to become extremely large in the years immediately before the war, were steps in the same direction. This in no sense implied that the army was becoming more democratic or that it was sensitive to popular demands. It was a purely defensive move designed to preserve the sectional interests of the army in a time of rapid social change. The implications of this changing attitude were to become apparent during the war when Hindenburg and Ludendorff established their form of a military dictatorship with popular support, against the wishes of the Reichstag and without the approval of the Kaiser.

7

The First World War

The news that the Austrian Archduke Franz Ferdinand had
been murdered by Serbian nationalists at Sarajevo on 28 June
1914 was welcomed by military circles in Berlin as offering the
golden opportunity for the preventive war for which they had
waited so long. The Saxon military plenipotentiary reported to
his war minister that the opinion in army circles was that it
would be a good thing if war was to come, as Germany's
position was favourable and was unlikely to get any better, and
that Germany should strike before Russia was given time to
prepare for war. The Kaiser wrote that it was 'now or never'.
The Austrian government was well aware that the military in
Berlin would welcome a war. On 5 July the Kaiser conferred
with his top military advisers and was told by the war minister
that the army was ready for war. Confident that the army was
ready to strike at a moment's notice, and having given the
Austrian government the assurance of 'Nibelungen fidelity', the
Kaiser went on his traditional cruise in the North Sea, the
chancellor, Bethmann Hollweg, retired to his estates at Hohen-
finow and Moltke, who had not even returned to Berlin,
continued his cure.

Excitement in the week following the murder of the Archduke was very high. The army was confident that their war plan
would succeed. Moltke had argued that the summer of 1914 saw
Germany at a considerable advantage. German artillery was
superior to the French and the Russians who lacked howitzers.
The German rifle was superior to those of the enemy. The

French army was in a state of disorganization as a result of the new military service law. But by the sixth of July the excitement was giving way to disappointment and even resignation. The exodus from Berlin continued. The quartermaster general, Waldersee, went on leave, as did the head of the 2nd department who was partly responsible for mobilization. Moltke remained in Karlsbad.

On 27 July the Austrian government prepared the declaration of war on Serbia which was delivered on the following morning. Meanwhile the vacationers had returned to Berlin, Moltke on the night of the 25th, Waldersee and Tirpitz on the following day and the Kaiser on the 27th. Immediately the general staff prepared a note for the foreign office to be handed to the Belgian government, which claimed that as the French were about to march through Belgium to attack Germany, the German army would be obliged to march through Belgian territory. Thus Moltke and the staff made it clear that they hoped and believed that the war between Austria and Serbia would lead to a European war.

By the 29th the war minister and the general staff chiefs were pressing for war, arguing that the longer Germany waited the less would be the chance of success for the Schlieffen plan which depended on surprise and speed. The chancellor and the foreign office, although sympathetic to this point of view, wanted to wait for a while, so that Russia would appear as the aggressor. Moltke summed up his position in a memorandum to the chancellor on the 29th in which he concluded with the words: 'The further our neighbours' preparations go, the sooner their mobilization will be finished. The military situation will thus worsen from day to day, and may, if our potential opponents continue undisturbed to prepare for war, have disastrous consequences for us.' He was particularly worried about the report from the Prussian military attaché in Petersburg, who suggested that if Germany did not hurry up with its mobilization Russia could well defeat Austria before Germany had even moved, and then the eastern front would be left defenceless.

On the following day Moltke told the Austrian military attaché that Austria should mobilize against Russia, and that Germany too would mobilize in support of Austria. The attaché at once related this message to Vienna, and when it landed on Conrad's desk he read it to Foreign Minister Berchtold who made his famous remark: 'Who rules: Moltke or Bethmann?' Indeed Moltke had jumped the gun. News that Russia had mobilized did not reach Moltke until 7 a.m. on the 31st, yet the day before he had informed the Austrians that Germany would mobilize, and for the German army mobilization meant war. Once the decision to mobilize had been made the army urged that the war should begin as soon as possible. On 1 August there were rumours that Britain and France might remain neutral and that the war might be localized, but Moltke insisted that the war plan which envisaged a swift attack on France could not possibly be changed. He was getting increasingly nervous with the prevaricating attitude of the Kaiser and Bethmann, and on 2 August he told Tirpitz that it was about time that the general staff took over the political control of the Reich. But on the following day such anxieties were allayed. Germany declared war on France.

In the July crisis of 1914 the German military played a decisive role. Military leaders had been pressing for a preventive war for decades, and they were now determined that the golden opportunity offered by Sarajevo should be exploited and not frittered away as similar situations had been in the past. In 1909 Moltke had urged the Austrians to be firm in the Balkans, and had guaranteed German support even if this were to lead to a European war. For years the general staff had insisted that Russian mobilization would automatically lead to war, although there was no evidence for this assertion. Moltke's telegram to Conrad on 30 July was one of the decisive steps towards war. Most serious of all Germany had only one war plan which meant that a war would be on a European scale and could not be localized and contained. This meant that the German government had no freedom of action as the crisis mounted, and had the diplomatists seriously wanted to avoid a large-scale war there was little that they could have done about it. The army was certainly not solely responsible for the war, but they played a decisive part in bringing it about.

At first the German war plan seemed to work smoothly, and there was widespread optimism that France could indeed be defeated within six weeks. The field army of 84,000 officers and

2,314,000 NCOs and men was rapidly and efficiently mobilized. The railway system was used to maximum efficiency, transporting over 2,000,000 men, 400,000 tons of war material and 118,000 horses in less than three weeks. On 2 August Luxemburg was occupied, and two days later the German army crossed the frontier of Belgium. The French army seriously underestimated the strength of the German right wing, considering it impossible for reserves to attack with the field army, and thus northern France, through which the right wing was to sweep, was left almost empty of defending troops. The first sign that everything was not going exactly according to plan was the attack on Liège which took rather longer than had been anticipated. The army had hoped that the Belgians would capitulate rather than fight against hopeless odds, and they had not brought up their heavy artillery to Liège. The Belgian defence of the city was determined, and it was not until the 42-cm and 38-cm artillery was employed that the city fell on 16 August.

With the fall of the fortresses at Liège the German army continued its advance with little opposition. By 20 August Brussels was reached, and on the same day the spearhead of the German army crossed the Belgian border into France. By 25 August most of Belgium was occupied, the German right wing was surging forward and the left flank had withstood the French attacks and had managed to make substantial gains. The mood at German headquarters was understandably jubilant, and the chief of the operations staff, Colonel Tappen, announced that 'the whole thing will be over within six weeks'.

The German 1st Army, on the extreme right flank, continued its advance towards the north-west of Paris, where it was to begin its swing to the south and east so that Schlieffen's dream of a giant Cannae would be realized. The British expeditionary force was defeated at Le Cateau on 26 August, as was the French 6th army at Péronne on the Somme two days later. The allies had failed to stop the German right wing, and now withdrew to the south and the south-east to avoid being outflanked. On 2 September the German High Command (OHL) ordered the right wing to pursue the allies and not to continue the advance towards Paris. Meanwhile the French, realizing the growing weakness of the German right wing due to supply problems and exhaustion, began preparations for a counter-attack.

The German 1st army under von Kluck ignored the OHL's commands to turn south and continued towards Paris in an attempt to outflank the British, but von Kluck succeeded merely in further exhausting his troops and in messing up von Moltke's changed plans. By 5 September Kluck was talking of taking Paris which was a mere 30 miles away, but the German army was by now tired and under-strength. Two corps had been sent to eastern Prussia to stem the Russian advance. Several divisions had been forced to remain behind to continue the sieges of Maubeuge and Antwerp. The troops were exhausted after a long march in hot weather and often with fierce fighting – the 1st Army had covered nearly 400 miles in under three weeks. There were no reserves to give extra weight to the attack. But the most serious danger of all was created by Moltke's strategic mistake in shortening the sweep of the German right wing. The German army now ran a serious risk of being outflanked, for it was marching straight into a sack, the opening of which stretched from Paris to Verdun roughly along the line of the Marne. On the left near Paris was the French 6th army and the British, on the right the 3rd, 4th and 9th armies. As long as the French line from Verdun to Nancy and Toul could hold off the German advance from Alsace-Lorraine, the French position was far from hopeless, although the country was under very great strain indeed.

On 4 September Joffre gave the order for a counter-offensive to begin on the 6th, a desperate attempt to close the sack around the German right wing. Moltke seems to have been unaware of the seriousness of the situation, and von Kluck, ignoring orders once again, pushed on south over the Marne, thus reaching deeper down into the sack. On 6 and 7 September Kluck had to scramble back to avoid being trapped, but as the Entente pushed forward over the Marne the 1st army was badly exposed and was threatened with being crushed between the French 6th army and the British. By 9 September the Germans were in a perilous situation. Casualties had been very high, and there were no reserves. The commander of the 2nd army, Bülow, ordered a retreat to the Aisne, having consulted with the representative of the OHL at the front, Colonel Hentsch. This left Kluck's 1st army in a hopeless situation, and he too was forced to retire to the Aisne line. Only the failure of the French and British to exploit the gap between the German 1st and 2nd armies saved the Germans from the danger of a break through their front. In the next few days the Germans retreated to take up defensive positions on the Western Front. The Schlieffen plan had failed and the war of attrition began. On 14 September Moltke was replaced by Falkenhayn as chief of the general staff.

Falkenhayn, who remained war minister as well as being chief of the general staff, was well known as a tough and outspoken man, and was quite different from Moltke who was often plagued with doubts and fears. In spite of the serious reverses in France Falkenhayn still believed that the war would be decided in the west, and therefore began planning for a new offensive. As this was to take place with exhausted and badly depleted forces it was even more risky and hazardous than was Schlieffen's original plan, and had even less chance of success. After the failure of numerous limited offensives on the Western Front the 'race for the sea' began. By the beginning of October most of the fighting was on the northern sector of the front between the Oise and the Channel coast. Both sides tried to outflank the other in an attempt to gain the initiative and break the deadlock of trench warfare. Neither side succeeded, but in the course of these operations the Germans were able to seize Antwerp, Lille, Bruges, Ghent and Ostende.

Unable to outflank the French in the 'dash for the sea', Falkenhayn now attempted to punch a hole in the Entente's lines around Ypres in the hope of then being able to roll up the front. The battle began on 20 October from La Bassée to the coast. German losses, particularly in the reserve corps, were dreadful, and the offensive ground to a halt. At the same time Conrad was making ceaseless demands for reserves from the Western Front to help stem the Austrian retreat from southern Poland. Falkenhayn still insisted that the Western Front must have priority, and on 4 November ordered that the attacks should be continued so that Ypres could be captured and Dunkirk used as a German U-boat base. The second battle of Ypres lasted from 10 to 24 November. The French and British defence of Ypres was determined and unwavering, German losses were very high, particularly at the senseless attack at Langemarck which was to become part of right-wing mythology after the war. There was a serious shortage of munitions. The troops suffered severely from typhoid and dysentery. Above all the battle of Ypres showed the great superiority of the defence in trench warfare and the extraordinary difficulty of punching a hole in the opposing line. Thus by the end of 1914 the two sides faced each other from their trenches from the Channel to the Swiss border.

In the east the Germans had been somewhat more successful. With the rapid advance of the Germany army in the west, Britain and France urged Russia to mount an offensive on East Prussia in the hope that this would force the Germans to move more troops from the Western to the Eastern Front. The Russian plan was for a two-pronged attack on the German forces in East Prussia from the north-east and the south of the Masurian lakes. The 1st Russian army under Rennenkampf pushed the Germans under Prittwitz back across the Vistula, but Rennenkampf did not exploit this situation and the Germans were able to retreat to defensive positions in good order. But Prittwitz also panicked, fearing that he would not be able to hold off Rennenkampf. The junkers were filled with alarm that the whole of eastern Prussia might be lost, and demanded action. The OHL replaced Prittwitz by Hindenburg and Ludendorff, and sent reinforcements from the Western Front so that the remainder of eastern Prussia might be won back from the Russians. Hindenburg and Ludendorff's plan was to exploit Rennenkampf's hesitation by attacking the Narev army of Samsonov to the south, leaving only scant forces on the defensive against Rennenkampf. In fact during the battle there was only one cavalry division opposing the Russian Njemen army. The battle of Tannenberg began on 23 August. By 28 August the Russian Narev army was trapped in a pincer movement by the German 8th army. Seventy-five per cent of the Russian troops, some 120,000 men, were lost. The remainder retreated across the Narev.

There is no doubt that the battle was a masterly piece of military leadership. The weaknesses of the Russians had been brilliantly exploited and the battle was the 'Cannae' for which the general staff had hoped in the west. But like the original battle of Cannae it did not settle the campaign. Eastern Prussia had been saved for the time being, but the situation for the Central Powers in the east was far from satisfactory, particularly in Galicia where the Austrians were in serious difficulties. The most important aspect of the battle was that it created a myth. The very name suggested that it was a revenge for the defeat of the Teutonic knights in 1410. Hindenburg and Ludendorff were puffed up by chauvinist propagandists as the saviours of East Prussia and as infallible geniuses of the order of Hannibal or Moltke. As German hopes of victory in the west were dashed on the Marne, men looked to Hindenburg and Ludendorff to bring that victory which had so far eluded Moltke and Falkenhayn. Tannenberg was the most successful military operation of the First World War, but its military effects were limited. Its political and psychological effects, however, can scarcely be over-estimated.

Thus by the end of 1914 the Germans had met with some success in the east, whereas in the west they had become bogged down in a war of attrition. Falkenhayn realized that unless Germany was able to reach a separate peace with Russia there was little chance of defeating France. After the failure of the German offensive in northern Poland to bring victory in the east Falkenhayn argued that the only way to force the enemy to sue for peace was through limited operations which would gradually wear down Germany's opponents. Whereas Hindenburg and Ludendorff remained true to the Schlieffen concept of a war of annihilation, Falkenhayn argued for a skilfully planned war of attrition. He felt that Germany did not have the resources to fight the kind of war that Hindenburg and Ludendorff wanted. In this he was perfectly correct, but his own ideas were equally mistaken. Germany did not have the economic or human resources to fight a successful war of attrition against such overwhelming odds. Falkenhayn's attempts to solve this problem were intelligent and ingenious, but in the final analysis there was nothing he could do to alter this fact.

Falkenhayn believed that Germany should concentrate her efforts on the Western Front. Hindenburg and Ludendorff, supported by the Austrians, argued for a major offensive in the east which would lead to the defeat of Russia. But Germany and Austria did not have the resources for such an offensive, and

Falkenhayn only sent further reserves to the east when Russian successes in eastern Prussia and the Carpathians threatened the position of the Central Powers.

In January 1915 Falkenhayn was forced to give way to the demand for an offensive in the east. The Austrians were hardly able to hold the Carpathian front. Some success was needed in the east to relieve the pressure on the Habsburg monarchy which was threatening to fall apart under the stress of war, to dissuade the Italians and Rumanians from joining the Entente and to persuade the Bulgarians to support the Central Powers. A plan was thus developed by Hindenburg and Ludendorff along with Conrad to attack the Russians on the two fronts, the Carpathians and East Prussia. On 20 January the Kaiser decided that four army corps of reserves should be sent to the east for this offensive.

From the outset there was a misunderstanding between the OHL and the 'Easterners' over the aims of this operation. Falkenhayn saw the offensive as a means of relieving the pressure on the Eastern Front and strengthening the determination of the Austrians to continue the fight. Hindenburg, Ludendorff and Conrad aimed to smash the Russian army and secure a total victory. In fact the Austrian offensive in the Carpathians made very little headway, and the losses were terrible. Within a few weeks the Austrians lost 600,000 men, among them 100,000 dead. Russian losses were twice as high, but they stopped an Austrian breakthrough and kept up ceaseless counter-attacks.

To the north Hindenburg and Ludendorff were somewhat more successful, although a decisive victory eluded them. An attempt to encircle the Russian forces, as at Tannenberg, failed, and by 27 February the offensive had to be halted, although substantial gains had been made. The Russian army kept hammering at the Austrian front, so that the OHL was obliged to agree to a further offensive, this time at Gorlice, to ease the pressure on the Austrians who had suffered so much in the recent offensive. Conrad still dreamed of a gigantic encirclement of the Russian army, but Falkenhayn insisted on a more limited objective, a break through the Russian line at Gorlice. This offensive, led by General von Mackensen, whose chief of staff was Colonel von Seeckt, was a considerable success. The

Russian lines from the Carpathians to the Vistula were broken, and the German and Austrian armies advanced some 120 miles. This placed the Central Powers in a favourable strategic position for further operations in Poland, and the Austrian front in the Carpathians was relieved of the almost unbearable pressure. Falkenhayn determined to continue the attack in the east across the San, and sent further reinforcements from the Western Front. By keeping up the momentum of the advance he hoped that Russia might be forced into making a separate peace, so that then the full weight of the German army could be exerted on the Western Front. By the end of June Mackensen had captured Lemberg and won back most of Galicia, but Russia was far from defeated. The Entente decided at Chantilly in July to mount offensives on the Western Front to relieve the pressure on Russia. Falkenhayn was now forced to think of moving troops from the Eastern Front to the West, and was also concerned with the situation in the Balkans where German troops were badly needed. But he decided to conclude operations in the east before moving these reserves.

The operation proposed was a pincer movement, Mackensen's army moving up from Galicia, Hindenburg's down from the Narev, trapping the Russians along the line from Warsaw to Brest-Litovsk. Once again there were bitter arguments between the OHL and High Command East. Falkenhayn wanted the pincer movement on a limited front; Hindenburg and Ludendorff pressed for a massive operation on a broad front. Although Falkenhayn now felt that it might be possible to defeat Russia, rather than just seriously weakening her, he could not spare the reserves from the west needed to implement Hindenburg's grandiose plan. Falkenhayn's plan was eventually adopted, and was a tremendous success. Warsaw and most of Congress Poland was taken, as were Lithuania and Courland. On 27 August the Germans established the General Government of Poland and began the systematic exploitation of Polish resources. But the operation did not bring peace with Russia. Although the Russians lost 750,000 men, on 3 August the Tsar turned down a proposal for a separate peace.

With the offensive in the east Falkenhayn was unable to mount any major offensives on the Western Front. Attempts by the French in the Champagne and the British in Flanders to break through the German lines were failures. Losses were exceedingly high, the gains minimal. Falkenhayn was thus confident that the Germans could withstand any further attacks of this nature, and was prepared to send further troops to the east where the offensive was so successful. The Anglo-French offensive in Artois in May and June was massive and gave Falkenhayn some anxious moments, but the Entente lost nearly twice as many men as the Germans and by the middle of June the offensive had to be called off.

By the summer of 1915 the relative strength of the Entente was growing, Falkenhayn had to be forced to stop the offensive in the east and was unable to mount a fresh attack in the west, the U-boat war had not proved successful and the Allied blockade of Germany was beginning to hurt. The operation against Serbia was successful, opening up the route to Turkey and enabling supplies to reach the Turkish army which was being hard pressed at Gallipoli. But the campaign showed that there were serious differences between the Germans, the Austrians and the Bulgarians, and the improvement in the overall situation of the Central Powers was not nearly as great as had been hoped. The operation showed that the Central Powers were able to achieve considerable limited successes, but that they were not strong enough to force a decision on either the Eastern or the Western Front.

In September 1915 the Germans entered Wilna, but the offensive of Hindenburg and Ludendorff into the Baltic states did not result in the capturing of as many Russian prisoners as they had hoped, nor could it be used as the first stage of a further massive operation against the Russians that would lead to victory in the east. A series of further operations pushed the Russians back, so that the Central Powers controlled vast areas in the east, but the decisive victory over the Russian army for which they had been hoping eluded them.

Falkenhayn had assumed that the Entente was not in a position to mount any further large-scale offensives in 1915, but in this he was mistaken. In September two massive attacks were launched, in Artois and in the Champagne. Although the Entente made minimal gains, the OHL was obliged to send troops from the east and from Serbia in order to provide the necessary reinforcements to the badly battered German lines. It was a serious mistake by the Entente that they began their offensive at a time when the Germans had completed their operations in the east, and were thus able to spare the reserves. By the end of 1915 the Germans had had considerable success. They had occupied large areas in the east, the allied attack on the Dardanelles had been driven back, Serbia had been defeated and Bulgaria had joined the Central Powers. In the west the Entente's attacks had been repulsed. But these successes led to exaggerated hopes. Although the Germans were killing more Frenchmen and Englishmen than they were losing, the Entente was far from being seriously worn down by this war of attrition. In the east the Russians had not been defeated, and the army could not therefore be used to fight the final victory in the west.

In spite of this relative success then, Falkenhayn had to find some new strategic plan that would bring Germany nearer to victory. Hindenburg and Ludendorff still believed that a decisive victory in the east was possible, if only Falkenhayn would give them the reserves. They were supported by the Austrian chief of staff Conrad, who constantly pestered Falkenhayn for more reserves so that he could launch a full-scale offensive in northern Italy which would force Italy to sue for peace, so that then a joint attack on the Western Front could be mounted. The reasoning behind the positions of both Conrad and the High Command East was faulty. Conrad was willing to admit that he needed a victory in Italy more for psychological reasons than for any genuine strategic significance. He was afraid that without some successes the Austrian army would fall apart. Hindenburg and Ludendorff totally failed to realize how hard pressed were the German troops in the west, and how serious the situation had been in Artois and the Champagne. A campaign such as they envisaged could not be operationally mounted without considerable reserves, and these reserves would largely have to come from the Western Front. It was not until they were appointed to the OHL that they realized that the reserves could not be spared, and thus they implicitly had to admit that their vicious attacks on Falkenhayn had been unjustified.

But Falkenhayn's arguments were no better. He was correct in rejecting the arguments of Hindenburg and Ludendorff, but his own strategy of attrition was based on equally faulty principles. Germany had done extremely well in using its human and economic resources to the full, but in the long run it was bound to reach the limits of its resources long before the Entente, and all the desperate attempts in the next three years to overcome this hard fact were doomed to fail.

Thus Falkenhayn was to realize that a decisive victory in the east was not possible, and that limited operations on the Western Front were not likely to break the will of the Entente. He knew that a breakthrough, such as Mackensen and Seeckt had achieved at Gorlice, was not possible in the west. He therefore began to think in terms of a new strategy which was, in a sense, a compromise between the Easterners' 'strategy of annihilation' and his own 'strategy of attrition'. He hoped that such a strategy would give Germany the initiative and exploit the realities of the situation to maximum advantage. This new strategy was ingenious and imaginative, but it also ignored certain essential considerations. True to his western strategy, Falkenhayn proposed a massive attack on the fortresses of Verdun. The idea was that the French would send all their reserves to defend Verdun, where they would be destroyed by constant bombardment and limited operational attacks. The French army would be drawn into Verdun and destroyed in this trap. For such a plan to work he insisted that the fortress did not have to be taken, but rather that it should be constantly threatened so that more and more Frenchmen would be drawn into the trap.

The attack on Verdun was part of a wider strategy. Falkenhayn was expecting the Entente to mount a fresh offensive near Arras in the spring. If the Verdun offensive worked this offensive would be left to the less experienced British troops. He hoped that the attack would be repulsed, and that a counterattack might lead to a break in the Entente's lines. Four weeks after the beginning of the Verdun offensive he hoped that unrestricted submarine warfare would begin which, combined with the difficulties at Arras, would lead Britain to realize the hopelessness of their scheme to defeat Germany. Thus the aim of this strategy was chronically to weaken France and to force Britain to sue for peace.

This plan had a number of serious flaws. Britain, France and

Russia were nowhere near the end of their strength as Falkenhayn believed, and although they had all suffered terrible losses, their reserves and their determination to continue the war were still very great. The belief that the submarines could inflict such serious damage on Britain was illusory. The Verdun concept itself was a reversal of the experience of the war up until that time, for it was the attacker rather than the defender who had the heaviest casualties. It was therefore unlikely that the action, even if it was successful, would have the effect that Falkenhayn hoped. Most serious of all, there was considerable ambiguity in the plans for the attack on Verdun. Local army commanders were determined to take the fortresses rather than menace them, and this was not merely the result of personal ambition but of the failure by Falkenhayn to make his intentions perfectly clear.

The attack on Verdun was begun on 21 February, but in spite of many initial successes it soon threatened to become another Ypres. The German strategy degenerated into a bloody slogging match, and the losses on both sides were appalling. Falkenhayn had clearly failed, but he refused to call off the operation, fearing that such an admission of failure after such high losses would have serious consequences. German losses at Verdun were so high that they were unable to exploit any weaknesses in the French lines at other points on the front. Indeed the Entente's offensive on the Somme placed the German forces in a very serious predicament. Kitchener's army was far more formidable than the Germans had imagined, and the first successful use of tanks by the British army was a new and serious threat. In the east the Brussilov offensive threatened to destroy the Austrian army, which lost 200,000 prisoners and had to evacuate southern Galicia and the Bukowina. The Italians were also successful against the Austrians, and in August 1916 they captured Görz. Shortly afterwards Rumania declared war on the Central Powers.

Militarily the initiative was now clearly in the hands of the Entente. Politically the position of the Central Powers was dangerously weak. The Austrian army was in disarray, there had been mass desertion, and the war minister, Krobatin, feared that a catastrophe was imminent. In Germany there were the first political strikes against the war, clear indication that the political truce of August 1914, the *Burgfrieden*, was wearing extremely thin. On the extreme right the pan-Germans and the heavy industrialists were planning to overthrow Bethmann Hollweg and Falkenhayn who they felt were standing in the way of a victory which would enable them to realize their imperialist aims for a German-dominated Europe. These aims could not be achieved without a victory, and thus it was natural that the right should look to Hindenburg and Ludendorff, the victors of Tannenberg and popular idols, as the obvious successors to Falkenhayn whose strategy had clearly failed.

Falkenhayn had many enemies. In the army he was not particularly popular. Chief of the general staff at fifty-two, he was a younger man than any of the army commanders, and was regarded as something of a careerist and pusher. The failure of his strategy confirmed suspicions that he did not have the abilities needed for his position. Among the politicians he was equally unpopular. As war minister he had been haughty and disdainful, his name closely associated with the excesses of Zabern in 1913 when the army had acted in a brutal fashion against innocent civilians. Bethmann Hollweg also favoured the replacement of Falkenhayn by Hindenburg, hoping that his appointment would bring about a separate peace with Russia and that he would then complete the victory in the west with unrestricted submarine warfare. Hindenburg was still the man of Tannenberg, Falkenhayn of Verdun. Hindenburg's appointment would paper over the divisions in German society, silence the criticisms of the left, placate the chancellor's pan-German critics and restore the *Burgfrieden*. Such were Bethmann Hollweg's calculations. His determination to oust Falkenhayn was strengthened by the latter's refusal to approve the appointment of Hindenburg as supreme commander on the Eastern Front, and he shared the view of the war minister, General Wild, that such perversity on the part of the chief of general staff was robbing the Central Powers of the chance of a victory against Russia.

Criticism of Falkenhayn continued to mount. The foreign office was provided with ample ammunition against him by Ludendorff, who was actively engaged in trying to secure the appointment of Hindenburg. The military cabinet supported Hindenburg. The army commanders on the Western Front were sharply critical of Falkenhayn's conduct of the Verdun offensive. The Kaiser continued to support Falkenhayn against his critics, but in July and August bitter complaints against the chief of the general staff came from all quarters. On 27 August news that Italy had declared war on Germany and that Rumania was about to join the Entente plunged the Kaiser into deep despair. He was momentarily convinced that the war was lost. At last he dropped his objections to the dismissal of Falkenhayn. On 29 August Hindenburg and Ludendorff were appointed to the High Command.

This decision was the result of both military and political considerations of profound importance. Militarily it was a rejection of Falkenhayn's *Ermattungsstrategie* and an affirmation of Hindenburg's *Vernichtungsstrategie*. Victory in the east would, it was hoped, be followed by a crushing blow in the west. Without such a decisive victory Germany would be unable to secure the extensive war aims of the ruling class, which were deemed essential not merely for economic advantage but to preserve the social *status quo*. The enormous popularity of Hindenburg which had been assiduously fanned by official propaganda had given him the stature of a national father-figure. United behind him the nation would achieve the 'Hindenburg victory' which would provide the answers to the acute social divisions which, under the strain of war, were threatening the whole structure of society. William II was painfully aware of the consequences of the appointment. By giving way against his better judgment to public clamourings he feared that he was conceding to 'democratic' forces which threatened the power of the crown. Hindenburg and Ludendorff were prepared to mobilize public opinion in a way which would have appalled Bismarck. Theirs was a radicalized and militarized form of Bismarck's bonapartism. It is precisely this complex interaction of military, political, social, and economic forces that makes the regime of Hindenburg and Ludendorff so important a stage in the course of German history since Bismarck.

If the Hindenburg victory were to be achieved there had to be a substantial increase in the production of war materials. Up until 1916 there had been little inclination to interfere with the workings of private capitalism because the war had been relatively successful for the Germans and the 'battle of materials' was only just beginning. Heavy industrialists, who had played an important part in securing the appointment of Hindenburg and Ludendorff, favoured a high degree of government planning which would strengthen their hands against the consumer goods industry, and lead to higher profits and an increased tendency to monopolization. Among the most politically active heavy industrialists was Hugo Stinnes who had been in touch with Hindenburg and Ludendorff since 1915. At the OHL Colonel Bauer forged the close links with heavy industry which were to be so important when Falkenhayn was dismissed. During the August crisis heavy industry chiefs kept Hindenburg and Ludendorff informed of their thinking, and after their appointment they were inundated with visitors such as Krupp, Duisberg and Rathenau.

Two days after his appointment to the OHL Hindenburg wrote to the war minister outlining his ideas on industry. He pointed out that faced with the almost limitless resources of the Entente powers Germany would have to increase industrial output drastically, but not at the expense of curbing the size of the reserves. As every man was needed at the front, women, children and the war wounded would have to do the bulk of the work, and only the highly skilled workers could be exempted from military service. Priority would have to be given to heavy industry. Hindenburg's aim was for a hundred per cent increase in the production of ammunition by the spring, and a threefold increase in the production of artillery and machine-guns. The army intended to use its authority under the law on the state of siege to militarize and coerce German labour. Hindenburg's proposals aimed at establishing control of the economy by the OHL and the large monopolies. The effects of the 'Hindenburg Programme' would be further to regiment and exploit the workers, to destroy many small companies, and to establish the hegemony of the huge heavy industrial firms. Bethmann Hollweg was well aware of the implications of these proposals, and was deeply concerned that the powers of the civilian government would be further curtailed by the OHL. He also feared that the militarization of the labour force would further depress the morale of the country, and that a major structural change in the economy would make it all the more difficult to restore peacetime prosperity once the war was over. Bethmann and his economic adviser Helfferich hoped for co-operation between capital and labour, rather than state intervention in the free workings of the economy. The war minister was also concerned about the proposals, for the OHL and the industrialists were quite determined that economic problems should no longer be controlled by the cumbersome bureaucracy of the war ministry, but should be directly under Hindenburg and Ludendorff and their economic adviser Colonel Bauer.

With the enunciation of the Hindenburg Programme there followed a period of often acrimonious discussion between its protagonists and its detractors. The OHL and the heavy industrialists called for the regimentation and militarization of labour, the concentration and monopolization of industry, substantial interference with the free workings of the economy and a maximization of war output. The war ministry and the civilian government, from the chancellor down, feared that such a drastic programme would create severe political dissent and labour unrest, and that it would cause a major structural change in German industry which would be extremely difficult to reverse after the war. In economic terms this was a struggle between monopoly capitalism and economic liberalism; politically a clash between authoritarian statism and liberal conservatism; militarily part of the long struggle between the general staff and the war ministry and between the civilians and the military.

As a result of these debates a number of compromise solutions were found. Although the OHL was not able to gain direct control over the economy or push through its most radical demands, its position was nevertheless significantly strengthened. A new institution, the war office (*Kreigsamt*), was created under General Groener to implement the Hindenburg Programme. Groener's responsibilities included the procurement and allocation of raw materials, the production of guns and ammunition, fuel, and the control of labour resources. Although nominally under the war ministry, Groener was subjected to constant interference and cajoling from the OHL. He also worked closely with the 'War Committee of German Industry', a representative body of heavy industry, to the considerable advantage of the monopolies. This new organization was in many ways unsatisfactory: a large bureacratic apparatus had been reshuffled in a new form with ill-defined fields of competence. But for heavy industry results were satisfactory. Profits soared. The great chemical combine BASF was given 400 million marks credit, not repaid until 1923 when the mark was almost valueless. Control over the large firms was minimal, so that far too many different types of guns were produced, causing endless trouble with ammunition and spares.

As a further part of the compromise Bethmann agreed to the dismissal of Wild as war minister in return for the OHL not pressing its most extreme demands for placing everyone from the age of fifteen into the army. Wild's successor was Stein, a man who was much more willing to follow the orders of Hindenburg and Ludendorff. Having secured the dismissal of Wild and having created the *Kriegsamt*, the OHL now devoted most of its energies to an Auxiliary Labour Bill (*Hilfsdienstgesetz*). This law passed the Reichstag in December, after it had been somewhat amended from the original drastic version of the OHL. All male Germans between the ages of seventeen and sixty were obliged to perform what was termed 'auxiliary labour' for the duration of the war. The definition of what kind of work was essential to the war effort and therefore qualified as 'auxiliary labour' was hopelessly vague. In practice it only applied to the working class and to some sections of the lower middle class. The bourgeoisie had no difficulty in showing that whatever they did was for the good of the war effort. A worker was not allowed to leave a job without permission, but a certificate could be obtained if the worker could show that 'suitable improvement of working conditions' would result from his changing employment. Fines and prison sentences could be given to workers who refused offers of employment. Workers' Councils were established under the terms of the bill. They were celebrated as a triumph by the unions, greeted as a step towards 'war socialism' by the social democrats and bemoaned by the right. But they were little more than empty tokenism, and were no more a step towards industrial democracy than were similar institutions under the Nazis. Workers' Councils were to be established in any firm which employed more than fifty workers, and their function was to 'promote a good understanding among the workers and between the workers and their employers'. Thus the law significantly reduced the workers' freedom of movement and greatly strengthened the position of the industrialists.

The *Hilfsdienstgesetz* failed to cure Germany's economic ills and could not enable the OHL to meet the unrealistic goals of the Hindenburg programme. By January 1917 the target figures had to be reduced, and even Ludendorff realized that with the chronic shortage of transport and coal no amount of regimentation could bring the desired result. Industry began to complain bitterly that the *Hilfsdienstgesetz* had been so watered down by the Reichstag that it was creating more problems than it solved, and the OHL soon joined in the chorus of complaints against the bill and against Groener's activities at the *Kreigsamt*, which they construed as being pro-labour. Eventually all Germany's economic ills were blamed on the bill: rising wages in some sectors, inflation, swollen profits, industrial unrest and shortages of materials and food. The OHL and the heavy industrialists made the ridiculous assertion that the bill had delivered the German economy into the hands of an irresponsible, unpatriotic and selfish working class. The bill was considered a disaster, and it would have to be changed.

Faced with the fact that their own measures had failed and that the *Hilfsdienstgesetz* had not solved Germany's problems, the OHL now decided to use it as a weapon in their struggle against Bethmann Hollweg. The OHL proposed using force, through the law on the state of siege, to settle any labour disputes and to keep the workers in order. Bethmann continued to urge caution and co-operation, but in the spring of 1917 the situation seemed to call for some rather more drastic measures. A series of events happened which made the crisis more threatening. The Russian February revolution was a tremendous encouragement to the left; the food situation was still very serious after the 'turnip winter' of 1916–17. On 7 April the Kaiser issued his Easter message which promised reform of the Prussian franchise, and in such a situation the contrast between the miserable conditions at home and the extensive war aims of the government was becoming all the more intolerable. The hopes and the disappointments of the working class were spontaneously expressed in a series of strikes throughout the country, and these strikes continued throughout the summer. Groener, who had gained the quite unjustifiable reputation of being the 'red general' by urging a degree of conciliation between capital and labour, came increasingly under fire from the OHL and heavy industry. He had also begun to make noises about controlling excessive profits in heavy industry which certainly did nothing to increase his popularity in that sector. So on 16 August 1917 Groener was given a new posting as a divisional commander.

Groener had been dismissed, but the OHL was unable to pursue its policy of outright repression against labour. By September 1917 the OHL had come round to a position very similar to that of Groener. They now argued in favour of co-operation with the unions, and discussed the possibility of a capital tax on war profits. The trade union leaders told Hindenburg and Ludendorff that they were anxious to stop any strikes or disturbances, and the OHL was impressed with these reassurances. Hindenburg still regarded strikes as tantamount to treason, but there is no doubt that his attitude towards the workers was beginning to mellow slightly. On the other hand the dismissal of Groener led to the virtual dismemberment of the *Kriegsamt*, and this in turn meant that many of its functions devolved to the commanding generals. They, in turn, were hardly sympathetic towards labour, and most of their economic activities were of a reactionary and repressive nature.

When preparations began for the German spring offensive in 1918 the OHL once again paid particular attention to economic affairs. They proposed to cut back profits and intervene in industry, and also to cut back wages and take further steps to regiment the workers. This attitude antagonized both capital and labour. They took an intransigent attitude towards the strikes in January, partly because there were already adequate reserves of ammunition. Acting in close liaison with the commanding generals, the OHL quickly suppressed the strikes. But this policy of 'one step forward, two steps back' since the dismissal of Groener was doomed to failure. No amount of regimentation or legislation could overcome the chronic shortage of men and materials which were the necessary result of a prolonged war. In spite of the *Hilfsdienstgesetz* and the Hindenburg Programme industrial production in Germany continued to drop, although it can be argued that it would have dropped even more sharply if these programmes had not been instigated. In 1916 industrial output was sixty-four per cent of the 1913 level, in 1917 it was sixty-two per cent and in 1918 fifty-seven per cent. The army became increasingly short of men and there was constant pressure to send more skilled workers to the front. As the situation grew steadily more hopeless during the summer of 1918 the OHL made wild accusations and demanded draconian measures, but their policies were now hopelessly unrealistic. Colonel Bauer even went as far as to say that 'we will win the war when the home front stops attacking us from behind'. Thus the failure of the OHL's economic policy provided rich material for the 'stab in the back legend' which was to play such a powerful ideological role in the Weimar republic.

Politically the main concern of the OHL in the first few months after the appointment of Hindenburg and Ludendorff was that Bethmann Hollweg might be tempted to accept a 'cheap' peace settlement. For this reason the OHL tried to force the chancellor to list his maximum and minimum war aims, but the chancellor was determined not to be tied down to a strict formula which might make negotiations exceedingly tricky. This was, of course, precisely the intention of Hindenburg and Ludendorff who wished to stop any peace feelers until the 'Hindenburg victory' had been won.

After a series of complicated negotiations a maximum war aims programme was agreed upon at Kreuznach on 23 April 1917. These aims included the annexation of the Baltic provinces; the military, political and economic domination of Poland; the annexation of a frontier strip to secure the Silesian industrial region; the exploitation of the oil resources in Rumania; in the west the annexation of the Flanders coast and Bruges, the annexation of Liège and southern Belgium, control of the Belgian railway system and military occupation of Belgium until 'effective treaties' were signed; Luxemburg to become part of the Reich; the annexation of Longwy-Briey and 'frontier rectifications' with France. Questions of the Balkans, Asia Minor and the colonies would be discussed at a later date. Bethmann agreed with these aims, and they accorded with his own thinking on war aims since September 1914, but he was reluctant to make an open declaration of war aims which might have an unfortunate propaganda effect on the Entente and might antagonize Germany's allies. Unlike the OHL, Bethmann was just as interested in indirect as direct annexations. Thus the quarrel between the chancellor and Hindenburg was tactical rather than fundamental.

On 17 and 18 May a conference was held with the Austrians at Kreuznach, and Bethmann managed to gain the Austrian government's consent to the OHL's war aims. It was clear that such a policy would make a separate peace with Russia impossible, unless Russia were totally defeated. Therefore on 16 June the German government published a declaration in the *Norddeutsche Allgemeine Zeitung* saying that the Petrograd formula for a peace without annexations and contributions did not stand in the way of peace between the Central Powers and Russia. Ludendorff thought this was going too far, and was not entirely convinced that Bethmann still intended to respect the Kreuznach agreement.

The OHL quarrelled with Bethmann not only over economic policy and war aims in the east, but also over western policy, particularly the question of Belgium. Hindenburg and Ludendorff were determined to exploit the resources of Belgium to the full. The OHL suggested that rations for workers could be reduced in Belgium so that workers would be forced to come to Germany to help the Hindenburg programme. They further demanded 200,000 Belgian workers to work behind the German lines, which was not actual deportation and therefore was not a flagrant violation of international law. Bethmann tried to have the best of both worlds. He wanted to win over the Flemish Belgians for a policy of close association with Germany, but he was not wholly averse to the idea of deporting workers. The OHL won their case by October 1916. Belgian workers were rounded up in camps and then deported to Germany as 'volunteers'. Indeed more Belgians were deported than German industry was able to absorb, and so the OHL demanded the deportation of machinery and raw materials rather than men. They bitterly attacked the General Governor of Belgium, General Bissing, for not exploiting the country to the full, and they tried to bring Belgium under the direct control of the OHL. This they were unable to do, and the realization that Belgium, however much it was exploited, could not provide the answer to Germany's problems made the OHL all the more bitter and frustrated.

Bethmann's belief that some political concessions would have to be made to lessen the domestic political tensions which had greatly intensified as the war continued, was bitterly opposed by the OHL. Hindenburg was tempted by the idea of ousting Bethmann and establishing a military dictatorship, as the extreme right – the Adlon Group – demanded. Bethmann proposed a reform of the Prussian franchise, which was long overdue. He won over the Kaiser to this view, and did not inform the OHL of his intentions. Thus the Kaiser's Easter message caught the OHL by surprise and was greeted with howls of protest. For Ludendorff it was 'a kow-tow to the Russian Revolution' and a pathetic gesture of appeasement, when force and the firm hand were what was needed. Colonel Bauer remarked that the best answer to universal suffrage was machine-guns. The OHL fought a bitter and prolonged battle against the reform of the franchise, but the most they could do was to make sure that the issue was not finally decided until after the war. At that time Bauer hoped to be able to use his machine-guns against the democrats, but by a supreme irony it was the German social democrats who were to use the machine-guns against the socialists.

Militarily the position of Germany in August 1916 was far from satisfactory. The Verdun offensive had failed, and the best that could be expected on the Western Front was that the line could be held against further attacks by the Entente. The strain on the Western Front was such that there were no reserves available for a further offensive in the east. Thus Hindenburg and Ludendorff were forced to admit in a memorandum of 22 November 1916 that the war was a war of attrition, or in Ludendorff's phrase a war 'of exhaustion', and that until there was a significant change in the situation there could be no further major offensive operations.

The OHL hoped to find a way out of this *impasse* by unrestricted submarine warfare. This issue was discussed by Hindenburg and Ludendorff almost immediately on their appointment to the OHL. At a Conference in Pless they suggested that unrestricted submarine warfare should not be commenced before the situation in the land war had become more stable.

First Rumania had to be defeated before troops could be withdrawn from the east to meet a possible threat from Holland and Denmark who might join the Entente if unrestricted submarine warfare were to begin. The chief of the admiralty staff Holtzendorff and the state secretary of the admiralty Capelle both argued that unrestricted submarine warfare should begin at once, and they attempted to show by highly dubious statistics that Britain could be defeated by the end of the year if only submarines were employed at once. Helfferich and German Secretary of State Jagow argued that by bringing America and possibly the neutrals into the war, Germany was likely to be defeated. Bethmann Hollweg made a serious mistake at Pless in that he accepted Hindenburg's arguments that from the military point of view the time was not yet suitable for unrestricted submarine warfare. He thus ignored the highly important political issues involved and left it to the OHL to decide if and when unrestricted submarine warfare should begin.

The admiralty were well aware that the OHL was the decisive factor in the decision, and an intensive campaign was mounted to convince Hindenburg and Ludendorff that the unrestricted submarine war should begin as soon as possible. By the middle of September 1916 they seem to have succeeded. But although the OHL was convinced that unrestricted submarine warfare should be used, they still insisted that the land war had first to be stabilized. By 6 December 1916 the Central Powers had entered Bucharest, and the military objections to unrestricted submarine warfare which the OHL had raised at Pless no longer held good. Hindenburg therefore began to press the Kaiser for a timetable which would state exactly when unrestricted submarine warfare could begin. Bethmann tried to ward off these attempts and at the same time pursue his own political chimera, the 'third way' – an extension of submarine warfare which would not necessarily bring America into the war. The chancellor's peace move was thus designed to provide the diplomatic cover for stepping up the submarine war, whereas Hindenburg wanted to step up the submarine war to stop the peace move. Holtzendorff, who had some concerns about America entering the war, and thus some sympathy for Bethmann's position, now fully supported Hindenburg and Ludendorff. But Holtzendorff would not attack Bethmann directly, preferring to hide behind the backs of Hindenburg and Ludendorff. It was not until January 1917, when he was told by Admiral Scheer, the chief of the high seas fleet, that he no longer enjoyed the confidence of the navy, that he finally screwed up his courage to demand of the chancellor that unrestricted submarine warfare begin on 1 February. Hindenburg, Ludendorff and Holtzendorff were now determined that unless Bethmann agreed to their demands then he would have to be removed. On 9 January 1917 Bethmann arrived in Pless for the fatal meeting. Having agreed that the unrestricted submarine war was essentially a military question he had already thrown away his trump cards. Faced with the arguments of the OHL and the admiralty he could only remark, rather lamely: 'Yes, when success is on the horizon, we must act.' At a crown council meeting that evening the matter was settled in favour of unrestricted submarine warfare.

Having won this victory over Bethmann, the OHL was determined to press its advantage. On 10 January Hindenburg asked the Kaiser to dismiss Bethmann, saying that he was weak and indecisive and that the OHL found it impossible to work with him. For the moment the chancellor was saved, for it was argued that if he were to be dismissed at that time the seriousness of the rift over the issue of the unrestricted submarine war would become apparent, and the effect of the campaign might well be lessened. For the moment the OHL was prepared to accept these arguments.

Unrestricted submarine warfare was the third great *va-banque* play of the war. The Schlieffen plan, and the Verdun offensive had both failed. Now Hindenburg and Ludendorff made their own desperate attempt to secure the breakthrough which alone would enable Germany to gain her extensive imperialist objectives. In military circles Major Wetzell of the OHL was almost alone in warning of the enormous military and economic potential of America. Hindenburg and Ludendorff brushed such concerns aside. Admiral Capelle announced that every American transport to Europe would be sunk. In fact two million Americans arrived safely in Europe, and not a single troopship was sunk by submarines.

The OHL's victory over Bethmann Hollweg, and their demand that he be dismissed, made it perfectly plain that unless the chancellor had some major success in the next few months he would indeed be removed. In the course of the summer of 1917 Bethmann's luck deserted him. Unrestricted submarine warfare failed to bring Britain to her knees, and the chancellor had to bear much of the responsibility for this failure. His hopes for a separate peace with Russia after the February revolution were dashed. On the home front prices were rising at an alarming rate and the labour movement was becoming increasingly radical. By the end of June he was told that war credits were exhausted and that the debate in the Reichstag over new credits was likely to be stormy. Talk of reform of the Prussian franchise made him extremely unpopular in conservative circles. On 6 July the Catholic politician Erzberger declared that the military situation was precarious and that a peace initiative should be begun at once. The SPD pressed for acceptance of the Petrograd formula for peace without annexations or reparations. To the OHL this was all proof that the chancellor had lost control of the situation, and that he would have to be removed. They therefore began a massive campaign against Bethmann.

The OHL's intrigues against Bethmann Hollweg were long and devious. Gradually the Kaiser was forced into an intolerable position. It was obvious that the chancellor and the OHL could not work together, and no amount of administrative changes could alter this fact. If he dismissed Bethmann he would be giving way to open threats from the OHL that they would otherwise resign, and would therefore establish a dangerous precedent and undermine his own prerogatives as Kaiser. On the other hand the dismissal of Hindenburg and Ludendorff would create such a scandal and public uproar that it might seriously undermine the war effort, and it would make Bethmann's own position untenable. Eventually on 13 July 1917 Bethmann submitted his resignation just before Hindenburg and Ludendorff arrived in Berlin for a final showdown. The Kaiser was so relieved that this painful scene was avoided that he forgot for the moment that Bethmann had been hounded out of office by the OHL. Hindenburg and Ludendorff arrived in Berlin in time to give their approval to the appointment of a successor to Bethmann, Michaelis, even though they had not the slightest constitutional right to do so. The result was that a man became chancellor who had no desire to take the post and who, because of the circumstances surrounding his appointment, was opposed by most of the senior civil servants. The OHL had thus managed to secure the dismissal of the chancellor and the appointment of a successor. Its power was at its height.

Among the many issues which divided the OHL and Bethmann the question of the future of Poland was one of the most important. Hindenburg and Ludendorff wanted an 'independent' Poland – a euphemism for a Poland dominated by Germany – which would be willing in return for this spurious independence to provide troops for the Central Powers. Bethmann agreed with this in principle, but had a number of concerns: about the timing of any such declaration of independence which might imperil his peace move towards Russia, about the exact delineation of an 'independent' Poland, and about the particularly sensitive question of Austria's reactions to such German proposals. Hindenburg and Ludendorff had little sympathy for such niceties, and in September 1916 they set about trying to bully the Austrians into submission. They found themselves without their usual political support on this issue, as the conservatives favoured outright annexation of Poland to indirect domination. But the conservatives were effectively silenced, and Austrian concerns about their hold over the area of Poland centred on Lublin, which they controlled as occupying power, were brushed aside. On 5 November 1916 the proclamation of Polish independence was issued by the governors of Warsaw and Lublin.

On November 9 a call for Polish volunteers was published, but the response was minimal. Julian Marchlewski summed up the attitude of the Polish left: 'Today's improvisation on the Vistula by Hindenburg and Ludendorff is unique, a joke the likes of which the world has neither seen nor dreamed. An "independent" state with unknown frontiers, with an unknown government, with an unknown constitution and, oh horror, oh shame, a kingdom without a king!' Austrian fears that the Poles would realize with the publication of the request for volunteers that the declaration of independence was a hoax to obtain cannon fodder for the German army were soon confirmed. Demonstrations were held in Warsaw, and among the more frequent slogans were: 'Without a Polish government, no

217

Polish army' and 'We do not want to be German mercenaries, but Polish soldiers'.

'Independence' had failed and the rivalry intensified between Austria and Germany over Poland, each determined to strengthen their hold over the Polish 'condominium'. The OHL, realizing that its Polish policy was a failure, now tried to use it as a weapon against Bethmann, just as they used the failure of the *Hilfsdienstgesetz* as a stick to beat the chancellor. By the summer of 1917 the OHL argued that they had been presented with a *fait accompli* on the Polish question which they had resisted. Hindenburg and Ludendorff's attacks on the chancellor for the failure of a policy for which they were largely responsible make truly astonishing reading, and the government's attempts to defend itself against this onslaught were pathetic.

Bethmann tried to settle the differences with Austria at a conference at Kreuznach on 17 and 18 May 1917, where it was agreed that Germany should be given control of Poland, and Austria would be given Rumania, allowing the Germans substantial economic rights there. Austria was also obliged to agree to a customs union with Germany which would amount to economic control of the Dual monarchy by Germany. Attempts by the Austrians to wriggle out of this agreement and to revive the Austro-Polish solution were vehemently opposed by the OHL. But in the autumn of 1917 the Kaiser visited Rumania, and was so impressed with the sight of the mountains and oil fields of Campina that he immediately wanted to annex the country. The problem now was to win over the OHL to the Austro-Polish solution, which would have to be the necessary *quid pro quo* for German control of Rumania. This proved exceedingly difficult. Hindenburg argued that Poland was needed as a deployment area in the east, and that the Austro-Polish solution would strengthen Austria far too much. Eventually Hindenburg was prepared to accept the solution provided that the Austrians agreed to certain terms. These included far-reaching economic penetration of Poland by Germany, a German naval base on the Adriatic, control of the railway from Silesia to Hungary and Rumania, the expulsion of the Jews from the Polish frontier strip and unconditional support by Austria for all Germany's war aims. This brought the

OHL back in line with the thinking of the conservatives and the heavy industrialists on Poland, for they would never accept an 'independent' Poland, nor would they tolerate a Poland dominated by Austria. They were also supported by the Kaiser who told his ministers that Poland 'looks like the Jüterbog artillery ground', and that Austria should be hit with conditions that would 'really make their eyes roll'.

The Austrians were obliged to revise the Kreuznach agreement and accept the Austro-Polish solution as proposed by the German government, but as this was all done without even consulting the 'independent' Polish state it made a further mockery of the declaration of 5 November. Meanwhile the October revolution with its call for the self-determination of peoples helped to strengthen the desire and the determination for genuine Polish independence. The OHL's plans for 'frontier rectifications with Poland', which amounted to a further partition of Poland, were opposed by Foreign Minister Czernin as a barrier to a peaceful settlement in the east. But the Austrian foreign minister's attempts to undermine the OHL were all doomed to failure. As relations between Germany and Austria became increasingly strained, particularly during the negotiations for the treaty of Brest-Litovsk, Ludendorff began to insist that Germany could do without Austria. He told the Bundesrat committee on foreign affairs: 'We do not need Austria any more, Bulgaria no longer has any significance, and Turkey is a military burden. Our own strength is enough.' The German foreign secretary Kühlmann tried to find a middle way between the OHL's position, which by now had become violently anti-Austrian, and the Austrian version of the Austro-Polish solution, which would not allow for annexations by Germany of vast tracts of Poland. The solution he proposed was the indirect domination of Austria by means of economic and military alliances. The OHL replied to this tactic by stepping up its demands for frontier rectifications, and now called for the annexation of Dombrowa, which would leave Poland without adequate supplies of coal. Hindenburg and Ludendorff kept up this attack until the summer of 1918, by which time Austria was in such an advanced state of collapse that even the most enthusiastic supporters of the Austro-Polish solution were beginning to have serious doubts. The OHL then suggested a small Poland which would be forced to share the costs of the war, and which would accept the frontiers as drawn up by the OHL. The railway system would be under German control. But the defeat of the Central Powers put an end to these dreams and to the endless arguments between Austria and Germany over the Polish question.

The OHL's policy towards Poland was part of a wider eastern policy in which the Baltic provinces played a very important part. Hindenburg and Ludendorff's interest in this area dated back to the time when they were at *Oberkommando Ost*. Occupied Lithuania and Courland were under direct military administration, unlike the occupied areas of Poland and Belgium. As Ludendorff told Zimmerman: 'since they have taken Poland from me, I must find another kingdom for myself in Lithuania and Courland.' The OHL's plans for this kingdom was to drive the Russians, Latvians and Jews from the area and then settle Germans into 50,000 new farms. The Baltic provinces were to provide the vital link in the new frontier from Germany to the Ukraine, which would encircle Poland by shortening the frontier between Poland and Russia. Bethmann Hollweg agreed with these ideas in principle, but wished to grant the Baltic provinces formal autonomy while placing them under the closest possible military, economic and political control of Germany. The OHL then developed plans for the annexation of the provinces of Lithuania and Courland by setting up puppet regimes which would then appeal to the king of Prussia for protection. These ideas were accepted by the foreign office at a conference in Bingen held on 31 July 1917, and later approved by the new chancellor Michaelis. Shortly afterwards the two autonomous states were created, although the vast majority of the population were vehemently opposed to Germany.

With the extension of the Bolshevik regime to Livonia and Estonia, there was mounting pressure from the Baltic Germans for the German government to annex these two provinces. This idea was warmly supported by the OHL. Representatives of the Livonians and Estonians were therefore selected to send cries of help to the Kaiser to provide the excuse for military intervention. The Germans moved swiftly and by 23 February 1918 the provinces were occupied and the Baltic barons saved for the moment from being expropriated by the Bolsheviks.

Lithuania proved somewhat more difficult to annex. The Lithuanians had to be forced by the OHL with threats of outright annexation, or of being handed over to the Soviets, before they would agree to some of the German terms. After a somewhat pathetic gesture of defiance against Germany during the negotiations for the treaty of Brest Litovsk, it was agreed that Lithuania should become independent provided that the first act of the Lithuanian government would be to seek the 'protection' and 'support' of Germany, and thus renounce her independence. The Lithuanians simply had to bow to the inevitable. The other Baltic provinces had come under German control, Russia was unable to help, and the Entente regarded Lithuania as a Russian province and were therefore hardly interested. On 23 March Germany recognized the independence of Lithuania. It remained under German military control, and the Lithuanians were allowed no say in the government of their country.

Throughout the summer of 1918 discussions continued about the future of the Baltic. What were the exact relations between the provinces and Germany to be? What was the correct delineation of civil and military authority in the east? Who was to be king of Lithuania? Should the army control the University of Dorpat? Such questions became increasingly absurd as the situation on the Western Front deteriorated. Prince Max von Baden terminated the civil administration of the Baltic the day before revolution broke out in Berlin. But this was only the end of a chapter in the history of German attempts to dominate the Baltic.

But for all the importance of the Baltic and Poland, it was Russia which was the great stumbling block to the OHL's ambitions in the east. Without the defeat of Russia the east could not be reorganized under German control. The problem, however, was how could Russia's defeat be achieved. On their appointment to the OHL Hindenburg and Ludendorff realized that troops could not be spared from the Western Front, and that Falkenhayn's arguments against such a move were substantially correct. Things began to look much more promising with the February revolution in Russia, which was taken by the OHL as a sign that Russia was on the verge of collapse and that therefore troops could be removed from the east and sent to the

Western Front. But the Lvov-Miliukov government was determined to continue the war, and the German government, realizing that the establishment of bourgeois liberal government in Russia would strengthen her ability to continue the war, now decided to support the socialists in their bid for power. Thus the Lvov goverment, which had come to power largely because the Russian people were war weary, earned the implacable hatred of the Russian workers and peasants organized in the Soviets. The Bolsheviks were for peace, therefore Hindenburg and Ludendorff had no objection to arranging the return of Lenin and his revolutionary supporters to Russia from their exile in Switzerland. On the night of 10/11 April the emigrés passed through Germany with the blessing of the OHL. The intoxicating vision of a peace with annexations blinded Hindenburg and Ludendorff to the serious danger to Germany of a proletarian revolution in Russia.

At first it seemed that the calculations of Hindenburg and Ludendorff were correct. On 28 November the Russians asked for a general armistice, and on 22 December 1917 the Brest Litovsk conference opened. The OHL's representative at Brest Litovsk, Hoffmann, was given instructions to make the following demands of the Russian government: Germany was to annex Lithuania and Courland; Poland was to be closely associated to the Central Powers; the Russians were to evacuate Finland, Estonia, Livonia, Bessarabia, Eastern Galicia and Armenia; Germany was to reorganize the Russian transport system and to have close economic co-operation with Russia; Russia was to provide Germany with oil, grain and other raw materials 'at favourable prices'; and Russia was to pay compensation for prisoners of war held by the Germans. Both Kühlmann and the chancellor, Hertling, were concerned that these extensive demands could not in any way be reconciled with the notion of a peace without annexations and reparations, which the German government had accepted as a principle for purely propaganda reasons. When the Soviet delegation protested that the forcible annexation by Germany of eighteen Russian provinces could hardly be described as a 'peace of reconciliation' as the Germans quaintly called it, Hoffmann replied that as this was the result of appeals to the German government by the provincial governments, it was fully in accordance with the principle of the self-determination of peoples which the German government had agreed to respect. As Kühlmann supported Hoffmann's position on this issue the Soviet government had to face the very real prospect of having to break off negotiations. The OHL, although it had won acceptance for its views, was still furious at Kühlmann for his prevaricating attitude and his attempts to wrap up the real intentions of German policy in subtle diplomatic language. Thus during the adjournment of the conference the OHL mounted a massive attack on Kühlmann, accusing him of conducting the conference in a dilatory and complaisant fashion.

In a series of conferences and exchanges over eastern policy the OHL stepped up its attacks on Kühlmann and the foreign office, and Hertling desperately tried to restore some semblance of unity between the OHL and the civilians without which the German delegation when it returned to Brest Litovsk would be seriously weakened. Hindenburg and Ludendorff realized that for the moment they would have to put up with Kühlmann, so they concentrated their efforts on securing the dismissal of Valentini, the head of the civil cabinet, whom they regarded as an evil influence responsible for the leftward swing in domestic policies. Although the charges against Valentini were preposterous and though he enjoyed the confidence of the Kaiser, William was forced to ask for his resignation as Hindenburg and Ludendorff threatened to resign if he was not removed. Thus by dismissing Valentini at the behest of the OHL, and against his own better judgment, William II further weakened the position of the monarchy and gave way to the bonapartism of the OHL, who were using their power and popularity to secure their own authoritarian political ends. Indeed the OHL was able not only to get rid of Valentini, but also to name his successor, the arch-reactionary Berg. When it was rather too late the Crown Prince, who had played an important part in securing the dismissal of Valentini, woke up to the fact that he was helping to undermine the authority of the crown which he hoped to inherit. To Hindenburg and Ludendorff he said: 'You cannot demand of my father that he dismiss a statesman every five minutes just because you don't like him.'

When the negotiations resumed at Brest Litovsk it became immediately apparent that the differences between the Germans and the Soviets had become even greater during the interval. Hindenburg and Ludendorff argued that the Soviet delegation should be faced with the simple choice that either they accept German demands, or the armistice would be revoked. Kühlmann and Hertling managed to hold the OHL back for the moment, but it was Trotsky who made the next move by denouncing the German peace terms as imperialist and annexationist, ordering the demobilization of the Russian army – this was against the orders of Lenin and was countermanded by the Council of People's Commissars – and returning to Petrograd with the Soviet delegation. The OHL immediately demanded that the war should continue so that German peace terms could be secured and Poland and the Baltic provinces saved from the danger of Bolshevism. Kühlmann opposed this suggestion, for although he wanted to see the destruction of the 'centre of revolutionary pestilence' he did not believe that this was possible. He feared a long protracted guerilla war and the massacre of the Baltic barons. He further argued that without a large army of occupation a peace settlement dictated in this fashion would be meaningless. Külmann's hopes were for an alliance with the anti-Bolshevik forces in Russia, who would agree to satisfactory peace terms in return for help against a common enemy. These conflicting views were discussed at a crown council in Homburg during which the Kaiser supported the OHL, saying that Bolshevism was part of a world-wide Jewish conspiracy and that 'Bolsheviks are tigers, round them up, and shoot them'. Finally it was agreed that when the armistice ran out on 17 February 'police actions' should be carried out to secure 'law and order' in the occupied territories. The OHL was delighted with this outcome, because the term 'police action' was so vague that it was open to almost any interpretation, a fact which made Kühlmann exceedingly depressed.

On 17 February 1918 fifty-two German divisions began their advance eastwards. Dünaburg was reached on the first day, Pskov five days later, and on 1 March German troops entered Kiev. On 18 February the Central Committee agreed by a very narrow margin to accept German peace terms.

On 1 March negotiations began again in Brest Litovsk, but they were hardly worthy of the name. The Soviets had come to sign a treaty and not to negotiate. Kühlmann had already left for Bucharest to negotiate the peace treaty with Rumania. The result was a triumph for the OHL, and there was little trace of the foreign office's policy of indirect annexation. Lithuania, Courland and parts of White Russia and Poland were taken away from Russia. The Russians were to evacuate Estonia, Livonia and Finland. The Ukraine was to be recognized as a separate state by the Soviet government. The eastern Anatolian provinces and the districts of Ardahan, Kars and Batum were to fall under Turkish domination. Thus Russia lost one million square kilometres of territory with fifty million inhabitants. She lost ninety per cent of her coal mines, fifty-four per cent of her industry, thirty-three per cent of her railway system, thirty-two per cent of her agricultural land, thirty-four per cent of her population and virtually all her oil and cotton production. It is therefore hardly surprising that the OHL were satisfied for the time being and did not press their demands for an assault on Petrograd. But some politicians felt that the treaty was too generous to Russia. Among them was Gustav Stresemann.

While the treaty was being signed at Brest Litovsk another was being negotiated in Bucharest. This presented many extremely difficult problems. Questions of the relations between Austria and Germany and the future of Rumania and Poland were still not resolved. Kühlmann's schemes for a German-dominated *Mitteleuropa* were opposed by the OHL who were thinking in terms of an eventual war with Austria to settle the issue of control of central Europe, and were therefore not prepared to make any concessions to the Austrians. Hindenburg and Ludendorff wanted complete German control of the Rumanian economy, because Rumanian oil was deemed a military necessity, and also some concessions to Bulgaria on the Dobrudja to win her as a useful ally in the future struggle against Austria. At the same time the OHL was not prepared to make concessions to Austria in Poland which might have made their demands on Rumania more palatable to the Austrians. The ensuing negotiations were extremely complex, and the OHL was unable to achieve all its aims. The Dobrudja question was left unsettled, although Bulgaria did win back the area lost in 1913. Constanta did not become a German port as the OHL wished, but became a free port, although the distinction between the two was somewhat academic. Germany was able to make a profit of about 2½ billion marks by insisting that money to cover the new currency – the 'German lei' – be deposited in Berlin banks. Germans had the right of veto over every Rumanian ministry, and control over the railways, telegraph and post. An army of occupation remained. Rumanian oilfields were to be controlled by a consortium of the '3 D-banks' – the Deutsche Bank, Discontogesellschaft and the Dresdner Bank. All 'surplus' agricultural produce was to be delivered to the Central Powers. Up until the very last moment the OHL tried to torpedo the negotiations on the grounds that this peace was too weak, and the determination of Hindenburg and Ludendorff to remove Kühlmann was reinforced.

The OHL now mounted a vicious smear campaign on Kühlmann. He was accused of playing 'an American game of chance by the name of poker'. He had gone off duck shooting instead of negotiating with the Rumanians. A phoney picture was produced of him in a state of drunkenness, waving a champagne glass and accompanied by a notorious Bucharest whore. In the course of a libel suit that Kühlmann brought against the *Deutsche Zeitung* which printed these stories, it emerged that they had come from Kühlmann's chauffeur who was a paid agent of the OHL. Kühlmann was able to hold on, partly because these accusations were blatantly ridiculous and false, and partly because the Germans were not particularly successful on the Western Front, and therefore the OHL was obliged to be a little quieter than usual.

On 24 June 1918 Kühlmann spoke in the Reichstag on foreign affairs. It was not a particularly remarkable speech, and he was careful to conceal his differences with the OHL. But it contained a remark that without diplomatic discussions with the Entente it would not be possible to end the war by purely military means. This was greeted with howls of protest from the right, and the OHL at once seized the opportunity to go into action against Kühlmann. Hindenburg and Ludendorff let it be known that they had no doubts that a military victory was possible, and argued that Kühlmann's remarks had done much to undermine the fighting spirit of the army. Hindenburg and Ludendorff told the Kaiser that it was impossible for them to continue working with Kühlmann. Hertling's defence was very weak. On 8 July 1918 Kühlmann resigned, and his place was taken by Admiral von Hintze, who was suggested by Berg as he was a pan-German who enjoyed the confidence of the OHL. Hintze was in fact rather more of his own man than the OHL hoped. He continued Kühlmann's policies, but managed not to alienate the OHL. But then his task was so much easier. Kühlmann had to contend with the OHL at the height of its powers, Hintze was to witness the gradual waning and final collapse of the German army.

The treaties of Brest Litovsk and of Bucharest by no means ended the OHL's ambitions in the east. Indeed one of the most extraordinary episodes in the history of Hindenburg and Ludendorff's collaboration was their eastern policy in 1918. The basis for this policy was established at the Bad Homburg meeting of the crown council on 13 February 1918, in which it was decided to engineer 'cries for help' from the Baltic, Finland and the Ukraine so that the Germans would have a pretext for intervention. The Rada government of the Ukraine, which had no popular support and was severely threatened by the Bolsheviks, realized that it could not survive without help from the Germans, and therefore appealed for help on 15 February according to the Homburg formula.

The German advance into the Ukraine was very swift. General Groener, who was chief of staff to Field Marshal Eichhorn, used his unique understanding of the military use of the railways to maximum advantage. By 1 March the Germans entered Kiev, and the campaign gathered such momentum that by the end of April the Crimea was captured and in the following month the Germans seized control of Rostov and the Donetz basin. Within a few weeks the generals had carved out a gigantic empire in the east. The Ukraine was nominally under civilian control through Mumm von Schwarzenstein who was appointed diplomatic representative to the Rada. But in fact it was Groener who was in effective control. The main problem for Groener was that the Rada was utterly worthless, and was not even a workable marionette. He therefore negotiated with General Paul Skoropadsky, an immensely wealthy landowner, Tsarist officer and fervent anti-socialist, to organize a coup which would remove the Rada, undo the Rada's land settlement and establish an authoritarian and compliant regime. Skoropadsky agreed, muttering that it was better to 'sell cheaply to the Germans than to give everything away free to a lot of landless peasants'. On 3 May the new government was formed under Hetman Skoropadsky after a bloodless coup. The civilian government in Berlin was glad to see the last of the Rada, but was alarmed to see the army carrying out *coups* without any authority to do so. Hindenburg and Ludendorff were delighted with Eichhorn and Groener and congratulated them for their initiative.

But for all this success the results of the German occupation of the Ukraine were disappointing. They had gone there to get food and raw materials. In fact there was barely enough surplus to feed the occupying troops, and in spite of taking the Donetz basin 80,000 tons of coal per month had to be exported from Germany to the Ukraine to keep the railways running. The reason for this was the determined opposition of the Ukrainian people to the German occupation. This was met by the Germans with great brutality. Mass executions took place and villages were burned to the ground. The Ukrainians became even more determined to resist, while the Germans became increasingly frustrated and violent.

Politically the army favoured the anti-socialist groups such as the Cadets, the Don Cossacks and the Volga Cossacks even though they were sympathetic to the Entente. Regardless of Kühlmann's objections, the army delivered 11,000 rifles, 46 guns, 88 machine guns, 100,000 rounds of artillery ammunition and over a million rounds of rifle ammunition to the Cossack army and a subsidy of 15 million roubles. All this was part of the futile attempt to create a 'South Eastern Alliance' of Cossacks, Georgians and Ukrainians who would be anti-Bolshevik and pro-German.

German industrialists had long looked upon the manganese, oil, ores, cotton and wool of the Caucasus with greedy eyes, and firms such as Gewerkschaft Deutscher Kaiser, Albrecht and Co., and Siemens und Halske made repeated demands for the securing of economic interests in the Caucasus. Ludendorff was attracted by this idea, and would have liked to establish a German bridgehead to India, but for once he exercised some restraint. To the foreign office he wrote in unusually modest terms: 'I am afraid that we want too much and will end up with nothing.' But within a few weeks, by the beginning of June, the

OHL changed its attitude towards the Caucasus. It now agreed with heavy industry's assessment of the economic potential of the area, and was concerned that it might come under Turkish control. The OHL now proposed an 'independent' Georgia under German 'protection'. This would form the basis of a non-Slav, anti-Russian and pro-German federation, so that Germany would be able to contain Russia in future from its bases in Finland to the north and the Caucasus to the south. This policy succeeded in making the Turks so angry that the pro-German Enver Pascha threatened to resign, which would leave the field open to those Turks who seriously contemplated changing over to the side of the Entente. This threat brought even Ludendorff to his senses. But even the news that the economy of Georgia was so disrupted that there was nothing much to exploit, and if there was anything to exploit there was no means of transporting it, did not end German dreams for dominating the Caucasus. Among the more madcap schemes discussed as late as October 1918 was that of sending dismantled submarines and motor torpedo boats by rail from Batum and Baku to establish German naval supremacy in the Caspian. All these activities made the Soviets threaten to renounce the supplementary treaty of Brest Litovsk which the Germans were flagrantly ignoring, and the Turks felt that they had been deliberately deceived by the supplementary treaty and therefore refused to ratify it. It was the collapse of Bulgaria which brought an end to the imperialist visions of Turkey and Germany, at least for the time being, and the dangerous tensions between Russia, Turkey and Germany over the future of the Caucasus were overshadowed by the collapse of the Western Front.

The German army's advance into the Crimea was also a violation of the treaty of Brest Litovsk, but the OHL argued that it was in answer to the attacks by the Russian fleet on the German positions in Nikolayev and Kherson, and that the naval nase of Sebastopol was a 'pirates'' nest'. Ludendorff developed a number of schemes for a puppet regime in the Crimea, and dreamed of establishing a 'German riviera', but these ideas had to be abandoned with the signing of the supplementary treaty of Brest Litovsk.

The key to German policy in the north-east, the base for the future containment of Russia, was Finland. From August 1914 there was a mounting desire in Finland for independence from Russia, and the Germany army had trained Finnish volunteers fully aware that Germany could use the independence movement to her own advantage. After the Russian February revolution Kerensky refused to give Finland full independence. The policial situation became highly polarized, the economic conditions were appalling, and by January 1918 full-scale civil war had broken out with the Finnish Red Guards controlling Helsinki, the Whites the north.

At first the civil war did not go particularly well for the Whites, and the OHL, against the express orders of Kühlmann, sent arms and ammunition to Finland. At the same time the *Reichsbank* froze Finnish assets, keeping them as a bargaining counter to use to extract economic concessions. As a pretext the bank insisted that Germany was still legally at war with Finland, for the treaty of Brest Litovsk was yet to be signed. The Homburg meeting of 13 February established the principle of 'cries for help' to give the pretext for German occupation of the east. A somewhat fraudulent appeal for German intervention was engineered and a series of treaties signed which would tie Finland closely to Germany economically, militarily and politically. The OHL managed to overrule all the objections of the chancellor and the foreign office to sending an expeditionary force to Finland. The Germans landed in Finland in April under the command of von der Goltz, and reached Helsinki on 13 April. Mannerheim resigned as commander of the White army, fearing that Germany would lose the war and that Finland had become too closely associated with the losing side. But President Svinhufvud was strongly pro-German and offered little resistance to the OHL's determination to see that the demands of German heavy industry on the Finnish economy were indeed met. These demands became so excessive that the foreign office became seriously worried that they might undermine the economic treaties with Finland which offered almost unlimited chances to exploit Finnish resources.

In the course of the next few months the OHL planned to seize Petrograd and overthrow the Bolshevik regime by an attack from Finland and the Baltic, an operation in which Finnish troops would be involved. This plan, given the code name *Schlusstein* (coping-stone), was not cancelled until 27 September 1918 when the situation on the Western Front had become so desperate that there could be no more talk of this final act of German policy in the east. Schlusstein had been opposed by the foreign office as a serious over-extension of German forces, but there can be little doubt that had it not been for the collapse of the Western Front the OHL would have triumphed once again over the 'ink-pot men' in the Wilhelmsstrasse.

In July 1918 the German position on the Western Front began to look very serious. The French, aided by the Americans, had broken through the German lines at Villers-Cotterêts and penetrated to a depth of four miles. The position of the German army on the Marne was now seriously endangered. Ludendorff became increasingly irritable and nervous, and no longer seemed to be quite in control of the situation. A number of officers at the OHL became highly critical of his conduct of affairs and were very pessimistic about the general military prospects for the Central Powers. This was the beginning of the formation of an opposition group within the OHL which was to play a most important role in the next few weeks.

Over the next few days the situation stabilized somewhat. But on 8 August the Entente broke through the German lines on the Somme, and faced with a massive attack by tanks some units of the Germany army lost their nerve and fled in panic. This was the *dies ater* of the German army. One of the most serious aspects of this débâcle was that the German 2nd Army was experienced and well rested, and a guards division had jeered at a division of Württembergers who were about to launch a counter-attack with epithets such as 'strike breakers' and 'prolongers of the war'. The large number of prisoners taken was also clear indication of a serious loss of morale.

The Kaiser now argued that the army had reached the limits of its endurance and that the war would have to be ended. Ludendorff agreed that there was now no hope that an offensive would succeed, as he had imagined in July, but felt that if the German army were to go on the defensive the Entente could gradually be worn down. The OHL still clung to the belief that Germany could secure an annexationist peace, even though it was blatantly obvious that the military preconditions for such a peace did not exist. To make matters worse Ludendorff fell into a deep nervous depression, and much of his work had to be done by Colonel Heye who became head of the operations division of the OHL. Heye, far from being an unthinking yes-man, as many feared, proved to be a stong-minded and ener-getic officer who soon became the leader of the opposition group to Ludendorff within the OHL. Heye, Stülpnagel, Merz, Bockelberg, Brinckmann, Posek and the later chancellor, Schleicher, all agreed that Ludendorff's powers would have to be drastically reduced and that the army would have to face the fact that the war was probably lost. They were in favour of close liaison with the majority parties in the Reichstag and the opening of armistice discussions before the military situation degenerated still further. Ludendorff still persisted in viewing the overall situation with unjustified optimism, and argued that the outbreak of Spanish flu in the French army would turn the tide.

The Heye group decided that it was time to act. They invited Secretary of State Hintze to Spa without consulting Ludendorff, saying that the military situation was hopeless. They told Hindenburg that an armistice was essential, and Ludendorff agreed. At a meeting at 6 p.m. on 28 September Hindenburg and Ludendorff discussed the question of an armistice, and they agreed that it could not be long delayed. But Ludendorff's attitude was still highly unrealistic. He thought of an armistice as a breathing-space which would allow Germany time to recover its strength. He realized that territorial ambitions in the west would have to be abandoned, but he still hoped that it would be possible to use anti-Bolshevism as a screen for annexations in the east. Neither man would admit that Germany had been defeated.

On 29 September Ludendorff told Hintze that an armistice would have to be signed immediately, and he agreed with Hintze's concept of a 'revolution from above' – limited demo-cratic reforms that would convince the Entente and particularly President Wilson that the war had indeed been fought for democracy. An armistice should be negotiated on the basis of Wilson's fourteen points, which they hoped to manipulate as they had the Petrograd formula for a peace without annexa-tions. Hindenburg still hoped to annex Longwy and Briey, but

Ludendorff pointed out that this was no longer possible. On 30 September the Kaiser signed a document announcing that Hertling had resigned as chancellor and that a new government would be formed of men who 'enjoyed the confidence of the people'. The Austrian and Turkish governments were informed that the German government was obliged to open armistice negotiations on the basis of Wilson's fourteen points.

Ludendorff, supported by Hindenburg, began to look around for scapegoats. They were not hard to find. The socialists had systematically undermined the morale of the army, the foreign office was responsible for the collapse of Bulgaria, and the war ministry had not enforced the auxiliary labour law with due rigour. He told the OHL: 'I have asked His Majesty to bring those people into the government who are largely responsible for things having turned out as they have. We shall therefore see these gentlemen enter the ministries, and they must make the peace which has to be made. They must now eat the soup which they have served to us.'

Prince Max of Baden wished to delay the armistice for a while, fearing that precipitate action would be regarded by the Entente as a confession of serious weakness. He was delighted to find that Ludendorff was largely in agreement with him, and that he was not carried away by Rathenau's ridiculous proposal for a *levée en masse* which had gained a certain popularity in extremist circles. At the OHL Bauer now plotted against his old friend and colleague, arguing that Ludendorff had lost his nerve and was sick and weak.

Meanwhile an exchange of notes between the German government and President Wilson began. Hindenburg and Ludendorff viewed this with great alarm, and decided that Wilson's terms amounted to a demand for unconditional surrender. Ludendorff was outspoken in insisting that Wilson's terms be rejected. On 25 October he travelled with Hindenburg to Berlin, threatening to resign if his conditions were not met. This time he made a serious miscalculation. The Kaiser accepted his offer to resign when he repeated it in the course of an audience, and contrary to Ludendorff's expectations Hindenburg did not offer his resignation. This to Ludendorff was betrayal, and he travelled back to Spa in a towering rage. He was now almost without a friend. To the left he was a dangerous extremist, and the right felt that he had become hopelessly weak. He retired from the army and devoted the rest of his life to cranky *Völkisch* politics of a dangerously irrational kind.

Groener was appointed as successor to Ludendorff, but by now nothing could be done to save the situation. Military discipline was breaking down, desertions were frequent and the Entente was taking increasingly large numbers of prisoners. At home a revolution loomed large. For Groener the fault lay with the home front: 'The army stands splendidly; the poison comes from home.' The Kaiser and some of his closest advisers began to think in terms of turning the army against the enemy at home and mounting an anti-socialist crusade which might still bring territorial gains in the east. But clearly such ideas were absurd. Most of the junior officers at the OHL now realized that the Kaiser would have to abdicate if an armistice were to be signed and if revolution were to be avoided. Groener first toyed with the romantic idea of letting the Kaiser find a hero's death on the front, but after some thought William II rather understandably turned this down. On 9 November 1918 Groener told the Kaiser that he no longer enjoyed the confidence of the army, Hindenburg having refused to bear this message. A few hours later the Kaiser was on his way to Holland and many years of exile.

8

The Army and the Weimar Republic

On 9 November 1918 General Groener was determined to ride the political storm rather than making a futile and heroic last-ditch stand on the Western Front, or precipitating a bloody civil war. His main concern was to preserve the unity of the officer corps and maintain discipline in the army. To this end concessions had to be made to the new government of Ebert and the Council of People's Representatives. On 10 November Hindenburg announced that he was prepared to co-operate with Ebert 'in order to stop the spread of terroristic Bolshevism in Germany'. At the same time he ordered the formation of councils (*Vertrauensräte*) in the army which would deal with complaints, and which were designed to take the place of the politically dangerous soldiers' councils which threatened democratic reform in the army. Ebert who hated revolution 'like the pest' was prepared to accept these terms and agreed to support the army's anti-Bolshevik position.

The pact between Ebert and Groener halted the revolution in its tracks. Ebert in the chancellory remained in daily telephone contact with the OHL. Throughout Germany there were incidents of violence and brutality by units of the army against the revolutionaries. On 8 December, immediately after a counter-revolutionary *putsch* attempt in Berlin by army units, Hindenburg presented a list of political demands to Ebert. These included the calling of a national assembly, which would automatically cancel the power of the workers' and soldiers' councils, the reaffirmation of the officers' right of command, the abolition of soldiers' councils and the creation of a reliable police force. Ebert was not prepared to accept all these demands at once, for the determination of the Berlin workers against the army on 6 and 7 December showed that a more gradual approach against the workers' and soldiers' councils was advisable. But he made a major concession to the OHL when, on the following day, he allowed General Lequis to march into Berlin, his troops issued with live ammunition. On 10 December Ebert greeted nine guards divisions at the Brandenburg gate with the words: 'we welcome you back home with joyful hearts, the enemy did not defeat you!' The social democrat Ebert thus accepted the main contention of the 'stab in the back' legend.

The workers' and soldiers' councils were determined to fight back against Ebert, who they felt had betrayed the revolution, and against the army which they knew was determined to crush them. On 18 December the Congress of Workers' and Soldiers' Councils passed a resolution, known as the 'Hamburg Points' as it was suggested by a delegate from Hamburg, which called for the creation of a people's army. Power of command was to be vested in the people's representatives and in the local soldiers' councils. Badges of rank were to be abolished. Officers and NCOs were to be elected by the men. The standing army was to be abolished, and officers were to declare their allegiance to the revolution. The OHL immediately told Ebert that this resolution was unacceptable, and that Hindenburg and Groener would resign if Ebert accepted it. Groener and Schleicher went to Berlin to discuss the matter with the Council of People's Representatives, and in return for a rather feeble assurance that the army was not thinking in terms of a counter-revolution the council agreed not to respect the Hamburg Points. Groener had certainly over-reacted to the Hamburg Points, for there was little chance that Ebert would have accepted them anyway. But by reacting so violently he had made it quite plain that the army would not tolerate any interference from the politicians or the people, and by meekly giving way to the OHL the Council of People's Representatives had further strengthened the position of the army.

On 23 December Ebert telephoned the OHL and said to Schleicher, 'You promised that you would help me. Now act.' Ebert made this somewhat panic-stricken appeal because he wanted the army to dislodge the revolutionary 'People's Marine Division' from the royal palace. The OHL ordered Lequis to force them out, but Lequis' troops after bombarding and storming the palace were suddenly faced with a large and determined crowd which had been armed by the independent socialist police chief Emil Eichhorn, and which forced the army to retreat. 'Bloody Christmas' was a severe setback for the OHL which realized that the forces at their command were dwindling. But in the long run their position was strengthened. The three USPD members of the Council of People's Representatives resigned in protest against Ebert's actions against the Marine Division. The USPD abandoned its attempt to co-operate with the majority socialists, and moved closer towards the Spartacus group of Rosa Luxemburg and Karl Liebknecht. Gustav Noske joined the Council of People's Representatives with responsibility for military affairs. Noske's lapidary statement, 'Someone has to be the bloodhound, I'm not afraid of the responsibility', was soon put to the test. On 5 January 1919 the Spartacus revolt began, an ill-organized and spontaneous outburst against the steady erosion of the revolutionary achievements of November by the regime of Ebert, Scheidemann and Noske. The revolt was crushed by units of the Free Corps, the regular army and irregular forces, all under the overall command of the OHL. Rosa Luxemburg and Karl Liebknecht were brutally murdered by members of the *Garde-Kavallerie-Schützen-Division*. Captain Waldemar Pabst, the general staff officer who ordered this murder, was personally congratulated by Noske. The official SPD newspaper *Vorwärts* rejoiced at the news that Luxemburg and Liebknecht were dead. Noske told his colleagues: 'You have got nerves like old women. War is war.'

By calling upon the Free Corps, a band of ultra-reactionary and vicious enemies of democracy, to defend them against their enemies on the left, rather than relying on their own loyal forces, Ebert and his associates left the preservation of 'law and order' in the hands of their own worst enemies. By strengthening the Free Corps they also ensured that the anti-democratic elements of the old army would form the nucleus of the Reichswehr of the Weimar republic. Not only was no attempt made to create a republican and democratic army, but the anti-republican and anti-democratic aspects of the military were encouraged and strengthened. In their panic the social democrats betrayed the heritage of fifty years of struggle against Prussian and German militarism. Groener had every reason to be satisfied. His policy of 10 November, which had been so frequently attacked by his critics on the right, now bore rich fruit.

But the future of the army was still undecided in January 1919. The exact relationship between the army and the government had to be formalized, and the subject became the topic of a bitter debate between the two Württembergers Groener and Reinhardt, the latter of whom had been appointed war minister on 3 January 1919 at Noske's insistence. Reinhardt wished to make some concessions to democratic principles. He accepted the notion that the power of command was vested in the Council of People's Representatives, and that the war minister was responsible to the Council. He was also prepared to allow the soldiers' councils certain rights. Groener was furious. He insisted that the soldiers' councils should be abolished, because they undermined military discipline, were dangerously political and were bitterly opposed by experienced soldiers. Groener also rejected the idea that the army should be nothing more than the willing tool of the Council of People's Representatives. Officers such as Groener and Seeckt felt that it might be expedient to support the SPD for the moment, particularly against their common enemy on the left, but they felt that Reinhardt was going too far in the direction of democratic republicanism.

Reinhardt, with his schemes for a strictly limited democratization of the army, stood sadly alone. Throughout Germany Free Corps units smashed the power of the workers' and soldiers' councils, crushed spontaneous outbreaks of working-class unrest and discussed plans for the economic and political reconstruction of Germany on authoritarian lines. But whereas Reinhardt was prepared to compromise with the majority socialists to a degree which was unacceptable to Groener, the question of the acceptance of the Treaty of Versailles saw these roles reversed. Groener argued for acceptance, thinking that the preservation of the territorial unity of the Reich was of paramount importance, whereas Reinhardt entertained rather romantic notions of retiring to the eastern provinces and continuing the struggle against the Entente. These were the two poles of the dilemma which faced the army. On the one hand there were few officers who felt that the terms of the treaty could be accepted, but on the other hand most of them realized that resistance was quite hopeless. Between these two positions there was no possible compromise, as Groener found when he suggested acceptance provided that the 'shame' paragraphs of the treaty were removed, only to have this promptly rejected by the Entente. Groener's position on the acceptance of the terms of the treaty made him increasingly unpopular in the army, but his critics had no reasonable alternative suggestions. Groener answered the attacks of men such as General Luttwitz by saying that the army should respect its traditions of being apolitical, and that any political decisions should be left to the military elite. Finally Groener's arguments had to be accepted as the only possible course open to Germany. On 16 July 1919 the National Assembly accepted the terms of the Treaty of Versailles.

The treaty severely limited the size of the army. It was not to be more than 100,000 men, and the number of officers was restricted to 4,000. So that reserves of trained men could not be built up, officers and men had to serve for a fixed number of years – twenty-five years for officers and twelve years for the men. The myth of the *Krümper* system was still very much alive. The general staff and the war academy were abolished. Aircraft were forbidden, as were submarines, tanks and gas. Germany was not allowed either to import or to export war materials and armaments. All weapons that were forbidden by the treaty had to be handed over to the Entente. The army, which at that time was about 500,000 men, had to be reduced to 100,000 by 31 March 1920. An inter-allied control commission was established to ensure that the terms of the treaty were respected. The treaty was written into German law, so that any violation of the terms of the treaty was automatically a violation of the law.

The Treaty of Versailles necessitated a change in the organization of the army. Under the terms of the constitution, adopted in August 1919, the president had the power of command over the army, but he delegated much of this authority to the war minister. With the abolition of the general staff, which had been the most powerful institution of the army since the days of the older Moltke, a struggle for power took place for control of the new German army. Hindenburg resigned in protest against the terms of the Treaty of Versailles. Groener remained at the OHL. Reinhardt as ex-war minister was determined to establish the authority of the new war ministry, as was constitutionally correct. Groener resisted these attempts, and denounced Reinhardt as a '*Schweinehund*'. A number of officers appealed to Noske, saying that they had little confidence in Reinhardt, and as a result of this intervention Seeckt was given the task of reorganizing the army.

Seeckt wished to revive the general staff, giving it the new name of Military Office (*Truppenamt*). This would be largely independent of the war ministry. Reinhardt wished to establish a central administrative office (*Heeresleitung*) which would obviate all the confusion that had existed between the various organizations of the old army. Reinhardt was thus prepared to give considerable power to the war minister, at that time the civilian Noske, whereas Seeckt wished to avoid any political control over the army.

Reinhardt was appointed *Chef der Heeresleitung* under Noske, a somewhat unsatisfactory and *ad hoc* position as quasi-secretary of state. Groener was furious and began a virulent campaign against him, being determined to strengthen Seeckt's position. He was unsuccessful in his attempt to overthrow Reinhardt, even though he used some highly dubious tactics against him. In September 1919 Groener retired, and played no significant political role for the next few years.

If the attempts of those who wanted to stop a degree of civilian control over the army had been temporarily frustrated, this certainly did not mean the end of the political activity of the army. Throughout the summer of 1919 there were constant demands that the army play a more active role in crushing the left, and some even suggested overthrowing the government. In many units there was a rebellious discontent which could become exceedingly dangerous if sufficiently provoked. The army was far from being the servant of the new state. In the Baltic army units were still fighting against the Soviets and against the newly formed governments in the Baltic provinces. Attempts by the German government and by the Entente to force the army to return to Germany were bitterly resented and taken as proof that the Weimar government was, in its heart of hearts, Bolshevik and anti-German. To Reinhardt men such as von der Goltz used arguments which were very similar to those he had used against Groener over the debate on the acceptance of the Versailles treaty. The anti-Bolshevik crusade in the east could be used to strengthen Germany to the point that she might reject the treaty and break the stranglehold of the Entente. Such arguments were difficult for Reinhardt to counter. He, like Groener and Seeckt, did not want the Reichswehr to be the subordinate instrument of the politicians, and he was as eager as Goltz to find a way round the restrictions of Versailles. But the tactics he chose were different. He wanted an end to the bitter political strife within the army. He wanted to establish the unchallenged authority of the *Heeresleitung* over all military units. Most important of all he felt that more could be achieved in co-operation with the government than by ceaseless criticism and mumblings of revolt. Thus in the final analysis the differences between Reinhardt and his critics from the right were tactical rather than fundamental, but that made them none the less bitter.

German operations in the Baltic brought up the major question of future relations with Russia. This was a matter of great concern to Seeckt. In February 1920 he outlined his ideas on the future of Russo–German relations. Seeckt believed that the Soviet regime was there to stay and that whatever the government and the generals might think about communism, it was vital for the two countries to work closely together to frustrate the plans of Britain and France. Germany would have to restore the frontiers of 1914, partition Poland which the Entente had established as a 'thorn in the flesh' of Germany, and establish a common frontier between Russia and Germany. The alliance with Russia, whatever its political regime, was the essential basis from which Germany would regain her position as a great power. Seeckt was to remain faithful to these ideas for the remainder of his career, and they were to have a profound effect on German foreign policy in the Weimar republic.

For the moment grandiose schemes of an alliance with Soviet Russia were of secondary importance. The pressing concerns of early 1920 were the reduction of the army according to the stipulations of the Treaty of Versailles and ending the lawless and dangerous activities of the Free Corps. Both of these questions were highly political and liable to lead to a serious confrontation between Reinhardt, Seeckt and the hotheads on the extreme right who regarded any concessions to the Entente as treason. General von Lüttwitz, the commander of the troops in Berlin, set about systematically sabotaging the demobilization orders. Lüttwitz was particularly determined to save the 'Brigade Ehrhardt', one of the most extreme right-wing formations under his command, from being demobilized. He went directly to Ebert, demanding that Reinhardt be dismissed and that Ehrhardt's brigade should continue under his command. Ebert refused these and other political demands. Rumours flashed around Berlin that a *putsch* was imminent. On 11 March Lüttwitz was suspended from his command, and when he refused to comply with the order a warrant was issued for his arrest and that of his fellow conspirators, Kapp – the murderer of Luxemburg and Liebknecht – Pabst and Colonel Bauer, the *eminence grise* of the OHL under Hindenburg and Ludendorff. On the following day the Ehrhardt brigade marched into Berlin. There were no troops loyal to the government to oppose them.

As Ehrhardt marched towards Berlin the army was thrown into confusion. Reinhardt and the Social Democrat Noske wanted to call upon loyal units to fight the insurgents. Seeckt violently disagreed; he did not want 'an exercise between Potsdam and Berlin with live ammunition'. Reinhardt found that there were few units on which he could rely and therefore resigned, as the Ebert government ordered the army not to resist the *putsch*, not that it would have followed his orders in any case. Seeckt preferred to play a waiting game. He took leave of absence, but also handed in his resignation from the army. Seeckt had considerable sympathy for the aims of the Kapp–Lüttwitz putschists. Their programme calling for the prohibition of all political and economic strikes, for the abolition of unemployment insurance benefits, for 'work and order' and for the rigorous repression of the left appealed to the general, but he did not approve of their means. He feared that a *putsch* might seriously divide the Reichswehr in a conflict of loyalties which would be harmful to it. As he said on the night of 12 March as Ehrhardt marched to Berlin, 'troops do not shoot at troops'. But by remaining neutral Seeckt in fact was supporting the coup.

Seeckt's concern was, as Heye put it later, that the Reichswehr would become so seriously divided that it would only benefit a third party, Ebert and the Weimar government. Meanwhile the government had left Berlin, and the counter-revolutionaries were in control. Seeckt's position of trying to avoid choosing between Kapp and Ebert was now hopelessly unrealistic. Units of the army demonstrated their allegiance to the Kapp–Lüttwitz government, while others remained loyal to the Ebert regime. Generally speaking, units in northern and eastern Germany tended to be sympathetic to Kapp. In the rest of Germany the army was either neutral or for the Weimar government. There is sufficient evidence to suggest that the majority of the army either supported the *putsch* or showed a benevolent neutrality towards it. No attempt was made to save the Weimar republic.

The republic was saved not by the army but by the workers. On 14 March a general strike broke out throughout the country. The country came to a standstill. Three days later Kapp left Berlin, handing over his government to Lüttwitz. In a series of somewhat mysterious negotiations between Lüttwitz in Berlin and Ebert in Stuttgart, in which a number of senior officers played an important role, Seeckt was given command over the Reichswehr. Seeckt was determined to reunite the Reichswehr in a battle against the forces of the left. In the struggle against Kapp and Lüttwitz the communists, the independent socialists and the majority socialists united, seized some of the armouries of the Free Corps and in some districts overcame the Reichswehr. The workers' councils took on a new lease of life. The flight of Kapp and the resignation of Lüttwitz encouraged the left to make further political demands. The extreme right had been defeated, it was now essential to make sure that such an attempt would not be made again. As the SPD in Berlin announced, 'We must learn the lesson of the last few days. We demand a government which will continue and end the struggle against German-National and militarist reaction with iron determination.' In the Ruhr a Red Army had been formed of 100,000 men. On 18 March it stormed Essen, and in the next few days the Reichswehr was driven out of Germany's richest industrial area. On 18 March Seeckt said that the Reichswehr was now engaged in a struggle for existence against Bolshevism and a Soviet government. Seeckt and his officers now began a campaign to get rid of Noske. On the right his name was associated with the general strike which in turn had led to the radicalization of German labour. Noske's pathetic insistence that his name had appeared on the strike proclamation without his consent did not convince his opponents. To the left Noske was still the 'bloodhound' who had failed miserably to create a Reichswehr that was loyal to the republic. Indeed Noske was ultimately responsible for the anti-democratic stance of the army in 1920, and his failure to create a loyal officer corps was to have a profoundly dangerous effect on the course of the republic. The new Reichswehr minister was Dr Gessler, who had been mayor of Nürnberg and founder of the Democratic Party. He was to stay in the position of Reichswehr minister for the next eight years despite the many changes of government. Seeckt was appointed chief of the *Heeresleitung*, and was given considerably more power than had been vested in Reinhardt.

Thus the Kapp *putsch* led to the dismissal of the two men, Reinhardt and Noske, who had been prepared to save the republic. It brought to power General von Seeckt who had sympathized with Kapp and had broken his oath to defend the republic against its enemies. The Reichswehr crushed the paramilitary units of the left with great brutality, the reaction against the army in many areas was very strong and some units were close to mutiny at being ordered against those who had risked their lives to save the republic. Seeckt called Ehrhardt to him, and said that he admired the discipline of his division and hoped that he could count on them in the struggle against the revolutionary left. In this situation it is hardly surprising that General von Möhls, commander of the Reichswehr in Bavaria, told his men that 'Kapp feels that his mission is accomplished and has resigned. He is convinced that in this moment of danger we will unite against Bolshevism.'

In 1920 there was a real chance that the army could be reformed, its ranks purged of those who opposed the republic. In fact the reverse happened. Very few officers who had supported the *putsch* were dismissed. A number of those who had loyally supported the government were removed on the grounds that they had disobeyed orders from superior officers even when those officers supported the *putsch*, and although their oath of allegiance obliged them to support the legally constituted government of the republic. The fact that the Reichswehr had to be further reduced in size, according to the stipulations of the Treaty of Versailles, gave the army a golden opportunity to purge its ranks of republican officers and men. A parliamentary committee of investigation established to examine the conduct of officers during the *putsch* was successfully rendered innocuous by Seeckt's intervention and robbed of its right to dismiss officers. By appointing Seeckt to the *Heeresleitung* Ebert had renewed and strengthened the pact of 10 November 1918. Ebert and the government feared the left so much that they were prepared to place the fate of the republic in the hands of those who were either critical or outright hostile towards the government of Weimar. Under Seeckt the army remained aloof from the republic, and its conservative and anti-democratic elements were strengthened. For the Reichswehr and for Seeckt the Kapp *putsch* was indeed a success. The attempt by Noske and Reinhardt to establish a working relationship between the army and the republic, and to allow a degree of civilian control over the army, had been defeated. By withdrawing into itself and proclaiming that it was unpolitical, the army was to play an active and harmful political role in the years to come. When asked whether the Reichswehr was politically reliable, Seeckt replied: 'I have no idea whether it is reliable or not, but it obeys me.'

From 1920 to 1926 Seeckt was the dominant figure in the Reichswehr, and for all his protestations that he had no political ambitions, he was one of the most important political influences on both domestic and foreign affairs. He was born in 1866 the son of a general, member of the Pomeranian aristocracy. He was educated in Strasburg and then joined an exclusive guards regiment. During the First World War he had a brilliant career as one of the outstanding staff officers, serving mainly on the Eastern Front. He was a man of considerable intelligence and with wide-ranging interests, from horse breeding to art and from military history to beautiful women. In society he could be a charming host and a witty conversa-

A Military History of Germany

tionalist, with politicians he was usually exceptionally cautious, suspicious and abrupt. Most who knew him were impressed and somewhat perplexed by him. Politically he was anti-democratic, hostile towards parliamentary democracy and determined to isolate the army from those tendencies of the modern world which he despised and rejected. In foreign affairs he was more open-minded, prepared to use any means to restore Germany's power and influence and circumvent the restrictions of the Treaty of Versailles. He was a difficult man who could not tolerate being criticized or contradicted, but he was admired and respected by most of his subordinates.

The corner-stone of Seeckt's foreign political ventures was the establishment of close working relations with the Soviet government, so that the two 'pariah' states could co-operate to their mutual benefit. From as early as 1919 tentative and in-formal feelers had been made from both the Soviet and the German sides. In the summer of 1921 a group of German specialists, led by a rather romantic figure, Oskar von Nieder-mayer – who was known as the German Lawrence on account of his adventures in the Middle East during the war – visited Russia to inspect armaments factories. Niedermayer was a fluent Russian speaker and had an insatiable appetite for adventure and intrigue, and was thus felt to be an admirable choice to head the mission. His task was to investigate the possibilities of Albatros building aircraft, Blohm and Voss submarines, and Krupp sundry forbidden guns in Soviet factories. Niedermayer's group reported back that conditions did not appear suitable at that time. This was by no means the end of discussions between the two sides. In September further talks were held in the apartment of Major Schleicher, another officer whose taste for conspiracy was to become unbridled, and the Soviet delegation was strongly in favour of Germany building aircraft in Russia. Seeckt began a series of talks with the Russians in the next few weeks, but they did not get very far. German industry was unwilling to put up the money for large investments in Russia, and the chancellor and finance minister Josef Wirth was also unwilling to commit large sums at that early stage. Seeckt was also somewhat alarmed at the Russian suggestion that the Reichswehr should support a new attack on Poland, for he knew full well that Germany was in no

246

position to withstand an attack from France and Czechoslovakia. The best he could offer was benevolent neutrality. A further mission went to Russia in December under Niedermayer, who made a number of promises to Trotsky and Chicherin which he was in no position to make and which Wirth had to disavow.

Money was still the major problem, but in early 1922 Wirth gave the Reichswehr 150 million marks to cover initial investments in Russia. A few days later Radek appeared in Berlin calling for close military co-operation with Germany and for the manufacture of aircraft which could be used for an attack on Poland, which he claimed was planned for the spring. Immediately after these discussions Junkers was given money by the Reichswehr to set up a factory in Russia, and construction began in April.

Seeckt was delighted with the Treaty of Rapallo, and his representative Major Hasse was a very active member of the German delegation who, as a leading member of the group of officers which had been negotiating with the Russians, was in an excellent position to present the army's point of view to Wirth. In September 1922 Seeckt wrote a memorandum which outlined his thinking on foreign policy and his reactions to Rapallo. For Seeckt 'Poland's very existence is intolerable, and irreconcilable with the vital interests of Germany'. Poland would have to 'disappear', and could be made to disappear if Germany and Russia were to co-operate. The strengthening of Russia would lead to the strengthening of Germany, and by strengthening Russia Germany would not be running the risk of becoming Bolshevized. In spite of the 'ridiculous slogan: "No More War"', war with France seemed imminent. Seeckt did not think that Britain would support France, and considered a possible alliance between Britain and Germany. Indeed Seeckt's thinking in 1922 is strikingly similar to Hitler's in 1939. The same fanatical hatred of Poland, the same hope of driving a wedge between France and Britain and the same opportunist alliance with the Soviet Union.

Seeckt's desire to prepare the ground politically and militarily for Germany's 'struggle for existence' was highly alarming to the German ambassador in the Soviet Union, Brockdorff-Rantzau, whose appointment he had tried to stop. Brockdorff-

Rantzau was also shocked that Seeckt and Wirth had been discussing military policy with the Soviets and had even built factories in Russia without informing President Ebert, but he lacked the courage to tell the president himself and contented himself with dropping a few hints. Hasse argued that as Brockdorff-Rantzau was an opponent of Seeckt's policy in Russia, future negotiations should be carried on behind his back, and the foreign office should not be informed.

German activity in Russia increased in the following months. With guaranteed state loans German industry was now prepared to risk investing in Russia, and the whole enterprise was centralized under one organization in Berlin under the name of *Gefu*, which controlled investments for the production of poison gas and aircraft in Russia. A complicated series of negotiations continued between the Red Army and the Reichswehr, and neither Ebert nor the new chancellor Stresemann knew quite what was going on, though they made it plain that they disapproved of such schemes, and the missions continued to work behind the ambassador's back. That these activities had in no way affected Seeckt's virulent anti-communism was soon to be shown in his reaction to domestic upheavals in the crisis year of 1923.

Chronic inflation which rendered the mark valueless, mounting unemployment, the occupation of the Ruhr by French and Belgian troops, the threats to the republic from the left and from the right, and the policy of 'passive resistance' which virtually closed down the Ruhr and with it the major source of German wealth, all served to create the most severe crisis which the republic had yet to face. With the risk of civil war or even a war with France, it was obvious that the Reichswehr would play a vitally important role in the crisis. And it was well equipped to do so. Seeckt had the army under close control. The Wirth government had been replaced by a right-wing government under Cuno. The Cuno government was closely associated with big business – Cuno was managing director of the Hamburg–America Line (*Hapag*) – and his closest advisers were men such as Stinnes and Helfferich. It was the most reactionary government that the republic had yet seen. For the army this new government was ideal. Cuno was a friend of Seeckt, and the government co-operated closely with the army.

After the occupation of the Ruhr Seeckt attended cabinet meetings, and his views were taken very seriously by a government in which Seeckt felt comfortably at home. Some hotheads in the army were in favour of attempting to drive the French from the Ruhr, but Seeckt agreed with the government that such an action would be foolish in the extreme. German rearmament had simply not reached the point where such a serious risk could be taken. On the other hand Seeckt was prepared to support sabotage acts against the French in the Ruhr, which were carried out under the auspices of the Reichswehr. Nor could he ignore the possibility that such actions in the Ruhr might provoke an armed conflict with the French. Thus he began to organize reserve forces, well beyond the limits set down in the Versailles treaty and to buy weapons abroad. 100 Fokker fighters were bought in Holland; other planes were made in Stockholm. A guerilla army, the *Feld-Jäger*, was trained to fight behind enemy lines. Negotiations were opened with the para-military units of the extreme right, such as Stahlhelm and the National Socialists, but they were not particularly satisfactory for either party. Seeckt naturally wanted these men to follow army orders, while the *Verbände* wanted to remain independent and were often highly critical of the government and of Seeckt's handling of the Ruhr crisis. In Bavaria, where particularist and ultra sentiments were running very high, even the Reichswehr units were becoming increasingly suspicious of Seeckt's motives. His centralist ideas were rejected by many officers who saw Bavaria rather than the Reichswehr as their *Vaterland*.

As the crisis grew the Cuno government was forced to resign. Faced with a wave of strikes and mounting criticism it was obvious that the government had to be extended to include the social democrats. In August a new coalition government was formed under Stresemann. Seeckt was angry at the change, feeling that it was a kow-tow to the French and to the communists. His only consolation was that Gessler remained as Reichswehr minister and was as subservient to him and as remiss in his constitutional duties as ever. Indeed Seeckt was so suspicious of the new government that all Stresemann's efforts to establish cordial relations with him were to little avail. At a time of national crisis Seeckt called for an iron hand, not a compromise with the social democrats whom he despised. Soon his worst fears were confirmed. Hilferding, the prominent social democratic theoretician and minister of finance in the new government, threatened to stop payments to the Reichswehr because of their adventures in Russia. Rumours were also circulated in Berlin that Seeckt might well be replaced by an officer who was more sympathetic to the republic, and Reinhardt's name was frequently mentioned. As a final insult Stresemann ordered an end to passive resistance in the Ruhr, which was harming Germany far more than France. Stresemann had a realistic understanding of Germany's weakness. Seeckt and many senior officers allowed their fervent nationalism to cloud their judgment, and began to mutter about another lost war, with Stresemann and the social democrats stabbing the nation in the back. To the chancellor Seeckt uttered the somewhat ominous words: 'The Reichswehr will follow you, Mr Chancellor, if you pursue a *German* course.' Stresemann had no reply to this astonishing piece of insubordination, so reminiscent of the way that Hindenburg and Ludendorff had treated Bethmann Hollweg, and he tried to placate Seeckt. It was all to no avail. Seeckt worked behind the chancellor's back, maintaining close contact with right-wing extremist politicians, who in return suggested that Seeckt should become chancellor. Seeckt was flattered, but his closest political advisers warned him against this course. A dictatorial chancellor supported by the *Deutschnationale Volkspartei* had little chance of survival. Such a combination would meet the determined opposition of the left and the republicans. Seeckt was at first annoyed, for he found it difficult to accept the fact that he might be wrong and resented even the most circumspect criticism. But the fanaticism of some extreme right-wing politicians, particularly men such as the pan-German Heinrich Class, was little to his taste, and gradually he gave up his political ambitions and returned to his usual stance of preserving the unity of the Reich and the independence of the Reichswehr.

The preservation of the unity of the Reich was soon to become a matter of pressing concern. On 26 November Kahr was appointed as virtual dictator of Bavaria, where separatist feeling was running high and where some extremists, among them Hitler, were plotting a march on Berlin. Stresemann's reaction was to use the emergency powers of article 48 of the constitution to give Gessler as Reichswehr minister absolute powers. As it was well known that Gessler was completely subservient to Seeckt, this amounted to giving the Reichswehr dictatorial power. Thus Seeckt had gained the power which he had been coveting, but without having to rely on the support of a political movement which lacked wide popular support. Instead a military dictatorship had been established by a social democratic president and with the approval of a coalition government. Seeckt was understandably delighted.

The first major crisis with which Seeckt had to deal once he had been granted these emergency powers was a threat from the right. Free Corps units, the so-called 'Black Reichswehr', feeling that the government had betrayed the national interest by ending the struggle in the Ruhr, made an abortive attempt to seize government buildings in Berlin, and then tried unsuccessfully to capture the fortresses of Spandau and Küstrin. These attempts were easily crushed by the Reichswehr and they confirmed Seeckt's worst suspicions of the extreme right. He knew all too well that the extremists regarded him as little more than a tool of the system, the willing lackey of a government they detested. Such criticisms hurt, and he was determined to keep his distance from Stresemann and his coalition. On the other hand he did not approve of the radicalism and fanaticism of many of the Free Corps leaders and found much of their rhetoric vulgar and distasteful. He continued to refuse to choose between the republic and its enemies on the right, but such a position was dangerous and uncertain. A disciplined and controlled Reichswehr was the most attractive guarantor of the social status quo to those who were alienated by the pseudo-revolutionary and anti-monopolistic posturings of the petit-bourgeois ultras, and who were even more alarmed at the prospect of revolutionary socialism. Provided that Seeckt could keep the Reichswehr from the influence of the radical right, and the experience of the last few days indicated that this was possible, and provided he silenced his critics on the right by a violently anti-socialist posture, he would enjoy the support of influential sections of the ruling economic and political elite. It was an exceedingly difficult position. As Seeckt wrote to Kahr, the Weimar constitution was a denial of all his fundamental principles, and it was well known that he despised Stresemann for being too soft on the socialists. But he also had little sympathy with those on the extreme right who wanted to plunge Germany into a civil war in which the left would be exterminated. Hasse summed up this problem very clearly when he said at the end of October: 'Stresemann must go, otherwise the Reichswehr will be caught between two revolutions.' Thus the Reichswehr had to make a right incline and begin an offensive against the socialists.

Seeckt went to see Ebert and told him that the Reichswehr intended to work closely with the right, and that Stresemann should be dismissed. Ebert feebly protested and suggested that Seeckt should say this to Stresemann in person. Without hesitation he then went to Stresemann, and in a close paraphrase of the words Groener had used to William II he told the chancellor: 'Mr Chancellor you cannot lead the struggle. You do not enjoy the confidence of the troops.' Then Seeckt must have suspected why Ebert had sent him to Stresemann, for his answer was: 'Is the Reichswehr no longer loyal?' To this masterly question Seeckt had no reply, and he left the chancellor in a towering rage. It was not the generals but the Reichstag which was to unseat Stresemann. On 23 November a vote of no confidence was passed and he was obliged to resign. For all his efforts against Stresemann, Seeckt was still regarded by some officers as being too close to the government, and there were those who wished to see him replaced by an officer who would take a stand against the prevarications of Stresemann and the coalition.

Nowhere were criticisms of Seeckt louder than in Bavaria. The National Socialists' organ *Völkische Beobachter* roundly denounced the dictatorship of Seeckt and Stresemann, who were regarded as Siamese twins who were steering the country on a disastrous and anti-national course. Gessler at once ordered that the *Völkische Beobachter* be suppressed, and the Reichswehr commander in Bavaria General von Lossow was ordered to see that this command was carried out. Lossow refused, and a serious conflict began between him and Seeckt. For Seeckt's taste Lossow was far too pro-Bavarian, too closely associated with the right-wing *Verbände*, and now outright insubordinate. Gessler tried to negotiate a resignation from

Lossow, but this was refused, whereupon Lossow was dismissed. Kahr refused to accept this order, and said that henceforth no orders from the Reichswehr ministry would be respected. The 7th Bavarian Division separated from the Reichswehr to form in effect an independent Bavarian army. Having thus broken with Berlin Lossow began negotiations with the *Verbände* suggesting that all para-military organizations should unite under the leadership of Lossow's Reichswehr division. Lossow painted in glowing colours the prospect of a march on Berlin and the establishment of a national dictatorship, but most of the *Verbände* refused the offer. Lossow was a somewhat unimpressive figure, and the Reichswehr, even when it had openly defied Berlin, was regarded with deep suspicion in many extremist Bavarian circles. The fact that many para-military leaders did not wish to lose control over their little empires also played a role.

These developments in Bavaria showed how precarious was Seeckt's political position. On the one hand it was an open secret that he favoured the same programme as Lossow and Kahr. He hated the republic and supported the idea of a dictatorship, but unlike the Bavarians he wanted to achieve this by legal means. Like the OHL in September 1918 he wanted a revolution from above, he did not want to risk a revolution with riff-raff like the national socialists. Thus ties between Munich and Berlin were by no means completely severed. The *Heeresleitung* continued to finance the 7th Division, pretending that only Lossow had been dismissed. On 3 November the Bavarian Colonel Seisser had a long political discussion with Seeckt, acting as an emissary of the Bavarian Reichswehr. He was given a cordial reception, and Seeckt told him that their political differences were ones of timing, not of the final aim. Seeckt assured Seisser that he did not want to fight the war of 1866 all over again, and that the thought of sending Reichswehr units against Bavaria, which would have to be supported by the Proletarian Red Hundreds from Saxony and Thuringia, was utterly repugnant to him. Troops, in other words, were not going to shoot at troops. At the same time Seeckt told Seisser that the Reichswehr would be sent against the Red Hundreds in Saxony and Thuringia. He thus had no second thoughts about crushing the organizations of the left, whereas those who had openly defied him and had broken their oath of allegiance as soldiers were left unpunished. In a letter to Kahr dated 2 November Seeckt wrote that the Weimar constitution was certainly not a *noli me tangere* as far as he was concerned, and that he opposed Stresemann and sympathized with Kahr. He warned Kahr that he did not want a situation to arise where the Reichswehr might be forced to take action against those with whom they were essentially in sympathy, and he therefore warned Kahr against any precipitate action.

Hitler's *putsch* in Munich on 8 November helped to solve Seeckt's dilemma. The Reichswehr had marched into Saxony and Thuringia, and therefore the Bavarian *Verbände* who were spoiling for a fight with the Proletarian Hundreds and for a march on Berlin after the fashion of the Italian fascists, now found their way blocked by the Reichswehr. Hitler's *putsch* also forced the Bavarian units of the Reichswehr to make a choice between Hitler and Berlin. Most of the 7th Division opposed the *putsch* and helped to defeat it. Seeckt, however, refused to accept Lossow's offer to let bygones be bygones, and insisted that as he had disobeyed orders he would have to be dismissed. The new commander of the 7th Division was Kress von Kressenstein, a loyal supporter of Seeckt. There was no more talk of separation of the Bavarian Reichswehr from control from Berlin.

On the day after the Hitler *putsch* Seeckt was given dictatorial power by Ebert. The powers that had been vested in Gessler by paragraph 48 were now formally given to Seeckt. Those who were pressing for a military dictatorship under Seeckt were temporarily silenced, for this had been legally achieved by the provisions of the constitution. The left-wing united front governments of Saxony and Thuringia had been violently overthrown by the Reichswehr. Hitler's *putsch* with its internal dissensions between fascists and monarchists and without much popular support was bound to fail, but its failure solved Seeckt's problems in Bavaria. He was now at the pinnacle of his power. But he was still frustrated. Stresemann remained chancellor, and Seeckt's attitude towards him had not changed. His relations with Ebert were becoming increasingly strained. The right was becoming impatient, hoping that Seeckt would play a more active political role. When Stresemann was eventually replaced by the Catholic Centre Party leader Julius Marx, Seeckt was not consulted, and although he had hoped for a cabinet post in any new government he was ignored. At the level of the divisional commanders, all of whom were given great political powers, there was a high degree of uncertainty and even naïvety. Right-wing politicians, particularly from the DNVP, were quick to exploit this situation, and the relationship between the party and the army in 1923 was very close. Only General Reinhardt in Stuttgart resisted their advances. He was certainly not a man who was in any way sympathetic to the left, but he was strongly opposed to the idea that the Reichswehr was an instrument of party politics, and was more aware than most other officers that there were serious dangers inherent in giving the Reichswehr the political role which it was now called upon to play.

Some historians still argue that Seeckt and the Reichswehr saved the Republic in 1923, but this argument is highly dubious. The Reichswehr did not save Germany from a communist revolution, nor from a fascist coup, nor from falling apart under separatist pressure. The communists in Saxony and Thuringia, although understandably impatient with their new allies in the SPD, acted in a strictly constitutional manner much to the chagrin of their own left wing. The KPD was badly split in 1923 on the proper course of action to take in this moment of severe crisis. The Comintern's plans for revolutionary action were revoked, and the revolt in Hamburg was the result of faulty communications between the party headquarters and the local branch. The action of the Reichswehr against the legally constituted governments of Saxony and Thuringia, far from saving Germany from revolution, was part of a systematic policy of repression against the labour movement which included ending the eight-hour day, which was a major achievement of the November revolution, and abolishing the right to strike. As Germany entered a period of relative prosperity and economic stability, it did so with a seriously weakened labour movement. This was to have fatal consequences when in 1929 the growing menace of fascism was not countered by a determined and united left.

The Hitler *putsch*, although perhaps a somewhat exaggerated episode in the context of 1923, was not crushed by the Reichswehr. In Bavaria the Reichswehr units had connived with the putschists, and Lossow played a highly ambiguous role. The right-wing *Verbände* were armed and trained by the Reichswehr, and whether army units in Saxony and Thuringia would really have stopped a determined 'March on Berlin' is dubious in the extreme. The *putsch* itself was stopped by a salvo from the police, not by the intervention of the Reichswehr. In the Rhineland separatists such as Adenauer pursued their treasonable ends without the Reichswehr in any way intervening, for they had no rights in the occupied areas and few wanted to risk a war with France.

Far from preserving Germany, Seeckt weakened the country. By constantly intriguing against Stresemann, by quarrelling with Ebert and by openly expressing his disgust of the republic and its constitution he can hardly be said to have aided the republic. He was ever eager to placate the right, and by crushing the left he tilted the political balance dangerously in favour of the *putschists* and adventurers who were out to destroy the republic. By using his emergency powers to such an extent that even his admiring biographer talks of 'tyrannical brutality' Seeckt helped further to isolate the army from the people and to steel it as an anti-democratic weapon. As an American observer commented, Seeckt was loyal to the republic because the republic let him do whatever he wanted. For this Ebert and the politicians of the majority parties must bear a heavy responsibility.

Once the crisis was over Seeckt was anxious that the army should no longer play a direct political role and therefore he asked Ebert to rescind paragraph 48. Traditionally the army had always preferred to conceal its political activities and to work behind the cover of the civilians. Ludendorff had referred to the chancellor as a useful lightning conductor, and this was an attitude shared by Seeckt. Like so many political generals, part of him was eager for direct political power, and like Waldersee before him he was strongly tempted by those who suggested that he might become chancellor. But in the end he realized that by keeping out of the political limelight and avoiding open political struggles, he could exercise far greater influence. Many of his supporters, particularly from the DNVP, were annoyed at this attitude. Once again Seeckt was careful to explain his attitude to his critics on the right, and he was particularly sensitive to the charge that he was soft on social democracy. Thus his political support was dwindling. He had earned the implacable hatred of the left, and was regarded as a traitor by the extreme right. The liberals were uncertain in their attitude towards the army. With their traditional concern for individual liberty they were unhappy with the use that had been made of paragraph 48. To the right the DNVP were divided, many feeling that Seeckt had been too restrained in his use of emergency powers. Under these circumstances it is perhaps not surprising that Seeckt gave up his powers, but he did so with many regrets. He felt that by retiring from centre stage he might be able to improve his political image, and there is evidence to suggest that he had his eye on the presidency of the republic at some future date.

In 1924 Seeckt's main concerns were again with foreign policy. The big question was whether or not Germany should become a member of the League of Nations. Stresemann, who remained foreign minister in various governments until his death in 1929, saw entry as an essential part of his policy of fulfilment, and the Dawes plan of 1924 and the Locarno treaty of 1925 were the main steps in this policy. Eventually in 1926 Germany entered the League of Nations. Seeckt opposed this policy. He was particularly anxious that if Germany were to enter the League armaments controls would become more rigorous than those of the singularly ineffective Inter-Allied Commission. He was also concerned that Stresemann's conciliatory moves towards the western powers might hinder his eastern policy. Some officers were even more outspoken in their criticisms of Stresemann. Freiherr von Fritsch, who was to become a rather improbable martyr in the national socialist period, saw this policy as part of a 'massive attack on the National Idea, and an attempt to bring about the final victory of the Internationals – capitalism, socialism and pacifism'. But Fritsch's antidote to the Internationals was hopelessly unrealistic – war with France. Seeckt's opposition to Stresemann was by no means so outspoken; indeed he accepted the Dawes plan as a helpful step towards a settlement of the reparations problem. Using Schleicher as his political agent, he tried to persuade the DNVP to accept the Dawes plan. Schleicher spent

257

much of his time in the corridors of the Reichstag, but he was not entirely successful. The Dawes plan was accepted by the Reichstag, but a majority of the DNVP voted against the measure. There were fears in the army that the *Schweinhund* Ebert (the phrase is from Fritsch) might dismiss Seeckt under pressure from the French, and again there were murmurings of a military dictatorship. But in February 1925 the *Schweinhund* died. Seeckt still thought of himself as a possible candidate for the presidency, but he was anxious not to appear too eager. He had wanted to present himself as a candidate in 1926 when the next presidential election was due, but his plans were disrupted by Ebert's early and sudden death. With the election of President Hindenburg, Seeckt's position was considerably weakened. Under Ebert there was a certain separation of powers between the civilian and the military, and Seeckt used his position as a professional soldier to the utmost, making Ebert feel at times like an ingorant civilian. There was a sense in which Ebert was president by grace of the army, and Seeckt did not hesitate to rub this in. With Hindenburg this tactic could not possibly work. Hindenburg was almost the personification of the army, and certainly did not treat a mere general as an equal. Hindenburg discussed only military matters with Seeckt. He seldom touched on matters of wider political importance. A political general like Hindenburg knew all the tricks, and was not likely to be out-smarted by Seeckt. Seeckt for his part realized this, and complained bitterly that his political influence had been considerably reduced.

But he was certainly not reduced to a mere cipher. With the president he had lost ground, but he continued to attend cabinet meetings and to attack Stresemann's policies. He still had no patience with Stresemann's policy of attempting to undo the Versailles settlement by diplomatic negotiations and by demonstrations of good faith. His views were simplistic in the extreme. Germany should be strengthened, should rearm and should prepare to fight to win back all the territory lost in 1918. Thus he opposed Stresemann's policy at Locarno, and was against entry into the League. Some meaningless changes in the question of command over the Reichswehr, in which Seeckt lost some of his formal rights to the Reichswehr minister Gessler, were taken by Seeckt as proof that Stresemann was hopelessly subservient to the Entente who were understandably somewhat concerned at the power of the *Heeresleitung*. For Seeckt any negotiations with the western powers were bound to benefit them at the expense of Germany, and if this premise were accepted Stresemann was systematically undermining the strength and independence of Germany.

Differences between Seeckt and Stresemann had extremely important military consequences. In 1923 when there was the possibility of civil war, and even of a war with France, the Reichswehr had been strengthened by flagrantly violating the Treaty of Versailles. Weapons had been bought abroad, volunteers had been signed up into the army on a short term basis and links with para-military organizations had been strengthened. After 1923 when Stresemann's fulfilment policy was in full swing, it was logical that these measures should be abandoned. But Seeckt, by stressing the fundamental antagonisms between France and Germany, was determined to strengthen the army well beyond the limits laid down in the Treaty of Versailles. His plans were very extensive. As the years went by the number of men of a suitable age for military service who had served in the war was steadily diminishing, and it was estimated that by 1933 this reservoir of manpower would be virtually exhausted. Thus a secret training programme was to be set in motion aiming to increase the number of infantry divisions from seven to twenty-one, and creating thirty-nine 'border guards divisions'. Vast stores of weapons were to be made, airmen trained, and special short training programmes established for the reserves in universities and boys' clubs. The Interallied Control Commission was quite incapable of mastering this situation, and sent rather pathetic reports back to its governments. In 1927 it was finally abolished, having achieved nothing. On the other hand Stresemann was concerned that this illegal activity by the Reichswehr, some of which was known to the Entente, was hampering his efforts to come to an understanding with France and Britain as the necessary first stage of his revisionist policy. Thus quarrels between the two men over foreign policy were part of a struggle over the future size, organization and nature of the army.

Seeckt was able to ignore most of Stresemann's objections. The training and arming of para-military organizations under the supervision of the Reichswehr continued, causing endless conflicts with government departments, particularly the Prussian ministry of the interior under the social democrat Severing. This in turn obliged the army to be a little more devious and careful than it had been, but it certainly did not bring such activities to an end. In his foreign policy Seeckt remained an opponent of Stresemann, but his opposition to German entry into the League of Nations was shared by Brockdorff-Rantzau, so that the conflict between these two men became less intense and both men believed that closer relations with the Soviet Union offered the best possibility of revising the Treaty of Versailles. By no longer opposing Seeckt's Russian policy Brockdorff-Rantzau was able to exercise considerable political control over his clandestine policies, and the army no longer had to work behind the ambassador's back. A German military mission was established in Moscow with overall responsibility for the activities of the German army in the Soviet Union. The officer in charge of the mission, Colonel Thomsen, established cordial relations with the German ambassador, thus further smoothing relations between the army and the Moscow embassy. The work of the German army in Russia continued apace. After long and difficult negotiations a tank school was established at Kama near Kazan which opened in 1929. A flying school was built at Lipetsk at which pilots and aircrew were trained, new models of airplanes were tested and various aeronautical experiments were conducted. Economically the Soviets had driven a very hard bargain. The Lipetsk installation was a rather modest return for German investments in the Soviet Union, but Seeckt's main concerns were political rather than military. The eastern orientation of his foreign policy was aimed against 'appeasement' of the western powers, against Stresemann's policies, against the Versailles settlement even in a sharply revised form, and for the destruction of Poland and the restoration of the frontiers of 1914.

Yet for all this activity in the Soviet Union it was clear that Seeckt's authority was waning. With the election of President Hindenburg there was no question of Seeckt playing the role of '*ersatz* Monarch', a part which Hindenburg played to perfection. The clandestine activities of the Reichswehr, both at home and abroad, were opposed by many ministers who desperately tried to control them. Seeckt had many enemies, and were he to make a serious slip a determined effort would be made to secure his dismissal. On 27 September 1926 the Seeckt crisis began. A small local newspaper in southern Germany reported that Prince William, the eldest son of the Prussian crown prince, had attended the manoeuvres of the 9th Infantry Regiment – the rather unglamorous new title of the old guards regiment. It took a whole week for this news to break in the Berlin press, but when it did a virulent campaign against Seeckt was immediately instigated. Seeckt seems to have lost his nerve. He told Gessler that he had known nothing about Prince William's activities, and that the whole affair was a plot by the extreme left to get rid of him. Neither of these statements was true. Seeckt did know all about the affair, and some of those who were most outspoken in demanding his resignation came from the middle of the political spectrum, or from supporters of the Reichswehr who were angry that Seeckt's extraordinary lack of caution had given its enemies considerable ammunition. Seeckt had been extremely offensive to Gessler and had also lied to him, and the minister was understandably furious. He now looked back on the many years he had worked with Seeckt, and remembered how badly he had often been treated by him. Schleicher tried to placate Gessler and urged Seeckt to be conciliatory, but realizing that he had failed he abandoned Seeckt, knowing that it was only a matter of time before he would be dismissed. Seeckt resigned, hoping that Hindenburg would refuse to accept the resignation, or that he might become a martyr to the anti-republican forces. Hindenburg, who disliked and resented Seeckt, was glad to get rid of him. He had no intention of provoking an officers' Fronde or of arresting Seeckt and making him a hero. All he was prepared to do was to offer him a post as ambassador. Among Seeckt's closest associates only Fritsch advised resistance, but with his extremist ideas of an armed *putsch* he stood alone. Seeckt was wise enough to know that a right-wing *putsch* had no chance of success in 1926. Thus his resignation was accepted without any serious political complications.

The Reichswehr was to a very considerable extent the creation of Seeckt. After the brief period when Reinhardt had considered building a bridge between the army and the republic Seeckt had systematically cut off the military from the republic and the government of the republic, to make it an almost autonomous body which served his notion of the state – an abstraction which had nothing to do with the political reality of Weimar. Seeckt paid minute attention to the details of promotions and appointments, and the officer corps became a clique in the worst traditions of the Wilhelmine army. Many senior officers who were sympathetic to Seeckt were highly critical of the lack of young and talented officers and resented Seeckt's byzantine personnel politics. His traditionalism stood in the way of essential innovations and the Reichswehr seemed to many to be little more than the old army in miniature.

Officers were recruited from traditional sectors of society. The proportion of aristocrats in the officer corps was lower than it had been before the war and remained at about 21 per cent, but as the percentage of aristocrats to the total population was a mere 0·14 per cent the figure is significant. As in the Wilhelmine army the aristocracy tended to congregate in certain regiments. In 1926 45 per cent of the officers in the cavalry were aristocrats, but in the pioneers only 4 per cent. Some 85 per cent of officers came from families of ex-officers, senior civil servants, academics and professional men. The traditional antipathy towards industry and trade was still very strong. Only 6 per cent of the officer corps came from the families of factory owners and merchants. The 'tradesmen's entrance' remained firmly closed in the Reichswehr. As in the Wilhelmine army the bourgeois officers were certainly no less conservative in their outlook than the aristocrats. The officer corps was carefully separated from the rest of society, and Seeckt was particularly careful that only very few NCOs were able to obtain commissions. The gulf between officers and men was to remain as wide as ever.

This socially exclusive officer corps remained apolitical, in the euphemistic military sense of the term. It rejected the squabbles and factionalism of parliamentary democracy. It was highly critical of the revolution, of the republic and all who served it. Just as the Wilhelmine army had found its political ally in the conservative party, the Reichswehr worked closely with the DNVP which was the old conservative party under a new and more radical guise. But the DNVP was so highly critical of the Weimar system that co-operation with such a party did not mean that the army was prepared to make any concessions to the new political order.

After Seeckt's resignation a successor had to be found who would continue his work. Reinhardt was one of the two most senior officers in the army whose experience had been such that he seemed the most qualified choice. But he was rejected. The appointment of Reinhardt would have amounted to a rejection of Seeckt's concept of the Reichswehr. After further negotiations General Heye was appointed. He had been at the OHL during the war, and subsequently was one of Seeckt's closest advisers. Heye agreed completely with Seeckt's views. He was not a particularly strong-minded person, unlike Reinhardt, Hasse or Lossberg – who were the most likely candidates for the post. Thus the army would continue on its old course, but with a weaker leadership.

The critics of the army were determined to exploit this new situation to the full. The politicians, particularly the social democrats, tried to achieve the maximum degree of control over the army. Seeckt when he heard of this said that all Heye had to do was to say that he had one hundred thousand men behind him and he was not going to budge. Heye replied that it would be all right for Seeckt to say such a thing, but he could not. Gessler, who remained in office, assured the social democrats that things would change now that Seeckt had gone, and that the clandestine training of the para-military organizations of the right would stop. Such was the situation when on 3 December 1926 the *Manchester Guardian* published a feature article on German military activities in the Soviet Union. The article was translated immediately and appeared in *Vorwärts* two days later. On 16 December Scheidemann gave a rousing speech in the Reichstag denouncing these activities.

The social democrats were not only concerned with the illegal rearmament programme and the way in which the army was clearly working without consulting the government, but they were also determined to establish a degree of parliamentary control over the recruitment policies of the army. The bias, particularly in the appointment of officers, was all too obvious, and it was pointed out that the army recruited the vast majority of its men from the ranks of the para-military organizations of the extreme right. Löbe, who was the social democratic president of the Reichstag, suggested that the Austrian recruiting system should be adopted, whereby a list of medically fit men was made and recruits taken in order, the system being checked by parliamentary commissioners. The army was incensed at this suggestion and argued that if company commanders were no longer responsible for recruitment the *esprit de corps* of the army would be destroyed. Gessler supported this argument, saying that political considerations played no part in recruitment. But this certainly did not convince the critics of the army.

Heye had shown a degree of readiness to compromise with the republic, through weakness rather than conviction, and Gessler had announced a 'new era', but the rapid succession of attacks on the army from the left forced them on the defensive so that hostility between the army and the republic grew rather than diminished. Indications that the army wished to allow democrats and republicans to serve in the territorial army (*Landesschutz*) which had been exclusively rightist and which was organized in a way which violated the terms of the Treaty of Versailles, were bitterly opposed by many officers who were appalled at the idea of 'bolshies and pacifists' worming their way into the illegal formations of the Reichswehr. The *Landesschutz* played a vital part in the military planning of the Reichswehr and there could be no question of its being abandoned or even seriously modified. Those officers in the general staff who merely suggested that these illegal formations should not be exclusively right wing, and that they should become genuine republican institutions, were branded as 'reds' and either dismissed or silenced.

Heye was unwilling to compromise, particularly when any steps in such a direction occasioned such a violent response from the army. But he did keep the government far better informed of the army's activities than Seeckt had done. Funds for illegal armaments were granted by the treasury, the *Landesschutz* was debated by the cabinet and the foreign office was kept reasonably well informed of the Reichswehr's activities in Russia. This policy paid off handsomely. The government spent ever increasing sums on the Reichswehr. From 1924 to 1928 expenditure increased from 459 million marks to 728 million marks. Thanks to Scheidemann's 'treason' in his Reichstag speech and the reaction of the Entente to the *Manchester Guardian* article, the *Gefu* had to be abolished. But the Reichswehr continued with its activities in Russia, supported by the government to the point where Brockdorff-Rantzau bitterly complained to Stresemann that he was pushing military activities in Russia and not keeping him properly informed of what was going on. Thus under Heye relations with Russia were strengthened in spite of the scandal in 1926.

Seeckt's resignation was followed very shortly by that of Gessler. The Reichswehr minister who had survived so many changes of government and who seemed to be almost immune to the vicissitudes of political life in the Weimar republic was implicated in a scandal involving secret naval funds handled by Captain Lohmann. Gessler had signed a guarantee for a loan for one of Lohmann's highly dubious enterprises. In 1927 the Lohmann scandal broke in the press, and Gessler had to resign.

His successor was General Groener, a man who had been absent from the political scene for some years, and who had devoted much of his time to writing on military topics. The army had wanted a soldier as Reichswehr minister, and Groener seemed an ideal choice. He had been Hindenburg's right hand man in the final stages of the war. He was Schleicher's patron in the OHL, and none had worked harder than Schleicher to secure his appointment. He had considerable experience of politics and was respected by many politicians. His reputation for liberalism was undeserved, but he was prepared to compromise with the republic, unlike so many of his more conservative colleagues. Yet there was in Groener a degree of common sense which was sadly lacking in so many other leading military figures of the time. Unlike Seeckt he thought that the idea of another war was ridiculous, for even a limited war – which could only mean a war against Poland for which so many soldiers hoped and which some chauvinists in the Red Army were prepared to support – would lead to the intervention of the Entente. For Groener the contemporary variation of the slogan 'better dead than red' – 'better dead than a slave' – was pure nonsense. His aim was for a close association between the Reichswehr and the nation, in the tradition of Seeckt and in terms that were almost as vague, and for Germany to be sufficiently armed for no state to risk a war. Like so many other generals, Groener painted a lurid picture of military preparations in Poland for an eventual attack on Prussia, and he used this bogey to argue for increased armaments. A major problem was that Groener's requests for a strengthening of the Reichswehr came at a time when the depression was already having a serious effect on the German economy. The SPD government was reluctant to meet Groener's wishes, the more so as the decision to support the building of the pocket battleship 'A' had been strongly criticized by many party members. Groener got his way, once he had agreed to a relatively small cut in his original demands, and the resulting budget deficit which was partly the result of this excessive expenditure on the army and navy led to the resignation of Hilferding, who had unsuccessfully urged Groener to exercise a certain moderation. Groener was prepared to accept the republic as a fact, and was critical of the extreme right with its endless intrigues and its sentimental hankering after days that had long gone. He hoped that the gulf between the army and the republic could be bridged, but the demands he placed on the state, particularly when the depression was beginning to have a critical effect, helped to weaken the state and to provide grist to the mill of the right-wing fanatics whom he disliked and resented. Similarly the social democrats, by not producing a satisfactory military policy and by compromising with Groener's demands, caused a split within their own party which further weakened the main political support of the Weimar republic at a critical stage in its history.

Groener was a man of considerable organizational talents. During the war he had attempted to centralize many of the disparate procurement offices under the *Kriegsamt*, and on his appointment to the Reichswehr ministry he was determined to co-ordinate the efforts of all those departments which were immediately under the minister. For this purpose he created a ministerial office (*Ministeramt*) which was commanded by his 'elective son' General Schleicher. Schleicher had pressed for the creation of such an office in the days of Seeckt, and there is no doubt that he saw himself as the most suitable candidate to head the new organization. This position gave Schleicher's unbounded political ambition ample scope. Groener trusted his political judgment uncritically, and soon Schleicher was able to make an exceptionally powerful position for himself. These political activities, which were given the full support and backing of Groener, resulted in a considerable strengthening of the influence of the Reichswehr ministry. As Heye at the *Heeresleitung* was not a particularly forceful character this resulted in a movement of power away from the *Heeresleitung* to the ministry, so that the position of Seeckt and Gessler was soon to be reversed. The Reichswehr ministry was soon to be run by a trio of officers, all of whom had held important positions in the OHL during the war – Schleicher, Stülpnagel and Bussche. Heye bitterly resented his own loss of power and criticized the trio, but there was very little he could do. In the press there were murmurings against this clique, and many officers resented their excessive powers and the fact that they had been unusually rapidly promoted. One officer did not quite fit in to the Schleicher group, the chief of the *Truppenamt*, von Blomberg. Schleicher managed to secure his resignation in a singularly underhand manner over a scandal involving the *Landesschutz*, and in his place Kurt Freiherr von Hammerstein-Equord was appointed. Shortly afterwards his brother Günther was given Stülpnagel's position, for 'Stülp's' political stance was not entirely in accord with that of Schleicher and Groener. It was now only a matter of time before Heye was replaced, because the chief of the *Heeresleitung*'s position was becoming intolerable. It was openly discussed in messes that Heye was little more than a puppet of the Reichswehr ministry and he was rapidly becoming a figure of fun. Groener said of him: 'The good old uncle was not a tough guy, and was led around by the nose by lieutenants.' Stülpnagel was regarded as the most likely successor to Heye, but he no longer enjoyed the confidence of Schleicher – in spite of profuse assurances to the contrary. Kurt von Hammerstein-Equord was given the post and a new clique was established – ex-officers of Hindenburg's old regiment the 3rd Footguards, in which Hammerstein, Schleicher and Hindenburg's son Oskar had all served.

Schleicher's position was now exceedingly powerful. He had greatly strengthened the Reichswehr ministry, he had placed his nominee in the *Heeresleitung* and he enjoyed the full confidence of Groener. In the early months of 1930 he worked frantically behind the scenes as Groener's *cardinal in politics*, preparing for the change-over of government from Müller's coalition government. Schleicher had little sympathy for the extreme right from Hugenberg to Hitler, for he felt that they were particularly dangerous in that they disguised their demands for radical change by nationalist rhetoric. His sympathies lay with the moderates in the DNVP, with the 'tory-democrats' of the *Volkskonservativen* and with the right-wing of the catholic centre party under Brüning. Hindenburg liked Müller even though he was a social democrat, and was prepared to give him emergency powers under paragraph 48. Schleicher opposed this, threatening that Groener would be forced to resign as such an action would be not acceptable to the Reichswehr. Hindenburg then accepted Schleicher's suggestion of Brüning as chancellor, having first been reassured that he was, after all, a respectable reserve officer. Schleicher now hoped that the Brüning government, which was friendly towards the Reichswehr, which represented the bourgeois parties and which seemed as if it might be tolerated by the extreme right and by the social democrats, would be able to achieve the degree of political stability that the Reichswehr leadership deemed essential.

The onset of the depression in 1929 and the subsequent radicalization of politics forced the Reichswehr to face the problem of national socialism. The question of what were officers' attitudes to national socialism in 1929 and 1930 is extremely hard to answer. From the available evidence it would seem that initially senior officers were unsympathetic towards a movement which they considered too radical and vulgar and whose pseudo-revolutionary rhetoric they found potentially dangerous. Senior officers, such as Colonel Ludwig Beck, who were enthusiastic supporters of Hitler and who resented Schleicher's and Groener's opposition to national socialism, were few and far between. The younger officers seem to have been far more favourably disposed towards the Nazis. They had not been brought up in the traditions of the Wilhelmine officer corps with its antipathy to mass movements and with its old-style authoritarianism. They were impatient and dissatisfied and were easily attracted by the powerful slogans of the national socialists. To such young officers men like Schleicher and Groener were feeble and indecisive, and criticism of the

Reichswehr leadership became more and more outspoken in some circles. Thus the political question of attitudes towards national socialism quickly became one of military discipline.

In 1929 three young officers, Scheringer, Ludin and Wendt, published a leaflet which was sharply critical of the 'bureau-generals' and which expressed much of the conventional ideological clap-trap of the Free Corps and the radical right. Scheringer and Ludin subsequently went to Munich and established contacts with the national socialists. Their professed aim was now to revolutionize the Reichswehr so that it would support any Nazi attempts at a coup. When the Reichswehr ministry heard of these activities the three lieutenants were arrested on a charge of conspiring to commit high treason. Groener made his position quite clear in two orders, one published before their arrest, the other after it, which stated that as the NSDAP aimed at overthrowing the constitution and at undermining the discipline of the Reichswehr, support for the movement could not be reconciled with a soldier's oath of allegiance to the constitution. Any national socialists were therefore to resign from the army. The three officers were tried in the High Court (*Reichsgericht*) shortly after the September 1930 elections which brought Hitler's first major electoral victory. Hitler appeared as a witness and gave a characteristic speech. The three were given eighteen months' jail, during which time Scheringer became a communist.

The case of the officers of Ulm seriously divided the Reichswehr, showing that the political homogeneity, for which Seeckt, Heye and Groener had striven, did not exist any longer. Many officers, even those who were unsympathetic to national socialism, felt that the trial was an unwarranted political interference in the internal affairs of the Reichswehr, and that the leadership of the Reichswehr had failed miserably to stop the politicians from meddling in their affairs. Groener and Schleicher were accused of steering a 'left course' and of betraying the national cause for which the Reichswehr stood. Groener for his part realized that the trial had caused a serious split in the Reichswehr, but he seems to have seriously underestimated the strength of feeling among junior officers, and his notion that these difficulties could be made to disappear by publishing 'pastoral letters' to the Reichswehr was curiously naïve. Neither

Groener nor Schleicher was able to understand quite what German fascism was all about. Groener was utterly perplexed why anyone on the right should doubt his patriotism, and Schleicher came to the absurd conclusion that there was little to choose between communism and national socialism.

Hammerstein, who was given the misleading title of 'the red general', partly because his three daughters were active members of the communist party, was particularly bitter at the attacks on the Reichswehr leadership which came from its erstwhile allies on the right. He hoped to steer a middle course between the extremes on the left and right, and win support for this moderate policy from a wide sector of society. He hoped that the political and social isolation of the Reichswehr could be ended and that it could work in close co-operation with the moderate forces in the country. By late 1930 such ideas were becoming increasingly utopian, for the political basis for this programme was rapidly disappearing. Hammerstein was also not a politician, and tended to leave political manipulation to Schleicher. Groener also relied on Schleicher's political advice, and Schleicher became increasingly intimate with Hindenburg to the point where he was virtually a special adviser to the president. Hindenburg became extremely cool towards Groener when the Reichswehr minister committed a serious breach of the army's code of honour by marrying a lady who was already pregnant shortly after his first wife had died. Thus by late 1930 Schleicher was the single most powerful man in the Reichswehr.

The elections on 14 September 1930 did not give Brüning the parliamentary majority for which he was hoping. The real victors of the elections were the national socialists who won 107 seats – in the previous parliament they had only twelve. As Schleicher saw the gradual disappearance of any chance of a parliamentary coalition of the moderate right, which would support the demands of the Reichswehr, he began to think in terms of a presidential dictatorship which would exclude the Reichstag which could no longer provide a majority government. A particular thorn in Schleicher's flesh was the Prussian government, whose SPD ministers had tried to control the illegal activities of the Reichswehr. He revived Seeckt's plans of 1923 against 'red Prussia', arguing that the power of the central government should be greatly strengthened, and that the

Prussian government should disappear. Within the Reich government Schleicher hoped to secure the appointment of Groener as minister of the interior, which with control over the police was a critically important position, and thus strengthen the position of the Reichswehr. There is also some evidence to suggest that he was thinking of attempting to make Groener chancellor. The key figure in any such schemes was President Hindenburg, and Schleicher met his son almost every day during this time to discuss the political situation.

The army leadership was beginning to lose some of its hostility towards the Nazis, and Hitler was particularly careful to repeat the assurances he made at the trial of the Ulm trio that he had no intention of undermining the Reichswehr or of seizing power by violence. Hammerstein was convinced by these assurances. Schleicher believed that there was much that was praiseworthy in the Nazi Party, if only it would drop its radical rhetoric and show a certain degree of responsibility. From this he drew the fatal conclusion that if only the Nazis were given some share in the responsibilities of government they would lose their *élan* and their appeal to the extreme radical right. He argued that just as industry elected the most tiresome shareholder to the board of directors, so the government could tame the national socialists just as the British ruling class had tamed the labour party. In less than two years Schleicher was to see how appallingly false these analogies were.

In the course of 1931 Hitler strengthened this impression that he intended to remain within the bounds of the law. Groener was impressed, and found Hitler to be personally sympathetic. 'A modest, decent person who wants the best', was his impression. By January 1932 the Reichswehr permitted soldiers to attend national socialist meetings, and national socialists were allowed to join the army. General Seeckt, who was now a Reichstag member for the *Volkspartei*, had said in a newspaper interview as early as December 1930 that Hitler's partnership in a coalition government was both desirable and necessary. Seeckt's enthusiasm for Hitler was such that he voted for him, and not for Hindenburg, in the presidential elections of 1932. Thus by 1932 Groener, Schleicher, Hammerstein and Seeckt were all in favour of Hitler joining the government. But this did not mean that they were any less ambivalent in their attitudes towards

271

the para-military force of the Nazi Party, the SA. The terrorist outrages committed by this band of fascist rowdies were such that there was widespread popular revulsion against them, and the well publicized details of the homosexual activities of Röhm and his cronies had caused some unfavourable comment in respectable circles. Many officers were alarmed at the radicalism of the SA and at their fraudulent socialist rhetoric. Severing in Prussia, and most of the other interior ministers of the German states, demanded that the government ban the SA. Groener felt that there should be a ban on all such para-military units. Schleicher was less positive, for he had long been in negotiations with Röhm, and was eager to use the SA as a reservoir of manpower for the Reichswehr. He was also concerned that by banning the SA the small right-wing parties would have even less chance in the elections in Prussia. Groener hoped, quite unrealistically, that if the SA were banned 'decent' members would join organizations of the Reichswehr such as the Sports Association.

The pressure on Groener was mounting. The interior ministers of the states were threatening to act on their own, and Groener, who had become Reich's minister for the interior in October 1931, wanted to avoid this at all costs. On 13 April 1932 Groener agreed to ban the SA. The reaction in the army was very strong, and Schleicher told Groener that he was a 'dead man'. In the right-wing press the attacks on Groener were unbridled. He was the man who had betrayed the Kaiser and had helped to create the Jewish-socialist republic, and by banning the SA but not the republican *Reichsbanner* he had shown his true colours. Groener was now caught between two stools, between the Reichswehr and their right-wing supporters, and the government which had to rely to a certain degree on the benevolent neutrality of the social democrats. On 10 May Groener defended his position against the SA in the Reichstag, but the speech was not a success. Hammerstein viciously told his colleagues that Groener was senile. Schleicher said that the whole Reichswehr leadership would resign if Groener did not go. Groener's position was now intolerable, and on 12 May he handed in his resignation as Reichswehr minister. Brüning offered the post to Schleicher who, as he was busily engaged in negotiations with Hitler and the national socialists in plotting a new government in which the Nazis would be represented, prevaricated whilst giving profuse professions of loyalty to the chancellor. Thus Schleicher continued in the illusion that he could lead the Nazis around by the nose – as Groener bitterly commented – even though the SA ban had been a temporary setback for this policy. The resignation of Groener plunged the Brüning government into a serious crisis, and Schleicher did much to undermine the President's confidence in the chancellor. Schleicher had reached a tacit agreement with Hitler that the government should be replaced and the SA ban rescinded. Since Brüning stood in the way of this programme he would have to be dropped. He blindly followed his disastrous policy of trying to tame the wild man and find popular support for a government of the moderate right.

Apart from the traditional argument that the army no longer had confidence, in this case in Groener, Schleicher had also argued to Hindenburg that his anti-Nazi policy seriously handicapped the work of the border guards, because the national socialists provided the bulk of the men. This was utterly untrue. Relations between the Reichswehr and the Nazis in the *Landesschutz* and *Grenzschutz* were strained, and the army much preferred to work with the *Stahlhelm*. But Schleicher was preparing the ground for lifting the ban which he felt made it impossible for him to draw the sting of the national socialists and was making them even more radical. Having secured the dismissal of Groener, Schleicher was then able to secure the appointment of his candidate as chancellor, Franz von Papen. Papen was something of an outsider, a member of the extreme right wing of the centre party and a proponent of an authoritarian, nationalistic and anti-parliamentary system of government. He had had a disastrous career as military attaché in Mexico and Washington from 1913 to 1915, and after the war he had been in the Prussian *Landtag* where he had successfully managed to smash the coalition between the centre party and Braun's social democrats. His friends, among whom Schleicher was prominent, regarded him as a harmless dilettante. Those who were less charitable considered him to be a dangerous fool. The historical record supports the latter view.

Schleicher was made Reichswehr minister in Papen's government and was the most powerful man in the new cabinet. He regarded this government as a stepping stone to a new coalition in which the Nazis would be partners following a new election. Such a policy was astonishingly naïve, because it compounded the error of trying to tame the Nazis by demanding new elections at a time when the extreme right was rapidly gaining support and would exploit the situation to the utmost. Hitler was delighted with the deal which he made with Schleicher immediately after the Papen government was formed. Schleicher promised that the ban on the SA would be lifted and that there would be new elections. Hitler promised to tolerate the Papen government until election time. Hitler had gained all he wanted, Schleicher a vague assurance that the NSDAP might consent to join the post-Papen government.

The major political act of Papen and Schleicher was the *coup d'état* against Prussia. The destruction of 'red Prussia' had long been the aim of the Reichswehr, and Papen's record in this respect was quite impressive. On 20 July 1932 Papen was made *Reichskommissar* of Prussia through the emergency presidential powers of article 48. Martial law was proclaimed in Berlin and Brandenburg, and General von Rundstedt was given emergency powers in case of resistance. By supporting this act of violence against the legitimate constitutional government of Germany's largest state the Reichswehr fatally weakened the democratic forces in Germany and eased the way for Hitler's rise to power. By actively assisting in the destruction of democracy in Germany by a government which enjoyed the support of 5·9 per cent of the electorate, Schleicher was frantically sawing off the political branch on which he was sitting. This was made abundantly clear in the election results of 31 July.

The National Socialists won 230 seats, more than doubling their previous total. There could now be no question of Hitler meekly accepting a subordinate position in a new government, and he demanded nothing less than the post of chancellor along with other key ministries such as the interior, justice, agriculture and education. Schleicher discussed these questions with Hitler at the beginning of August and agreed to support Hitler's candidature for chancellor. At first he was somewhat uneasy, but he seems to have been convinced by the argument that if Hitler remained outside the government while some of his followers were in the cabinet, then the *Führerprinzip* would dictate that they would have to seek his permission before acting, and this would make government unworkable. Schleicher was simply following the logic of his early arguments in a changed situation. By making Hitler chancellor he would become respectable. If he remained outside the government the national socialists would become increasingly radical and irresponsible. In the cabinet Schleicher argued that either the government would have to exclude the Nazis and attempt to win popular support by decisive and effective action, or Hitler's Party would have to be given a share of governmental responsibility. He argued that the latter course might well lead to a split in the ranks of the NSDAP between the politicians who accepted office and therefore would become respectable, and the paramilitary formations of the SS and SA who would continue to press their radical demands. There was a grain of truth in this idea, as was to be seen two years later, but the basic notion of taming the fascists was as foolish as ever, particularly when it was combined with determined efforts to smash the anti-fascist forces in the name of a national government. For the moment it was mere speculation, because Hitler refused Papen's offer of the vice-chancellorship and some cabinet posts for his followers.

Papen was incapable of mastering the situation. His economic measures were unpopular, and his meagre support was dwindling. Schleicher became concerned that Papen's reactionary policies and his talk of establishing some form of dictatorship might lead to the Reichswehr's having to give military support to a regime that was without popular support. He still believed that some form of working arrangement could be made which would include the Nazis, and therefore he moved steadily away from Papen. The problem for Schleicher was how to get rid of Papen.

The opportunity was offered by the Reichstag elections of 6 November. The results showed that the national socialists were losing ground. They gained two million fewer votes, and lost thirty-four of their seats in the Reichstag. The general feeling that the Nazis had been irresponsible in not co-operating with the Papen government was shared by many senior officers in the Reichswehr, who were beginning to feel that the Nazis were just another collection of political chatter-boxes who shied away from accepting responsibility. Nazi support for the Berlin transport strike which occurred just before the elections and in which the communist party played a leading role led many voters to believe that perhaps Hitler's anti-Bolshevism was not sincere, and that he was not the only alternative to the Bolshevization of Germany. The sight of fascists and communists standing shoulder to shoulder, denouncing the union bosses and engaging in sabotage against the transport system, led Schleicher to order the preparation of a study to see what would be the effect of widespread civil unrest in Germany and whether the Reichswehr would be able to maintain law and order against the combined forces of the left and the right. The notion that the fascists and the communists would in fact combine in this way was absurd, and it is extremely hard to determine whether the Reichswehr undertook this study for purely cynical political reasons, or whether they really believed that the nazis were disguised Bolsheviks. The study, which was conducted very hastily, painted a gloomy picture in which the Reichswehr was unable to maintain order, and the Poles would overrun eastern Prussia. The whole study was so ridiculous that one is tempted to regard it as nothing more than a clumsy weapon against Papen. There was no sign that the fascists and communists would combine, no evidence that the Poles would attack and most of the arguments used in the study were blatantly false.

Determined to oust Papen, Schleicher now felt that he was the most suitable candidate for chancellor. On 23 November he asked Hitler if the nazis would be prepared to support a Schleicher government, but Hitler refused point-blank. Hindenburg also was not in favour of a Schleicher government, and was annoyed that Schleicher had been intriguing with Hitler. Schleicher continued to negotiate with leading political figures, arguing that Papen's determination to strengthen his proto-fascist dictatorship would plunge Germany into a civil war in which the armed forces would be inadequate to keep control. These gloomy prognostications had their effect. The majority of ministers were convinced by Schleicher's arguments and therefore opposed Papen's schemes. To Papen Hindenburg said that he was too old for a civil war, and that therefore 'in

God's name we must let Mr von Schleicher try his luck'. On 2 December 1932 Schleicher was appointed chancellor.

Schleicher's position was certainly not enviable. He had virtually no support in the Reichstag, and even the loyalty of the army was no longer certain. As Groener told him in a bitter letter, for an authoritarian government one did not need Schleicher; Hitler would do the job better. To the left Schleicher was the man of 20 July, the officer who had legalized the lumpenproletarian riff-raff of the SA and SS, the unprincipled politician who had been in constant contact with the fascists and who had urged that Hitler join the government. The attempt by the SPD leadership to negotiate with Schleicher failed owing to the determined opposition of the rank and file. There could be no question of an accommodation between Schleicher and the organized working class, even at this moment when the republic was in danger of collapse and the fascist menace a ghastly reality. Schleicher still had many friends among the political and military elites, but they were generals without an army.

His one hope seemed to be the Nazis. He had still not given up hope of persuading Hitler to support his government. For the first few days of the new government the nazis supported Schleicher. In the Reichstag they voted against a motion of no confidence and agreed that the Reichstag should be adjourned. In a desperate attempt to win support Schleicher wooed Gregor Strasser, the *Reichsorganisationsleiter* of the NSDAP and leader of the 'left' faction of the party. Strasser's political position was hopelessly muddle-headed and his political sense was strictly limited. He was tempted by Schleicher's offer, and had the support of a number of industrialists who were more impressed by Strasser's anti-marxism than his vague anti-capitalist rhetoric. Schleicher hoped to combine the support of the Strasser wing of the nazis with the unions under the banner of social reform. But he could gain the support of neither faction. Hitler had not lost his grip over the party in spite of a setback at the polls and, supported by Goering and Goebbels, he acted swiftly. Strasser had far less support in the NSDAP than either he or Schleicher had supposed. He resigned his party membership and his seat in the Reichstag. Hitler took over the task of party organizer and appointed a notorious drunkard, Robert Ley, as his second-in-command. The unions also refused to answer Schleicher's call. They had no reason at all to trust Schleicher: for most of the labour movement Schleicher was little more than the pathfinder for fascism. The SPD and KPD voted for the no-confidence motion, and subsequent efforts by Schleicher to contact the moderates in the SPD failed.

Yet in spite of the total failure of his plan Schleicher did not lose his confidence or his optimism. His schemes to create new jobs and employment for youth did not, however, win much support. He hoped that if only he could hang on to power his opponents might become exhausted and divided and his own position would become stronger. But this too was a miscalculation. Particularly in the circles of heavy industry there was growing discontent with Schleicher's government. The growth of working class unrest and the failure of Schleicher to find any adequate solution to the problems of the country made them ready to support Hitler at a time when his fortunes were waning and his coffers becoming alarmingly empty. The liaison man between the industrialists and the fascists was none other than Franz von Papen, who was now a decided opponent of Schleicher and was determined to come back to power. Hitler met Papen on 4 January 1933 in the house of the Cologne banker von Schröder. By this time industry enthusiastically supported Hitler's economic policies and his determination to smash the labour movement. The meeting was most satisfactory for Hitler. Papen promised to support a new government in which Hitler would be chancellor and to remove all 'Bolsheviks, social democrats and Jews' from leading positions. Industry was delighted. Immediately after the meeting one million marks were paid to the NSDAP by sympathetic industrialists.

All that now stood in the way of creating a new cabinet with Hitler as chancellor was Hindenburg. Papen began a series of negotiations with Oskar von Hindenburg to persuade the president to dismiss Schleicher and appoint Hitler. Schleicher, who always had his ear close to the ground, immediately went to Hindenburg and asked for authority to dismiss the Reichstag and ban the NSDAP and the communist party. Hindenburg replied dryly that Schleicher had been made chancellor largely because a civil war had to be avoided as the Reichswehr could not deal with a confrontation with the NSDAP and the KPD. Schleicher replied that times had changed and that volunteers would support the Reichswehr as would the Reichsbanner and the unions. Hindenburg was not impressed by these arguments, and probably felt that he had been deceived on 2 December. He also liked Papen, the smooth aristocratic cavalry officer, and preferred him to Schleicher who was altogether too much of an intriguer and politician for his tastes. Schleicher could now no longer rely on Hindenburg's support.

Within the Reichswehr there was growing opposition to Schleicher. Younger officers, many of whom were Nazis, were sharply critical of the army leaders whom they regarded as a group of self-serving careerists who were tinged with dangerous parliamentary-democratic ideas. Some senior officers also felt that the time had come to establish a 'national' government with Hitler as chancellor. General von Blomberg, commander of the East Prussian Division, whose general staff chief von Reichenau was a fervent national socialist, went directly to Hindenburg without consulting Schleicher. The arguments which Blomberg used against Schleicher were much the same as those Schleicher had used against Papen. The Reichswehr would not be able to control serious civil unrest, because if there was an armed conflict with the SA and the SS the army would be seriously divided and would probably be defeated. Therefore a new government would have to be formed with Hitler as chancellor. Blomberg thus told Hindenburg that the Reichswehr no longer had confidence in Schleicher, and that Hitler was their preferred candidate. Hitler and Papen were delighted with Blomberg, and in return for his services they decided to offer him the post of Reichswehr minister in a Hitler cabinet. This suggestion was acceptable to Hindenburg. Clearly Schleicher had lost control of the Reichswehr and was no longer properly in touch with the troops. He seemed almost helpless against these intrigues.

Unable to win support by splitting the labour movement and the national socialists, and uncertain of the support of the army, Schleicher had no alternative but to try once more to persuade Hindenburg to grant him emergency powers. But Hindenburg would not change his mind. Hammerstein warned the president that there were two disastrous alternatives if Schleicher were to fall – either a minority Papen government which would have enemies ranging from Hitler to the communist party leader Thälmann in which case the Reichswehr would have to stand up against the opposition of ninety-three per cent of the German people, or a Hitler government the danger of which Hammerstein painted in vivid colours. From this discussion it would seem that Schleicher and Hammerstein had no idea of the negotiations between Papen and Hitler, and thought that either Papen or Hitler would be the next chancellor. Thus Hindenburg's famous remark that he would not make the 'Austrian corporal' chancellor did not answer the question whether Papen would be appointed.

Schleicher had exhausted all his possibilities. On 28 January he ceased to be chancellor. He now gloomily agreed with Hammerstein that the only possible successor was Hitler. Any of the other alternatives would probably lead to a civil war in which the Reichswehr would be trapped between the Nazis and the communists. Their great fear was still that Hindenburg might appoint Papen, and that negotiations with Hitler were simply a cover for this move. There was even wild talk of a military coup against the president if he refused to appoint Hitler. Thus Schleicher and the Reichswehr leadership wanted Hitler as the lesser of all possible evils, and Schleicher hoped that he would remain in the cabinet as Reichswehr minister.

On 30 January General Blomberg returned to Berlin from the Geneva disarmament conference. Waiting for him at the station were Oskar von Hindenburg and Hammerstein's adjutant. Both men had orders for Blomberg, the first that he should go at once to the President, the second that he should report to the *Heeresleitung* in the Bendlerstrasse. Blomberg was now faced with a choice between accepting the orders of his military superior or going to the president to accept the position of Reichswehr minister in a government with Hitler as chancellor. Blomberg went with Oskar and thus gave the army's approval to the appointment of Hitler. Blomberg was sworn in as the first minister of the new cabinet. A few hours later Hitler made his oath of allegiance to the constitution. In September 1933 Hitler thanked the army for the part it had played in the 'revolution', saying that if 'the army had not stood at our side, we should not be standing here today'.

9

The Second World War

The day of Hitler's 'seizure of power', 30 January 1933, was on the whole greeted with enthusiasm by the army. Many of the principal components of fascist ideology were to be found in the conventional wisdom of the military. The Versailles treaty was regarded as a monstrous injustice – no thought was given to the German imperialist policies which were responsible for the treaty's existence. Parliamentary democracy was rejected out of hand as a hopelessly inefficient, corrupt and divisive system – but not a word was said of the forces that had set about the systematic destruction of democratic institutions, among the most powerful of which was the Reichswehr. The irrational concept of community (*Volksgemeinschaft*) awoke a powerful response in the army, for it had long been an ingredient of military ideology, particularly since the war. The idea of the 'community of field grey' was claimed to transcend all social and economic differences. The military wanted a highly structured authoritarian state, and although they were put off by the plebeian and lumpenproletarian rank and file of the fascist mass movement, and looked down upon them with haughty disdain, they were still prepared to accept an uneasy alliance with the fascists as the most likely means of achieving their aims. Most attractive of all for the army was the emphasis placed by the Nazis on military virtues and their determination to ignore all restrictions on armaments imposed by the Versailles treaty. The younger officers were enthusiastic about the youthful activism of the NSDAP and were attracted by its

281

vague idealism and its talk of 'renewal' and 'rebirth'. The objections of the more senior officers were largely to Hitler's style which, considering their agreement in principle with his main aims, can hardly be regarded as a serious political objection to the man and his policies.

The exact extent of the army's support for the new government cannot be accurately measured, but it was clearly considerable. Blomberg spoke of a 'wave of enthusiasm' throughout the army and told army commanders that the government was an expression of 'national will' and was the 'realization of that which many of the best men had wanted for years'. Reichenau enthusiastically supported the army's determination to use terror to destroy all that was rotten in the state, particularly the socialists. Colonel Beck was delighted with Hitler's appointment, as was Colonel Keitel. Lieutenant Claus Graf Schenk von Stauffenberg donned full dress uniform and marched through the streets to celebrate Hitler's appointment, insisting on the parallel between 1933 and 1813.

The new Reichswehr minister Werner von Blomberg proved to be a willing accomplice of the new chancellor. He was a man of conservative views but was far more sympathetic to the Nazis than most officers of this type. To Hindenburg he appeared to be an admirable non-political soldier, a war hero (he had won the *Pour le Mérite* during the war) and an aristocratic gentleman. Hitler appreciated his efforts to bring the Reichswehr and the NSDAP into a working relationship and found him easy to influence and control. His friends stressed his considerable diplomatic skill and the spontaneity of his conversation. But he was too much of a trimmer and he was weak-willed and excessively romantic. He was so impressed by the Red Army which he inspected in 1928 that he even considered becoming a communist, but instead he found solace in the philosophy of Rudolf Steiner. However it would seem that he felt that the Soviet relationship between army, party and state could, in his view, be transferred *mutatis mutandis* to Nazi Germany. For all his impeccable military exterior Blomberg was politically naïve and impulsive. For Hitler he was an almost ideal choice. He quickly became utterly subservient to the chancellor, and acted as a valuable link between the Nazi Party, the president and the Reichswehr.

Blomberg, who detested Schleicher, quickly appointed an officer to replace von Bredow as chief of the *Ministeramt*. His new right-hand man was, predictably enough, von Reichenau. He was a clever man, hard-headed, highly ambitious, and Machiavellian. But in spite of this ruthless streak he was charming and open-minded and was quite different from the old-style aristocratic and snobbish officer. He was strongly anglophile, affecting tweed clothes and speaking English at home. He was attracted by Hitler, who in turn admired the modernity of Reichenau's thinking, particularly in the development of blitzkrieg strategy. But he had reservations about the Nazis and felt that the army should keep a certain distance from the party. His basic argument was that the new state offered tremendous possibilities to the Reichswehr and therefore it would be wise to co-operate closely with Hitler. On the other hand the army would have to avoid being swamped by the NSDAP. Reichenau's concerns were therefore tactical rather than political, and he hoped to use the Nazis to secure their common military aims.

Blomberg and Reichenau thus supported the new regime, and were determined that the Reichswehr should co-operate with the Nazis. Hammerstein, who remained chief of the *Heeresleitung* for the time being, was less enthusiastic. His attitude towards the Nazis was one of aristocratic arrogance. He was scoffing and scornful, and carefully cultivated the impression of indolence and indifference. He was against the Nazis, but he lacked the courage and determination to do anything very much about it. Reichenau openly coveted Hammerstein's position, and relations between Hammerstein and Blomberg became increasingly strained. Hammerstein was determined to hang on to his position as long as possible to try to strengthen Hindenburg's opposition to Nazi interference with the army. For the moment he was saved by the fact that his dismissal would probably be construed in the army as being an exceptional political interference with the army, but it was obvious that he was unlikely to survive for very long.

Hitler was anxious to put forward his ideas to the generals as soon as possible after his appointment as chancellor. On 3 February a meeting was arranged in Hammerstein's apartment. He told the generals that he was determined to conquer

Lebensraum in the east, and to pursue a policy of ruthless germanization. He promised a large rearmament programme which would pay no heed to the dictates of the Versailles treaty. Marxism and democracy would be smashed and the forces of 'pacifism' eradicated. A matter of some concern to the army was the question of the future role of the SS and the SA for there were those, like Röhm, who wanted to see the SA as a National Socialist army, replacing the old reactionary Reichswehr. Hitler assured the generals that the SA would be 'purely political' and the army would be 'purely military' and would have no political role. Hitler thus cunningly appealed to the idea of a non-political army which had long been the ideological expression of its conservative and reactionary stance. The reaction to these remarks was on the whole positive, although some voiced a concern that some of Hitler's language was a trifle excessive. Hammerstein was not impressed, telling the French military attaché shortly afterwards that he would not tolerate any military units in Germany other than the Reichswehr. But this was an empty threat. The Reichswehr accepted Hitler's offer that the army should remain aloof from politics, and in return would be given every help and encouragement to become an effective military force.

In March Blomberg announced to his commanding generals that the Reichswehr would show 'benevolent neutrality' towards Nazi brutality, anti-communist excesses and the establishment of a centralized dictatorial state by the policy of *Gleichschaltung*. In the tradition of Seeckt, Blomberg argued that the Reichswehr had to serve the nation, not just a section of it, and that as the final aim was the preparation for a war nothing should be allowed to stand in the way of establishing the unity of nation and army. For this reason the swastika flag, the Hitler salute and the Horst Wessel song would not be allowed in the army. If any officers wished to become political soldiers then they should leave the army and join the SA.

Blomberg was treading on exceedingly thin ice. To many the distinction between benevolent neutrality and support for the regime was very fine indeed, particularly at a time when the fascist dictatorship was not yet fully established. Certainly Hitler was little concerned with such niceties. The pretence of a 'non-political' army became increasingly hard to believe. The army leaders were perfectly well aware of Hitler's long-term aims from the moment of their first meeting in Hammerstein's apartment. As the Nazi dictatorship established itself and began to influence all aspects of life it was impossible for the army to remain uninfluenced by the world around it. An army can never be divorced from the social milieu in which it is embedded, and this is doubly true under a totalitarian dictatorship.

By July Blomberg announced that the 'time of the un-political is over and there is only one thing for us to do: to serve the national movement with the utmost dedication.' The steps towards the politicization of the army were remarkably rapid and were simply disguised by the continued talk of a non-political army. Blomberg accepted the idea that the NSDAP was the only legitimate political party and wished to see the other parties vanish. Gradually concessions had to be made to the party. Military bands were allowed to play Nazi marches in spite of Blomberg's declaration in March. The swastika was incorporated into military insignia. As part of the *Gleich-schaltung* the army lost its monopoly of control over the secret service and counter-espionage. Nazi indoctrination began to play an increasingly important role in the education of soldiers. In July the *Wehrmacht* schools were given 'national political instruction', in other words pure Nazi propaganda. Nazi propaganda material was also allowed into the barracks. As early as June 1933 Blomberg announced that the Reichswehr should cease to be politically neutral and should 'serve the national socialist movement without reserve'. Blomberg and Reichenau appreciated Hitler's 'two pillars theory' by which the state was supported by the Nazi party and the army. But they seemed unable to grasp the simple fact that the political element was clearly dominant and that the army was becoming increasingly subservient to the political leadership. That this submission was voluntary and even enthusiastic did not alter the fact that the pillar was becoming a tool.

Appointments to key positions in the Reichswehr went to men who were faithful to the National Socialist regime. Such a man was General Beck who had created a favourable impression in Nazi circles by his appearance at the 1872 Leipzig treason trial and was openly sympathetic to many of the aims of the new regime. He was appointed chief of the *Truppenamt* as a successor to General Adam, and thus became Hammerstein's right-hand man. Beck, for all his brilliance as a military thinker, was withdrawn and reserved and lacked the force of character which was needed if his ideas were to survive in the new environment. It was matters of a purely technical and strategic nature which were gradually to force Beck into opposition to the regime, not a rejection of the premises of fascism.

A far greater problem than finding a successor to Adam was the question of who should replace Hammerstein at the *Heeresleitung*. Blomberg had successfully kept Hammerstein away from Hindenburg and had undermined his position. Hindenburg was not particularly fond of Hammerstein whom he regarded as one of Schleicher's creatures, and was therefore prepared to let him go. But he was particularly anxious that the question of a successor should be decided by him in his capacity as commander-in-chief of the armed forces and should not become a political matter. Thus when Hitler and Blomberg suggested that Reichenau should be appointed he was furious. Reichenau was far too much of a party man for Hindenburg's taste and he considered that his military experience was inadequate. Blomberg then threatened to resign if Reichenau was not appointed. Hindenburg was furious, saying that Blomberg was free to resign as Reichswehr minister at any time for political reasons but that as this was a purely military matter Blomberg's conduct was grossly insubordinate. Hindenburg discussed a possible alternative to Reichenau with Papen. Hindenburg's position was thus illogical. Blomberg clearly had responsibility to some degree for appointments in his political capacity as minister, and Hindenberg accepted the suggestion of Papen, a civilian and a politician. Papen's candidate was Fritsch, an officer who was widely respected in the army. Fritsch was eventually appointed even though neither Hitler nor Blomberg was particularly enthusiastic about him. He was an ultra-conservative traditionalist, and his outspoken opposition to the Weimar republic has already been mentioned. He was a devout and slightly hysterical Christian, had an excellent military mind and was politically singularly naïve. Unlike Blomberg and Reichenau, he believed that the army should remain as aloof as possible from the fascist state, although it should approve it from a distance. This was a variation of Seeckt's political attitude during the Weimar republic. Although Fritsch approved many of the aims of the Nazis he was highly critical of most of the leading figures in the party and of the SS and SA. His snobbery and his sarcasm soon won him many enemies, and even Hitler was curiously inhibited in his presence. His closest friend and associate in the Reichswehr was Beck, for they were men of a similar cast of mind.

Although the appointment of Fritsch rather than Reichenau was a modest victory for Hindenburg and the majority of the army against Hitler and Blomberg, and although some felt that this indicated that Fritsch's hopes of separating the army from the state were realistic, in fact the nazification of the army progressed rapidly. Blomberg constantly harped on the theme that there was an identity in basic ideology between the Reichswehr and the national socialists. In both movements the traditions of the front-line soldier (*Frontkämpfer*) were very strong. Both the army and the party had stood up against the forces of socialism and Bolshevism and Blomberg painted a glowing picture of their common stand in 1923, a picture which showed some interesting distortions of historical perspective. Although the Nuremberg race laws were not published until 1935 the army insisted that only those of proven 'Aryan' descent could serve. The traditional anti-semitism of the army was such that the fascists found willing accomplices in the Reichswehr for these criminal racist policies. The army was flattered by the way in which the fascists used the soldier as an ideal type of man, the army as an exemplary form of political and social organization, and war as the realization of man's highest potential. The belief in virtues of hardship, renunciation, courage, sacrifice, manliness, obedience, power and discipline were common to fascist and militarist ideology. Fascism and militarism complement and strengthen one another, and in this situation the belief that the army could somehow remain aloof from politics was sheer fantasy. This identity of aims can be clearly seen by comparing the 1930 and the 1934 editions of *The Duties of the German Soldier*, the official bible of the Reichswehr. In the first it is stated, 'The Reichswehr serves the state, not the parties'. In the second this passage reads: 'The Wehrmacht is the arms bearer of the German people. It defends the

German Reich and fatherland, its people which are united by national socialism, and its *Lebensraum.*'

Whereas relations between the Nazi party and the army were becoming increasingly cordial, those between the army and the SA were very strained. At first the army regarded the SA as a useful source of manpower, and a number of agreements were reached between the two. The gist of these agreements was that the Wehrmacht would respect and salute members of the SS and the SA and their colours. In return the SA and SS were placed under the control of the army in military affairs. Hitler was also repeatedly to insist that the army was the 'sole bearer of arms in the nation' and thus snubbed the SA in their desire to become a national socialist army. The SA was annoyed by the avuncular attitude of the army and was determined to remain as independent as possible from its control. Before long the tensions between the SA and the army became increasingly severe as the question of the position of the SA in the Nazi state led to a severe crisis in the regime.

Röhm never lost sight of his aim of creating a new army under his leadership. As he phrased it, 'the grey rock must be drowned in the brown flood'. Far from the SA providing the Reichswehr with manpower, Röhm wished to reverse these roles. The Reichswehr was to become the training ground for his own national socialist militia. This notion of a 'revolutionary' army was part of the radical rhetoric of the Nazi extremists who were demanding the 'second revolution', and the SA was the organizational spearhead of this movement. The political demands of the SA radicals were that the official party programme should indeed be implemented. They wanted the destruction of consumer co-operatives, the end of the chain stores, elimination of monopolies and cartels and drastic changes in the structure of the banks and the corporations. Hitler's reply to this was that: 'The ideas in our programme do not oblige us to act like idiots and overturn everything.' Almost as soon as Hitler gained power steps were taken to neutralize the radicals and the SA. Big business paid protection money against possible attacks by the SA by means of Krupp's 'Hitler Donation'. The 'Fighting Organizations' of the little businessmen were abolished. When Keppler, who had played such an important role as liaison man between big business and the NSDAP, became Hitler's economic adviser in June 1933 the party's hold on economic affairs was weakened and the crack-pot ideas of the party's economic luminaries tended to be ignored. In these early stages the party, big business and the generals had a common economic plan. Their aims were military equality with the great powers, national autarchy in economics, economic rearmament, the destruction of the labour movement and the invigoration of capitalism after the depression. In such a programme there was no place for the reactionary anti-capitalist rantings of the radicals, and Blomberg heartily agreed with Schacht's dictum that spinning wheels and folk dancing were very nice and pretty, but only big business could produce guns and submarines.

This economic policy, in which the Reichswehr played an important role, hurt the little men who had supported the Nazi party and many of them now seemed doomed. The depression had reduced unit costs and therefore had strengthened the big firms against the little ones. Interest rates had risen sharply. The petit bourgeoisie had no labour unions to fight for their demands. The national socialist economic programme tended to make this situation worse. The rising share of public investment in total investment delayed the reduction of interest rates and the destruction of 'interest slavery'. Private parties became increasingly excluded from the capital market. Private consumption was reduced by deliberate fiscal policy and by the reduction in the production of consumer goods. Wages were frozen and real wages declined. Imports were restricted except for those goods needed for military purposes. Big business was delighted, for, as Max Weber said, 'In general, and at all times, imperialist capitalism, especially colonial booty capitalism based on direct force and compulsory labour, has offered by far the greatest opportunities for profit.' The little men were bitterly disappointed. Given little more than the right to destroy Jewish property, they began to clamour for a 'second revolution'. The very reverse happened. In July 1933 Schmitt, the general director of the largest insurance firm in Germany, was appointed minister of economics. In his programme he guaranteed business against what was termed 'interference by the NSDAP', business was given further tax incentives, wages were restrained, but price controls were dropped. Robert Ley's labour front was instructed not to press the demands of labour, and the labour act of

January 1934 established the 'leadership principle' in the factories, thus giving legal sanction to the domination of labour by capital. To appease the radicals who were strongly opposed to finance capitalism, a commission was established in April 1933 to examine banking. Chaired by Schacht, the committee consisted largely of bankers, with the usual assortment of pliable academics. The net result was that there was an increased degree of governmental control over the banks which enabled them to make even bigger profits. In spite of all the rhetoric about 'hereditary farms' and 'blood and soil', the Junkers and their allies in the military were largely able to stop the breaking up of the large estates and the land reform which the radicals wanted. A solution was later to be found by grabbing the land of other nations. Fascist imperialism and racism were thus adequate substitutes for old-style 'National Socialism'.

This growing split within the system was further exacerbated for Hitler by the fact that in conservative circles there was much talk of restoring the monarchy when Hindenburg died, and as the president was not likely to live much longer a succession crisis was looming. In order to combine the post of chancellor with that of president without there being any serious opposition, the attitude of the Reichswehr was critical not least because of the enormous prestige of the army in conservative circles. In his fight against the 'revolutionary' Nazis and the SA Hitler could be certain of the support of the Reichswehr. The army wanted a forced rearmament programme, and thus had no sympathy for the folk dancing and spinning wheel brigade, quite apart from their hostility to anything that smacked of socialism. The increasing friction between the army and the SA, and Röhm's ambition to control the military, had resulted in the army now being firmly opposed to the SA. The stage was set for an agreement between Hitler and the army.

On 28 February 1934, Schlieffen's birthday, when the general staff had its annual dinner, Hitler addressed the generals at a meeting in the general staff headquarters in the Bendlerstrasse. He announced that the revolution was over and that he had no intention of approving a militia as proposed by Röhm. He argued that Nazi economic policy had brought an end to unemployment but the economic boom would last for only eight years. Therefore living space would have to be seized in the east. This aggressive war would begin with a swift attack in the west followed by a lightning strike in the east. For this purpose the Reichswehr alone was suitable. Röhm's militia was no substitute for a highly trained professional army armed with the most modern weapons. The SA would still have a useful function in pre- and post-military training and for political indoctrination, but the Reichswehr was the sole bearer of arms.

Röhm and the SA were furious at this move and some harsh criticisms of Hitler were voiced. Röhm contacted Schleicher in the search for allies but little came of this. In conservative circles some hoped that the SA crisis would become so severe that the Reichswehr would be put in the saddle, and this would be the first stage in bringing back the monarchy. But Blomberg and Fritsch saw no point at all in this. Hitler gave the army everything it wanted and supported it against the SA. The conservatives simply failed to realize that although there was a split between the Reichswehr and the SA, this did not mean that there was a split between the Reichswehr and the NSDAP.

On 17 June 1934 Papen delivered his Marburg speech which criticized the regime from a conservative perspective. Hitler was now determined to act. On 24 June Himmler and Heydrich called a meeting of SS leaders and told them that they would have to co-operate closely with the Reichswehr to smash a revolt by the SA. Lists of those who were to be liquidated by the SA were carefully fabricated, and included leading figures in the Reichswehr so as to ensure their support. On the same day the Reichswehr began preparations for the *putsch*, and some units were alerted. On 29 June the *Völkische Beobachter* published an article by Blomberg packed with professions of loyalty to Hitler and the national socialist state. He wrote: 'Today the soldier plays a conscious part in the political life of the German people which has become bound together in unity.' There was no longer any talk of 'two pillars' or the separation of military and political power. Reichenau co-operated closely with Himmler and Heydrich in preparing the action against the SA and other opponents of the regime. The murders were committed on 30 July 1934 by members of the SS who were given the enthusiastic support of Reichswehr units.

Some 150 to 200 people were slaughtered, among them Schleicher and his right-hand man General von Bredow.

Thus the Reichswehr, by giving its full support to this criminal act, played a vital role in strengthening Hitler's dictatorship at a time when it faced mounting criticism from the left and the right. Blomberg praised Hitler and his gangster methods in an army order published on 1 July which read: 'With soldierly determination and exemplary courage the Führer has attacked and destroyed these traitors and mutineers. The Wehrmacht will show its gratitude by its dedication and fidelity.' He forbade any discussion of the murder of Schleicher and Bredow, and no soldier was allowed to attend the funeral. It is to Hammerstein's credit that he ignored this order and attended in full-dress uniform. There was absolutely no evidence that the SA and its allies were planning a coup as Hitler claimed, and thus the Reichswehr, by conniving in an illegal act, helped to legalize terror and to strengthen the dictatorship, and ultimately ensured that it would in future at all times be the willing accomplice of the fascist regime. Blomberg, Reichenau and Fritsch were in no sense hoodwinked or deceived; they acted with their eyes wide open, fully aware of the consequences of their actions. The identity of aims of Hitler and his generals was complete.

Having so successfully mastered the SA crisis and having won the complicity of the Reichswehr in this criminal act with only a few murmurs of discontent from generals such as Adam, Witzleben, Rundstedt and Leeb, who felt that the murder of Schleicher and Bredow was going a bit too far, Hitler could look forward to the succession problem with a certain equanimity. On 2 August 1934 Hindenburg died. The way had been carefully prepared for Hitler to combine the offices of chancellor and president. The cabinet had already prepared a bill to this effect which was clearly unconstitutional in that it ignored the restrictions placed on such arbitrary acts by the emergency law which formed the legal basis of the Nazi dictatorship. The Reichswehr had also prepared for this intended change by drafting a new oath of allegiance. This was the work of Reichenau who disliked the old oath to the constitution which was becoming increasingly anomalous as Hitler clearly had no intention of being bound by any constitution. On the very day when Hindenburg died the Wehrmacht swore its oath of allegiance to Hitler: 'I swear to God this sacred oath, that I will unconditionally obey the Führer of the German Reich and people, Adolf Hitler.' Hitler was now supreme commander of the armed forces with the power of command effectively at his disposal. In fact he scarcely bothered to use it until 1938, but by supporting Hitler against the SA on 2 August and by taking the new oath of allegiance the army had prepared the ground for their 'nemesis of power'. To critics Blomberg insisted that Hitler was determined to build up the army, and therefore the army would have to be prepared to take the rough with the smooth. Fritsch, although he remained passive, began to have some second thoughts that perhaps the army was giving up too many of its independent rights to the regime. Hitler realized that the Reichswehr had done much to help him consolidate his power. In a letter of thanks to Blomberg on 20 August 1934 he wrote:

Just as the officers and men of the Wehrmacht have dedicated themselves to the new state embodied in me, so I will always consider it to be my highest obligation to stand up for the continuation and the independence of the Wehrmacht in accordance with the testament of the deceased Field Marshal and with my own desire to secure the Wehrmacht as the sole bearer of the nation's arms.

The Wehrmacht showed its dedication to Hitler and the new state by playing a prominent role in the party rally held in September, which was designed as a massive display of solidarity after the events of July and August. The official film of the rally, *Triumph of the Will*, showed the army marching along with the Nazis, and the 'Wehrmacht Day' at the end of the rally was an enormous success. Any tensions that might have been growing between the army and the national socialists were skilfully concealed.

After 30 July 1934 the Reichswehr broke off all contacts with the SA which now sank into relative insignificance. The real winners of 30 July were the industrialists and bankers, who now no longer had to fear the radicalism of the left Nazis, and the SS. As a reward for their sterling services Hitler created the SS *Leibstandarte Adolf Hitler* as a separate regiment which was independent from the Reichswehr. Thus the army found that they had helped to put down one rival only to be faced with another. Tensions between the army and the SS soon became acute, and rumours began to circulate that the Reichswehr was planning a *putsch* which would be led by Fritsch, who had realized that the army's victory on 30 August had been pyrrhic. On 3 January 1935 Hitler called a meeting of party and military leaders at the State Opera unter den Linden. In his speech Hitler told his audience that he needed a strong and powerful army in order that Germany's place in the world might be secured. Therefore it was essential that there should be unity between the party and the Wehrmacht. He announced that his faith in the army was 'unshakable' and that he refused to believe that any of his generals were working against him. This speech did something to ease the tension for the next few months. Blomberg and Reichenau did everything possible to avoid conflicts with the SS, bending over backwards to avoid charges that they were 'reactionaries' and lukewarm in their enthusiasm for the national socialist regime. Fritsch, however, took a much stronger line against the SS and against encroachments from the party. Like Blomberg he agreed that the Führer was beyond all criticism and that they were bound to him by their almost religious oath of allegiance. Fritsch was, however, much more aware of the fact that the army was menaced to a degree by the SS and the NSDAP. Blomberg's solution was to give rousing demonstrations of loyalty, and assurances that the army was national socialist to the core. He said: 'He who cannot follow a national socialist *Weltanschauung* has no place in the ranks of the Wehrmacht, and must be removed.' This 'more Hitler than Hitler' approach was too much even for Reichenau who, like Fritsch, wanted to preserve a modicum of independence for the army. As the army expanded rapidly, and as the demands of the totalitarian state became more pressing, Fritsch and Reichenau found themselves increasingly powerless to combat the nazification of the army. There seemed to be no alternative to the toadying attitude of Blomberg, for none of the senior officers would think of a determined revolt. There was no reason why they should do so, for whatever their grumbling they agreed that the state was giving them almost everything they wanted, and putting up with the jibes and pinpricks of the SS and the party was the price that had to be paid.

In May 1935 the army command structure was reorganized. The Reichswehr minister was now named war minister so that his task would not be obscured by any euphemisms; the chief of the *Heeresleitung* became commander-in-chief of the army (*Oberbefehlshaber des Heeres*). The chief of the *Truppenamt* was called chief of the general staff of the army. In October Reichenau's position was taken by Keitel, a hard working and unimaginative organization man who was totally subservient to Hitler and whose political naïvety was almost unmatched in the German Army. Keitel's son was married to Blomberg's daughter and this close family tie was combined with a common conviction that they were both serving the greatest revolution in world history. The reorganization of the army placed it directly under Hitler, for Blomberg as war minister was no longer responsible to the Reichstag.

Until the end of 1937 the army's strategic thinking was mostly cautious. Von Manstein's section of the general staff prepared a strategic plan, 'Plan Red', in 1935. It was a defensive scheme against the French and the Czechs, the main emphasis of which was on holding the Rhine against the French and having only modest forces against the Czechs. As the non-agression pact had been signed with Poland it was not considered necessary to deploy troops on that sector of the eastern frontier. As Hitler's policies became more and more daring there was growing confusion, disagreement and rivalry in the upper echelons of the Wehrmacht. These differences were tactical and methodological; they cannot possibly be construed as an opposition to fascist policies as some historians have suggested. Beck, and most of the leading officers, urged caution. They feared that the murder of Dolfuss, leaving the League of Nations, or the 16 March – the date on which conscription was introduced in defiance of the Treaty of Versailles – might lead to serious conflicts which Germany, with its rearmament programme incomplete, might not be able to survive. For similar reasons Fritsch opposed German intervention in the Spanish civil war in 1936 (Plan Richard) and Beck objected to the notion of armed intervention in Austria in the following year ('Plan Otto'). That Beck had nothing in principle against an unprovoked attack on Austria can be amply seen in the enthusiasm with which he greeted the *Anschluss* in 1938. His objection to

'Otto' was that German rearmament was as yet insufficient for such an undertaking.

On 5 November 1937 Hitler called Blomberg and Fritsch to attend a conference in the Chancellery at which Neurath, Goering and Raeder were present. The record of the meeting was kept by Colonel Hossbach and can be studied in the 'Hossbach Memorandum'. Hitler talked for more than four hours, indulging in flights of social-Darwinist and racist fantasy. The gist of his speech was that he was determined to secure living space for the German people, and that this would be possible only in Europe, for he denounced colonialism as being too liberal. He insisted that this would not be possible without a war, and announced his unchangeable determination to fight this war not later than 1943/45 under favourable conditions. His territorial demands were for Austria and Czechoslovakia. Blomberg and Fritsch were alarmed at these ideas, and now realized that Hitler's rearmament programme was not just to amuse the generals. Again their concerns were technical, for they feared that Hitler was forcing the pace. Fritsch departed for two months' recuperation in Egypt and Blomberg quickly adapted his thinking to these ideas, so that there was once again no question of opposition.

Without any directives from Hitler Blomberg ordered a revision of the general staff's strategic plans. The result was 'Plan Green', which was completed on 21 December 1937. The plan contained a clear declaration of intent: 'When Germany is fully ready for war in all areas the military preconditions will be met for an aggressive war against Czechoslovakia and thus for a solution of the German space problem which will be successful even if one or other great powers should attack us.' 'Plan Green' was clearly a response to Hitler's remarks on 5 November, and the phrase 'fully ready' might possibly have been intended to give the army the final decision as to whether a war should be fought or not and under what circumstances. But it would be absurd to argue that the generals had been seduced by the demonic powers of Hitler. The plan was a swift, enthusiastic and unsolicited response to Hitler's guidelines.

The attack on the army leadership, which began in January 1938, was mounted not by Hitler, who had every reason to be satisfied with the army, but by three of his most ambitious paladins, Himmler, Heydrich and Goering. Relations between the army and the SS had always been strained. The SS resented the army, thinking it to be stuffy, snobbish and reactionary. The army found the brutality and radicalism of the SS distasteful and felt menaced by the Gestapo and the *Sicherheitsdienst*. Goering had been locked in battle with Blomberg and Fritsch over the expansion of the Lutwaffe which the army had opposed, and wanted not merely to win this battle but also, if possible, to weaken the army so that he might be appointed commander-in-chief of the armed forces.

Their chance came on 12 January 1938 when Blomberg married his second wife, one Fräulein Erna Gruhn, who had been a typist in his office. Blomberg had acted perfectly correctly. He had asked Hitler's permission, and the wedding had taken place with Hitler and Goering as witnesses. It was not until after the wedding that rumours began to circulate that Frau Blomberg had been a prostitute, and Goering was given a file which showed that she had indeed been convicted of posing for pornographic photographs. Goering had been given the file by Keitel, who was either exceedingly foolish or had his reasons for wanting to get rid of Blomberg. The file had been given to Keitel by the police in the hopes that the army would be able to sort out the affair without the SS becoming involved. But Keitel's action made it certain that the SS, which was already poised to strike at the army, would exploit the Blomberg scandal to the full.

Himmler decided that an attack on Blomberg would be combined with a renewed effort to remove Fritsch. In 1936 Heydrich had tried to get rid of Fritsch by presenting Hitler with a file designed to show that he was a homosexual. Hitler ordered the documents to be destroyed and said that he wished to hear nothing more of the matter. The Gestapo prudently copied the file which was now prepared carefully, with extra material added, and given to Goering. On 24 January Goering informed Hitler of the dubious background of Frau Blomberg and of the accusations against Fritsch. Hitler quickly made up his mind that Blomberg had to go. During Blomberg's final interview with Hitler he suggested that Hitler should become war minister as Goering was not acceptable to the Führer who considered him too idle, and there was no outstanding candidate. When Hitler asked Blomberg who could then run the staff he replied that Keitel was hardly suitable as he was a mere bureaucrat. Hitler exclaimed: 'He's just the man I am looking for!' Thus on Blomberg's instigation Hitler decided to take over supreme command of the armed forces and to have an utterly subservient and unimaginative officer as his right-hand man.

Fritsch resigned on 4 February, but in the course of his trial it became abundantly clear that the evidence against him was sheer fabrication. There were those such as Oster, Gisevius, Dohnanyi, Goerdeler and Schacht who wanted to use the Fritsch crisis in order to discredit the SS and the Gestapo and to restrain some of the more excessive elements in the regime. Others wanted varying degrees of 'satisfaction' for the wrong done to Fritsch. Fritsch, however, did not want to get involved in any way with any such political moves and resisted all attempts to enlist his support against the regime. When the Fritsch trial ended in a verdict of 'not guilty' this did not cause any great sensation. Men's minds were occupied elsewhere with Hitler's march into Austria and the conclusion of the *Anschluss*. This was a major triumph for the regime, and there was no hope of mobilizing opinion in favour of a general who was hardly known to the public. The would-be conspirators and malcontents had to be satisfied with collecting money to buy Fritsch a new house, a very modest gesture of protest which was totally without effect. Fritsch died in the early days of the war from a sniper's bullet in Poland. Since 1945 there have been attempts to make him into an anti-Nazi hero, but however unjust the charges against him were he is unsuitable material for these purposes. He suffered in the hands of a regime which he supported and which he had helped bring to power. He did nothing to embarrass the Nazis in spite of the treatment he received. His opposition to Hitler's war plans were caused by differences over means rather than ends.

On 4 February 1938 Hitler announced a reorganization of the army. The post of war minister was abolished. General Keitel was appointed chief of the armed forces high command (OKW) with a status equivalent to the other Reich ministers and with much the same functions as the former war minister. The army high command (OKH) was given to General Brauchitsch. Hitler clearly wanted Reichenau to be Fritsch's successor. He knew he was an enthusiastic supporter of the regime and hoped he would give the army the dynamic leadership which it had lacked under Blomberg and Fritsch. There was considerable opposition to this idea in the army because Reichenau was considered to be too much of a party man. Rundstedt told Hitler 'in the name of the army' that Reichenau was not acceptable, and once again this well-worn formula worked. Hitler, having gained complete control over the army, was prepared to compromise. Even Keitel opposed the appointment of Reichenau. Brauchitsch was an ideal candidate for Hitler, for he had a brilliant military record, admired Hitler greatly, had a fanatically Nazi wife and was clearly likely to be a pliable and willing subordinate. He was also quite acceptable to the army. Brauchitsch eagerly accepted Hitler's offer even before Fritsch had been tried, thus making it more difficult for there to be an effective opposition by the army to these attacks on the high command.

The affair of Fritsch and Blomberg was a serious setback for the army. Hitler was now in full control and Keitel at OKW and Brauchitsch at OKH were completely subservient to him. Himmler and the SS had been greatly strengthened by their victory over the army. The change in the leadership of the army removed many of those who had expressed concern about the course of German policy since 1936 with its emphasis on economic autarchy and on rearmament for blitzkrieg which would obviate the need for a long war in which the economic superiority of Germany's enemies would lead to its defeat. Those who hoped to use the Fritsch scandal to embarrass the regime were mainly those who favoured the idea of a war in the east, if necessary with the Soviet Union and even with France, but who were concerned that Germany should have some outside economic support, preferably from the USA. They were also concerned that the pace of rearmament was creating severe inflationary and foreign exchange problems, and that therefore rearmament should be more gradual. With the reorganization of the army in 1938 a further step was taken towards war.

On 9 March 1938 Schuschnigg, the Austrian chancellor, announced that there would be a plebiscite on 13 March which was designed to snub Hitler and show Austria's determination to resist the Nazis. On the following day Hitler called Beck and his operations chief Manstein to ask them their ideas on the military occupation of Austria. It took them a mere five hours to prepare the plan so that orders could be issued in time for the army to cross the border on 12 March. The operation was hardly a masterpiece of military planning. Tanks had to refuel at commercial petrol stations in Austria, while their divisional commander plotted their route to Vienna just like any tourist with his Baedeker. The army's role in the *Anschluss* was thus kept as minimal as possible.

The annexation of Austria had occurred without the intervention of any of the powers as some pessimists had feared. This strengthened Hitler's determination to move swiftly to grab *lebensraum* in the east. The general staff chief, Beck, became increasingly alarmed at the trend of Hitler's imperialist policies. In March 1938 he composed a careful memorandum which argued that there would be a general European war if the problem of Czechoslovakia was not settled in a way which was acceptable to Britain. Germany would have little chance of victory in such a war and Italy was hardly an ally to inspire great confidence. Brauchitsch and Keitel were reluctant to pass on this memorandum to Hitler, and the version which they did show him was severely pruned. Hitler was furious with Beck and told his miliary advisers that he lacked 'objectivity' and seriously over-rated the strength of the enemy. Beck's views were certainly not influenced by any love for Czechoslovakia or any fundamental opposition to Hitler's policies. In a further memorandum dated 29 May he argued that Germany needed *lebensraum* both in Europe and in the colonies, that Czechoslovakia in its present form was 'impossible' for Germany and that a solution had to be found by war if necessary. The problem for Beck was that he feared that Britain and France would support the status quo in Czechoslovakia and that Germany was in no position to fight a war on this scale. Little did he realize that the British and French governments would actively help Germany to destroy Czechoslovakia, thus removing the ground from under the feet of the miliary opposition to Hitler's more excessive plans.

Beck greatly overestimated British understanding of German policy, and underestimated the anti-Soviet thrust of appeasement politics, but for all his agreement in principle with much of Nazi politics he was more realistic and sober in his thinking than any other leading military figure in Germany at the time. He realized that Hitler's policy was risking a world war, and that in such a war Germany, in the long run, had no chance of success. By July Beck was proposing a kind of generals' strike if Hitler were to lead Germany into such a war. He wrote: 'Military obedience reaches its limits when one's conscience and sense of responsibility forbids the execution of a command.' This did not mean that Beck was now a firm opponent of the regime. He hoped that national socialism would be reformed, that there would be an end to what he called the 'Cheka methods' of the Gestapo and SD, and that the SS would be held in check. This was not strictly opposition to national socialism, indeed it showed a naïve misunderstanding of the true nature of fascism, just as his objections to Hitler's Czechoslovakian policy were based on a lack of comprehension of British and French policy.

At the beginning of August Brauchitsch, at Beck's insistence, called a conference of senior army commanders to discuss these concerns about 'Plan Green'. In his opening remarks Brauchitsch echoed Beck's concern that a German attack on Czechoslovakia would lead to the intervention of Britain and France which in turn would lead to a disaster for Germany. There was general agreement that these ideas came directly from Beck, who probably wrote the memorandum which Brauchitsch read aloud. The generals, with the exception of Reichenau and Busch, agreed that the army was not ready for such a war and that the general feeling in the army and in the country was against war. Brauchitsch ended with the statement that war would mean the end of German culture, but when he conveyed these thoughts to Hitler he soon collapsed. Brauchitsch was certainly not the man to lead a generals' strike.

Hitler, who had heard of these murmurs of discontent among the generals, called the army leaders to a meeting at the Berghof on 10 August. They were treated to a long rambling monologue on national socialist ideology, but the main point Hitler made was that he was convinced that the western powers would not intervene if Germany were to attack Czechoslovakia. Five days later he told a group of generals that he was determined to

301

attack Czechoslovakia in the autumn, and that as long as Chamberlain and Daladier were still in power there would be nothing to fear. This was too much for Beck who realized that there was now nothing to stop Hitler as Brauchitsch seemed almost mesmerized by him, his will completely paralysed. His position was hopeless. He was convinced that war with Czechoslovakia would lead to the defeat of Germany, and realized that there was nothing he could do about it. On 18 August 1938 Beck handed in his resignation which Hitler eventually accepted.

With the resignation of Beck there was no longer any chance that the army would be able to control, restrain or even influence Hitler. Basically Beck's struggle had been to secure the position of the army in the Third Reich. He believed that the army should participate in decision-making on vital matters of state such as war and peace. This was intolerable to Hitler. Beck insisted that the army possessed a technical expertise which politicians could not afford to ignore and which gave the army the right and the obligation to participate in policy-making. The tragedy for the victims of Nazi aggression was that Beck and those who thought alike had no fundamental critique of national socialism, no valid alternative to offer, and thus their criticisms were mostly tactical, technical and in the short term completely wrong. Hitler's assessment of the European political situation was far more realistic than Beck's, and his early and brilliant successes blinded men to the objective inevitability of the defeat of fascism.

Beck's successor was General Franz Halder. He came from an old Bavarian military family and was an outstanding staff officer. He was a highly intelligent, clever and even witty man, but like so many of the leading generals of the time he suffered from a curious paralysis of the will. One historian has wickedly suggested that in this respect he confirms Bismarck's aphorism that 'a Bavarian is a cross between a man and an Austrian'. Politically he was a dyed-in-the-wool conservative who shared Beck's concerns with Hitler's lack of restraint, but he put even fewer obstacles in the way of Hitler than did his predecessor. After 1945 Halder spent much of his time creating a legend of the determined opposition to Hitler by the general staff from September 1938 onwards, much of which has found its way into the literature. But the truth is rather more complex and confusing.

By September 1938 it was obvious that Hitler was heading for war and an opposition group was beginning to form which was determined to stop him. The aim of the conspirators was to arrest Hitler and place him on trial as soon as he gave the orders to implement 'Plan Green'. The whole business was extraordinarily jejeune and showed a lamentable lack of understanding of the situation either in Germany or abroad, not to mention the slipshod planning of the actual coup. The coup was planned by Witzleben who was responsible for the military side, and by Oster who would supervise the police. Halder was drawn into the opposition group by Oster, Weizsäcker and Gisevius. He led an extraordinarily schizophrenic existence for the next few days. On the one hand he was busily polishing up the plans for the destruction of Czechoslovakia, and on the other hand conspiring with the opposition. He agreed to give Witzleben advance notice of Hitler's order to attack Czechoslovakia and promised that he would not pass on the order. At this point a group of Young Stahlhelm, formed into a commando troop, would break into the chancellery and arrest Hitler. The monarchy was to be restored and war would be averted. The basic political ideas of the conspirators were exceedingly authoritarian, and the whole enterprise was exceptionally badly planned.

Brauchitsch made a further attempt to persuade Hitler to change his mind, but was treated with a torrent of abuse. Accusations of cowardice were levelled at the army by Hitler and Goering. Keitel lectured his staff at OKW telling them that he would not tolerate any doubts or criticisms. Jodl with his unshakeable belief in the 'genius of the Führer' fully supported Keitel and condemned the other generals as a bunch of doubting Thomases who failed to realize that the little corporal was the greatest statesman since Bismarck. The conspirators, smarting under these accusations, continued to plan the attack on Czechoslovakia.

The attack was to begin on 30 September. On 28 Brauchitsch implored Keitel to try to stop Hitler from marching into the Sudetenland. At 4.15 that afternoon Chamberlain announced that he would go to Munich the next day. The conspirators' plan was to mount the *putsch* when Germany was on the verge of war. Chamberlain's decision to go to Munich and betray the Czechs meant that these ideas could not be put to the test. The British government, which had been informed of the conspirators' plans, did not take them very seriously and anyway thought that they were a bunch of reactionary Wilhelminians – for once showing a reasonably accurate understanding of German affairs. Some members of the Foreign Office thought Hitler was a moderate who acted as a restraining influence on hotheads like Ribbentrop, and, as Henderson argued, if he was given the Sudetenland he would be a good boy. The British were far more concerned with building a *cordon sanitaire* against the Soviet Union, with the state of British armaments and with the problems of the British economy than they were with the romantic notions of a handful of generals and bureaucrats or the fate of a small and distant nation.

After Munich Halder gave up the idea of active resistance and lapsed into complete fatalism, interesting himself solely in the technicalities of military planning. Beck was furious with Halder for adopting this attitude and continued to argue as he had done during the Czechoslovak crisis that the western powers were bound to intervene and that if it came to a world war it would be too late to avoid a calamity. Halder argued that the western powers were even less likely to save Poland than they had been to help Czechoslovakia, and that therefore there would be no war. The conspirators continued with their planning and plotting but they were as ineffectual as ever. The *Reichskristallnacht* on 9 November 1938 when Nazi hooligans destroyed valuable Jewish property appalled most senior officers. In spite of the traditional anti-semitism of the officer corps, this mindless destruction of property seemed to them utterly senseless. But once again they did nothing. Gradually men like Witzleben and Goerdeler began to have second thoughts about a 'generals' strike'. As representatives of the reactionary wing of the resistance they had a deep suspicion and distrust of the working class, and they feared that such an action would simply trigger off a pro-Nazi general strike, a kind of Kapp *putsch* in reverse. It was not until much later, too late indeed, that some officers realized that it was only in cooperation with the working class that a genuine anti-fascist front could be formed. In any case the idea of a generals' strike made little sense because most of the generals were convinced that war would be avoided by diplomacy.

The Sudetenland was occupied in September 1938 and in the following March the remainder of Czechoslovakia was occupied. On 23 May Hitler sketched his further plans to his generals. He argued that Germany's economic problems could be solved only by a war of annexation, and that his policy was directed not at Danzig but at *Lebensraum* in the east. Indeed the economic problems of Germany, the result of forced armaments, were considerable. The capital goods sector was increasing at four times the rate of consumer goods, so that the German consumer was forced to pay a heavy price for rearmament. The dependence on imports from abroad was particularly high in the armaments industry: 7·5 per cent of iron ore was imported, 90 per cent of zinc and 99 per cent of bauxite. In spite of the improvement of the synthetics industry 65 per cent of the mineral oils, 85 per cent of the rubber and 70 per cent of the raw materials for textiles had to be imported. The demands placed on the economy by the armed forces were considerable. They consumed 30 per cent of the steel, 14 per cent of the rubber, 14 per cent of the fuel and 45 per cent of the cement produced in the country. Between 1933 and 1938 Germany increased military expenditure by 2,000 per cent, and by 1938 armaments accounted for 62 per cent of the budget, or 16 per cent of the GNP. By 1938 the overall level of consumption had not reached the 1929 level. From 1933 to 1936 industrial profits rose by 433 per cent, but there was a reduction in real wages and an increase in the intensity of labour. The national debt had reached the catastrophic level of 30·7 billion marks by March 1939 and the situation could be only temporarily checked by the wildly inflationary policies of the Reichsbank. The frantic need for foreign currency, occasioned by the rapid increase in the import of materials needed for armaments, could only be met by an aggressive export programme and the unscrupulous use of blocked accounts and dubious currency agreements. This in turn served to heighten the antagonisms with other trading nations, particularly Britain and the USA. That the Nazi regime did not win the enthusiastic approval of all Germans is shown by the fact that by 1939 more than one million people had been, or still were, in concentration camps. Thus war in the east was not merely to realize the plans that Hitler had been concocting since the 1920s, but also to find a solution for the pressing economic problems, which really required a drastic reordering of society and its priorities and values. Poland was an attractive prize. The capture of the economically developed areas of Upper Silesia and Dombrowa would increase Germany's coal holdings by 28 per cent, and iron and steel by 24 per cent, not to mention the holdings of zinc, sulphur, manganese and oil.

Thus on 3 April the OKW gave orders for a plan for an attack on Poland, known as 'Plan White'. The attack was to be capable of being launched at any time after 1 September 1939. The plan was for a sudden and violent attack on Poland on the second day of mobilization. Only weak forces would be left in the west against a possible French attack. There was no protest against this plan by the generals, for they had now come to share Hitler's belief that Poland could be seized without a general European war. A long-standing aim of the generals would then be achieved – the destruction of Poland. As Seeckt had said: 'The very existence of Poland is unbearable, and irreconcilable with the vital interests of Germany.'

In the late spring and summer the German government made frantic preparations for war. Diplomatic and economic agreements were made with a number of states with the most cynical of motives. The economy was geared to war. The non-aggression pact with Poland and the Naval agreement with Britain were renounced by Hitler in a characteristic speech in the Reichstag. In August, when the army was told that the attack on Poland would begin at any moment, Hitler's thoughts were already devoted to the next step in his *Lebensraum* plan. To Carl J. Burkhardt he said that everything he did was aimed against the Soviet Union, and if the western powers were so stupid as to fail to see this, then he would be forced to defeat them in the west before attacking the Soviet Union so as to seize the Ukraine so that Germany would not starve. On 25 August Hitler cancelled his orders for an attack on Poland. On 31 August he issued the order for the attack to begin the following day at 04.45 hrs. This time the order was not cancelled.

With the outbreak of the war there were certain organizational changes in the army. Overall responsibility for the conduct of the war, under the direct control of Hitler, was with the Armed Forces Office (*Wehrmachtsführungsamt*) of the OKW under Jodl. Jodl tried to co-ordinate the staff work of the three armed forces and of Germany's allies. He was responsible for implementing Hitler's orders and for keeping him informed of developments as well as preparing position papers for Hitler to use as the basis for his decisions. Jodl had complete faith in Hitler's genius, and rarely took advice from other officers. His motto, which he confided to his diary, was that 'we shall win this war, even if it goes one hundred times against the doctrine of the general staff'. Jodl tended to ignore his own staff, and that staff was never large enough effectively to master all the work that was demanded of it. The result was that there was a serious lack of co-ordination and agreement at the top of the armed forces throughout the war which, combined with traditional inter-departmental and inter-service rivalries, made the military leadership inefficient and allowed Hitler to exercise even more power than would otherwise have been possible. However the notion that the generals were a lot of mindless puppets who were totally mesmerized and manipulated by Hitler is nothing more than a legend designed to abrogate them of their responsibilities for the crimes of German fascism.

The army leaders preferred to turn a blind eye to the excesses of the SS and the Gestapo and were mainly concerned that they would not be held responsible for their criminal acts. Thus in occupied Poland the army was largely outmanoeuvred by the SS so that when the extent of the atrocities committed in Poland was known, the army had few grounds for effective complaint. Many of the generals in Poland were disgusted at the barbarous activities of the SS and protested that as much of this was happening in areas which were nominally under military control they should be stopped at once. The supreme commander east, General Blaskowitz, complained directly to Hitler, who went off into a long tirade against the 'salvation army' attitude of the military. In May 1940 Hitler managed to get Blaskowitz removed from his command, and was able to avoid the appointment of General Ulex who had also been highly critical of German policies in Poland. The quarrels and rivalries between the general governor, the civilian administration, the SS and the army continued. The commander in Poland, General von Gienanth, continued to protest to Keitel about the excesses of the SS and the police, but was told to stop concerning himself with matters which were not his business. Keitel, Jodl and Brauchitsch, by failing to stand up against the SS, weakened the relative position of the army and became accessories to the murderous activities of the SS.

The army failed to protest against the growth of the *Waffen* SS and Himmler, skilfully exploiting the rivalries between OKW and OKH, was even able to get the army's support for his plans to expand the military side of his empire. The subservient attitude of the army towards Himmler was clearly shown in its attitude to his order of October 1939 calling on soldiers to produce illegitimate children to secure the 'eternal life of our blood and race'. The SS journal *Schwarze Korps* insisted that any girl who refused to bear such a child was guilty of desertion. The army was horrified at this order and felt that it was grossly immoral, but it refused to do anything very much about it. Indeed General Groppe, who was strongly critical of the order, was forced to retire from active service because Himmler felt that he had been insulted by these criticisms.

On 27 September 1939 Hitler summoned the commanders of the three services and announced that he intended to attack the west that year. The army was alarmed at this news, for it was convinced that Germany was in no position to attack France at that time. A few days previously General von Stülpnagel had completed a study which indicated that an attack on the west could not be launched before the spring of 1942. Brauchitsch and Halder drew up a long list of reasons why Hitler's order for an early attack was likely to lead to disaster. The army needed more time to recover from the Polish campaign. There was a shortage of ammunition. The violation of Belgian and Dutch neutrality which Hitler proposed would turn world opinion against Germany. Bad weather would make effective use of tanks and aircraft impossible, and there was a serious shortage of fuel. General Thomas pointed out the economic problems of Germany, particularly a shortage of 600,000 tons of steel per month. The Ruhr was not adequately protected against French attack. Halder warned that the French army was greatly superior to the Polish army and that a campaign in the west would not be a repeat performance of the campaign in the east. Hitler took no notice of these objections and ordered that 'Plan Yellow' – the attack on the west – should be mounted on 12 November. Discussions of 'Plan Yellow' reactivated the opposition among the general staff, those officers who were in contact with Beck and the civilians such as Goerdeler, Schacht and Weizsäcker. Once again their plans were hopelessly vague and naïve. Hitler knew of the murmurings of the 'Zossen activists', although he had no idea of the extent of their plans or of their contacts with foreign powers. On 23 November, 'Plan Yellow' having been postponed due to bad weather, Hitler called the army commanders and told them that he knew all about the 'spirit of Zossen' and of the defeatist attitude of the generals. Halder was panic-stricken, and fearing that Hitler knew the full extent of the plots against him, determined to have nothing more to do with the opposition. Brauchitsch offered his resignation, but Hitler refused, telling him that he should obey orders and do his duty, which Brauchitsch continued to do. In spite of this dramatic confrontation the basic difference between Hitler and his generals was not whether the west should be attacked, but when. Just as in the debates over the attack on Poland, the army had no fundamental and radical critique of Hitler's policies. By concentrating on the feasibility of plans rather than on their political, economic and moral import, the resistance of the generals was based on shaky foundations. All Hitler had to do was to bully them, and they were soon compliant.

Thus once again Halder and the general staff busied themselves with the details of the 'Plan Yellow'. It lost none of its authority as the central planning agency for the attack in the west. An exception to this rule was the attack on Denmark and Norway, 'Operation *Weserübung*', which was planned by Jodl's staff at the OKW and was thus directly under Hitler's supervision. *Weserübung* was designed to secure the flank against any possible threat from developments of the Soviet-Finnish war, and also to secure adequate supplies of ore which were becoming seriously depleted. The usual route for military planning, both strategic and operational, was for the general staff to take the initiative and to work out a detailed plan which would then reach its final form when it had been worked over

by Jodl's staff, generally in consultation with the staffs of the
navy and airforce. This was the case in the planning of Order
No. 8 (attack on the west) and Order No. 21 (attack on the
Soviet Union). Specialized air or naval operations were planned
by the staffs of the Luftwaffe or the navy, but as the war was
essentially a land war it was the general staff which was largely
responsible for planning. As supreme commander of the
Wehrmacht Hitler kept a close watch on the army and frequently interfered in its operational planning. But the army
remained the senior service, and this close association with the
Führer gave it added prestige and authority.

The attack in the west eventually began, after innumerable
delays, on 10 May 1940. The campaign was a brilliant success,
and the generals' fears that it might lead to disaster were shown
to be groundless. On 15 May the Dutch army capitulated, on
29 May the Belgians. The British expeditionary force along with
allied troops were trapped at Dunkirk. That they were not
destroyed was partly due to von Rundstedt, the commander of
army group A, who wanted to give his troops a rest in preparation for the defeat of France, and who did not think that his
tanks were suitable for operations in Flanders and therefore
asked that the advance be halted; and partly due to Goering
who wished to use the Luftwaffe to deliver the *coup de grace* to
Britain. Hitler accepted these arguments partly because he still
believed that an arrangement could be made with Britain which
he regarded as a natural ally of the Third Reich. By 4 June
340,000 men were evacuated in the course of a remarkable
action which was greatly assisted by the weather, along with the
exceptional courage of RAF fighter pilots, to frustrate Goering's
plans. The British army had not been defeated, but it was out
of action for a considerable time to come. Germany had taken
1·2 million prisoners and shot down 1,800 airplanes. On 14
June the army entered Paris. On 22 June France capitulated.

A plan for the invasion of England (Operation Sealion) was
developed, largely by the Lutwaffe and the navy, but it had to
be postponed. The Luftwaffe failed to gain air supremacy over
England, and the navy was still unlikely to be able to match the
Royal Navy. In spite of the catastrophic upset at Dunkirk
British morale was high and it was clear that they would resist
Hitler's 'New Order' with their last ounce of strength. If

'Sealion' were to fail the result would be disastrous for the German fascists who relied on success after success to paper over the contradictions within the Third Reich. Without the co-operation of General Franco, and with Italy as an unreliable ally, the Mediterranean was hardly a likely theatre for a new success. Hitler now turned to the Soviet Union to seek his final spectacular victory. If the Soviet Union fell, then Britain would be unable to continue the struggle and the whole of Europe would be under German domination.

The destruction of the Soviet Union, the crushing of 'Jewish Bolshevism' and the capture of *lebensraum* in the east had long been the guiding principle of Hitler's politics. The decision to attack the Soviet Union was thus not a sudden improvisation, but the necessary outcome of carefully considered politics. Contrary to the legend which can be found in all too many books on the subject, the generals were not principled opponents to such an attack. As early as 1937 Fritsch had welcomed the idea of an attack on the Soviet Union. Beck considered *lebensraum* in the east 'essential'. In April 1939 the OKW discussed the seizure of the Caucasus with representatives of IG Farben, the chemical monopoly. Halder regarded the German–Soviet pact as a 'pact with the devil', and the occupation of Poland as the first step towards an attack on the east.

In June 1940 Halder heard that Hitler was showing increasing interest in operations in the east, and he at once ordered strategic and operational studies of an attack on the Soviet Union. When on 21 June Hitler made a formal request for such studies the general staff had already begun on its own initiative. The army thus approved of the idea of an attack in principle; once again it was simply a question of when and how this attack was to be launched.

The first serious mistake which the general staff made in planning an attack on the Soviet Union was to underestimate the Red Army and the war industrial potential of the Soviet Union. It had very little understanding of the true nature of the Soviet state, and its thinking on the Soviet Union was seriously distorted by national socialist race theory which insisted that all Slavs were inferior, stupid and irresponsible. The quality of Soviet armaments was also underestimated, particularly their tanks. Guderian was to call the T34 the best tank of any army up to 1943. The KV tanks, Russian field artillery and aircraft were to provide some unwelcome surprises to the invaders. By August 1941 Halder was to realize the error of these assessments and admitted that the Soviet Union had almost twice the number of divisions the general staff had imagined, and that they were of far greater quality than had been thought and were backed by massive economic and human resources. But by that time the die had been cast and it was too late.

There was considerable debate as to the best way to launch an attack. OKH thought in terms of a powerful thrust into the Soviet Union which would turn back to hit the Red Army in the rear and force it to fight on a reversed front. Halder favoured a thrust to the north, others a thrust to the south. Hitler, however, wanted a two-pronged attack, one prong aimed towards Kiev, the other towards the Baltic provinces and on to Moscow. Whereas Halder's ideas were developed and refined at OKH, OKW produced a plan by Lossberg for a three-pronged attack with two army groups in the north, and the third attacking the Ukraine.

In December 1940 Jodl's staff produced the final plan on the basis of these ideas and discussions. Hitler was particularly concerned that the Baltic provinces should be properly occupied, whereas Halder felt that this was a side-show which should not be allowed to slow down the impetus of the main attack towards Moscow. The final plan was given the code name 'Barbarossa'.

Barbarossa called for an attack by three army groups. The main force would be Heeresgruppe Mitte which would attack Moscow from two sides. Heeresgruppe Süd was to encircle and destroy the Soviet forces in the Ukraine. Heeresgruppe Nord was to work with the Finnish army and attack Leningrad.

This massive blitzkrieg operation was extraordinarily risky and adventurous. War games conducted by General Paulus showed that if the Red Army was not seriously defeated in the early stages of the operation there was no chance for the Germans to be victorious. But the fact that the forces available to Germany relative to those of the Soviet Union were seriously out of proportion with the aims of the operation was never seriously debated either at OKH or OKW. Brauchitsch felt that the operation would be more or less decided in the first four weeks, after which there would be only 'slight resistance'.

After Hitler's meeting with Keitel, Jodl, Brauchitsch and Halder on 31 July 1940, when it was decided that the Soviet Union would be attacked the following May, a massive armaments programme was begun. The war industrial capacity of Germany was stretched to the limit. Even the vicious exploitation of the occupied areas did not relieve the situation as much as had been hoped, for there was soon a serious shortage of raw materials, particularly iron, steel, rubber, oil, coal, copper and aluminium. The drain on manpower was also considerable, and 150,000 workers had to be released from duty in the Wehrmacht in order to meet the increased demand for manpower in industry. Some of these shortages were met by supplies from the Soviet Union under the terms of the trade agreement with Germany, but Stalin knew how to make a hard bargain. In return for these shipments Germany delivered machine tools, machinery, weapons and motor vehicles, and thus a further strain was placed on the German economic preparations for war. On balance, and given that Germany was planning an imminent attack on the Soviet Union, these exchanges favoured the Soviet Union more than Germany. Germany's economic failures in the war were thus not the result of inadequate planning, but because Germany's resources were no match for those of the Soviet Union.

Military preparations for the attack began in the late summer of 1940. In August the plan 'Eastern Build-up' was ordered and the concentration of German troops in Poland, on the Soviet border, began under various disguises. By October 1940 there were forty German divisions on the Polish-Soviet border. In April 1941 the German army attacked the Balkans, overrunning Jugoslavia and Greece and capturing Crete. The build-up of forces in the east were excused as part of the Balkan operation, and also as a feint to disguise preparations for an attack on Britain. The movement of ships was also disguised as part of these plans in 'Operation Shark' and 'Operation Harpoon'. The troops were given intensive training for the attack, although the goal was kept carefully concealed. Ideological indoctrination was also stepped up with particular emphasis on the need for *lebensraum*, national socialist *Weltanschauung* and the brilliant successes of the German army in the recent campaigns in the Balkans and North Africa. The fanatical anti-Bolshevik and anti-Slav component was not added until immediately before the attack was mounted.

The OKW was determined to work closely with the SS in the Soviet Union so that there would be no repetition of the problems that had arisen in Poland. The army agreed that it was a question of the 'final battle between two opposing political systems', and that the SS had a valuable role to play. Thus the army was prepared to aid and abet the criminal activities of the SS. But they were also prepared to throw international law overboard themselves. An order of May 1941 on courts martial in the Barbarossa area enabled the army to treat the Soviet people with almost no regard to legal norms. Brauchitsch's concerns about this order were simply that it might lead to the troops running amok. He insisted that such acts of barbarism should be collective acts under proper military control, and not be simply individual acts of brutality. Similarly plunder would have to be properly organized. If individual soldiers started plundering, then military discipline would soon break down. The army leadership's concern with military discipline has often been taken as evidence that they wished to restrain the policies of Hitler and the national socialist elite. But the racist violence of many army orders shows that this was not the case. The army agreed with Hitler's aims, but they were genuinely concerned that military discipline might well disintegrate in an orgy of violence. The determination not merely to win the campaign, but also to destroy the 'Bolshevik *Weltanschauung*' can also be seen in the 'commissar order'. As the 'perpetrators of a barbaric Asiatic method of fighting' they were to be instantly shot. Once again although the 'commissar order' was a typical brain child of Hitler the attempts to show that it was either resisted by the army leaders, or was foisted on them as part of an ideologizing of the army, are not particularly impressive. Hitler could count on the virulent anti-communist and anti-Soviet attitude of the generals, and although some protested against this monstrous order, it was usually because they feared that military discipline would be affected if such disregard was shown to the conventions of war.

The War Economics and Armaments Bureau of the OKW

also played an important part in planning the economic exploitation of the Soviet Union. A new organization was formed, the 'Economic Staff East', which was designed to control the economy of the Soviet Union to a line drawn from Archangel to Astrachan. The Economic Staff East planned for the provision of food and fuel for the Wehrmacht from Soviet sources, and for a surplus to be shipped back to Germany to secure against the effects of the allied blockade. The staff coolly considered that millions of Soviet citizens were likely to starve to death if their plans were put into operation. The staff also worked closely with the leaders of industry and showed themselves willing to accommodate their most outlandish requests.

The fundamental opposition of the generals to Hitler's plan to attack the Soviet Union is a legend, and the idea that the generals were blinded by the demonic power of the Führer is little more than a convenient excuse, but there were those who had serious doubts about the timing of such an attack. Keitel and Jodl did manage to persuade Hitler in July 1940 to postpone the attack until the following spring. There were those who warned that to begin a two-front war before Britain had been defeated would be disastrous and would simply prolong the battle with Britain. In this spirit Rudolf Hess flew to Scotland in the hope of winning the support of those members of the British ruling class who were prepared to capitulate to Hitler's 'New Order' and thus obviate the need for a two-front war. Hitler, fearing that this action would be seen as a sign of weakness, declared Hess insane. His arguments against those who wished to postpone the attack on the Soviet Union for military reasons were somewhat more substantial. In July 1940 he argued that the submarine war and the bomber raids on England would take a long time to have a real effect. He reckoned it would take up to two years, during which time Britain would have to rely on the support of Russia and America. If Russia were defeated, America would no longer support Britain, and Germany would be the master of Europe and the Balkans. It was Hitler's firm conviction that the best way to defeat Britain was first to destroy the Soviet Union, and he constantly reiterated this theme. Thus when Halder returned from his Christmas holidays on 16 January 1941 Hitler again insisted that it was impossible to invade England and that Germany therefore had to establish an invincible position on the continent before the final struggle with Britain and America.

Further plans were made in February 1941 for operations to follow Barbarossa, which included a march towards India through Afghanistan and the defeat of the British in the Mediterranean by attacks through Egypt, Turkey, the Trans-Caucasus and 'Operation Felix' against Gibraltar. Switzerland and Sweden were also to be overrun in two swift operations: *Tannenbaum* and *Polarwuchs.* Thus the Soviet Union would be destroyed, the British driven from the Mediterranean, Europe firmly under German control, and Germany could then look forward with confidence to the final battle with the Anglo-Saxon powers.

The essential precondition for these plans was that the Soviet Union should be defeated. At first the situation looked promising. At 0.315 hours on 22 June 1941 Germany attacked the Soviet Union. The Heeresgruppe Nord under Field Marshal von Leeb pushed forward through eastern Prussia and the Baltic provinces and approached Leningrad. The Heeresgruppe Mitte under Field Marshal von Bock pushed the Red Army back towards Minsk and Smolensk, seriously threatening Moscow. The Heeresgruppe Süd under Field Marshal von Rundstedt advanced towards Kiev and the Donetz basin. Within three weeks the German army had advanced more than four hundred miles. In the battles of Bialystok and Minsk the Germans had taken 323,898 prisoners and captured 3,332 tanks and 1,809 guns. In spite of Stalin's call for the 'Patriotic War' and the mobilization of all available forces for the defence of the country, and although the Soviet airforce was still intact and the partisans were beginning their heroic efforts behind the German lines, the Wehrmacht had every reason for optimism. Barbarossa was going like clockwork. On 3 July Halder wrote in his diary that the war could well be won within two weeks, and all that would remain were some mopping-up operations.

The German advance continued. At the beginning of August the Heeresgruppe Süd broke through the 'Stalin Line', trapping the main bulk of the Soviet forces in the south in the area around Kiev, and taking 103,000 prisoners. In spite of the extraordinary efforts of the Red Army the Heeresgruppe Mitte also broke through the Stalin Line and in the battles around Smolensk took 348,000 prisoners, but the Red Army had managed to slow down the tempo of the German advance, and although the cost had been dreadfully high valuable time was won for the defence of Moscow. To the north the Germans continued their advance, helped by the Finnish offensive towards Wiborg and Leningrad. On 8 September the 900-day siege of Leningrad began.

By August the Germans realized that their excessive optimism was misplaced. The advance was far slower than had been anticipated. The Red Army for all its shortcomings had fought with exceptional courage, defending positions to the last man so that reserves could be brought up and the advance slowed down. The enormous distances that had to be covered placed a tremendous strain on supplies and equipment, and motorized units which were so vital to the blitzkrieg strategy were seriously hampered by mud, dust and rough terrain. The Russian winter was approaching and the great question now facing the Germans was how to break the resistance of the Soviet Union before the winter set in.

Brauchitsch and Halder argued that the decisive battle should be fought around Moscow. They argued that the Red Army would send all available men to the defence of the capital, for not only would its loss be a crippling psychological blow to the Soviet peoples, but also it was a vital transport centre. If Moscow fell the Soviet armies in the north would be separated from those in the south, and the Germans would then be able to roll up the two flanks. Hitler and the OKW would not accept these arguments. He insisted that Leningrad had to be taken so that the Soviet Union would have no access to the Baltic, and in the south the Donetz basin and the Ukraine, the Crimea and the oil fields of the Caucasus would have to be captured so that the Red Army would be without adequate economic support and the Germans would be able to use the industrial and natural resources of the country to overcome their own shortages and deficiencies. Thus on 21 August Hitler ordered a considerable section of Heeresgruppe Mitte to turn south to help the capture of Kiev and to enable Heeresgruppe Süd to continue its advance towards Rostow. Only when the Germans had joined with the Finns in the north, and the main objectives in the south had been met, would Hitler permit the advance towards Moscow to continue. Brauchitsch and Halder gave way to Hitler's order, but relations between Hitler and the OKH were now very tense.

On 20 September Kiev fell, and in the gigantic battle of encirclement in the south the Wehrmacht reported that 665,000 prisoners had been taken, with 884 tanks and 3,718 guns. But the operations in the Ukraine held up the advance on Moscow. On 30 September 'Operation Typhoon' was launched against the Soviet capital. The Germans advanced to within twenty miles of the city. Military experts solemnly declared that the Soviet Union was defeated. On 3 October Hitler told the German people that the enemy was broken and would never recover. The initial stages of the operation were again tremendously successful. The Wehrmacht report listed 662,000 prisoners, 1,242 tanks and 5,452 guns. The government left Moscow, but Stalin remained behind to urge every man and woman to put their last effort into the defence of the capital. On 7 October the rains began. The roads were impassable for all but tracked vehicles. Shortages of supplies, particularly food, ammunition and gasoline became acute. The German advance slowed down. The pause was used to the full by the Soviets. Reserves of men and material were brought up to Moscow. The transport system was improved. Emergency defence groups were formed. When the frost began and the mud hardened von Bock ordered the advance to continue and further gains were made. But the Germans were beginning to feel the strain. In spite of their confidence and high morale, their effectiveness was seriously diminished. In some panzer divisions only one-third of the tanks were operational. They had no reserves which could be used. The weather got steadily colder, and the Wehrmacht was not adequately equipped for a campaign in the Russian winter. The superhuman efforts of the Red Army, the partisans and the Soviet citizens were beginning to have a disastrous effect on the Wehrmacht. Towards the end of November the Red Army had begun a series of successful counter-attacks. On 1 December von Bock reported to OKH that the enemy could not be defeated in one final effort. Although Halder was reluctant to admit it, Operation Typhoon had failed. On 5 December the Red Army launched a counter-attack near Moscow. The Wehrmacht had lost the strategic initiative.

Heeresgruppe Nord and Heeresgruppe Süd had also not achieved their objectives. Leningrad had not fallen, and in the south the Germans failed to take Rostow before the winter set in. Hitler refused to agree to Rundstedt's request for a strategic withdrawal to prepare for a new offensive in the spring. Rundstedt resigned his command, and von Reichenau was appointed to take his place. Reichenau also realized that a withdrawal was necessary. Hitler flew to Mariupol to examine the situation, and was convinced that Rundstedt and Reichenau were correct. Heeresgruppe Süd was therefore withdrawn to the Mius. On 8 December Hitler issued Order No. 39 stopping all offensive operations on the eastern front. The withdrawal to defensive positions and the intensification of the Red Army's counter-attacks led to serious German losses. In early December the Wehrmacht lost 120,000 men, 1,300 tanks and 3,000 guns. At some points the front was pushed back as much as 150 miles.

The failure of these plans caused a severe crisis in the military leadership. The OKH called for a strategic withdrawal behind the Dnieper and for a flexible and elastic defence until a new offensive could be mounted in the spring. Hitler violently opposed these ideas, fearing the psychological effect of such a withdrawal both on the Wehrmacht and the home front. On 16 December he issued his 'Halt Order' forbidding any withdrawal and calling for 'fanatical resistance' and the defence of positions to the last man. Three days later Brauchitsch, who had been the subject of bitter attacks by Hitler, resigned. Hitler himself became commander-in-chief of the army. Von Bock also resigned, for 'health reasons', and was replaced by von Kluge. Guderian and Hoepner, the tank specialists, were both dismissed from their commands for refusing to obey the Halt Order to the letter, and Hoepner was dismissed from the army. Hitler thus tried to find scapegoats among his generals, just as later historians have tried to find them in 'General Mud' and 'General Winter', but neither is adequate to explain the swing of the balance in favour of the Red Army in the winter of 1941.

In the spring of 1942 the Red Army continued with its offensives, and scored a number of significant successes. The Wehrmacht was forced to concentrate all its efforts on the

Heeresgruppe Süd so that the resources of the Donetz basin and the Caucasus could be exploited. Manstein's 11th Army occupied the Crimea. Marshal Timoschenko's counter-attack at Kharkov was beaten back with heavy losses to the Red Army. Thus on 28 June the great summer offensive, 'Plan Blue', began under what seemed to be highly favourable conditions, and with Rommel's desert army storming on towards Alexandria the army was in a confident mood. The plan went well. On 5 July the Don was crossed, and on 24 July Rostov fell. But the Germans failed in their main objective, the destruction of the Soviet forces in the south in a vast battle of encirclement, the Cannae of which Schlieffen had dreamed. The Heeresgruppe Süd was divided into two sections. Herresgruppe A to the south was commanded by List, Heeresgruppe B to the north by von Weichs. They seized the Donetz basin, but they did not trap the Red Army. On 23 July Hitler issued Order No. 45, 'Operation Braunschweig', in which Heeresgruppe B was ordered to capture Stalingrad and to secure the Volga from Stalingrad to Astrachan. Heeresgruppe A was to destroy the Red Army to the south of Rostov, capture the eastern shores of the Black Sea and control the Caucasus. Hitler said: 'If I do not get the oil of Maikop and Grozny I shall have to liquidate the war.' But this plan placed an almost intolerable strain on the German forces in the south. Men like Halder became increasingly alarmed at Hitler's underestimation of Soviet forces and his unthinking reactions to momentary events. In July Halder wrote in his diary that it was no longer possible to do any serious work at OKH, adding that he considered Hitler's attitude to be 'sick'.

But once more the campaign seemed to be successful. Heeresgruppe A pushed forward. On 21 August the German standard was planted on the highest mountain of the Caucasus in a symbolic gesture which was exploited to the full by Goebbels' propagandists. But Soviet resistance was increasingly determined, and the Germans faced severe logistic problems. On 10 September Hitler dismissed List and took over the command of Heeresgruppe A himself, but not even the 'greatest field commander of all times' could make any further progress. To the north the Sixth Army under General Paulus reached the Volga on 23 August. By the beginning of September

German troops entered Stalingrad and the critical battle of the Second World War began.

At OKH Halder was increasingly concerned with the position of the Sixth Army. The flanks were badly exposed, the troops exhausted by the murderous fighting in the city. Hitler would not listen to these warnings, and was convinced that the secret of victory lay in 'fanatical will' and 'burning faith in national socialism' rather than in the more prosaic considerations of the art of warfare. On 24 September Halder was dismissed, his concerns over the over-extension of the German front in the south of the Soviet Union being dismissed as defeatism and fatalism. His place was taken by General Zeitzler who agreed with Halder and Paulus that the offensive against Stalingrad should be halted, but Hitler would not hear of such a suggestion. Thus the fighting continued, house to house. German losses were exceedingly high, and the Soviets continued to hang on to the vital bridgehead over the Volga whilst the Red Army prepared its counter-attack. On 19 November the Red Army broke through the Rumanian Third Army and on 22 November the encirclement of Stalingrad was almost complete. Some 220,000 men were trapped. That evening Hitler ordered the Sixth Army to stand its ground, but Paulus insisted that they did not have the strength or the supplies to defend their position. He requested permission to fight his way out of the encirclement, and this request was supported by von Weichs and by Zeitzler. On 24 November Hitler, having been assured by Goering that the Luftwaffe could supply the Sixth Army adequately, repeated the order that Stalingrad had to be held. Von Manstein was ordered to form a new 'Heeresgruppe Don' to stop the Soviet counter-offensive and to save the German position on the Volga, but he soon realized that the Sixth Army would have to abandon Stalingrad. Hitler rejected Manstein's plan for a break-out – 'Operation Thunderclap' – and neither Paulus nor Manstein had the courage to ignore Hitler's idiotic order. On 31 January and 2 February the German forces in Stalingrad surrendered.

The Germans had suffered a severe defeat. Between November and February they lost 800,000 men on the Eastern Front. By the end of January there were only 495 operational tanks on the whole front. The Luftwaffe lost 488 planes in the battle of

Stalingrad. The German advance had been stopped, and the Red Army was now beginning to push back the Germans to the positions they had held in the summer of 1942 before the offensive began. This defeat at Stalingrad was followed closely by a further victory of the allies in North Africa. On 8 November 1942 allied troops from America and Britain landed in Casablanca, Oran and Algiers as 'Operation Torch' began. After the victory of El Alamein Montgomery's Eighth Army pushed on, taking Tobruk on 13 November and reaching Benghasi a week later. By the beginning of February the Eighth Army crossed the border into Tunisia, so that the allied troops in Tunis could now co-operate with Montgomery's forces. Rommel was able to secure some successes against the inexperienced American troops, but after the battle for the Mareth line at the beginning of March he realized that his 'Heeresgruppe Tunis' would have to withdraw. Hitler flatly refused to allow the withdrawal. Rommel was ordered to go on sick leave, and his place was taken by General Sixt von Arnim who was forced to surrender with 252,000 men on 13 May 1943.

The defeats of the German army on the Volga, in the Caucasus and in North Africa were made all the more serious by the failure of the U-boat war in the Atlantic and the beginning of intensive bombing raids by the British and Americans. The allies were able to build far more ships than were sunk by the U-boats, and methods of U-boat detection, particularly with radar, were becoming so effective that by May 1943, when thirty-eight U-boats were sunk, submarine operations had to be severely restricted, and hopes of a slow strangulation of the allies were abandoned. After the Casablanca conference in January 1943 the air war against Germany was intensified, and although terror bombing did little to disrupt German war industry it undoubtedly had a severely damaging effect on morale. As early as April 1943 Goebbels confided in his dairy that he could see no way in which Germany could win the war. As the situation grew increasingly critical greater stress was placed on 'will power', 'fanaticism' and similar slogans from the slag-heap of national socialist ideology. Zeitzler thus stressed 'faith', 'fortitude', 'steadfastness' and other such irrational concepts, and castigated any officer who dared to paint a realistic picture of the true military situation. As it became all too apparent that objectively Germany was no match for the allies, a blind faith was placed in subjective factors. Thus Jodl told an audience of *Gauleiters* that although no one could foresee how the war would end Germany would be victorious: 'We must be victorious, because otherwise world history has no meaning.' The military leadership was gradually giving way to a fanatical *Götterdämmerung* attitude and attempts rationally to analyse the military situation were abandoned in favour of a criminally irresponsible faith in destiny and the German genius.

On the Eastern Front the OKW decided that the army should go on the defensive in the hope that the Red Army would gradually exhaust itself in a series of attacks against a highly flexible and mobile defence. By May 1943 the situation was more stable and the OKW began planning for a summer offensive, 'Operation Citadelle', aimed at the Kursk salient in which heavy Soviet forces were concentrated. The objective was a limited one. As Keitel said, 'We have to attack for political reasons.' There was no hope that Operation Citadelle, even if successful, would bring victory in the east. It was part of the new defensive strategy in the Soviet Union which, with its enormous concentration of forces on a very limited front, was reminiscent of the battles of the First World War, and had little in common with the Barbarossa strategy of a swift attack on a wide front. After modest initial successes von Kluge and von Manstein's attack at Kursk ground to a halt. German losses in the 'greatest tank battle of all time' were very high. Within a few days the Soviets began their counter-attack. On 10 July the allies landed in Sicily and some reserves had to be sent to the Italian front. On 13 July 'Operation Citadelle' was abandoned. In the subsequent Soviet offensive the Germans were forced to abandon the Donetz basin, and Heeresgruppe Mitte was pushed back to the west of Smolensk. The German army left behind it a trail of waste and desolation. The scorched earth policy of the German withdrawal was the culmination of the brutal exploitation of the Soviet Union in which the army had played such an active part. By the beginning of October the Red Army had reached the Dnieper on a broad front and had established some important bridgeheads over the river. On 6 November Kiev was liberated, and the German attempts to recapture the city were beaten back with heavy losses.

The summer offensive of 1943 was a resounding success for the Red Army. The Germans had been forced to abandon half of the occupied territory of the Soviet Union and had been pushed back between 300 and 900 miles. The Wehrmacht lost two million men, and although reserves were hastily mobilized the absolute loss of men and equipment was crippling. From the battle of Kursk the tide of the war had finally turned against the Germans. From then on they were steadily and remorselessly forced back by the Red Army. With the OKW order No. 51 of November 1943 the army hoped to strengthen the German forces in the west in preparation for the allied invasion, hoping that when this had been repulsed a decision might then be reached in the east. But this was largely wishful thinking. The German forces were badly depleted and essential raw materials were becoming increasingly scarce. In March 1944 Germany still produced 181,000 tons of aircraft fuel, but in September this had been reduced to 10,000 tons as a result of allied bombing. Thus the Luftwaffe was rendered almost useless, and tanks and trucks had to be used as little as possible to conserve petrol supplies. Adequate reserves of men and materials could not be sent to the western front without risking the collapse of the Eastern Front. As it was, the Red Army continued to push forward relentlessly. Leningrad was liberated from its 900 days of siege in which 600,000 men, women and children had lost their lives. At the beginning of April the Germans were forced out of the western Ukraine, and in the Crimea the German troops were trapped and destroyed. Hitler's answer to these catastrophes was a constant change in personnel. Men like Manstein and Kleist who wanted a flexible and operational defence were replaced by men like Schörner and Model who blindly followed Hitler's orders not to retreat one step. But however 'fanatical' the will power of the Wehrmacht commanders, nothing could now stop the momentum of the Soviet advance.

On 6 June 1944 the allies landed in Normandy, thus forcing the Germans to fight on two fronts. Within six weeks of the landing the bulk of the German forces in Normandy were defeated, when the Canadian army broke through from Caen to Falaise, cutting off 250,000 men of the German Fifth and Seventh armies. Although the allied advance eastwards was painfully and unnecessarily slow the German front was crumbling, and the national uprising of the French gave a new stimulus to the war. In the east the Red Army continued its advance until the front was temporarily stabilized in eastern Prussia and on the eastern border of Poland.

As 'Fortress Europe' began to collapse a fresh impulse was given to movements of national liberation and to the anti-fascist struggle at home. The Hitler regime was still supported by the vast majority of the people of Germany. With a mixture of brutal terror and cunning propaganda its hold over the population was still secure. A vivid picture was painted of the gruesome fate that awaited the German people if they were defeated, which was made all the more convincing by the often mindless and vicious bombing policy of the allies. As the allies advanced in the east and the west it became clear to all but the most purblind national socialists that unless some drastic action was taken Germany would be destroyed. Such was the background to the attempted *putsch* of 20 July 1944.

The main ideas of the resistance and of the leader of the various groups, Goerdeler, were hopelessly unrealistic, authoritarian and anti-democratic. Goerdeler's aim was to save what could still be saved by removing Hitler and his cronies, which he even thought could be done with their consent, and to establish a military dictatorship. He hoped to split the coalition against Germany by joining forces with the western powers in a crusade against the Soviet Union. Thus Germany would realize its true goal and historical mission as the defender of European civilization against the Bolshevik hordes. The German army would then form the nucleus of a European military force that would crush the Soviet Union and guarantee the independence of a free united Europe. Many of these ideas were attractive to senior officers, the most prominent of whom was Beck, who was the conspirators' first choice for head of state. As the military situation worsened and as Hitler became increasingly capricious in his leadership, they were anxious to act. But on the other hand they feared that a successful anti-fascist coup might unleash genuine democratic forces with which they had no sympathy. Furthermore the failure of previous attempts to remove Hitler made them cautious, and many were still

325

plagued with pangs of conscience that they would be breaking their solemn oath of allegiance to the Führer.

The German resistance to Hitler within the army was divided into many groups and factions. Among them were men of outstanding courage, deep humanity, vision and moral greatness. Men such as Colonel Claus Graf Schenk von Stauffenberg, who planted the bomb at Hitler's headquarters on 20 July, Fritz Lindemann, Henning von Treskow, Mertz von Quirnheim, Werner von Haeften, Friedrich Olbricht and Helmuth Stieff had little sympathy with the reactionary politics and endless humming and hawing of the Goerdeler group. Although most of them were from old aristocratic military families they had none of Goerdeler's fears of a thorough-going democratization of Germany and co-operation with the Soviet Union. Stauffenberg contacted the 'National Committee for a Free Germany' (NKFD) which had been formed in the Soviet Union in 1943 from prisoners of war, among them General Paulus and exiled German communists. He co-operated with underground communist organizations in Germany much to the alarm and disgust of Goerdeler. He also worked closely with left-wing social democrats such as Julius Leber and Professor Reichwein. Closely connected with the Stauffenberg group was the 'Kreisau Circle' of Graf Helmuth von Moltke, which included men like Adam von Trott zu Solz, Peter Graf York von Wartenberg and Fritz-Dietlof Graf von der Schulenburg. They were mostly young men from distinguished families who subscribed to a slightly idealistic Christian socialism. Like Stauffenberg they were impatient with Goerdeler's prevarications, and had little in common with his German national ideas.

Men like Stauffenberg and von Moltke realized that the only genuine alternative to fascism was a thorough-going democratization of the state. This separated them from those who by resisting fascism, at whatever personal cost, hoped like the OHL of 1918, to preserve the privileged position of their class by a 'revolution from above'. The conservative and church opposition to Hitler was paralysed by this fear of socialism, and by cutting themselves off from wide popular support they were doomed to failure. The progressive elements in the resistance were too small to be effective, and within the army there was little response to their ideas.

On 20 July 1944 Stauffenberg planted the bomb in Hitler's headquarters in eastern Prussia, but Hitler was only slightly injured. The effectiveness of the blast was diminished by the light structure of the building, and Hitler was protected from the bomb by a heavy table. The *putsch* was extraordinarily badly organized, and it was not until Stauffenberg reached Berlin from eastern Prussia that 'Operation Walküre' was mounted. In the meantime the government had had time to recover from the initial shock of the attempted assassination, and the OKW had countermanded all orders by the conspirators. Stauffenberg, Haeften, Merz von Quirnheim and and Olbricht were arrested and shot that evening, executed by soldiers of the army they had hoped to save. Then the SS and the SD began to round up all those who were in any way implicated in the plot. Thousands were murdered in a bestial manner in the dungeons of the secret police, and Hitler followed the slaughter of his opponents with eager interest. The more fortunate were able to commit suicide before appearing before Freisler's 'People's Court', among them Beck, von Kluge and Rommel.

The *putsch* attempt was a failure, and if anything it strengthened Hitler's hand, for many felt that the conspirators were mere traitors who had tried to stab their country in the back at a time of dire need. It enabled Hitler to purge the upper echelons of the officer corps of his critics and opponents and to reduce the remainder to mindless and time-serving obedience. The army was now obliged to give the Nazi salute. Guderian published an order as chief of the general staff that all staff officers had to be national socialists, and that character was more important than intellect. On August 4 the army humbly requested Hitler to be allowed to purge its ranks of all those who were involved in the dastardly deeds of 20 July. A special court of honour was established among the members of which were Keitel, Rundstedt and Guderian. It eagerly set about handing over officers to the 'People's Court' and to almost inevitable imprisonment, torture and death. The story of the following weeks is one of the most shameful episodes in the history of the German army. While brave men died for their convictions,

327

others saved their necks by cowardly betrayals of their colleagues in arms or by hastily changing sides. As the Third
Reich faced imminent military defeat there was nothing which
would hold it together but terror and the senseless sacrifice of
human life.

Even with a sixty-hour 'normal' working week and a lowering
of the recruiting age to sixteen, reserves of men and materials
were rapidly dwindling. In September 1944 in a frantic attempt
to revive the spirit of the wars of liberation, a *Volkssturm* was
created of men between the ages of sixteen and sixty. But these
units were hopelessly badly equipped and inadequately trained.
Only at the cost of appalling losses, particularly on the eastern
front, did the *Volkssturm* have much effect. Frantic propaganda
efforts by Goebbels stressing the dire consequences of defeat
had some effect, and the new weapons, particularly the V2,
gave some encouragement, but nothing could overcome the
growing weakness of nazi Germany. The *Gauleiters* were given
virtually dictatorial powers, and Himmler was made commander of the reserve army. In this way the Nazi elite
strengthened its hold on the country and forced the people to
make every possible effort to avert the inevitable defeat. But all
they could do was to prolong the death agony of the regime.

Hitler's final hope was one last offensive in the west which
might make it possible to move some reserves to the eastern
front to stop the Soviet advance. There was also still the hope
that if the offensive was successful the western allies might
agree to some form of anti-Soviet arrangement. This offensive
in the Ardennes led by von Rundstedt was a desperate final
effort. Initially the situation looked serious for the allies and the
Wehrmacht was able to break through the American lines, but
the momentum of the attack was soon lost and the Germans
were pushed back. In January the Red Army began its offensive
in Poland. A German offensive in the south-east was beaten
back and on 13 April the Red Army occupied Vienna. By the
end of March the allies had reached the Rhine and established
bridgeheads at Remagen and Oppenheim. The German army
began to collapse. Whole units surrendered rather than continue
a senseless battle, and desertions became increasingly frequent.
The OKW answered with drum-head courts martial following
which deserters were shot on the spot. Families of deserters

were frequently arrested. On 19 March 1945 Hitler issued the 'Nero Order' calling for the destruction of everything that might fall into the hands of the allies, but Keitel and Speer both issued orders that this should be ignored for they were already thinking of rebuilding Germany after the war. Keitel did, however, issue orders that every town had to be defended to the last man and that anyone showing a white flag was to be shot. None of these measures could stop the allied advance. On 25 April American and British troops met the Soviet forces on the Elbe at Torgau. The OKW's hopes that they would at once start fighting one another did not materialize. On 30 April Hitler committed suicide. On 8 May Keitel signed the unconditional surrender of the German forces at Berlin-Karlshorst. The German army was destroyed, the fate of the country in the hands of the allies. In the Potsdam Agreement signed on 2 August 1945 the four powers solemnly announced their intention to secure the full disarmament and demilitarization of Germany and the end of the production of the instruments of war by German industry. It seemed that the history of the German army had come to an end.

10

Aftermath

In 1945, even more than in 1918, there was a widespread feeling in Germany that every effort had to be made to create a new society on the ruins of the old which would be based on broadly democratic principles. The terrible consequences of Imperialism and militarism were clearly evident for all to see, and in many sectors of society there was a determination to break the power of the economic, political and military elites who were responsible for fascism and war, and to change fundamentally the social order which had given rise to these forces. Even the right-wing political parties agreed that such a fundamental change was needed. The Christian Democrats (CDU) solemnly declared that: 'The capitalist economic system is incommensurate with the vital governmental and social needs of the German people . . . The capitalist drive for profit and power cannot be the content and aim of this new social and economic order, but rather the prosperity of the whole people.'

At first it seemed that the allies were in full agreement with such aims. At the Nürnberg trials the guilt of the big industrialists and the generals was affirmed. Keitel and Jodl were executed, and men like Krupp and Flick imprisoned. The power of the junkers was finally destroyed by the agrarian reform in the east under Soviet auspices. The Potsdam agreements made it seem that the military caste would be unemployed. Those industrialists who were still at large were so convinced that major concessions would have to be made that they freely offered the unions full participation in economic decision making. In 1946 Adenauer said: 'We agree completely that we should be disarmed and that our war industry should be destroyed . . . . I would go even further and say that I believe that the majority of our people would agree if we followed the example of Switzerland and became neutral.' In 1949 Franz Josef Strauss said that the hand should wither that held the gun – a curious echo of Scheidemann's words in 1919. Yet within a few years West Germany was fully remilitarized, and a complete right-about-turn had been executed.

The reason for this reversal was that West Germany was fully integrated into the American-dominated anti-communist and capitalist bloc. Far from being a second Switzerland it became the outpost of the 'Free World', armed to the teeth in the front line of the struggle between two social systems. The remilitarization of Germany was the golden opportunity for those who were threatened by the general trend towards a thorough-going democratization of society, and was the keystone of the restorative policies of the post-war epoch.

The functional role of the military-industrial complex in late capitalism is so critical that without gigantic expenditures on armaments no advanced capitalist state can hope to overcome its cyclical problems of over-production without abandoning the principle of the private ownership of the means of production. Deficit spending on an astronomic scale on instruments of mass destruction is the most striking example of the irrationality of the system. As this system is forced increasingly on the defensive a huge military apparatus is needed in the hope of maintaining the status quo both at home and abroad. The war in Vietnam and the murder of students by the troops of the National Guard at Kent State University are but two examples of the determination to use the utmost violence to defend an international and social system of domination against its opponents, critics and enemies at home and abroad.

Clearly such a system has to find some justification for what would otherwise appear to be a senseless and highly dangerous waste. This is provided by the ideology of anti-communism. By painting a grotesque picture of the aggressive intentions of world communism an attempt is made to justify a world-wide system of military basis in which West Germany plays a critical role. Whatever one's view of communism, particularly in its

Stalinist form, there can be no doubt whatsoever that this world view is a serious distortion of reality and is a serious barrier to a rational critique of western military policy since the war. Such a view forgets that the extension of Soviet power in eastern Europe was the result of German, not Soviet, aggression. With the rejection of Trotskyism and the doctrine of 'socialism in one country' the Soviet Union abandoned its plans for a world revolution and concentrated its efforts on strengthening the new order at home. After the Second World War this tendency was stepped up, the resources of the eastern European countries being exploited to offset the industrial and military weakness of the socialist countries relative to the western powers. In the era of nuclear weapons none of the socialist countries has the slightest intention of risking the total destruction of what has been so painfully achieved. No rational planning can be based on the assumption that a lunatic might come to power, and the Soviet system offers as good a guarantee as any against such an eventuality. The communist parties in the capitalist countries have made no preparations whatever for a violent overthrow of the governments. In the under-developed countries the Soviet Union has studiously avoided exporting revolution, and violence, as in Vietnam, has more often been the result of western policies. When these factors are carefully weighed it becomes apparent that the military strength of the NATO powers, which is two to three times that of the Soviet Union, is out of all proportion to its declared intention as a defensive military alliance. Even if the Soviet Union and her allies were as aggressive as has been asserted, the extent of western armaments is unjustified.

The rearmament of West Germany was not a military necessity or a response to the acute danger of Soviet aggression. It was a deliberate political decision, designed to give some muscle to Adenauer's attempts to force concessions from the east and to win a place among the great western powers. As the present president of the Federal Republic, Gustav Heinemann, has shown in a series of penetrating essays this decision forced West Germany to follow the aggressive anti-communist policies of the United States, and made impossible any policy of peaceful détente and re-unification of Germany. It is small wonder that when faced with an army of 500,000 men, with the government of the day making loud demands for a sizeable chunk of Polish territory to say nothing of the GDR, and with equally strident requests for atomic weapons, the communist countries regarded the Federal Republic as the most dangerous and aggressive partner in the NATO alliance. By skilful propaganda these concerns have been used as further evidence of communist perfidy and aggressiveness.

Thus the rearmament of West Germany fulfilled several functions. It gave West Germany a powerful voice in the western alliance. Increasing expenditure on defence offered the attractive possibility of 'defence prosperity' and high profits. It enabled many of the old elite to regain their position which had been placed in serious jeopardy in 1945. And it enabled the restoration and strengthening of a conservative social order. The very fact that this policy created dangerous tensions in Europe and the world could be used as a justification for the policy itself by a bland application of the 'Catch-22' logic of the Dulles era.

This is not the place to recount in detail the history of the Cold War from 1945. As far as the rearmament of West Germany is concerned, the first significant step was the formation of the Brussels Pact on 17 March 1948. This was a defensive agreement between Britain, France, Belgium, the Netherlands and Luxemburg. As the anti-communist element of the pact increasingly outweighed the anti-German sentiments of the partners, informal discussions began about the possibility of a West German contribution to the containment of communism. In December 1948 Adenauer ordered General Speidel to write a memorandum on the possibility of German rearmament and Germany's future military needs. Speidel argued that in the event of a Soviet attack on western Europe it was essential for there to be troops as far east as possible. In other words a communist threat, real or imagined, was to be the justification of German rearmament.

For the time being there could be no question of a rearmament of Germany. Memories of the war were too vivid. Public opinion both in Germany and abroad was strongly against rearmament. On 4 April 1949 NATO was formed, but West Germany was excluded. Indeed in November the Adenauer government in the Petersberg Agreement solemnly declared that West Germany would be demilitarized, and that 'all

333

available means would be employed to hinder any such rearmament'. In the Bundestag debate of that month all parties rejected the idea of rearmament. But steps were already being taken in the direction of the active participation of West Germany in NATO. West Germany was regarded as being within the area defended by NATO, and in an interview with an American journalist in December 1949 Adenauer suggested that West German contingents within a European army were feasible. Such ideas were utterly unacceptable to the vast majority of Germans. An opinion poll of January 1950 showed that almost seventy-five per cent of West Germans were opposed to the formation of any sort of military units in Germany.

With the beginning of the Korean War in June 1950 the European situation became increasingly tense. Communist successes in the early stages of the war led to an almost hysterical fear of communist aggression in Europe. The NATO powers feared that the troops of the three western occupying armies in West Germany were insufficient to defend the country from attack. In August the European Council discussed Churchill's proposals for a European army in which there would be German contingents, along the lines outlined by Adenauer in December. Adenauer strongly supported this suggestion and proposed a German force of 150,000 men which would be integrated into a European army. Adenauer made this offer to the American High Commissioner, McCloy, without discussing the matter in the cabinet or the Bundestag. Gustav Heinemann, minister of the interior in Adenauer's cabinet, and a determined and courageous opponent of rearmament, resigned in protest against an action whch he felt was both high-handed and wrong. Adenauer's suggestions were discussed at the foreign ministers' meeting in New York in September 1950. Acheson and Bevin supported the idea, but it was rejected out of hand by the French foreign minister, Schuman. However, the foreign ministers agreed that the matter of a West German contribution to the western military alliance would be discussed at some future date.

Whereas most of the NATO powers were in favour of West German rearmament the French still had serious misgivings. In October 1950 René Pleven presented a compromise plan which was based on the suggestions made at the European Council in

August. Pleven called for a European defence community in which German troops would be integrated. Rather than being placed under NATO they would be controlled by a European defence minister. This was an ingenious compromise, for it would enable the western powers to draw on the military resources of Germany without arousing the understandable fears of a revival of German militarism. Pleven's suggestions were accepted by Adenauer and by the NATO powers as the basis for discussions on the nature and form of a German contribution to the western alliance.

In September 1950 General von Schwerin was appointed by Adenauer as defence adviser. After his resignation in October the task was given to the CDU Bundestag member Blank whose 'Blank Office' amounted to a shadow ministry of defence. Blank's principal military advisers were General Speidel and General Heusinger. Adenauer now began his political campaign for the rearmament of Germany. He insisted that it was a question not of remilitarization, but of the defence of peace and freedom which was threatened by the aggressive policies of the Soviet Union. He argued that Germany should be so strongly defended that the Soviet Union would never risk an attack, and that in return for this contribution to the defence of Western Europe West Germany should be given equal political rights with the other NATO powers. Rearmament would thus give the Federal Republic a powerful independent voice in world affairs. Of Adenauer one is tempted to say that had the 'communist menace' not existed it would have been necessary to invent it, for it is difficult to believe that a man of his cynical realism could seriously have believed that West Germany was capable of building up an army which could have withstood the determined efforts of the Warsaw Pact armies to overrun Germany. The political benefits of rearmament were undeniable; the question remained, however, as to whether they were worth the very high cost.

As rearmament was to counter the 'communist menace' Adenauer launched a campaign against the Communist Party (KPD) in the summer of 1950 which culminated in a total ban on the party's members holding positions in the civil service. The ban on party meetings and journals also silenced the most outspoken critics of rearmament. Throughout Germany massive

demonstrations were held against rearmament. Social democrats and communists, union leaders and churchmen, the
apolitical *ohne mich* man in the street, and the pacifists joined
together to protest against the proposals for the creation of a
new German army. Pastor Martin Niemöller's call for a
referendum on rearmament met with a tremendous response,
but the government forbade the referendum on the absurd
grounds that it represented a danger to 'constitutional order'
even though the right to hold referenda was guaranteed in the
basic constitutional law of the Federal Republic. In the spring
of 1952 the Bundestag agreed to rearmament within the frame-
work of the European defence community. In a speech in
Heidelberg on 1 March Adenauer said: 'I would ask you to bear
in mind that the danger of the neutrality of Germany is a very
great danger, and that we can only avoid this danger if we join
the defence community . . . . I like to think of developments
as follows: if the West is stronger than Soviet Russia, then the
time for negotiations with Soviet Russia has arrived. Then it
must be made plain to Soviet Russia that it is no good, that it is
impossible to keep half of Europe in slavery, and that by
debate, not by warlike debate, but by peaceful debate, conditions in eastern Europe must be changed.' For all the talk of a
peaceful détente in Europe, Adenauer's policies were based on
maximum tensions in Germany so that West Germany would be
firmly anchored into the western alliance. The way to reunification would be through the 'roll back' of Soviet forces by a show
of western strength. In this policy rearmament played a vital
role. It was, in Adenauer's view, the guarantee of a western
orientation of German policy, and the only possible way to
reunite a divided country. Having lost the war, the German
army was to help win the Cold War.

Ten days after this speech Andrei Gromyko, the deputy
foreign minister of the Soviet Union, handed the three western
ambassadors in Moscow a proposal by the Soviet government
for a peace treaty with Germany. The note proposed the withdrawal of all foreign troops from German soil, the creation of a
national German army which would not join any military
alliance and would guarantee the neutrality of Germany, the
signing of a peace treaty and the entry of Germany into the
United Nations. The Adenauer government refused even to

discuss these proposals, regarding them as a sign of Soviet weakness and proof that the 'politics of strength' was paying dividends. A genuine opportunity for a constructive détente was frivolously dismissed, and the preparation for the rearmament of West Germany continued.

Adenauer was able to find a comfortable majority in the Bundestag for his rearmament plans, although the opposition of the social democrats and the communists found strong support among wide sections of the community. In May 1952 representatives of the governments of France, Belgium, the Netherlands, Luxemburg, Italy and West Germany signed a treaty to form a European defence community. In March 1953 the treaty was ratified by the West German Bundestag, but on 30 August 1954 the French National Assembly refused to ratify it. Adenauer's plans for the rearmament of Germany seemed to be in ruins. Without the creation of the European defence community Adenauer could not get his 'General Treaty' which greatly extended the sovereign rights of the Federal Republic and made it virtually an autonomous state.

The American and British governments were particularly concerned to use the military potential of West Germany, and were determined to overcome French resistance to the rearmament of her powerful neighbour. At the end of September 1954 the nine-power conference in London, which included delegations from the United States, Canada and Britain, reached a compromise which was acceptable to the French government. The Federal Republic was to become a member of an extended Brussels Pact to be known as the Western European Union, and the way was opened to German membership of NATO. Germany was forbidden to manufacture ABC weapons, strategic bombers and large warships. The size of the new army would be restricted to 500,000 men. Once again, in spite of the SPD's warnings that the rearmament of West Germany would make the reunification of the country virtually impossible, and in spite of many large demonstrations against the treaties, the Bundestag ratified the agreements in February 1955 by a vote of 314 to 157. Ten years after the war Germany was once more rearmed.

The first intake into the army, the Bundeswehr, was in 1955 and consisted of more than 150,000 volunteers. There were

40,613 former officers of the Wehrmacht, 87,089 former NCOs and men and only some 10,000 who had had no previous experience in the army. Of 38 generals, 31 had been in the general staff of Hitler's army. The employment of men with such backgrounds meant that the officer corps was well trained and experienced, but there were many critics who were alarmed at what they considered to be the continuity of an unfortunate tradition, and who insisted that a new start should be made, even at the cost of military efficiency in the early stages. The screening process for these officers was inadequate, and there were too many Bundeswehr officers who had disreputable histories and who provided ample ammunition to the critics of the new army. For those who wished to create a democratic army the heavy preponderance of old Wehrmacht officers was a serious barrier and was to create a number of acute difficulties in the years to come.

In July 1956 compulsory military service was introduced so that the army could be increased to 500,000 men. With compulsory military service began the training of a new generation of army officers who will begin to hold leading positions in the Bundeswehr in the middle 1970s. These younger officers come from a slightly broader social base than the Reichswehr. Particularly in the increasingly important technical branches of the army, which were traditionally avoided by men from upper middle-class and aristocratic backgrounds, there is an increasing tendency for men from lower middle-class families to become officers. There are, however, strict limits to this democratization of the officer corps. The bias against the working class in the educational system makes it exceedingly difficult for a working-class man to achieve the educational standards required to become an officer. In 1970 although seventy-five per cent of the West German population can be broadly classified as 'working class' only fifteen per cent of the Bundeswehr officers came from this social group. An examination of the social backgrounds of the upper echelons of the officer corps shows that they are drawn from the top levels of the social pyramid. Thus although the Bundeswehr has undoubtedly broadened the social base of its officer corps, not least because the army officer no longer enjoys the high social prestige of the

338

pre-war years, there is still a long way to go before the officer corps is adequately representative of society at large.

With the creation of the Bundeswehr an attempt was made to clarify the relationship between the soldier and society and to analyse the role of the army in a democratic state. The principal idea of the ideological training of the army, the 'inner leadership' (*Innere Führung*), is the notion of the 'citizen in uniform'. The strong opposition to rearmament by a large section of German society, and the fears among the western allies of a resurgence of German militarism, made it essential for there to be some attempt to democratize the structure of the new army. Men like General Graf Baudissin realized that the increasingly technological nature of modern arms, and the changes in the nature of society itself, necessitated a change in military relationships. Only those civil rights which were in conflict with absolute military necessity would be restricted; the soldier would otherwise be a full member of a democratic state. It was argued that only if soldiers remained keenly aware of their democratic freedoms would they be prepared to fight to defend those freedoms. To expect a lot of square-bashing zombies to fight enthusiastically for the inalienable rights of the individual was considered altogether too much of a contradiction.

Baudissin's views were intelligent and liberal, and he raised fundamental questions about the relationship between the army and society in a parliamentary democracy. His answers were often incomplete and unsatisfactory, but they went too far for most of his conservative colleagues, and he was hastily posted to a command where he no longer had any influence on the 'inner leadership'. One of the basic problems he had to face was the fact that it was unrealistic to imagine that the Bundeswehr was starting from scratch. The traditions of the past, as well as the personnel of the new army, strongly biased the development of the new army. Most seriously of all Baudissin never squarely faced the problem of the fundamental differences between military society and civil society.

At times this lack of understanding reached levels of astounding naïvety. Baudissin seriously suggested that as a recruit and a general both enjoyed the same right to vote, both were equal. This was a strange echo from the propaganda of the Wilhelmine army where it was argued that the army had achieved true socialism, for in field-grey uniform all men were equal. That soldiers should be fully cognisant of democratic values, and should enjoy the widest possible democratic rights, is a praise-worthy but somewhat idealistic view. The concept of the citizen in uniform presupposes that there is a citizen in civilian clothes. The inner leadership programme assumed that all recruits were intelligent, well informed and active democrats. Many officers were bitterly disappointed to find that this was often not the case. Similarly the notion of 'intelligent obedience', rather than the blind instinctive obedience to orders bellowed in the best traditions of the Prussian drill sergeant, presupposed intelligent, educated and perceptive soldiers. Even then the effectiveness of such a concept is dubious. Clearly orders that are either criminal or insane have to be ignored, and with complex weaponry the active participation of the soldiers operating these weapons has to transcend blind obedience. But the notion that an order has to be intellectually understood before it can be obeyed comes dangerously close to being an empty slogan. The scorn of older officers towards an army of intellectual Hamlets is partly justified.

The wider question, which was largely avoided by the inner leadership, is whether or not the army is doomed to be to a certain degree a foreign body with a democratic society. With some notable exceptions sociologists have largely ignored the exceptionally interesting problem of the relationship between the army and society. Most research in military sociology has been devoted to positivistic studies of attitudes, inter-personal relationships and structural analysis with a view to making the military work more effectively, rather than critical studies of the functional role of the army in society. Sociologists who have tackled the problem, men such as Janowitz and Waldmann, have largely denied that there is any fundamental antagonism between a democratic society and its army. Janowitz has asserted that the military is becoming increasingly similar to civilian society, so that the army will one day become a glorified police force. Such a view is both sociologically and politically unsound. The prospect of the United States military as a world police force is not one which most people find attractive. The question of how far a police force itself is sociologically different from 'civil' society is ignored. Lastly this idea overlooks the extent to which wide sectors of industry, politics, science, technology and ideology have become militarized, or infused with essentially military ideas in the 'military-industrial complex' of the advanced societies. The phenomenal growth of military power in the decades since the last war, both directly and in the quasi-military institutions of secret police, spies, counter-insurgency and riot-control, clearly indicate that the optimism of men like Janowitz is misplaced. As the functional role of the military as a barrier against social change becomes all the more important, so the tensions between the army and civil society are likely to become more severe.

The more humane and democratic a society the greater is the discrepancy between civilians and military. Soldiers are expected to use extreme forms of violence which are regarded as taboo by that society. Soldiers are forced to accept an authoritarian and hierarchical social organization which is in sharp contrast to the avowed aims of a democratic society. Civilian notions of productivity and socially necessary labour are difficult to reconcile with the highly unproductive activity of armies. A social organization the aim of which is to kill other humans is bound to be based on somewhat different principles from those of one whose avowed aim is the maximization of human happiness. Lastly, the majority of people hold the subjective belief that there is indeed a difference between the military and the civilian, and a subjective belief which is so widespread becomes an objective fact. The notion of 'citizen in uniform' was thus misleading. It tended to become a slogan which attempted to obfuscate the real and necessary differences between civilian and military life. The moral worth of soldierly virtues, which are often quite different from civilian virtues, is always determined by the social goals and purposes to which these virtues are directed.

Baudissin was certainly aware of this fact. The Bundeswehr soldier was to be made fully aware that he was called upon to defend a free democratic state against the possibility of attack. He was to realize that his democratic rights could be guaranteed only if he willingly accepted the responsibility to defend them. He was to understand that the army was to serve the political needs of a democratic society, and that it was in no sense a 'state within a state'. This notion was fraught with problems. Critics of the inner leadership from the right argued that the army was an institution separate from civil society, that there were certain eternal soldierly virtues and that the task of an army was to be militarily effective, not to train a lot of sophisticated social scientists. This view was attractive, particularly to those who suffered from such acute ego-weakness that they welcomed the idea of becoming part of an elite and tough organization which was clearly separated from the rest of society. On the left it was pointed out that by raising the issue of the nature of the society the army was defending, the army was obliged either to indulge in a critical examination of that society or to fall back on propaganda in favour of the *status quo*. However laudable Baudissin's intentions, the inner leadership tended to deny real differences between civil and military society, and to degenerate into propagandistic apologies for the existing order. As such the inner leadership could all too easily become an ideological buffer between the army and society.

An essential part of the inner leadership was 'intellectual armament' *(geistige Rüstung)*, which became increasingly important as the problems and contradictions of the notion of 'citizens in unform' became apparent. 'Intellectual armament' was designed to draw a clear intellectual and psychological demarcation line between the Bundeswehr soldier and a potential enemy. An often grotesque picture of an agressive and totalitarian communism was painted which served to give a sense of purpose to the soldier, and which also was a convenient way of disguising and ignoring the deficiencies of West German society. The 'citizen in uniform' became less the defender of democratic rights at home than a crusader against a vicious dictatorial system which was held to be the enemy of all human rights. This manipulative use of anti-communism was particularly dangerous, for the Bundeswehr thrived in an atmosphere of tension and inner-German strife which rendered suspect the assertions that the army was designed to lessen international tensions. Furthermore in the guise of a struggle against communism, authoritarian, anti-democratic and traditionalist tendencies once again thrived in the army. The report of von Heye, the parliamentary military specialist *(Wehrbeauftragte)*, in 1963 gave an alarming insight into the failures of the inner leadership. Heye showed that the notion of thinking obedience was largely rejected, officers preferring to produce mindless robots. He also showed how Baudissin's democratic ideas were opposed by the majority of Bundeswehr officers and that the material used for instruction in the inner leadership was full of reactionary clichés and the traditionalist intellectual fare of the old army. The reaction to Heye's report was fierce. He was forced out of office, and in order to publicize his views he had to publish his report in an illustrated weekly magazine.

A discussion of the aims of the inner leadership leads necessarily to an examination of the domestic political role of the Bundeswehr. The passing of the 'Emergency Laws' (*Notstandsgesetze*) in June 1968 made possible the misuse of the Bundeswehr for domestic political purposes. The Bundeswehr can be used at home if the 'free democratic order' of the Federal Republic or a province of the republic is endangered, provided that there are insufficient police forces to deal with the problem. The discussions and debates on the emergency laws made it plain that their intention was not to meet the threat of aggression from the communist countries, but rather for domestic political repression. They were passed at a time when the remarkable economic prosperity of West Germany seemed likely to be plagued by increasing problems, and when the critical political consciousness, particularly of the youth, was becoming awakened. The emergency laws gave the Bundeswehr the legal right to act as a strike breaker and to march against the working class, even though, as the SPD pointed out, article 143 of the army law of 1956 clearly states that the Bundeswehr may not be used against Germans at home. The brutality of 30,000 policemen against a student demonstration against the Shah of Persia was hardly an encouraging example of the kind of thing that might be expected if the emergency laws were used by a determined government.

More insidious than the possibility of the direct use of violence for political ends at home, a prospect which, given the history of the German army, is far from pleasant, is the subtle manipulation of political attitudes of the members of the army. A study conducted in 1962 showed that of the officers between the rank of lieutenant and captain 74·6 per cent supported the CDU whereas a mere 4·8 per cent supported the SPD. Among

NCOs 74·2 per cent supported the CDU and 13·1 per cent the SPD. Among recruits 24 per cent supported the SPD and 47·5 per cent the CDU. The effect of political instruction and the inner leadership is clearly seen both by the fact that movement away from the SPD is greater the higher the rank, and by a further study which indicated that 16 per cent of the SPD supporters changed their political allegiance during their time of military service, which was true of only 6 per cent of the CDU supporters.

The reasons for this right-wing bias, even in an army which makes such pretensions to be a democratic 'people's army' are not merely to be found in the traditionally conservative, indeed reactionary, political attitudes of the warrior class. That citizens in uniform hold different political views from citizens in civilian clothes is due to a considerable extent to deliberate political indoctrination. A detailed study of the educational material of the Bundeswehr, the *Information for the Troops*, shows how far the lofty ideals of Graf Baudissin have been abandoned. 'Demoracy' is defined as being the political system of the Federal Republic, so that there can be no question of whether the Federal Republic is democratic enough, or how it could be made to be more democratic. Criticism of the system is denounced as 'belly-aching', and a compulsory stay behind the Iron Curtain is suggested as the best remedy. Great stress is placed upon the need for order, discipline and obedience both in civil and military life. Freedom is thus defined as subjection to authority. This definition of freedom is reconciled with the concept of democracy by insisting that: 'The democratic leader . . . takes responsibility for his fellow citizens and makes decisions on their behalf which they, through lack of strength, responsibility and understanding are unable to make . . . . These people make up the active part of a democracy. One could even say that they form an elite.' Underlying many of these pamphlets is a profound distrust of intellectual endeavour, and an insistence on the absolute value of essentially irrational concepts such as faith, self-sacrifice and idealism. An attempt is often made to counter critics of the Bundeswehr by insisting that in an age of advanced technology obviously the army needs intelligent soldiers and does everything to improve their thinking abilities. But such an argument avoids the central issue. The army encourages an instrumental rationality; a democracy needs a critical rationality.

The inner leadership, which in the eyes of Graf Baudissin was designed to overcome the differences between a democratic state and its army and to guarantee the full democratic rights of soldiers, thus degenerated into a revival of the old notion of the army as 'school of the nation'. Instruction in social studies was designed not to enlighten and to widen perspectives, but to reinforce and cement a given social order. Thus the Federal Republic was portrayed as being an exemplary democratic society, in which all but 'constructive' criticism was construed as communist propaganda. It stood at the forefront of western civilization in the defence of cultural values which were endangered by a barbaric, aggressive, Asiatic communism. The parallels with the Wilhelmine era are striking and alarming. It is greatly to be hoped that with the détente in Europe, which makes this vision of communism as the incarnation of everything that is evil altogether too absurd, and with a government headed by the SPD and with a president whose record as a critic of the excesses of the military is unblemished, there will be a significant change in the attitudes of the Bundeswehr. The 1970 White Book on the Bundeswehr called for commissions to study the problems of the inner leadership, but old attitudes die hard, and a profound and fundamental rethinking of the principles, possibilities and methods of the inner leadership is needed rather than patchwork on the old structure.

Initially opposition to a rapid and extensive armaments programme came from influential industrialists. With German industry working at capacity and with the work force fully employed, some concern was expressed that an excessive strain might be placed on industry and on the currency if rearmament were to proceed too hastily. Gradually, however, industry came to realize that high profits could be achieved in the armaments business, along with many other benefits, so that German industry could share in the defence prosperity characteristic of advanced industrial states. The military could be used as a doctor to tend the ailing branches of industry which were lagging behind in the extraordinary recovery of post-war German industry. The aircraft industry and shipbuilding were given large subsidies and contracts, without which both would

345

M

have been in serious difficulties. BMW was saved from a perilous financial situation by manufacturing jet engines for the ill-fated Starfighters of the German airforce. Similarly the Henschel Works was saved from most of its problems by being awarded contracts to build tanks. By the early 1960s almost all the leading German companies were actively involved in the armaments business. Industrialists were eager to lay their hands on the huge government subsidies for research and development which play such an important role in the economies of the USA and Britain. The myth that the most effective way to technological progress is through military research was widely broadcast. It was claimed that government research subsidies to private industry were for the public good, rather than for the private profits of 0·1 per cent of the population. But in spite of all these efforts government expenditure on research and development for military purposes has been relatively small, largely because a large number of American products have been built under licence – a fact which has caused some concern to the Americans who fear that the Germans are getting something on the cheap. There is still hope therefore that the Federal Republic may find some way of democratizing technological and scientific research so as to serve the true interests of the people, rather than the private interests of the large companies.

With the enormous volume of German goods exported the country soon had a massive balance of payments surplus. The import of armaments could therefore be used to reduce this surplus and to conclude favourable trade agreements with other countries. The import of military goods from countries such as the United States, Canada, Britain and France, as well as the less advanced countries such as Portugal, Turkey and Greece, plays an important part in the trade agreements between these countries. Without the import of military goods, which amount to about fifty per cent of the needs of the German armed forces, it is doubtful if Germany's forced export programme could have been so successful.

From 1956 discussions began in Germany about the possibility of arming the Bundeswehr with atomic weapons. The army welcomed the idea not least because of the enormous value of atomic weaponry as status symbols, giving the troops a great feeling of strength. Opinion polls showed that before long eighty-five per cent of the Bundeswehr soldiers were for atomic weapons. Atomic rearmament was also attractive to sectors of industry which stood to profit by enormous expenditure on advanced technology. For the politicians around Adenauer atomic weapons were deemed desirable as a necessary part of the politics of strength. In 1957 Adenauer tried to placate the increasingly large number of people who were highly alarmed at the idea of a German army armed with atomic weapons by saying that they were nothing more than artillery, and that the army could not do without the most modern weapons. On 12 April 1957 a group of prominent scientists, among them Max Born, Otto Hahn, Werner Heisenberg and Carl Friedrich von Weizsäcker, published the 'Göttingen Manefesto', a rousing attack on the idea of arming the Federal Republic with atomic weapons. Before long a large, loosely organized movement against atomic weapons for the Bundeswehr became increasingly active. In 1958 defence minister Strauss accepted the American offer of matador rockets for the Bundeswehr, rockets which could be armed with atomic warheads. Once NATO abandoned the idea of massive retaliation, an all-out nuclear response to a conventional attack, in favour of 'flexible response', demands by German generals for tactical nuclear weapons became louder, as they insisted that the response of the Bundeswehr also had to be flexible to meet any kind of military eventuality.

Proposals by the NATO commander, General Norstad, for a NATO nuclear force seemed to offer a possibility for the Bundeswehr to get a finger on the nuclear trigger. The concept was attractive to the United States government, for it was hoped that this multi-national atomic force (MLF) would help cement the NATO pact and lead to a cost sharing of the American nuclear contribution to NATO without giving the Europeans complete control over nuclear weapons. In spite of the opposition of France, which continued to build its own nuclear *force de frappe*, NATO continued with plans for the MLF, an idea which was enthusiastically supported by the Germans. In Ottawa in 1963 plans for a multi-national fleet which would be equipped with Polaris missiles were finalized. In 1964 the US destroyer *Biddle* was manned with a NATO crew to test the feasibility of the MLF. The Bundeswehr continued to press for an extension of the MLF which was seen as a necessary step towards the goal of a national atomic and nuclear force. As General Trettner said, the MLF was not the end of the line, but a means of convincing the Americans that the Bundeswehr could be trusted with nuclear weapons.

Adenauer and the Bundeswehr did not put all their eggs in one multinational basket, but also attempted to reach an agreement with the French on nuclear weapons. Strauss and Heusinger visited the French atomic testing grounds in the Sahara in 1957, and shortly afterwards joint research projects in ballistics, rockets, and in 1963 nuclear reactors were begun. The trend towards détente in the early 1960s strengthened the hand of the German 'gaullists', like Guttenberg, who hoped to reach an *entente cordiale* with France so as to frustrate British and American schemes for a European détente which marked a retreat from the sacrosanct 'roll back' theories of Dulles. The culminating point of this policy was Adenauer's special treaty with France in 1963. At that time de Gaulle was making loud anti-Soviet noises, refusing to join the Geneva disarmament talks and wrecking the test-ban treaty by letting off atomic blasts in the Sahara. He seemed to be an ideal partner for Adenauer, Strauss and the generals. The new chancellor Ludwig Erhard, who was not one of the gaullist group in Bonn, also feared that a military disengagement in Europe was possible, and sought to counteract it with closer ties with France. Guttenberg became the loudest and most articulate spokesman of those who wanted a 'European', that is Franco-German, nuclear force, which he hoped would put such fear and terror into Soviet hearts that the decision of 1945 could be revised and Germany reunited under the Bonn government.

Fortunately de Gaulle put an end to this dream. By 1965 he was in full swing with his own détente policy, blissfully independent from the Americans. He enraged his reactionary followers in the Federal Republic by recognizing the Oder-Neisse frontier and concluding a series of economic and cultural agreements with the GDR. At the same time he established closer relations with the Soviet Union and talked of the centuries-long sympathy and similarity of interests between the Russian and French peoples. In this changed situation he had no intention whatever of allowing such determined opponents of détente as Guttenberg and Strauss to have any share of his *force de frappe*. At the same time de Gaulle effectively torpedoed the MLF, so that both the 'gaullists' and the 'transatlantics' were bitterly frustrated. De Gaulle's policies left his supporters in Germany in complete disarray. All that was left for them to do was to raise hysterical objections to the proposed non-proliferation treaty which marked an important step forward in the moves towards a European détente. With the signing of that treaty the Federal Republic has undertaken 'not to receive the transfer from any transferor whatsoever of nuclear weapons or other nuclear explosive devices or of control over such weapons or explosive devices directly, or indirectly; not to manufacture or otherwise acquire nuclear weapons or other nuclear explosive devices; and not to seek or receive any assistance in the manufacture of nuclear weapons or other nuclear explosive devices'. Although there is a very long way yet to go, the treaty removes one of the greatest and most dangerous stumbling blocks to a true European détente.

Those politicians and generals who demanded nuclear weapons for the Bundeswehr simply refused to see that, in Rudolf Augstein's words, the only way for the Federal Republic to be defended was to ensure that there was no war. Nuclear weapons offer no such guarantee, for in the event of a war between the United States and the Soviet Union a NATO response, whether 'massive' or 'flexible' would almost certainly lead to the destruction of Germany. Even given that the 'balance of terror' gives the Soviet Union and the United States a certain security from one another, this does not guarantee the security of Europeans. Berlin could well be 'saved' in a crisis situation by being destroyed with nuclear weapons. Such defensive thinking is suicidal. The prospect of what is euphemistically called 'conventional' warfare is hardly less unattractive, particularly after the inhuman experiences of the Vietnam war. Clearly a drastic rethinking of the strategic and tactical role of the Bundeswehr is needed so that the political détente may be reflected adequately in military thinking, and that Germany may be saved from the horrors of full-scale or 'limited' war.

Most of the Bundeswehr is closely integrated into NATO and its strategic role is dictated by NATO. The key to the Bundeswehr's role is 'forward strategy'. With the strategic concept of massive response the Bundeswehr was to provide a vital part of NATO's 'shield', a defensive guard, whilst the nuclear forces of the United States and Britain would form the 'sword'. When NATO adopted the strategy of 'flexible response' the clear distinction between sword and shield began to disappear. The Bundeswehr generals therefore began to press their demands for atomic weapons, insisting that they were essential if the shield were to be effective. At the same time they argued that NATO's defensive line had to be pushed as far east as possible. The eastern defensive line was therefore moved to the River Weser in the hope that the highest degree of mobility could be maintained in the reserves behind this forward line. The Federal Republic is a relatively narrow strip of land which is densely populated, so that this aspect is a particularly pressing problem, and is the main argument used to support the forward strategy. As part of this strategy the Bundeswehr demanded that atomic mines be placed along the border of the GDR, and insisted that the United States should use its nuclear sword at the earliest possible moment after the commencement of hostilities, or else should give nuclear warheads to the Bundeswehr to strengthen the shield. In 1965 the defence minister von Hassel wrote in *Foreign Affairs* that if only conventional weapons were used the Bundeswehr would be unable to hold the balance, and the longer nuclear weapons were held back the greater would be the resistance to their use so that the opponent would have a clear advantage.

To the GDR and the Warsaw Pact states this 'forward strategy' is clear indication of the revanchist and aggressive intentions of the Bundeswehr and of the Bonn government. Although such a portrait of NATO and the Federal Republic undoubtedly plays something of the same role in the socialist countries as the grotesque picture of communism does in the west, and is as great a hindrance to a rational understanding of the present-day world, it would be a mistake to dismiss it out of hand as mere propaganda or communist paranoia. As Colonel Bogislaw von Bonin has shown, the structure and equipment of the present day Bundeswehr are offensive rather than defensive. Ten divisions are equipped with rockets that are designed to carry nuclear warheads. There are three brigades of paratroops. The F104G and G91 bombers can be equipped with nuclear weapons. The navy is also equipped with rockets. This extremely expensive equipment is quite unsuitable for the declared intention of the Bundeswehr to play a defensive role. Bonin has estimated that the size of the Bundeswehr could be reduced by one half, most of the expensive rocketry and tanks could be scrapped, and the Bundeswehr equipped with modern anti-tank weapons. A well-equipped force of 250,000 men, armed with defensive weapons, would be sufficient to deliver a serious blow to any attacker. The saving in men and equipment would be enormous. Germany would then no longer provide the deployment area and the expendable reserves for United States nuclear strategy. Liddell Hart argued along similar lines in 1967 when he told an interviewer of the German magazine *Stern* that the Bundeswehr should be reduced to about six divisions of highly trained professional soldiers equipped with defensive weapons. This highly mobile defensive army would be stationed in the western parts of the Federal Republic. The border areas would then be defended by a militia of 250,000 to 500,000 men armed with anti-tank weapons. All the Bundeswehr's rockets could be scrapped, compulsory military service abolished and huge sums of money would be saved.

With some steps towards a European détente and a far more realistic eastern policy by the Federal government, a drastic rethinking of the strategic role of the Bundeswehr is vitally important. If the Soviet Union is not planning a vast onslaught on the Federal Republic, then the military thinking of the Bundeswehr is without any rationale. Without access to nuclear warheads the rockets of the Bundeswehr are virtually useless. In the event of even a limited nuclear war, which the strategic doctrine of flexible response makes highly likely, the territory of the Federal Republic is liable to be laid waste. Only a limited force which is clearly designed for defensive purposes can give West Germany an adequate defence, and any other kind of force is liable to be a serious hindrance to further détente.

If the strategic role and structure of the Bundeswehr need to be fundamentally changed, so too must its self-image. The new army has been unable to find adequate historical models on which a new tradition can be based. The men of 20 July 1944 have been used for propaganda purposes to show that the army was not just a willing tool in the hands of Hitler. The praise lavished on men like Stauffenberg and Moltke at the annual ceremonies on 20 July often by men who held senior positions in the Wehrmacht, who played no part in the resistance and who willingly fulfilled their duties to Hitler, is an unattractive spectacle. Little attempt is made to analyse the political ideas of the men of 20 July, or to point out the serious differences between the various groups. Such often embarrassing questions are rendered innocuous by vague talk of the 'revolt of conscience' against an inhuman regime. By praising men who resisted a totalitarian regime the army imagines that it will automatically be seen as a thoroughly democratic institution. Thus Stauffenberg and his comrades provide an alibi both for the Wehrmacht and for the Bundeswehr.

The Bundeswehr is firmly placed under the political control of the elected representatives of the people in the Bundestag. Because of the defeat in the last war and the resistance of so many Germans to rearmament, it no longer enjoys the popularity and prestige of the old army and has found it extremely difficult to form an appropriate self-image. Great emphasis is placed on the heroic bravery of the Wehrmacht, particularly in the eastern campaign, so that Bundeswehr soldiers can feel superior to the soldiers of other nations and to the feeble civilians. Such an attitude may have a good effect on morale, but it is in marked contrast to the homage paid to the men of 20 July. The Bundeswehr prides itself on standing in the front line between east and west, guardian of the free world and of the interests of a divided nation. This attitude is dependent to a great extent on the functional pessimism of the Bundeswehr. Tensions and potential conflicts are made to seem as menacing as possible so that the Bundeswehr may be seen as the saviour of prosperity and freedom. This again hinders a rational assessment of the defence needs of Germany, for a small army playing a purely defensive role against a potential enemy which shows no sign of wanting to fight is not a particularly glamorous picture. The 'glittering army' threatens to become a drab police force.

An army whose strategic thinking is based on an anachronistic and manichean world view, whose structure and armaments are inappropriate for its professed role, whose ideological basis is suspect and whose functional role in post-war German society is open to severe criticism, is clearly in need of fundamental change. The possibility for such a change still exists. The lessening of east-west tension and an abandonment of extreme Cold War stances makes it possible to discuss the problem in a rational manner. The Bundeswehr is still under effective political control and is responsive to firm political leadership. The West German armaments industry has yet to reach the dimensions where control becomes exceedingly difficult. There are the clear delineations of a 'military industrial complex', but as yet the ruling ideology, the structure of social power and all levels of the social system have not become totally infected with the imperatives of the military, as is the case in the United States. The military industrial complex and the social system are as yet not identical, and this modern form of militarism has yet to become firmly established in the Federal Republic.

The way towards a genuine and meaningful reform will be long. Old traditions and established routines die hard. The mistakes of the past are often difficult to correct. Vested interests are not easily combated. Most difficult of all, military policy is always and at all times closely linked to social and political prerogatives. For there to be a genuinely new military policy the political leadership must be determined to pursue truly democratic ends. Disengagement necessitates the repudiation of the old demonology, disarmament genuine international co-operation. The structural violence of modern militarism as a means of maintaining decaying social systems must be repudiated, and the proliferation of weapons systems throughout the globe coupled with the intensive preparation for war by all advanced countries cannot possibly be given the name 'peace' but must be seen as the first wasteful stage of war itself. In the nuclear age the need for alternative methods for meeting violence, injustice and social tensions are more pressing than ever. Nowhere is this need more apparent than in the heart of Europe. It is devoutly to be hoped that the end of the history of German militarism will not be the tragic destruction of Germany, but rather the surpassing of the purely military to the realization of truly human and peaceful goals.

11

Conclusion

In the seventeenth and eighteenth centuries Prussian militarism helped to preserve a declining feudal system. The social and economic structure of the country was designed to serve the interests of the military system. Conversely, by the canton system the social relationships of feudal society were transferred and transformed into military terms. This system had to be kept in equilibrium. The cost of maintaining a large army was very considerable, and placed an intolerable strain on an already overburdened rural economy. Thus concessions to the economy had to be made in order that the army might survive. But those concessions could not be too great or too one-sided. If the aristocracy was allowed to become too powerful the peasantry was threatened, and without a healthy and vigorous peasantry the army could not function effectively. Thus *Bauernschutz* was introduced as *Soldatenschutz*. However greedy the aristocracy might have been for the land of the peasantry they had to accept the *Bauernschutz*, although ignoring it whenever possible, as the price that had to be paid for the preservation of the feudal system which guaranteed their own privileges against the inroads of capitalism. The officer corps of the army provided a means for the integration of a potentially obstreperous aristocracy into the authoritarian state of the Prussian kings. The independent power of the aristocracy was broken, and there was no question of a *fronde* in Prussia.

The aristocracy also had their problems. Frequently absent

from their estates on military duty, the rural economy strained by the incessant wars of Frederick the Great, they became more and more tempted to sell off their estates to the aspiring bourgeoisie. Once again the king stepped in, forbidding the sale of aristocratic estates and offering the junkers access to cheap credit. To the *Bauernschutz* was added *Junkerschutz* and the social structure of Prussia was put in quarantine. This placed severe restrictions on the possibility of growth in the Prussian economy. Sustained growth could not be maintained without ending the feudal relationships of production, but this in turn would threaten the military system. As far as possible the junkers used capitalist methods on their own estates, within a social system which remained feudal, thus creating the curious amalgam of capitalism and feudalism which was to characterize the development of Prussia.

Faced with the challenge of the French Revolution Prussia was presented with an acute dilemma. Its outmoded infantry tactics could not be changed without allowing the troops greater freedom and initiative; this in turn was not possible without a radical change in the social system. The military system could not be overhauled without a fundamental restructuring of the social system. But only a few men realized the pressing need for reform. Most officers were either so hidebound by the conventions of the past that they could think of nothing but drill and elaborate parade-ground manoeuvres, or they imagined that the Prussian army was invincible and that the rabble of Paris could easily be defeated. In 1806 the Prussian army was completely defeated, and there could be no question but that the military system had to be radically reformed if Prussia were ever again to be an independent state. The reformers, men such as Scharnhorst, Gneisenau, Boyen and Clausewitz, realized that a major social reform was the necessary precondition of an effective reform of the army. The enthusiasm, courage and resoluteness of the people had to be unleashed so that the army could draw on the moral reserves of the nation. The divisions between the army and the people, between rulers and ruled, had to be overcome to the highest possible degree so that the Prussian army could at last be a true match for the armies of Napoleon.

The crushing defeat of Prussia forced even the most conservative to realize that at least some of these ideas, which sounded so alarmingly jacobin, would have to be implemented. The serfs were liberated, the officer corps was purged of inefficient and cowardly officers, minimum educational standards for entry to the officer corps were set, and it was no longer to be an exclusively aristocratic preserve. Discipline was somewhat relaxed, and the sadistic punishments of the Frederican army were largely abolished. Military law was reformed. The army was reorganized, with a proper war ministry and the beginnings of an effective general staff. A major step forward was taken towards establishing the principle of universal military service, but strict limits were placed on this radical notion. A *Landwehr* was instituted which embodied some of the reformers' ideas of a people's army with its bourgeois officer corps and its popularity with the ordinary citizens.

The achievements of the reformers within such a short space of time, and against such opposition, were extraordinary. But once Napoleon was defeated the reaction set in, and even their modest attempts to alter Prussian society were under severe attack. The reformers were soon forced out of office. The political reaction of the Carlsbad decrees against liberal nationalism was coupled with a reorganization of the *Landwehr* which brought it under the close supervision of the regular army. Once again the army was cut off from the rest of society, was purged of its liberal elements and was prepared as an instrument of domestic oppression. In 1848 the army was put to the test. Although those who demanded an outright military dictatorship were frustrated in their aims, and although the army was initially humiliated by the Berlin crowd, it nevertheless played a vital role in suppressing the revolution. Thus throughout the pre-March when, particularly after the formation of the *Zollverein*, significant economic progress was being made, the army played an important role in stabilizing the power and authority of the junkers in a social environment which was becoming increasingly hostile, and in strengthening junker-capitalist agriculture. When this system was seriously challenged in 1848 the army ensured that the crown and the aristocracy preserved their exclusive political rights.

By crushing the revolution in 1848 the army gave the old ruling class a new lease of life. The middle class realized that if they pressed too hard for reform they ran the serious risk of being overtaken by the left, and they were thus beginning to accept the need for a compromise with the aristocracy. The army was now to achieve the national aims of the liberal bourgeoisie by 'blood and iron', and the 'revolution from above' would be the antidote to the 'revolution from below'.

After 1848 the main concern of the army was for the 'enemy at home'. The law on the state of siege gave the army wide powers in the event of civil unrest. The *Landwehr* was further purged of liberal elements. Even the humiliation of Olmütz was accepted as better than the risk of 'revolutionary' nationalism. After the economic crisis of 1857 the social question became particularly pressing, and plans for army reform were discussed which were designed to make the army an absolutely reliable tool of royal absolutism. The *Landwehr* was to be brought completely under the control of the regular army, the term of service in the regular army was to be three years rather than the usual two and the army was to be greatly increased. These schemes precipitated a major constitutional crisis as the liberal opposition demanded constitutional concessions and guarantees in return for support for the military reforms. In the army some hotheads pressed for a *coup d'état*, but cooler heads prevailed. Manteuffel wanted a show-down, but Roon was prepared to accept some kind of compromise with the *Landtag* and argued that foreign policy could be used to project the domestic crisis away from its true source. In September 1862 the situation reached complete deadlock when the *Landtag* refused to vote any further funds for reform of the army. In a last desperate move Bismarck was appointed minister president of Prussia with the task of solving the crisis.

Bismarck quickly realized that the liberals' main objection to the army was that it was chiefly designed for repression at home. An active foreign policy could thus be used to quell these fears and to divert the liberals' attention away from their obsession with constitutional questions. Thus he was brilliantly to exploit the Schleswig-Holstein crisis to strengthen the government's hand against the liberals at home, and Prussia's hand against Austria in Germany. His policies were supported by Moltke who, as chief of the general staff, was the architect of the defeat of Austria and France. Moltke, like Bismarck, believed that wars had to be as short as possible so that social unrest could be avoided. He had a mastery of the modern techniques of warfare which was unmatched; he was an open-minded intellectual, not a sabre-rattling militarist. But he was determined that the army should not be democratized for fear of unleashing social forces which might get out of control, and he was anxious that war should not unleash passions which might lead to social upheaval. He was ever conscious of the political effects of war, and was determined that they should be neutralized. He was the master of the limited war and a strong opponent of total war. Thus the often exaggerated differences between Moltke and Bismarck were tactical rather than fundamental. Both men knew that the 'political' and the 'military' could not be neatly divided, and Moltke accepted Bismarck's political concepts. Their quarrels, particularly during the Franco-Prussian war, were the result of temporary problems in the course of the campaign and differences over how they could best be overcome.

The victories of 1866 and 1871 greatly strengthened the Prussian army and the authority of the chief of general staff. After 1871 the superiority of the Prussian army over the armies of Bavaria, Saxony and Württemburg was firmly established. Although in theory the chief of the general staff and the war minister were Prussian authorities, *de facto* they acted as imperial ministers. Bismarck was anxious to cut back Moltke's power, but was only partly successful, for the relationship between the chief of the general staff and the Kaiser was particularly close. The Kaiser's dual function as king of Prussia and German emperor made Moltke's position both ambiguous and extremely influential.

But it was not just the army leadership that was strengthened. The Reich had been formed by blood and iron, and the prestige of the army was enormous. A commission in the army was an almost essential precondition for social and professional success. The army was the single most important stabilizing factor in an authoritarian, conservative and autocratic state. It served to preserve the rights and privileges of an aristocracy which found it increasingly difficult to maintain its unique position in a world which was becoming inimical to it.

Soon it became all too apparent that the great successes of

the army had not solved all the problems of Germany in Europe, Prussia in Germany or the aristocracy in Prussia. A further war was needed to secure Germany's place in the world, and to prevent radical social change at home. As these social, economic and political problems became increasingly acute the proposed means of overcoming them were more strident and virulent than ever. The army was greatly increased, allowing industrialists to make considerable profits and thus silencing their criticisms of the army as an illiberal institution. The control of the Reichstag over the army was reduced as far as possible. Through the institution of the reserve officer a large sector of the bourgeoisie was reconciled with the army and began to ape the manners of the aristocracy. Thus the army acted as a powerful means of social integration, but by placing a severe burden on the economy, by its aggressive military planning and by blocking institutional means of voicing discontent it helped to create the severe tensions which characterized the Wilhelmine era.

The career of General Waldersee showed that there was no danger of an outright military dictatorship or ultra right-wing coup. The army exercised the greatest influence when it operated behind the scenes, pretending that it was solely concerned with military affairs and had no desire to play a political role. But as the need for reform became increasingly pressing, the political role of the army was more pronounced than ever. The struggle against social democracy became one of the main concerns of the army. A massive propaganda campaign designed to turn the army into the 'school of the nation' which would teach young recruits the dangers of socialism was a miserable failure. So the army prepared for the revolution, studied street fighting tactics, and waited for the blood-bath which the Kaiser in his more expansive moments welcomed, but which the social democrats had no intention of provoking. While the ideologues of the army preached the necessity of war and imperialist expansion the general staff perfected its strategic planning with the Schlieffen plan of 1905. For all its brilliance the Schlieffen plan was a desperate bid for world power, an inflexible and essentially unrealistic strategic concept which had a disastrous effect on German diplomacy and accurately reflected the aggressiveness and instability of

Wilhelmine Germany. The army found itself caught in a serious contradiction between the imperatives of its strategic planning and its need for a socially exclusive officer corps. The Schlieffen plan required an enormous increase in the size of the army, but this could be realized only if 'unreliable' bourgeois elements were allowed into the officer corps and if an increasing number of townsmen were recruited into the ranks. Fearing that the officer corps might become dangerously liberal and the men would be social democrats, and that the army would thus no longer be reliable as an instrument of domestic oppression, the army rejected the general staff's requests for large increases. As a result the army did not have the men it needed if its strategic plan was to have a reasonable chance of success.

In the July crisis of 1914 the army was to play an important role in precipitating the war. The exigencies of the strategic planners' time-tables gave the diplomatists little room for manoeuvre. After the German defeat on the Marne a war of attrition began which gradually placed an almost intolerable strain on the German economy and society. The failure to find a way out of this impasse at Ypres and at Verdun led to the dismissal of Falkenhayn and the appointment of Hindenburg and Ludendorff to the High Command, in the hopes that they would be able to engineer the Tannenberg in the west which was needed if Germany was to win the war and secure her far-reaching war aims.

The Kaiser's reluctance to use his full sovereign powers during the war enabled Hindenburg and Ludendorff to establish their particular form of military dictatorship. They shamelessly appealed to popular support in a way which would have seemed incredible to the pre-war army. This pseudo-democratic rabble-rousing gave to the militarism of the High Command a peculiar bonapartist twist, so that the bonapartism of Bismarck was combined with a virulent militarism. But Hindenburg and Ludendorff had no desire to establish a direct military dictatorship, although they often discussed the idea, for they preferred to use the politicians as 'lightning conductors' for the unpopular measures and the failures of policies over which the High Command had ultimate control. The law on the state of siege gave the commanding generals almost dictatorial rights. The High Command used the censorship to pursue its own political ends. With the *Hilfsdienstgesetz* it was able to exercise a high degree of control over the economy. It was able to secure the dismissal of leading politicians from chancellors to foreign ministers down to the less exalted offices such as the war minister or the chief of the civil cabinet. In foreign policy its role was decisive, but for all the fierce and acrimonious debates between the High Command and the civilians on war aims there was an essential identity of aims, however great the tactical differences. German aims were out of all proportion to the means of attaining them, but the dim realization of this fact did not have the effect of making the High Command's ambitions more modest. On the contrary, it was used as proof that even more extensive war aims were essential to secure Germany's rightful place in the world. Hindenburg and Ludendorff insisted that there was a simple choice between world power and complete annihilation. But when the defeat came the blame was placed not on the army but on the politicians. The 'stab in the back' legend which was to play such a powerful role in the Weimar republic was a triumph of the 'lightning conductor' policy of the militarism of the High Command, and was also a powerful ingredient in the rise of fascism.

In 1914–1918 militarism had failed to secure the extensive war aims which were deemed essential for Germany's survival as a great power with an antiquated social structure, and had also failed to secure the social order against democratic change. But the army, however small and in spite of its crushing defeat, survived in the Weimar republic to play a profoundly important restorative and anti-democratic role. The pact between Ebert and Groener prevented any democratization of the army, made the social democratic government dependent on the army and thus stopped the revolution in its tracks. The Kapp *putsch* led to the dismissal of Reinhardt and Noske, the two men who had tried to save the republic and had tried to achieve a degree of compromise between the army and the social democratic regime. It brought Seeckt to power, the man who had refused to help the republic and who was determined to preserve the complete independence of the army and save it from political control. Seeckt pursued his policy of military co-operation with the Soviet Union in flagrant defiance of the Treaty of Versailles and behind the backs of the foreign office. In the crisis of 1923

Seeckt, far from saving the republic, tilted the balance dangerously in favour of the right. Although not sympathetic to the extreme right such as the national socialists, Seeckt, by crushing the forces of the left in Saxony, Thuringia and the Rhineland, dangerously weakened the labour movement which was the mainstay of the democratic republic. By undermining Stresemann's attempts to form a viable coalition government, by squabbling with President Ebert and by expressing his acute dislike of the republic to those who were bent on destroying it, he contributed to its downfall ten years later. He earned the hatred of the left, and those on the right who urged him to establish a military dictatorship were disappointed. He thus had ever-diminishing political support, and once Hindenburg became president, Seeckt's power was further lessened, for he could not hope to threaten Hindenburg with the displeasure of the army. In 1926 Seeckt was obliged to resign. His successor Heye was more ready to compromise with the republic, and so was the new war minister, General Groener. It seemed that the army was emerging from its isolation and its hostility to the republic, and that civil-military relations were entering a new and more constructive phase. But the more active the army became in day-to-day political intrigue the greater became the influence of General Schleicher whose appetite for plotting in the corridors of power was insatiable. Schleicher intrigued against Groener who had tried to ban the SS and SA. He helped to overthrow the legitimate government of Prussia. He helped to remove both Brüning and Papen from the chancellorship and won the office for himself. He tried to win over Hitler, and failing this he attempted to split the national socialist movement. Thus the army played a vital role in dismembering the republic, and did much to help bring Hitler to power.

Hitler's first Reichswehr minister, von Blomberg, and his right hand man von Reichenau, were completely subservient to the chancellor. Almost no resistance was shown to the steady inculcation of the army with national socialist ideology. The army gave decisive support to Hitler and the SS in their attack on Röhm and the SA, and thus gave their approval to terror, murder and totalitarian dictatorship. They readily set about planning the strategic details of Hitler's aggressive wars, became more and more outspoken in their support of the regime and allowed the army to become increasingly dominated by Hitler. In 1938 both Blomberg and Fritsch were removed and Hitler was able to strengthen his hold on the army by appointing General Keitel to the newly-formed OKW and General Brauchitsch to the OKH. Brauchitsch became concerned that Hitler was heading for a war for which Germany was not yet sufficiently prepared, but he was easily silenced by torrents of abuse from the Führer. This set the pattern for the military opposition. Both during the Czechoslovakian and the Polish crises there were those in the army who feared that Germany was not yet ready for war, but this opposition was not to the idea of a war of conquest but to the precise timing of the war. Hitler easily overruled their objections, and the spectacular successes of the early blitzkrieg operations silenced their tactical objections. Similarly, although some officers courageously objected to the criminal activities of the SS, particularly in the east, most officers preferred to turn a blind eye, whilst many senior officers actually supported these activities and issued orders which were flagrant violations of international law and of humane conduct. The same was true of the attack on the Soviet Union. There were those who thought that the attack was premature, or that the proposed plan of attack was faulty, but whilst they were 'resisting' Hitler they were busily putting the finishing touches on 'Operation Barbarossa' and discussing the exploitation of the resources of the Soviet Union with captains of industry.

When Barbarossa failed to reach its objectives Hitler began to interfere increasingly with the conduct of operations, becoming commander-in-chief of the army in place of Brauchitsch, and providing the generals with a splendid alibi for their failures after the war. Germany did not fail in 1941/42 because of Hitler's mistakes or the generals' incompetence or because of the severity of the weather conditions, but because the resources of Germany were not adequate for a successful campaign against the Soviet Union. Rather than admit this fact, the army resorted to appeals for fanaticism, heroism, self-sacrifice and other such slogans in the hope that will-power would overcome objective facts. Those who realized how absurd this attitude was drifted towards the resistance movement, but this movement offered no real alternative to the fascist regime. Only men of outstanding intellectual and physical courage, such as von

Stauffenberg and von Moltke, were able to realize that for fascism to be eradicated there had to be a thorough democratization of society.

With the total defeat of Germany a large section of society realized that Stauffenberg and Moltke had been correct, and that without democracy, international co-operation and the breaking of the power of the big corporations and the military and political elites which had been responsible for fascism, Germany could not be made immune against the resurgence of a political system the terrible consequences of which none could now deny. The rearmament of West Germany, which resulted from the Cold War, against the wish of a substantial section of society, was a major step backwards in that it enabled many of the old elite groups to regain their positions of power and influence, and halted the trend towards a further democratization of society. West Germany won a powerful position in the western alliance, and general prosperity reconciled many to the Bonn regime. But this prosperity was bought at a high price. Reunification became impossible. International tensions became acute. Germany ran the risk of being the target of a nuclear war. Further democratization was halted. An excessively large and expensive military establishment was created which was widely unpopular and was far greater than the defence needs of the country would warrant. In spite of many impressive efforts, the Bundeswehr has not managed to find a satisfactory role for itself either within Germany or in an international context.

Throughout its history the German army has been to a varying degree an instrument which has blocked social change and maintained the status quo. In the eighteenth century the balance between the military and the social systems was maintained so that the modernization of society was hindered. The crushing defeat of the old order by Napoleon enabled a group of reformers to tackle the problems of the relationship between the army and society in an imaginative and progressive way, but once Napoleon was in turn defeated the army again played a vital role in maintaining the old order and in reinforcing all restorative tendencies. In the revolutions of 1848 the army defended the old order against the threat from the new, and under Bismarck it helped to create an authoritarian bonapartist state. As the tensions within German society became more intense the army played a direct political role by propagandizing youth and by preparing for revolution at home and war abroad. The desperate bid for world power in 1914 which was designed to solve the social question and preserve the privileges of the ruling class failed, but the army survived to hamper the efforts of the Weimar republic to democratize. In Hitler the army found an ally who promised it power, prestige and glory, but who brought it defeat and ignominy. But within ten years the German army was revived and acted as a brake on further democratic reform.

There is no easy solution to the problem of the relationship between the army and society. An essential starting point is the examination of the historical record. The lessons are obvious. The army must at all times be under effective political control, and the sovereign political power must pursue rational and humane ends. It is very simple, but exceedingly difficult to achieve.

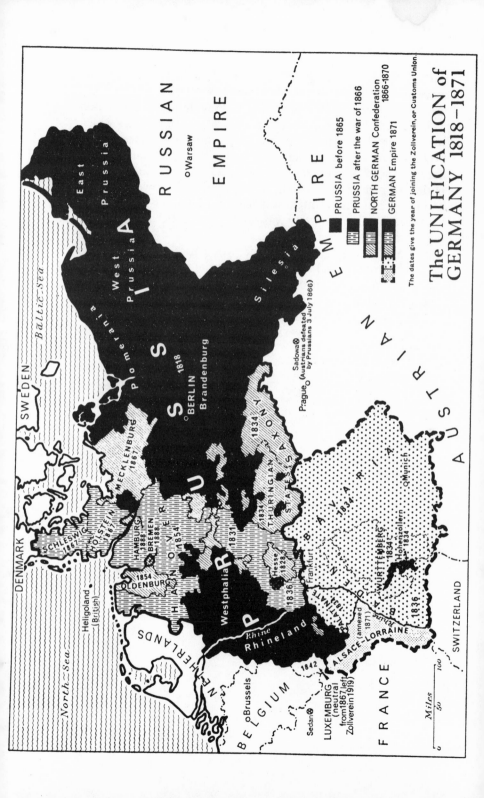

The UNIFICATION of GERMANY 1818–1871

PRUSSIA before 1865
PRUSSIA after the war of 1866
NORTH GERMAN Confederation 1866-1870
GERMAN Empire 1871

The dates give the year of joining the Zollverein, or Customs Union.

RUSSIAN EMPIRE

Warsaw

AUSTRIAN EMPIRE

SWEDEN

Baltic Sea

DENMARK

Heligoland (British)

North Sea

East Prussia

West Prussia

Pomerania

Silesia

PRUSSIA

BERLIN 1818
Brandenburg

Prague (Austrians defeated by Prussians 3 July 1866)

Sadowa⊗

MECKLENBURG 1861

SCHLESWIG 1867

HOLSTEIN 1867

HAMBURG 1888

BREMEN 1888

OLDENBURG 1854

HANOVER 1854

SAXONY 1834

THURINGIAN STATES 1834

Hesse 1828

1836

Frankfurt

1834

BAVARIA 1834

Munich

WÜRTTEMBERG 1834

Hohenzollern 1834

BADEN 1836

Westphalia 1831

Rhine

Rhineland

PALATINATE 1834

1842

ALSACE-LORRAINE (annexed 1871)

Sedan⊗

NETHERLANDS

BELGIUM

Brussels

LUXEMBURG (neutral from 1867 left Zollverein 1919)

FRANCE

SWITZERLAND

Miles
0   50   100

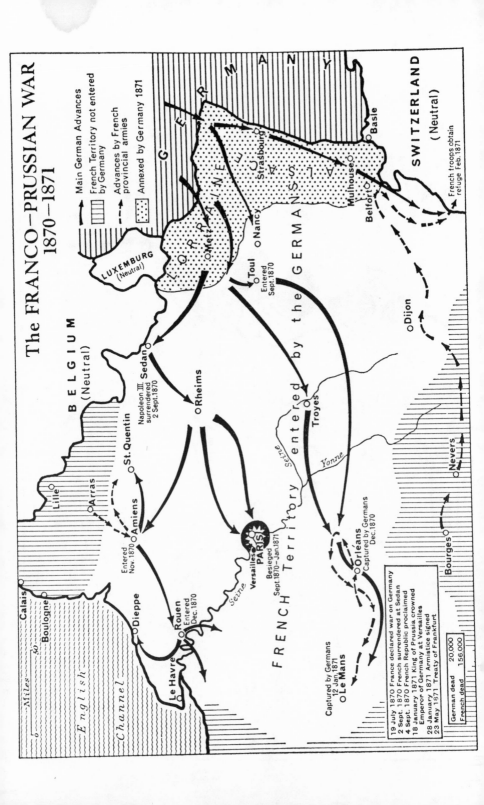

The FRANCO-PRUSSIAN WAR
1870–1871

Main German Advances →
French Territory not entered by Germany ▥
Advances by French provincial armies ⇠
Annexed by Germany 1871 ⋰

GERMANY

SWITZERLAND (Neutral)

BELGIUM (Neutral)

LUXEMBURG (Neutral)

Basle

French troops obtain refuge Feb.1871

Strasbourg

Mulhouse

Belfort

ALSACE

LORRAINE

Metz

Nancy

Toul
Entered Sept.1870

Sedan
Napoleon III surrendered 2 Sept.1870

Rheims

entered by the GERMANS

Dijon

Troyes

Yonne

Seine

St. Quentin

Lille

Arras

Amiens
Entered Nov.1870

Calais

Boulogne

Dieppe

Rouen
Entered Dec.1870

Le Havre

English Channel

Seine

Versailles

PARIS
Besieged Sept.1870–Jan.1871

FRENCH TERRITORY

Orléans
Captured by Germans Dec.1870

Le Mans
Captured by Germans 12 Jan.1871

Nevers

Bourges

Miles 0 50

19 July 1870 France declared war on Germany
2 Sept. 1870 French surrendered at Sedan
4 Sept. 1870 French Republic proclaimed
18 January 1871 King of Prussia crowned Emperor of Germany at Versailles
28 January 1871 Armistice signed
23 May 1871 Treaty of Frankfurt

German dead   20,000
French dead   156,000

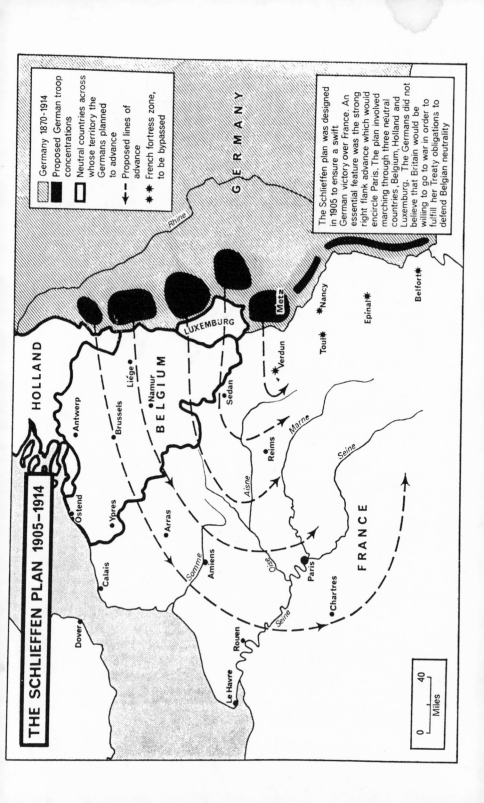

THE SCHLIEFFEN PLAN 1905–1914

Key:
- Germany 1870-1914
- Proposed German troop concentrations
- Neutral countries across whose territory the Germans planned to advance
- Proposed lines of advance
- ✳ French fortress zone, to be bypassed

The Schlieffen plan was designed in 1905 to ensure a swift German victory over France. An essential feature was the strong right flank advance which would encircle Paris. The plan involved marching through three neutral countries, Belgium, Holland and Luxemburg. The Germans did not believe that Britain would be willing to go to war in order to fulfill her Treaty obligations to defend Belgian neutrality.

GERMANY

Rhine

HOLLAND

BELGIUM

Antwerp

Brussels

Liége

Namur

LUXEMBURG

Sedan

Verdun ✳

Metz

Nancy ✳

Toul ✳

Epinal ✳

Belfort ✳

Ostend

Ypres

Calais

Dover

Arras

Somme

Amiens

Aisne

Reims

Marne

Seine

Oise

Paris

Chartres

FRANCE

Seine

Le Havre

Rouen

0   40
Miles

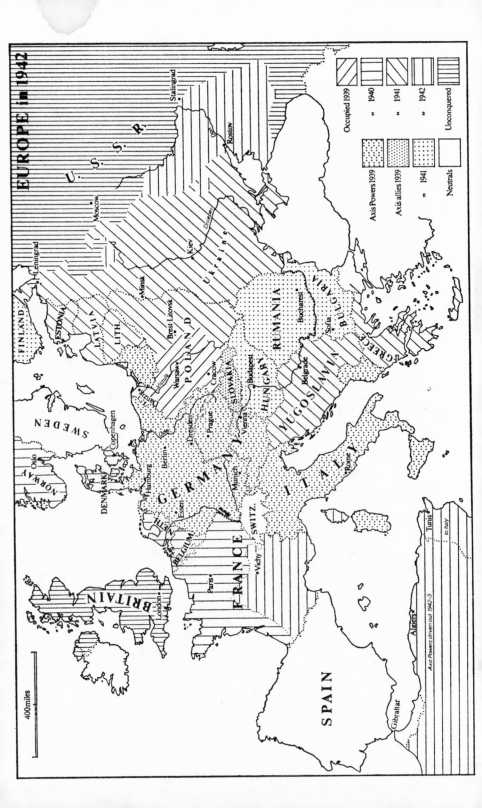

Bibliography

Students of the history of the German Army are fortunate in having two outstanding textbooks which cover the period from the middle of the seventeenth century to 1945. Gordon A. Craig, *The Politics of the Prussian Army 1640–1915* (Oxford 1955) is a brilliantly written synthesis of the major literature which also contains original research of importance. Although our knowledge of the period has increased greatly since the book was written it is still indispensable and highly enjoyable reading. For a more sociological approach, Karl Demeter, *The German Officer Corps in Society and State 1650–1945* (London 1965) is invaluable and provides an admirable supplement to Craig's book. Peter Bachmann and Kurt Zeisler, *Der deutsche Militarismus* (Berlin 1971) is an excellent selection of pictures. As yet only the first volume has appeared covering the period from the fifteenth century to the First World War. The text is lively and provocative, presenting a summary of the Marxist-Leninist viewpoint. Förster, Helmert, Otto and Schnitter, *Der preussisch-deutsche Generalstab 1640–1965* (Berlin 1966) is rather a mixed bag. It contains some good material but all too frequently lapses into harangues. Hajo Herbell, *Staatsbürger in Uniform 1789 bis 1861* (Berlin 1969) and Emil Obermann, *Soldaten-Bürger-Militaristen* (Stuttgart 1958) both examine the history of the question of the 'citizen in uniform', the former from an East German, the latter from a West German, perspective. The contrast is illuminating. Curt Jany, *Geschichte der Königlich Preussischen Armee*, 4 vols (Berlin 1928) is a standard work

370

which is very useful on the technical background, but is marred by uncritical admiration for the general staff. A summary of recent West German research will be found in *Handbuch zur deutschen Militärgeschichte 1648–1939* (Frankfurt am Main 1964) by various authors. Gerhard Ritter, *Staatskunst und Kreigshandwerk*, 4 vols (Munich 1959) is more illuminating as a study of the intellectual and moral problems of a distinguished conservative and nationalist historian than it is as a history of the German army. Starting with a completely unworkable definition of militarism, Ritter manages to tie himself up in some curious knots, but there is much valuable material in the book, particularly in the last two volumes which deal with the First World War. For the problem of militarism Alfred Vagts, *A History of Militarism Civilian and Military* (New York 1959) is a wise and humane book by a great historian.

For the eighteenth century O. Büsch, *Militärsystem und Sozialleben im alten Preussen 1713–1807* (Berlin 1962) is a brilliant book which provides a penetrating analysis of the relationship between the army and society. For background F. L. Carsten, *The Origins of Prussia* (Oxford 1954) and Hans Rosenberg, *Bureaucracy, Aristocracy and Autocracy, The Prussian Experience 1660–1815* (Cambridge, Mass. 1966) are invaluable. Two classics by Otto Hintze, *Die Hohenzollern und ihr Werk* (Berlin 1916) and *Historische und politische Aufsätze* (Berlin 1908), should also be consulted. Franz Mehring, the most consistently underrated and frequently plagiarized historian in Germany, has written some exceedingly stimulating essays which can be found in his *Gesammelte Schriften*, 14 vols (Berlin 1960). Gerhard Ritter, *Friedrich der Grosse* (Heidelberg 1954) has a useful chapter on Frederick the Great's strategy and tactics.

The reform movement is discussed in three interesting books: William O. Shanahan, *Prussian Military Reforms 1786–1813* (New York 1966), Walter M. Simon, *The Failure of the Prussian Reform Movement* (New York 1971) and E. N. Anderson, *Nationalism and the Cultural Crisis in Prussia, 1806–1815* (New York 1939). Franz Schnabel, *Deutsche Geschichte im neunzehn Jahrhundert* (Freiburg 1964) is a masterly textbook written in an admirable style, which is invaluable on the reforms and for the pre-March. Reinhard Höhn, *Scharnhorsts Vermächtnis* (Bonn

1952) is important but should be handled with extreme caution. The author's background as a national socialist ideologue is often all too apparent. Friedrich Meinecke, *Das Zeitalter der deutschen Erhebung* (Leipzig, no date) is an interesting essay by a major historian. Fritz Straube (editor) *Das Jahr 1813* (Berlin 1963) contains some valuable essays by East German historians. On the major figures Max Lehmann, *Scharnhorst*, 2 vols (Leipzig 1886–7) is a classic; Friedrich Meinecke, *Das Leben des Generalfeldmarschalls Hermann von Boyen* (Stuttgart 1895–9) is a mine of information; G. H. Pertz and H. Delbrück, *Das Leben des Feldmarschalls Grafen Neithardt von Gneisenau*, 5 vols (Berlin 1864–80) does not do Gneisenau justice. Peter Paret, *Yorck and the Era of Prussian Reform 1807–1815* (Princeton 1966) is good on the role of light infantry. Clausewitz is badly in need of a modern study. Roger Parkinson, *Clausewitz* (London 1970) gives an account of his life but makes no attempt to analyse his ideas. For a Clausewitz bibliography see Hans-Ulrich Wehler, *Krisenherde des Kaiserreichs* (Göttingen 1970) which is so comprehensive that it includes books not yet published.

The history of the army in the pre-March and in 1848 has also been neglected. Veit Valentin, *Geschichte der Deutschen Revolution von 1848–1849* (Cologne 1970) is by far the best study, although the truncated English translation is almost useless. Friedrich Engels, *Revolution and Counter-Revolution in Germany* is essential reading, the basis of all later work on the subject.

The best introduction in English to the conflict period is E. N. Anderson, *The Social and Political Conflict in Prussia 1858–1864* (Nebraska 1954). This should be supplemented by Ludwig Dehio's excellent articles: 'Edwin von Mantueffels politische Ideen', *Historische Zeitschrift*, CXXXI (1925); 'Die Pläne de Militärpartei und der Konflikt, *Deutsche Rundschau*, CCXIII (1927), and 'Bismarck und die Heeresvorlagen der Konfliktszeit', *Historische Zeitschrift*, CXLIV (1932). Gordon A. Craig, 'Portrait of a Political General: Edwin von Manteuffel and the Constitutional Conflict in Prussia', *Political Science Quarterly*, LXVI (1951) is an excellent essay. Horst Bartel and Ernst Engelberg (editors), *Die grosspreussisch-militaristische Reichsgründung 1871*, 2 vols (Berlin 1971) contains excellent essays on the conflict period, the role of the general staff in 1866 and 1870 and on Moltke and Waldersee by Konrad Canis, Heinz Helmert, Karl Schmiedel and Manfred Weien. The standard biography of Moltke is Eberhard Kessel, *Moltke* (Stuttgart 1957) which would be a much better book had the author not set out to write a literary masterpiece and had he been less in awe of his subject. Rudolf Stadelmann, *Moltke und der Staat* (Krefeld 1950) is a provocative study by a liberal historian. Heinz Helmert, 'Helmuth von Moltke under der preussische Generalstab in der Vorgeschichte des Krieges von 1866', *Jahrbuch für Geschichte*, 1 (Berlin 1967) is useful. For details of the wars of Bismarck and Moltke see Anneliese Klein-Wuttig, *Politik und Kriegführung in den deutschen Einigungskriegen* (Berlin 1934). Gordon A. Craig gives a good account of *The Battle of Königgrätz* (Philadelphia 1964), and Michael Howard's *The Franco-Prussian War* (London 1962) is a superbly written description of the campaign. For social and economic trends see Hans Rosenberg, *Grosse Depression und Bismarckzeit* (Berlin 1967), a model of concise and incisive scholarship. The same cannot be said of Helmut Böhme, *Deutschlands Weg zur Grossmacht* (Cologne 1966), but in spite of its failures in organization it is an important book. Hans-Ulrich Wehler, *Bismarck und der Imperialismus* (Cologne 1969) is essential reading for anyone wishing to go beyond the purely military aspects to the underlying social and political concerns of Bismarck's Germany.

For Wilhelmine Germany the best starting point is the essays of Eckart Kehr, *Primat der Innenpolitik* (Berlin 1965). I have learned more from these extraordinary pieces than from almost any other source. Their translation into English is long overdue. George W. F. Hallgarten, *Imperialismus vor 1914*, 2 vols (Munich 1963) in spite of many errors is an enormously influential book in the Kehr tradition. I have attempted to give an account of the Wilhelmine army in *The German Officer Corps 1890–1914* (Oxford 1968). For further details of the later period see Fritz Fischer, *Krieg der Illusionen* (Düsseldorf 1969), a very important study of the period 1911–1914.

The single most important work on the First World War in Germany is Fritz Fischer, *Griff nach der Weltmacht* (Düsseldorf 1964), a magisterial work which has triumphantly withstood the ferocious attacks of right-wing German historians. The English version is greatly shortened to encourage those reluctant to tackle 900 pages of German prose. On the early years of the war Karl-Heinz Janssen, *Der Kanzler und der General* (Göttingen 1967) contains much important material but is rather uncritical towards both the chancellor (Bethmann Hollweg) and the general (Falkenhayn). I have examined the politics of Hindenburg and Ludendorff in great detail in my forthcoming book *The Silent Dictatorship: The Politics of the German High Command 1916–1918*. For the economic policies of the army see Gerald D. Feldman, *Army, Industry and Labor in Germany 1914–1918* (Princeton 1966), a painstaking piece of work which is rather too kind to the army and industry and unsympathetic to labour. The East German co-operative effort edited by Fritz Klein, *Deutschland im ersten Weltkrieg*, 3 vols (Berlin 1968) is outstandingly good. A highly readable. and important book is the diaries of Admiral von Müller, edited by Walter Görlitz as *The Kaiser and His Court* (New York 1964), which gives excellent insight into the ruling elite during the war by a perceptive observer.

On the Weimar republic all previous books are surpassed by F. L. Carsten, *Reichswehr und Politik 1918–1933* (Cologne 1964) an outstanding work which combines meticulous scholarship with a strong moral commitment. The English version of the book is slightly shortened. Otto-Ernst Schüddekopf, *Heer und Republik* (Hanover 1955) is a useful collection of documents. Hans Meier-Welcker, *Seeckt* (Frankfurt am Main 1967) is unsuccessful as a defence of Seeckt but contains much useful material. For a general history of the period Arthur Rosenberg, *A History of the Weimar Republic* (London 1936) has yet to be bettered. A biography of Schleicher is lacking. Thilo Vogelsang, *Kürt von Schleicher* (Göttingen 1965) does not begin to get to the bottom of this extraordinarily complex character.

Relations between Hitler and the army are discussed in Robert J. O'Neill, *The German Army and the Nazi Party, 1933–1939* (London 1966), a very solid book. Some corrections of O'Neill are to be found in K–J Müller, *Das Heer und Hitler* (Stuttgart 1969) which covers the period from 1933 to 1940. Müller disperses a number of apologist myths, particularly those surrounding men like Beck and Fritsch, but creates some of his

Index

377

Index